ADOLPHUS STERNE

Hurrah for Texas!

The Diary of Adolphus Sterne
1838–1851

Edited
by
Archie P. McDonald

NorTex
Press

Fort Worth, Texas
An Imprint of
Wild Horse Media Group
www.WildHorseMedia.com

For Judy, Tucker and Christopher

First published in 1969 by Texian Press, Waco, Texas.

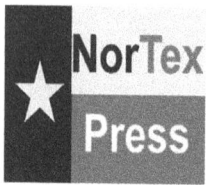

Copyright © 1986
By Archie P. McDonald
Published By NorTex Press
An Imprint of Wild Horse Media Group
P.O. Box 331779
Fort Worth, Texas 76163
1-817-344-7036
www.WildHorseMedia.com
ALL RIGHTS RESERVED
1 2 3 4 5 6 7 8 9
ISBN-10: 1-68179-084-X
ISBN-13: 978-1-68179-084-8

This printing of *Hurrah for Texas!*
is in celebration of
Nacogdoches' Tricentennial year.

Introduction to New Edition:
Hurrah for Texas!: The Diary of Adolphus Sterne, 1838-1851

To the delight of some, the consternation of a few others, and perhaps the bewilderment of the rest of the population, 2016 is the tercentennial (or tri-centennial if you want anyone to know what you are talking about) of the genesis of the city of Nacogdoches. That makes it the "oldest town in Texas," and I cannot think of a better "gift" to the city, the state, and the world than a re-issue of Archie McDonald's edited version of Adolphus Sterne's diary, *Hurrah for Texas!* McDonald did the public a great service when he gathered the contents of the entire Sterne diary in one edition, first in the original 1969 issue, and again in 1986 with a new printing. Sterne was one of the most consequential figures in Nacogdoches and Texas, and at the same time one that few people are aware, and even some that do know of him often fail to fully grasp his importance.

That's unfortunate because Mr. Sterne was so indicative of the men and women who came to Nacogdoches in those years immediately after the end of Spanish rule. A native German, like so many he fled the turmoil of early nineteenth century Europe for the United States while he was in his teens. He landed in New Orleans and began a mercantile career. However, again like so many before and after him, the siren call of what many of the day called "Texas Fever" led him to eastern Texas and Nacogdoches, which seemed like a good spot for a man with an entrepreneurial spirit. The frontier town became his home, but through business and in personality he remained attached to the United States, which led him to first become involved in the Fredonian Rebellion, and later drove his fervency in support of the Texian revolt against Santa Anna and Mexican rule. While Mr. Sterne honored his pledge to "never again take up arms against Mexico," which was the stricture the Mexican authorities placed on him after the Fredonian Rebellion, his money and influence helped to outfit and arm men who did join the fight against Santa Anna and his Mexican forces in 1835 and 1836. After the war, Sterne remained prominent in Nacogdoches until his untimely death in 1852.

I think that is one of the most astonishing things to many

people when they begin to learn about Adolphus Sterne: how much he accomplished and how prominent he became at such a young age. Once again, that was emblematic of others of his time. The frontier was not a place for the timid or the feeble; it was not an easy existence, which often made it the bastion of the young. Sterne was but sixteen when he landed in New Orleans, and only twenty-three when he made Nacogdoches his home. Before he was thirty he had taken made a small fortune and also taken up arms against his host nation, which resulted in a commuted death sentence. This young man of the frontier was not yet forty when he became a partisan of the Texas Revolution. When one sees photographs and renderings of Sterne I think he/she is often surprised at the young face, dark hair, and piercing eyes that stare back. Perhaps he knew that he would die just north of fifty, and that made him a man in a hurry.

The City of Nacogdoches has, to its credit, restored and maintained Mr. Sterne's former residence, the Sterne-Hoya House in historic downtown Nacogdoches. While it later became the residence of another prominent family in the city, the Hoyas, its historic significance was assured when Adolphus Sterne dwelled there. There were probably untold important conversations in its rooms, and it was no doubt the scene of more than one scheme, land deal, or other business transaction, some above board, and others—perhaps—"under the table." Visitors to the home are able to see an accurate recreation of life in early Nacogdoches, and a rendering of the past so rarely glimpsed these days. It is a symbol of what Nacogdoches was, and the past that they celebrate in 2016, this three hundred anniversary year. So, for those of you reading Sterne's words for the first time you are in for a treat, and for those of you becoming reacquainted with him, it will be like visiting an old friend. Enjoy.

M. Scott Sosebee

The Sterne House as it appears today.

INTRODUCTION

In Texas historiography the "Sterne Diary" is well known for its richness of material, its vividness of description, and its many incisive and human comments about the *dramatis personae* of the Republic of Texas. Any modern biographer or historian dealing with its period cannot afford to overlook it, yet all who use it must lament its inaccessibility.

The diary was retained in private possession until 1925, when it was given to the State of Texas by Charles Adolphus Sterne, the senior Sterne's eldest son and claimant to the title of oldest living native Texan. The five manuscript volumes, broken into the following periods, were then deposited in the State Library. Volume I contains materials from 1838 to 1840, Volume II from 1840 to 1841, Volume III from 1841 to 1843, and Volume IV from 1843-44. Volume 5 follows a seven-year gap with entries from 1851. Its abrupt end raises the possibility that there might have been a sixth volume. The diary was almost immediately edited for serial publication in the *Southwestern Historical Quarterly* by Harriett Smither of the Texas State Library. Its publication began with the second issue of Volume XXX in October, 1926 and continued through the third issue of Volume XXVIII in January, 1935. Eugene C. Barker is reported to have observed that when they ran out of copy they threw in a little more of the Sterne material. An examination of the installments would seem to indicate that this was not necessarily said with tongue-in-cheek. They vary in length greatly, and there is little coherence of thought in the various installments. Perhaps the most serious defect of the edition was the deliberate elimination of any material considered as "personal," particularly in relation to the birth of Mrs. Sterne's children, and the accidental deletion of many lines, even entire entries. Not infrequently entries were run under incorrect dates. These may be a nuisance, but their correction certainly would not justify a new edition of the diary. Indeed, every Texas historian is in the debt of Miss Smither and the *Southwestern Historical Quarterly* for making this material available. But it is precisely its form of availability that now calls for a new edition. Spread out over a decade in a magazine of limited distribution, the diary is unavailable to those who are not fortunate enough to be near a college library with back issues of the *Quarterly*. It is hoped that the present edition will correct these deficiencies, and by employing more modern techniques of editing, will enhance its readability.

The editor has sought in all instances to preserve the diarist's spelling, syntax, and quaintness of expression. Periods, a punctuation mark apparently unknown to Sterne, have been included to establish cohesiveness of thought. Miss Smither's interpretation of many near-illegible passages has been preserved, but brackets are used to indicate the presumptions of the editor or to indicate errors of the diarist. Sterne had a habit of capitalizing many common words and using lower-case letters for such words as "god" and "general." In the case of proper names the capital letter has been substituted. He also frequently misspells common words. Thus "monay" instead of "money," "send" instead of "sent," and "then" in place of "than" are left as originally inscribed.

The editor wishes to express his appreciation to Dr. James Day, formerly with the Texas State Library, and Mr. Charles W. Corkran, former director of the State Library's Archives Division, for their assistance in assembling the Sterne materials, to Miss Mildred Wyatt and Miss Grace Ramirez of the Stephen F. Austin State College Library for their generous help and suggestions, to the Hoya Library for permission to photograph Sterne materials, and to Milam Lodge No. 2, A.F.&A.M. for permission to reprint the portrait of Sterne used here as the frontispiece. My thanks must also go to Mr. Benjamine Smylie for his help in typing the manuscript, and to Mr. William J. Brophy for his timely suggestions and forbearance in the face of numerous questions.

THE DIARIST

Nicholas Adolphus Sterne, German-Jewish immigrant to the American and Texas frontiers, is an historical character of much complexity. He was an urbane, sophisticated man-of-the-world who was a mover and shaker in the early period of Texas history. Yet much of his personal history is confused in the myths and half-truths that spring from the memory of loved ones. One of the principal difficulties of trying to re-establish his biography is that most of the information, other than his diary and a few official documents, was provided by his children when they were in advanced years and working mostly from memory. Even so, the Sterne saga is an impressive one.

Sterne was born on April 5, 1801 in the city of Cologne, although some insist that the location was Alsace. He was the eldest son of Emmanuel Sterne an Orthodox Jew and his second wife, Helen, a Lutheran. Sterne was reared in a geography and an era of much turmoil and change. Early set to the task of helping to earn the family living, at the age of sixteen he was working in a passport office. When he learned that he was about to be conscripted for service in a German army, he forged the necessary papers and sailed to the United States. Sterne arrived in New Orleans in 1817 and sought employment in the mercantile establishments of the city. In his spare time he studied for the law, and although he never practiced it for a living, he was always on the periphery of the profession, acting as land agent and county judge after he came to Texas. It was while he was still in New Orleans that Sterne joined the Masonic Lodge including the Scottish Rite organizations available to him in the city. This affiliation would prove beneficial on many occasions after he moved to Texas.

The profits of itinerate peddling and merchandising appealed to the footloose Sterne, and in the early 1820's he used New Orleans as a base from which to market manufactured goods in the interior. He ranged as far north as Tennessee, where he met a young politician named Sam Houston at the Nashville Inn and over toddies formed a long-lasting, if somewhat rocky, relationship.

In 1826 Sterne opened a mercantile establishment in the Texas-Mexican frontier town of Nacogdoches. He had undoubtedly come to Nacogdoches earlier, thus causing many to assume that his year of immigration was 1824. He was soon in the thick of the complicated land dispute known as the Fredonia Rebellion. Despite pledges of loyalty to the Mexican regime made when he first came to Texas Sterne assisted his fellow immigrants in their attempt to break away from Mexico and establish, for economic reasons, an independent state. His assistance took the form of smuggling guns secreted in barrels of coffee. His activities were uncovered by the authorities and Sterne was tried for treason and sentenced to be shot. He was bound to a large iron staple in the Stone House in Nacogdoches while the circumstances of his case were reviewed by the military commander at Saltillo. He was apparently not closely guarded and he enjoyed many liberties while his appeal was being heard. Because of Masonic intercession from his New Orleans lodge brothers, Sterne's sentence was commuted and he was released on promise of renewed loyalty to Mexico and to never bear arms against his adopted country. Sterne's loyalty to this oath prevented his military participation in the battle of Nacogdoches in 1832 and the more important events of the Revolution, but it did not prevent him from assisting with its finance, organization, or propaganda.

Still going frequently to New Orleans on business, he usually traveled overland to Natchitoches, from whence he took passage on a river boat to the Crescent City. While in Natchitoches Sterne met a young German girl who attracted his fancy and ultimately became his wife. Eva Catherine Rosine Ruff was born in Eslenger, Würtenberg on June 23, 1809. At the age of six she and her family immigrated to America via the port of New Orleans. Both parents developed yellow fever from their stay in that city, a hazard to all who visited it, and died while in passage up the Red River to a permanent residence. The Ruff children were adopted by Monsieur Placide Bossier and his wife, who raised them in their home as their own. Eva was a Roman Catholic, and when she and Sterne married she succeeded in assisting Mexican law in converting him to that faith. References in his diary reveal that Sterne was more of a deist than anything else, but officially he was a Roman Catholic, a condition required for office holding in Texas. The Sternes were married on June 2, 1828, and they returned to Nacogdoches where Sterne built their home. A frame building located near the confluence of Lanana and Bonita creeks, it was developed into a garden spot and a seat of Nacogdoches hospitality by the amiable Sterne and the genuine friendliness and goodness of his wife. Seven children were born to them, including Eva Helena Eugenia, Charles Adolphus, Joseph Amador, William Logan, Placide Rusk, Laura Theresa, and Rosine Sterne.

One of the many important guests in the Sterne home was Sam Houston, who migrated to Texas following an aborted political career in Tennessee. Houston boarded with the Sternes, and it is one of the romantic legends of his career that he was converted to the Roman faith by Mrs. Sterne's gentle persuasions. Actually his reasons were purely political. Mrs. Sterne served as godmother at his baptism, which was performed in the parlor of her home. Sterne was not, however, the godfather, and one Jewish historian believes this was because the baptism occurred on *Erev Yom Kippur*.

Sterne was a strong supporter of the movement for Texas independence. Although restrained from participating actively because of his oath, he helped in the raising and financing of soldiers, particularly from New Orleans. As special agent there for the provisional government, in 1835 he financed the equipment and passage of two companies known as the New Orleans Greys under the command of Captain Thomas H. Breece, and preceded them to Nacogdoches where he entertained them when they arrived. Sterne's claim of $950 for these and other expenses went unpaid for many years.

Following the successful revolution Sterne was a supporter and then an opponent of Houston's policies, and they nearly came to a complete falling out over the Cherokee land question. Sterne commanded a company of militia in the Battle of the Neches, on July 15, 1839, which illustrates his attitude toward Indian ownership of land.

He remained active in the business and political life of Nacogdoches and Texas through the years of the republic and during the early years of statehood. In addition to above-mentioned duties, he became postmaster of Nacogdoches on February 19, 1840 and continued in that post for several years; he served as deputy clerk of the County Court until June 11, 1841, when he was elected associate justice; in 1841 he served as justice of the peace; he was deputy clerk of the Board of Land Commissioners and commissioner of roads and revenues; he served on a local board of health, and was an overseer of streets and roads in the Corporation of Nacogdoches. Finally, he was in 1847 elected to represent Nacogdoches in the House of Representatives of the Second Legislature of the State of Texas, returned to the House for the Third Legislature in 1849 and advanced to the Senate for the Fourth Legislature in 1851.

He was a member of many private organizations, including the Sons of Temperance, the American Legal Association, the Order of Eastern Star, both York and Scottish Rite bodies, and was a charter member of both Milam Lodge No. 40 (Louisiana Registry) and No. 2 (Texas Registry), and of the Grand Lodge of Texas. He served the latter as its first Deputy Grand Master and frequently filled the post of District Deputy Grand Master.

Sterne was a fun-loving, active man and worked with a real zest for life. He enjoyed dancing and an occasional drink, and was fond of playing whist. He was marked by the vices of his day, including the keeping of slaves, but he was free from hypocrisy. He was a substantial land owner. Estimates based on the Census of 1840 indicate that he owned or controlled about 16,000 acres of Texas land, although he continuously complained of not having enough "Monay." Mostly self-educated, he was extremely literate, and spoke, even occasionally as an official interpreter, English, French, Spanish, German, Yiddish, Portuguese, and Latin.

Sterne died in New Orleans on March 27, 1852 and following a brief interment there, was later reburied in Oak Grove Cemetery in Nacogdoches. In addition to two and one-half decades of personal service to Texas, his diary continues to be of service to those who trace its past. In any criteria of historical witnesses, Sterne is eminently qualified. Living in Nacogdoches during the years when it was both an important town and a port of entry, the panorama of Texas unfolded around him. He was therefore in a position to see, to understand what he saw, and his character and intelligence qualifies him as a reporter who could incisively and accurately chronicle his surroundings.

Sterne emerges from the pages of his diary as much more than the "rosy little Jew" that he is so often called by Houston biographers. He was a man, one imagines, who met his times with a powerful force for accomplishment. But above all, he was a man.

CONTENTS

ILLUSTRATIONS
(Following Page 132)

Drawing of the Sterne House in its original state.
— Drawing by Reese Kennedy

Introduction to the Second Printing

Much has happened to Nicholas Adolphus Sterne since this book first appeared in 1969. For one thing, *Hurrah for Texas!* proved sufficiently popular to go out of print several years ago. Since that time I have been asked by quite a few people where they could obtain a copy, and all I could do was refer them to a book search firm. Here in Nacogdoches at least, the book became something of a collector's item, especially after work began on the restoration of Sterne's house. So I am personally indebted to Robert E. Davis of the Texian Press for permission to reprint the diary, and to Ed Eakin for doing so.

While there is obviously some personal pleasure in seeing the diary in print again, most of my joy comes from the fact that more people will get to know my friend Adolphus Sterne. Nothing in the past seventeen years has changed my opinion that he was one of the most remarkable of all Texans and a person I would like to have known. Davis and Eakin are making a genuine contribution to Texas studies by allowing the daily observations of this most remarkable man to be available once more.

This is not my judgment alone. In a review in the *Dallas Morning News* on October 16, 1969, Thomas E. Turner of Baylor University said, "As long as Texas' past is studied, the daily chronicle Sterne kept for his adopted land will be a must." The late F. I. Tucker's review in the *East Texas Historical Journal* said:

> This volume for the first time places in one handy book Sterne's comments on the daily life of East Texas, as well as pertinent observations on the happenings in the Republic of Texas and the State of Texas as they impinged on the life of the diarist, as well as on other lives in the community of Nacogdoches.
>
> Adolphus Sterne speaks his mind in this diary as to the good and the bad. A careful reading will give the reader an excellent and interesting picture of the social and business lives of East Texans during this time. To any person interested in the history of Nacogdoches and [East Texas] at that time, or in the genealogy of the period, this volume should be both helpful and interesting. The pithy remarks about the citizens, the preachers, and the politicians are of much interest and throw considerable light on the thinking of the era.

In *Basic Texas Books: An Annotated Bibliography of Selected Works for a Research Library*, John H. Jenkins claims that "This diary is one of the most informative and complete that has survived for the period of the Republic of Texas. William Seale called it 'the most engaging one of its kind available on the subject of the Texas Republic.'" I think the response to the book I liked best came from Mrs. Samuel F. Johnson of Wimberley: "You may not have known that with the publication of *Hurrah for Texas!* you were literally making possible the answer to prayer, but that is the result nevertheless, and a gift so valuable — not only to all students of Texas History — but most particularly to Adolphus Sterne's direct descendants, of whom I am proud to be counted." With such stock being placed in Sterne's diary, it just had to remain in print.

In a larger sense, all contemporary Texans are Sterne's descendants, even if they do not carry the blood. He was one of the fathers of our republic and our state. An inquisitive, vital man, he lived his life at Texas's center stage in our infant years. He knew the other movers and shakers of that Texas and was known and respected by them and by ordinary people as well. He served his community with the spirit of boosterism and volunteering long before chambers of commerce institutionalized the former and President Ronald Reagan popularized the latter. Sterne was truly a renaissance man. He was competent in multiple fields, widely read, and interested in life and all that went on around him. It would have been a pleasure to have known him personally.

Another milestone that has happened since *Hurrah for Texas!* first reached print is the restoration of Sterne's home in Nacogdoches. That really should be stated as re-restored, for it has been kept more or less in repair and used as a library and museum for the city of Nacogdoches since 1956. But in recent years visitor traffic, the weight of books, and just plain aging took their toll. The Friends of Adolphus Sterne Home, working with the city-appointed library board, undertook the restoration of the building in the early 1980s, and the work on the house was completed by the summer of 1985. I think every member of the Friends board, of whom I am one, would give the full credit for the achievement to Captain Charles K. Phillips, USN Retired. Phillips was chairman of the board, restoration architect, foreman, and common laborer at every stage of the work. The restoration was financed by a fund drive and a few grants, with assistance from the City of Nacogdoches, allowing all of us to feel like we had a part in the project. But Chuck Phillips did the work and we all know it.

Phillips had the place sparkling for the official opening of the Nacogdoches Sesquicentennial program, a banquet in the style of the one Sterne gave for the New Orleans Greys on the same date, November 9, 150 years previously. The fare was duplicated as Herman Ehrenberg described it in his own diary, right down to the bear meat. Sterne recruited the Greys in New Orleans and paid for their trip to Texas so they could fight in the revolution against Mexico.

Portraits of Sterne and his wife were presented, recreationists impersonated the original Greys, and Squire Sterne himself, played by Stephen F. Austin State University English professor, Dr. Bill Cozart, addressed the assemblage. Mrs. Johnson was there, along with her brother Tracy Word, and other Sterne descendants. All left with the good feeling that they had gotten to know Sterne again, or perhaps to know him better.

If you could not come to the party, at least the diary is again available. It is my hope that even beyond the Sesquicentennial that many more Texans will come to know Adolphus Sterne, and will continue to *Hurrah for Texas!*

Portrait of Adolphus Sterne at age sixteen to eighteen.
— Courtesy Mrs. Samuel F. Johnson

CHAPTER I

". . . so here goes."

Nacogdoches September 28th 1840   Having sometime ago read Cobbets advise eta, & having seen my descd Friends Jas Ogilvy's[1] Diary & seen, and learnt its usefullness I come to the determination to Keep one, of such things as might be usefull, or interesting so here goes—this day obtained Letters of Administration on Jas Ogilvy's Estate, who died sometime ago at my House took the Oath as required by Law, went to my residence and took an inventory of the descd personal property.

Sepr 29th   handed in to the attorney of the Estate of C. S. Taylor[2] Espr. the inventory of the personal property of J. Ogilvy decd for the purpose of obtaining an order of sale from the probate Judge to pay funeral Expences eta.   Arranged the Papers of the Decd for the purpose of taking an inventory of them, wrote a long Letter to Luis Rueg[3] respecting his Business, with the Estate

---

[1]James Ogilvy, a ghostly shadow in Texas history, died sometime prior to September, 1839 in Adolphus Sterne's home, and Sterne became the administrator of his estate.   It was Ogilvy's diary, as he reveals here, that prompted Sterne's efforts to keep a careful record of his daily affairs for nearly eight years.   Ogilvy was an agent for the heirs of Dr. James Grant, who died on March 2, 1836 while leading the unfortunate Matamoros Expedition.   Ogilvy's efforts were less than successful.   For an account of his activities see Harriett Smither, "Diary of Adolphus Sterne," **Southwestern Historical Quarterly** (January 1927), 30, 219. Ogilvy's diary fell into Sterne's hands and was preserved among his own papers.   It was mistakenly published by Miss Smither as Sterne's diary. See **Ibid,** 139-155; 219-230; 305-324.   Miss Smither may be excused for assuming that the diary was Sterne's however, since it was so identified by A. G. Greenwood, attorney for Charles A. Sterne, when he presented the Sterne Papers to the State of Texas.   The handwriting is nearly identical.   Only internal criticism reveals the error, which Miss Smither corrected in the second installment of Ogilvy's diary published in the **Southwestern Historical Quarterly.**

[2]Charles Stanfield Taylor was born in London, England in 1808.   He emigrated via New York to Texas, and in April, 1930 became a citizen of Mexico.   For a time he boarded with Sterne, briefly was his partner in a mercantile enterprise, and by his marriage to Mrs. Sterne's sister, Anna Marie Ruff, became Sterne's brother-in-law.   Taylor served Nacogdoches County in many capacities, including membership in the **ayuntamiento,** land commissioner and county treasurer.   He also represented Nacogdoches County at the Convention at Washington-on-the-Brazos in March, 1836. and was one of the signers of the Declaration of Independence.   He was for many years Chief Justice of the Nacogdoches County Court.   He died on November 1, 1865.

[3]Louis Rueg was from Rolle, Switzerland.   He came to the United States about 1818 with his brother Henry, lived for a time in Louisiana, and after 1821 operated for a time a small mercantile business in Nacogdoches.   They also engaged in land speculation.

of Ogilvy [illegible] respecting six Blls whiskey, 8 Blls Sugar & 3 Stacks Coffee, Shipped by Ogilvy to Sam Norriss[4] on the 30th April last. Send Ruegs Letter by T. T. McIvor[5] who left this day with his waggon for Natchitochez, paid T. T. M'Ivor $40.00 Texas Monay on account of the Hire of the negro I have now in my Employ at $25, par money a month, paid old man Hyde[6] $5— Texas. Johnson the waggoner came in this Evening, no news.

Wednesday Sept 30 Wrote to C. Searles of Canton Missi. respecting my Business with Silverburg's Estate, send the Letter with a Mr. M. Teague who is going directly to the place, wrote to gen Henderson[7] on the same subject—much Law Business to[day] —R. F. Millard commenced 13 Suits against persons residing in this County, all for grog accounts!!! a, J. B. Springer was brought in, accused of stealing a Horse, and abduction of Negroes of Mr. Hotchkiss[8] was send to jail for want of security for $2000. saw Major Hollman[9] from Houston to day had a conversation with him respecting $100. J. K. Allen's Estate owes to Ygnacis Villegas—I think it a Slim Chance! . . .

Thursday October the 1st a child of Mr Millard's and one of Alexr McIvor's died last night, the weather is getting cool, had several fine rains lately—wrote to J. Pineda Bexar to inquire for a Daughter of the late Patricio de Torres, requesting him to get her to send me a power of attorney to act for her, in claiming her part of her Fathers' Estate. Joseph Nations delivered a Sack of Salt on a/c of the debt he owes me as administrator on the Estate of G Benard decd.

Friday the 2d October today the wind changed suddenly at 7 A.M. from a South, to a cold northern. Cloaks, and Shawls put in requisition, a Mr Wilson, Father in law of Reinhardt returned from lower Trinity cursing the Country as too sickly. two Negroes belonging to a Mr. .... of Alexandria La got away from the sheriff out on a hunt for them, "no catch em"—rain [in] the afternoon, fair towards night—very Cold. a negro I have hired

[4]Samuel Norris, a native of Maryland, was born in 1783. In 1803 his parents moved to the Attoyac River settlement near Nacogdoches. In 1825 he was elected **alcalde** of Nacogdoches, a partial provocation of the notorious Fredonia Rebellion when Martin Parmer, Norris' opponent for the office, refused to accept the decision of the election. Norris moved to Louisiana after the affair.
[5]T. T. McIver operated a saloon in Nacogdoches.
[6]Probably John H. Hyde.
[7]James Pinckney Henderson was born in Lincolnton, North Carolina on March 31. 1808. With both a legal and military background, he moved to Texas from Canton. Mississippi upon hearing news of the revolution. He served as a recruiter in the United States and as minister to both England and France, and helped negotiate the treaty of annexation to the United States which was originally rejected. In later years he served in both the Texas Legislature and the United States Congress. He died on June 4, 1858.
[8]Archibald Hotchkiss.
[9]Sterne may be referring to Colonel William W. Holman of the commissary department of the Texas army, who was from San Augustine, or to James S. Holman, who was a land agent from Houston.

called friday belonging to McIvor was kept at home since yester-day—Hunt, who has had my Horse since January last send him home to day in good order—

Saturday October 3d last night about ½ past Eight my wife, felt pains, incident to an event which will happen in the best of Families!—Send for Doctor Starr,[10] no news at daylight this morn-ing At 4 P.M. my wife was delivered of a fine girl, Doctor Starr in attendance.

Sunday the 4th Mrs. Stern remained from the birth of the child till ½ past Six this morning before the after birth took place, Doctor Starr here all night Mrs. Taylor who remained all night, 8 A.M.—Mother & Child well, the widow [of] Alexander H. Strong left here for Vicksbourgh at 9. this morning. wrote a few lines to Mr Holland[11] at San Augustin send by Sheriff Rusk[12] who takes a Horse Thief to San Augustine to be tried, the District Court is at present in session at that place. child no name yet, bothered what to call it— there's nothing in a name—! 8 P.M. Mrs. S. had a little fever during the day—made out my quarterly Post office returns and made them all ready to be forwarded in tomor-row's mail.

Monday October 5th last night at 12 oclock General Kelsey H. Douglass[13] died— was called by a Servant to go to the House, got there a little after his demise, helped to lay him out eta, Gen. D. Died of Consumption, his death was unexpected, in him this County has lost one of its best citizens, he was a good man, hon-est, liberal, & brave, he was a good Father, a good Husband a good neighbour, and a friend *in need*— Douglass my best friend rest in peace— . . . at 4½ P.M. interred Douglass with all the requisite Masonic Honours, the [longest] largest funeral seen here this Summer, received & dispatched the western and Southern Mails and attended to a good many suits brought before me, in all,

---

[10]Dr. James Harper Starr was born on December 18, 1809 at New Hart-ford, Connecticut. He briefly practiced medicine in Georgia, but came to Texas in 1837, arriving in Nacogdoches on January 17. Starr served the Republic and State in many capacities, including land commissioner under Sam Houston, secretary of the treasury under M. B. Lamar, and as an advertiser for prospective settlers. He also served the Sterne family as a physician. Starr died on July 25, 1890.

[11]John Henry Holland, former Grand Master of the Grand Lodge of Lou-isiana, and, following his immgration in 1839, a prominent attorney in Nacogdoches. He returned to New Orleans, and was still alive there in 1855.

[12]David Rusk, sheriff of Nacogdoches County from 1837 to 1847, was the brother of Thomas Jefferson Rusk. He came to Texas from Clarks-ville, Georgia in January, 1836, and fought at San Jacinto in Hayden Arnold's Nacogdoches company. He died in Orange County on Septem-ber 11, 1877.

[13]Kelsey Harris Douglass, who came to Texas prior to the Revolution to operate a mercantile establishment, was a supplier of goods to the Texas Army. He served in the First and Second Congresses of the Republic. His military title dates from his service against the Cherokees in 1839. The town of Douglass in Nacogdoches County is named for him. He died at his home in Nacogdoches on October 20, 1840.

— 3 —

this was a very busy day, I am perfectly exhausted and must go to rest.

Tuesday October the 6th Col Ransom[14] late private secretary to President Lamar arrived with dispatches from the war Department to Brigadier General Jim Smith to raise 470 men out of his Brigade to operate Against the Hostile indians, no matter what nation or what name they may bear; Col R. is quarter master general for the Eastern division, I understand that a general movement will be made throughout Texas; the general rendevous of the Eastern Division is the Nechas Saline Eastern mail arrived, no news . . .

Mrs Sterne is a little better to day; got a league & Labor location from W. A. Ferriss situated near the three forks of Trinity, for the Heirs of my Father in Law, John Eberhardt Ruff—the Heirs are—my wife, Mrs. C. S. Taylor, and Jeremiah Ruff—got also a league & Labor location from Ferries for J. H. Holland, on Susan Latham's Headright certificate issued at Shelbyville, gave my note for both for $194.00 payable in twelve months from this day. Taylor ought to pay the half of the League of the Heirs of J. E. Ruff, as his wife is one of the Heirs—paid Ferries $30 . . . Texas money equal to $6.00 par funds. to night is *erev Yom Kipur* [eve on the atonement] received from Elison 1 cart load of corn on a/c of rent of Plantation, this is the 4th Load—weather very fine.

Wednesday October 7 Weather very fine. Mrs Sterne is getting better, but very slow, rested bad last night, the infant unwell. got a pair of Horseman's Pistols belonging to Mr Rueg, loaned Mr von der Hoya[15] a Horse called Bill to go to Crocket paid Madame Carmel Mora $50. Texas Monay on Accot of rent for her part of Stone House.[16] received the monay from Bennett Blake[17]— Henry McNeil arrived from the U. S. news— France has declared war against England,—Ellison brought another load of Corn—

Thursday the 8th Cloudy weather at 8 A m. the old negro who lives on Rueg's Plantation came and requested me to write to Rueg, respecting the Farm, promised to do so, McNeil left for the west. wrote a Letter to L. Rueg respecting Ogilvy's Estate, and also the conversation had with the old negro respecting Rueg's Plantation, letter to go in to morrow's mail. was introduced to a Mr Compton from Alexandria, he has come to Texas to see the

---

14Colonel James B. Ranson.

15Francis von der Hoya.

16The origin of the Stone House, or Old Stone Fort, is shrouded in mystery. The usually accepted origin dates from 1779 and Gil Antonio Y'Barbo's reoccupation of the old mission site when he re-founded Nacogdoches. It served as a fort, jail, saloon, mercantile establishment and Sterne maintained an office in the east end room upstairs. It was razed in 1902, but a replica was reconstructed from some of its materials in 1936 and presently stands on the campus of Stephen F. Austin University.

17Bennett Blake was chief justice of Nacogdoches County during the Republic years. A native of Vermont. he was born there on November 11, 1809 and died in Nacogdoches on March 1, 1896.

Country. Agreably to Law had the personal Estate of James ogilvy appraised, was appraised at . . . . [blank] Bennett Blake, john Crutcher & john noblett appraisers—weather at dark very oppressively warm, times very dull—[Mrs. Sterne is getting better but has a very sore Breast, causing her excrutiating pains when giving suck to the infant]

Fryday the 9th October weather cloudy and Hazy in the morning, fair in the Evening—Arranged the Papers of James Ogilvie, and found some notes & accounts due him. found also a receipt of J. S. Roberts[18] for a fine pair of Pistols, Holsters, and Knift, valued at $65.00 good for that much—

Seth Sheldon arrived late this afternoon gave me four Documents in Spanish to translate, all concerning a League of Land granted to Sam Noris by the government of Coahuila & Texas, translated all of them before going to bed. Mrs wilson Reinhardts mother in Law died this morning, at John Thorn's House Send an advertisement to the San Augustine paper Cautioning all persons from trading for, or purchasing any note or notes given by me to one Mr. Roddy of Rohdy, they were obtained from me by fraud—

Saturday October 10th Weather very oppressive and Hot, felt unwell this morning took my translations I made last night up to the office, and received $40—Texas monay for my work. wrote a note to John Norriss promising that in case, on the return of Sheriff Rusk, I'll have a settlement with him & if Noris's Tax is not all paid to pay it— came home at Noon with a hot fever, 7 P.M. feel better addressed a note to Mr. Sheldon, requesting him to attend to the Business of Ogilvy's goods at Mr Sam Norris's which he promised to do, gave him a Bill of goods, (say)— the first cost in New Orleans and Expences up to Natchitoches amounts to $230.56 the following is a copy of the Bill—"Invoice of Sundries Shipped pr Hannibal consigned to Mr Norris.

1840

April 29th	3 sacks Coffee 545 11¼	$ 61.31
	8 Blls Sugar 1832 lbs 5¼	95.65
	6 Blls Whiskey 180 galls 27	48.60
		$205.56
Freight charges from N. Orleans to Natchitoc[he]s		
	17 Blls C 1¼	21.25
	Shipping	1.25
	Charges at Natchitochez	2.50
		$230.56

[18]John S. Roberts was born in Virginia on July 13, 1796. After serving under Andrew Jackson at the Battle of New Orleans, he remained in Louisiana and became sheriff of Natchitoches. He was in Nacogdoches during the Fredonia Rebellion, and led a company from there during the Battle of San Antonio in 1835. Roberts represented Nacogdoches at the Constitutional Convention in 1836, and was a signer of the Declaration of Independence. He died on August 9, 1871.

The Sheriff has lost his Boarders he had in jail they (2 negroes and 1 white man) broke out to day between 11 and 12 oclock—pretty bold—Mrs Sterne is getting better rapidly, my Son charles Sick—was his birthday to day he is 10 years old

Sunday October 11th the weather very dry & warm no news of the runaways of yesterday— mail arrived at noon brought no news of any importance, received a Letter from Louis Dufour, which is filed—Wrote to the Post Master general,[19] respecting mail route No 4 & 5— wrote to Doctor Levi Jones[20] Galveston respecting Major Allen Reynolds purchase of Bolivar Point in 1830 requested Dr J. to attend to my Tax I have to pay for my ten acre Lots; no simptoms of Fever to day, Mrs. S. still recovering—child well, . . .

Monday October the 12th last night was taken with an ague, had a hot fever all night untill noon to day.

Tuesday the 13th no fever but felt bad all day sessions of County Court, sold the Personal Effects of J. Ogilvy to day, sold for $103=82. received orders from Liut Col Todd[21] to draft every 5th man of my Company and one non commd officer, draft to be held 24th this month to rendevous here on the 6th next month, and the general rendevous to be at the Nechaz Saline on the 14th do to go on a 3 months tour against the Indians. mail arrived from the East brought no news at least not to me. paid Doctor Starr $13 par money on a/c of his Bill, general Houston passed for the west.

Wednesday the 14th passed a very restless night did not sleep at all, took the fever this morning at 7. left me at noon, went up town but was too Sick to attend to any business.

Thursday the 15th Very weak but no fever to day, attended to all Business as Justice, today, dispatched 21 cases, Mr. John Poe brought my plough home & paid me 280 bundles of fodder on a/c of 480 bundles he owes me, received a Letter from G. W. Smith Jasper respecting my Headright, also a Letter from Ambse Lompeyrae Sr Natchitochez, respecting the House & Lot on the Corner of Main & South Street at Present occupied by Mr Leusch, inclosed in Letter an old survey made by james gaines Esqr. of said Lot. filed among the Papers to which it belongs to wit—"Documents belonging to other Persons," Messrs J. V. Bossier Co. send me their receipt for 31 Dollars, rct filed also a Letter from jno. walker New Orleans which answered this Evening and mailed it for to morrows mail, a considerable south wind is blowing accompanied with rain 9 oclock P. m. went to bed with a sligh head ache . . .

Fryday October the 16 past a restless night, the wind changed

---

[19]John Rice Jones, Jr. served as Postmaster General under President M. B. Lamar from December 14, 1839 until the end of his term.

[20]Levi Jones was one of the founders of Galveston, where apparently Sterne owned several lots. Jones was the attending physician at the death of Stephen F. Austin.

[21]Probably Jackson Todd.

suddenly this morning to N. E. had a little rain, fair in the afternoon, did not have much fever, took medicine, remained at home
all day.

Saturday the 17th my well day, to day, yet am too weak to
walk to the office, went on Horseback and attended to several suits,
Old Pineda, wrote to me from Bexar. Letter handed to me by,
Mr. Dangerfield[22] a Lawyer of that place, made an arrangement
with him, to purchase on our joint account the right, Patricio de
Torres's Daughter (who lives at Bexar) has to her Father's Estate,
Mr D. informed me of the Death of R. R. Royall also that the
President of the Republic was so sick, that it is doubted, if he
would get over it a good many People in Town to day, but not
near as many as usual, there is one thing remarkable, that is—
very seldom is a drunken man seen—, thats something encourag-
ing anyhow— these bad times. a very strong south wind blew
all day, yet out of the wind, or in the sun it was very hot.

Sunday the 18th Anniversary of the Great Battle of Leipsic[23]
—rested well last Night, and thank God, had no simpthoms of
fever to day, mail from the W & S arrived, no news for me— nor
for any one else, wrote to John Walker N. Orleans, received some
old newspapers pr mail, spend the afternoon in reading them, set
in raining near night and looks like it would keep at it all night.

Monday the 19th Rained nearly all night, cloudy this morning, turned to be fair in the Evening, a Mr Lattimore from Red-
river County arrived, on his way to Austin was introduced to
him, I believe he is the one living on a League of Land of the El-
guezabal Claim nothing was said about it. Major Kaufman[24] arrived from San Augustin, Major Augustin[25] dito. no news.

Tuesday the 20th October all the Familie is well at present
I believe for the first time this summer Eastern mail arrived,
brought no news, Robert Potter[26] a Senator from Red River passed

---

[22]William Henry Dangerfield was born in 1808 at Alexandria, Virginia.
After attending the University of Virginia and practicing law in Maryland, he moved in 1837 to San Antonio and the following year was
elected mayor. Other posts included Commissary of Purchases for the
army, 1839, Bexar County's Senator in the Fifth and Sixth Congresses,
1840-42, Secretary of the Treasurer, 1842-44, and **charge d'affaires** in
the Netherlands, 1844-45. Dangerfiled died at his home in Prince County, Maryland in September, 1878.

[23]The Battle of Leipsig, "the battle of the nations" fought on October
16-17, 1813 was one of Napoleon's most decisive losses.

[24]David Spangler Kaufman was born in Boiling Springs, Pennsylvania on
December 18, 1833. A graduate of Princeton College (1833), he prac-
ticen law in Nachitoches, Louisiana before moving to Nacogdoches in
1837. He represented Nacogdoches County in the House of Representatives during the Third, Fourth and Fifth Congresses, and was Speaker
during the latter two terms. The title "Major" derives from his service
as aide-de-camp to General T. J. Rusk during the Cherokee War. Kaufman was elected to the United States Congress in 1845, and he served
there until his death on January 31, 1852.

[25]Henry W. Augustine.

[26]Robert Potter was born at Granville, North Carolina in June, 1799. Following a varied career in the navy, the practice of law, and service in
the United States Congress, he moved to Texas after serving two years

to day for Austin Our representative Major Kaufman also left to day for seat of government, John Sutherland formerly a resident of this place, now of Bexar arrived to day with a drove of mules—put them in my lot for the night, one of his servants is an Ex Colonel of mexico has come down from a high to a low station Sic transit gloria mundi— one of the mule drivers tells me that vicente Cordova is a Captain in the Centralist Army at Matamoros he also states that the late Outrage by the Comanchez at Linnville, was set on foot at Matamoros paid Mrs Holland $55. Texas monay for some Household furniture purchased of her.

Wednesday 21st Mr Southerland told me that J. Ogilvy is from Muryshire Banff Scottland John norris was here to day, brought in his Papers which he wants the Action of Congress on entrusted them to James Gaines Senator from Shelby & Sabine, paid Gaines $50. Texas Monay on a/c of Lots in Pendleton, all the members of Congress I have seen, are all for reform, a complete reorganization of the government, the government is in a desperate situation if this Congress cures all the complicated deceases it labors under, they will be skillful men, and will merit the sincere thanks of the People— had much Law business to day, got along very Smoothly, day very fine—, a cool Steady north wind is blowing at this time 7 P. M.

Thursday the 22d October 1840 fine cool weather— was introduced to a Mr Mitchel of New Orleans Mr Sherer of San Augustine who arrived this Evening from independence, and washington, brings Counter Orders from Felix Huston respecting the contemplated indian campaign, by the general good humor every one is in this Evening, I have reasons to believe that the measure was not a popular one, at least in this place.

Fryday the 23d nothing stirring to day, weather very fine, wrote to Seth Sheldon, pr mail.

Saturday the 24th Cold weather to day— my Brother Isaac left here to day for Alexandria La gave him $60 Texas monay and a fine Silver watch had nothing else to give him, but he is young and will work for a living like I have done wrote to John Walker, a sale of the Personal Effect of A. Rieman decd took place at my office, I bought a Silver Patent Lever watch gave $19.50 good bargain— a Mr Pucket from Colorado arrived late from indiana, he stays with me as I have some Business to transact with him, James Haverty died last night at Hyde's Tavern, was burried to day at 4 P. m.

Sunday the 25th very fine weather to day had a white frost last night, Mr Pucket left this morning to return in a few days he has become the purchaser of some lands I sold to J. D. Early of indiana in 1835 or 1836. mail arrived from galvezton, no news.

in prison for maiming two of his wife's relatives. Potter lived first in Nacogdoches and represented that county at the Constitutional Convention of 1836, and was a signer of the Declaration of Independence. He served in other public office, but was killed on March 2, 1842 as a consequence of his involvement n the Regulator-Moderator feud..

Monday the 26th October very cold last night very fine weather today, wind South this Evening—a child of Mr Lee's died last night received a long Letter from Mr Edward Salzman of New Orleans respecting his affairs with Mr Ogilvy, obtained Letters of Administration on the Estate of Patricio de Torres decd. took the Oath as prescribed by Law and entered upon the duties of administrator—

Tuesday 27 weather moderated to day, cloudy this Evening— Mail arrived from the US. received a Letter from Louis Rueg, one from the widow Patricio de Torres, and one from T. B. Stoddard of New York. paid to A. Jacobs $20— Texas for a claim on government of $37.50 God knows when I'll get it— paid out $20— Texas for Beef & other articles for the use of my Familie.

Wednesday the 28th begun raining last night and continued so all day to day, wrote a Letter to E. Salzman respecting Ogilvy's Estate. wrote to Louis Rueg, to Wm B. Stille, and to the widow Torres, gave to Corbin the County Depty Clerk, a mortgage to record, from George Wiede to myself, for ½ League of Land, originally granted to Juan Clemente Cortez's Heirs situated on 3 forks of Trinity said Land I sold to Wiede for $1650— payable in 3 months, with the above mentioned Mortgage, the note Wiede gave me of $1650=. is attached to the Mortgage, but is not to be recorded. Mrs. Sterne is a little unwell to day hope it is nothing serious—

Thursday the 29th October weather very fine Chriswell of Natchitochez passed through here to day towards the west, passed as sale before me to Judge Hart[27] for a Lot fronting the Public Square, between Thorn's and Engledow's House gave my letter to Luis Rueg, to a Mr O'Connor of Natchitochez gave him also Salzman's Letter to be mailed at that place, send $30. Texas to Sheriff of Houston County to pay Mrs Nancy Hamilton's Tax for her land and her late son E. E. Hamilton, directed the Letter to woods's or Springhill P. O. Examined Tax list and found James Ogilvy has given in Land last year as his own 13284 acres in the Republic— signed Bond to perform my duties as administrator on P. de Torre's Estate.

Fryday the 30th Weather continues fine, wrote to S. W. Blount of San Augustin, to send me some money he owes me, Manuel Guttierez came from Bayou Lea, has some verbal communication from the widow Torres, appointed 2 P. M. to morrow to meet me at my House, he is also a material witness, in the Land suit I have with the Heirs of Manuel Santos Coy. he knows when I made the trade with Ygnacio Santos for the Land on the Loco.

Saturday October the 31st. Thomas Puckett came late last night from San Augustin. this morning gave me a release dated yesterday for all the Lands I sold to John D. Early in New Orleans last time I was there 1836— for the purpose of giving Mr Puckett Titles to the same Lands in conformity with the Law of this

[27]William Hart.

— 9 —

country. he paid me $220. in Texas monay equal to $44. Texas Monay being the amount of Taxes I had advanced on a/c of said Lands for the year 1838 & 1839. wrote a letter by Mr Puckett to George Aldridge, also an introductory Letter to R. Potter Senator from Red River received $56. Texas monay to pay the Tax on Mr Puckett's Land in Harrison County and for recording the Documents belonging to J. M. Dor's Title, and said Pucketts sale— interpreted between General Rusk & Vital Flores respecting the Division of the Land left by said Flores's Parents to him and his Brothers & Sisters, Flores promised me for my services as interpetrer in said Business $50.00 if all goes to his satisfaction, and Rusk promised to relinquish 500 acres of Land which I gave him as a fee in my Case vs Heirs of Manuel Santos Coy to my youngest son Placide Rusk.— day very fine, many People in Town—

Sunday the 1st November Mr Puckett left this morning, wrote by him to Col Snively[28] respecting some discharges of a Soldier of Louis Sanchez's Company. wrote to Col. R. Potter, to D. S. Kaufman. and to Cap. D. C. Ogden respecting the public Stores he left with me, wrote to E. Salzman of N. Orleans respecting Ogilvy's Estate, E. J. Debard was here requested me to examine the Title Mrs Lazarin has for a Piece of Land on the Boteja— promised to do so to morrow, wrote to K. H. Muse of private Business. wrote also to Muse & Kaufan respecting this Lodge,[29] and such reform as ought to be made in the Grand Lodge of the Republic, particularly in the curtailing its Expences, which in our present situation is too grand intierly. mail from the west arrived, brought no news One Letter from P. Master Gel. which I answered.

Monday November 2d fine day, wrote to Martin Rumpf, of Austin. also to D. S. Kaufman, send off western mail, Mr J. H. Holland returned last night from San Augustin, District Court in session yet received back a contract made between Saml. Maas & myself for some San Leon Property, returned said Maas his note for $100.00 pr F. Von der Hoya his agent.

Tuesday 3d fine weather. Alexander McIvor[30] died last night at 9 oclock. was burried today at 4 P. m. a Horse which I loaned F. v. d. Hoya sometime ago, was so badly hurt by him, that I sold him for $40 to David Rusk on a years credid—Wm H. Dangerfield from Bexar, arrived invited him to spend the night with me, gave me a note of $85.75 to collect against Juan Bautista chirino signed

[28]Jacob Snively, a native of Pennsylvania, came to Texas in 1835. He held several military posts, including Paymaster-General and Acting Secretary of War. He is noted for leading the Snively Expedition in 1843, an unsuccessful attempt to capture the Mexican caravans running between St. Louis, Missouri and Santa Fe, New Mexico. In later years Snively moved further west to follow the mining frontier, and was killed by Apache Indians near Vulture, Arizona, on March 18. 1878.
[29]Milam Lodge No. 2, which Sterne helped to organize. He was at this time the immediate past Worshipful Master of the Lodge.
[30]Alexander McIver.

in 1826 in favor of John Cortez— Col Blount[31] of San Augustin, send me word by mail rider that he would be here on Thursday next, made Frederick T. Philipps an offer to let him [have] the Land trade between Old Jose de los Santos & myself in case he can get half the monay $125.00. the half of the Stone House (vicente Cordova's Part) was sold today at Public auction for the Benefit of the widow Finley[32] as indemnification of the loss of her Negroes, taken off by Cordova. Brichta gave up his Store to Roberts to day.

Wednesday the 4th November 1840 fine weather to day. Dangerfield left here to day in company with Ned Roberts, for Crockett, saw Mr. Flournoy from Canton Mississippi, who saw Mrs Silverberg, says the widow wants to come out here,—bought a Skeleton Lever watch of Mr Simpson[33] the watch maker, gave $82.00 in notes and Texas monay paid T. T. McIvor 13 dollars good monay for negro hire, said amount was paid in my assuming a debt McIvor owes to the Estate of A. Rieman—

Thursday 5th fine weather, signed a deed to one half of the Land purchased of Maria Cortez as Executrix and administratrix on the Estate of Juan Clemente Cortez decd. to Frost Thorn, said Land is Located on the Bois d'Arc fork of Trinity River Surveyed by Casey, being No 98. I have not settled with Thorn for said Headright. after allowing Thorn all he has advanced, say $180. from first to this moment, there is $20. coming to me from Thorn on that trade. Mr Flournoy goes to morrow, intends to bring Edward, Mrs Silverberg's oldest son here. Hoya mooved out of his Thorn's store to Roberts's Store. Orton[34] arrived with his Familie— Abram H. Scott came in from Angelina, had a conversation with him about the land he left with J. Walker to sell. hired a negro man of Mr Hunt at $1. or $6. Texas monay pr diem.

Friday the 6th November—1840 weather set in raining last night about 8 P. M. Hazy & Cloudy weather this morning. Wrote by Flournoy to Mrs. Silverberg, Saw Col. Carr of crockett. said county is filling up very fast. land becoming valuable. the Sun Saluted the Earth about 2 P. M.

Saturday 7th fine weather this morning F. T. Philipps announced to me that he was ready to go into the Speculation about the Santos Half League of Land, I offered him a few days ago— gave him my Papers I have from Santos, and the original Title to

[31]Stephen William Blount of San Augustine was a signer of the Declaration of Independence. He was born in Burke County, Georgia on February 13, 1808. He moved to Texas in 1835, and was an enthusiastic supporter of the revolution. He fought at San Jacinto. Blount served San Augustine, his adopted home, as County Clerk, First Judicial District Clerk, and Postmaster, and was active in Democratic Party affairs. He died on February 7, 1890, in San Augustine.
[32]Rebecca Collier Fenley, wife of Zachariah P. Fenley and step-daughter of John S. Roberts.
[33]The 1850 Census lists a W. P. Simpson whose occupation was listed as "silversmith." It is probable that this is the same man.
[34]Sidney Maury Orton.

make out a document from between himself & me, which he says
will have finished tomorrow morning— Mr P. returned to Town
this afternoon and paid me $32. in Silver the rest $40, in Silver to
be paid me by Mr Wm Jones. also $53— which is to be paid me
in coffe Sugar, whiskey, or any such groceries as I may want out
of Jones's Establishment. left all the Silver with Jones till I want
it next monday— signed a Bond to Philipps for the undivided half
of the half League of Land. wrote a contract in Spanish between
Vital & Policarpio Flores and Gel. Rusk, the Contract by consent of
Parties was left in my hands not to be given up till the contracting
parties are all together, placed the Document in the Package La-
belled "Documents belonging to other Persons" had a quarrell
with John Lussan, about Land, he wants to be right, and so do I,
we will both be right if left alone, the Law will do us Justice.

Sunday the 8th November 1840— fine weather today Major
Mayfield[35] arrived last night from San Augustin, Judge Richard
Scurry dito— all bound for Austin, Mayfield informed me he
knows that a Mr Dodd ownes 14 negroes, said Dodd owes me
$3500, of which Mayfield has a third and Mathew F. Sims a third,
if said money is collected. Mayfield before leaving here will have
the necessary Documents made out to bring suit against Dodd—
the circumstance is— Mayfield as my attorney in fact sold Dodd a
League and Labor of Land for $3500. Dodd paid him in Pearl
River worthless shinplasters, Dodd obligating himself to Mayfield
that said worthless paper was good as Silver that the Bank it was
issued from was a charted institution and Specie paying Bank all
of which has turned out to be a Humbug and for said fraud Dodd
is to be sued before the proper Tribunal— Wrote a deed for Vital
Flores in favor of his wife— Vital Flores obligated himself verb-
aly to deliver me next Spring a first rate gentle cow & calf for
such services as I have rendered him in writing the contract between him, his Son Policarpio & Gel Rusk, for fees due me in a
suit had before me yesterday about a Horse, and the writing of
the Deed above named, in failure of delivering a first rate cow &
calf he is to pay twenty seven dollars in Silver or its equivalent

Monday 9th November 1840— fine weather to day paid David
Rusk Sheriff— all the Taxes of 1839 and 1840— for myself— Mrs
Sterne— Genereux Benard's Estate, Jose de los Santos Coy &
Patricio de Torres & Wm K. English (for Mr Hazard) of Alexandria whole amount of Tax— $444.92½ got receipt for all, Mr
Blount of San Augustin arrived, also Mr. Gould. Judge Scurry
left for Austin. Lester Hotchkiss arrived last Evening, receiving
one months Rent $100. Texas money from Mrs Mongomery— on
a/c of Bernard's Estate. received $72.00 in Silver from Philipp
which I had left with him since we made the trade for Santos's
Land as already mentioned— Received of the Brothers Hoya 2

---

[35]James S. Mayfield, born in Tennessee in 1809, migrated to Texas in
   1837. He represented Nacogdoches County in the Texas House of Representatives from 1840 to 1842, and served briefly as Secretary of State
   under M. B. Lamar. Mayfield died on October 1, 1852.

notes for safe keeping sealed up in a paper and filed with the Package of "Documents belonging to other Persons" rented the House of Lompayrae, to Gel. Rusk for 18 months

Tuesday November 10th weather Cloudy, South wind, had a conversation with S. W. Blount told me that the Half League of Land claimed by his wife the widow of John S. Lacey, and sold as such was for my Special Benefitt, and that said Land would be conveyed to me in due form of Law as soon as I make to said Mrs Blount a deed for a League & Labor of Land granted to Jose Maria Alpando— (alias) Villalpando which I expect to do in a short time— Juan Bautista chirino Executed to me his notes for $55.00 payable in 4 months and one for $50. payable in 12 months, had a Deed for a tract of Land on which P. de Torres' Plantation is situated, Purchased of Jose Ma Mora, placed upon file for record in the county Clerks office.

CHAPTER II

"... no sleep, much drinking, and a little fighting ..."

Wednesday November the 11th 1840— had a storm and rain last night, fine weather to day. got ready to start to Grand Cane, and Shrevee Port, to morrow morning, O'Neil's Carriage came in to day to take Mrs Holland & familie to Natchitochez, to return from there to New Orleans, several strangers in Town to day, Emigration pours in, *en masse*

Thursday the 12th left home to John Norris[1] on attoyac, got him to accompany me. left his House at 2 P. M. and went to the widow Parmer's in Shelby county, had a wretched Lodging, and worse fare, paid one dollar Silver in the morning—

Fryday 13th— fine weather crossed the Sabine at Logans's Ferry, went to Aaron Fergusson, fared midling well for $3.00

Saturday the 14th left Fergusson's to Jose de los Santos's 5 miles. found him ready to leave for Natchitochez, got my Bill of Sale for a half League of Land, agreable to a Contract made with him on the 3d of February last, went to a Mr Nicholsons' on the Shreeveport Road, got Excelent fare & good Lodging for $2.50, the country we travelled trough to day is very poor—

Sunday the 15th November fine weather to day—left Nicholsons to a beutifull little Town called Summergrove 10 miles South of Shreveport at this place, we met with a Son of Saml. Norriss, who guided us trough, swamp morass, and water, to Nat. Norriss, was received in a friendly manner by him, nothing however was said about the late Rebellion in which he took such an active part. The goods which Mr Ogilvy send up to Sam Norriss are in Nat Norriss Posession. he N. Norriss, told me he had made an arrangement with Mr Louis Rueg to pay me for them, had no monay to give me, the arrangement is to be made trough Mr John Durst,[2] who is to pay $200. which amount N. Norriss says he loaned

---

[1] John Norris was born on November 22, 1800. He married Mary Celeste Stockman on November 6, 1826, and died on March 10, 1881. He was a brother of Samuel Norris

[2] John Durst, the natural son of wealthy trader Peter Samuel Davenport, was born on February 4, 1797 in Arkansas County. Missouri Territory. He enjoyed a varied career which embraced Indian trading, service in the legislature of Coahuila and Texas in 1835, and a captaincy under Rusk in the Cherokee War. He died on February 9, 1851.

Durst previous to the Rebellion, as I have not seen Mr Durst nor Mr Rueg, I know not how the matter stands, but if the Estate gets any thing I shall consider it as that much found— crossed in flat boat one of the Forks of Red River, to Mr Samuel Norriss, who lives on the Bank of the Main Red River, was well received by Mr Norriss and his amiable Familie

Monday the 16th remained all day at Mr. Norriss's the Steam Boat Washington passed up, John Norriss had never seen one before—

Tuesday the 17th November left, recrossed the River, swamps, eta passed by Summergrove to Thomas Norriss's, fared well at his House.

Wednesday the 18th passed trough Greenwood a beutiful village with a fine Acadamy build partly by the State of Louisiana and partly by subscription, the place is in a Languid state, in consequence of the belive that the place will be in the Limits of Texas, in fact all the inhabitants are *fearfull* they will be in Texas after the line is run— passed several large plantations to day, Lodged for the night at the House of a Mr John Jurdan, had good fare for One dollar

Thursday the 19th went this day to the Town of Shelbyville,[3] called on the County Clerk, and found my Headright purchased of the widow Susan Latham to be rejected by the Traveling Board of Land commissioners. However I know the claim to be a good one, I do not despair in getting it yet fixed all right—

Fryday the 20th left Shelbyville to the Crossing of Attoyac near Vital Flores's. here Mr Norriss left me for his House and I came home about dark— found a Letter from Alexander Philipps, One from Mr F Hazard of Rapide, and one from Mr James P. Kay, who inclosed a note of J. S Linn which he wants me to collect, nothing new has occurred during my absence, my Familie have been unwell, but are all thank God well at present—

Saturday Novr 21th heard that George Pollitt has died since I left home— many Strangers mooving to the west passed today, send a letter to Cable & Mears Natchitochez—saw R. F. McKinney of Galvezton, has a claim of upward of $3500 against Douglass—

Sunday Novr 22d Cold weather—wrote to D. S. Kaufman, to A. Philips of N. Orleans, to J. P. Kay informing of the rumor here about him, wrote to F. H. Hazard of Alexandria. mail from Austin arrived brought the Presidents massage, nothing very particular in it— Kaufman elected Speaker. Retrenchment & reform appear to be the Order of the day, nothing else is talked about, so says Kaufman.

Monday Novr 23 Cold but fine weather—wrote to Saml Norriss, also to Louis Rueg, paid the Sheriff $166.00 for Rueg's Tax for 1840 also $123.62 for John Norriss's Tax for 1840. had to bor-

---

[3]Shelbyville, in Shelby County, was originally called Nashville when it was founded by Tennessee immigrants in 1824. In 1837 it was renamed in honor of Isaac Shelby.

row the monay from chevallier[1] at an enormous interest, gave
David Rusk $25— Texas money to pay govt dues for my part
of the Headright of Jose Ma. Mora located in Houston County, Col
Ranson returned from Fannin County on the way to Houston, Mr
Woodward[5] Deputy Sergeant at arms of the House of Representatives, arrived from Austin with Supoenas from Congress for, John
S. Roberts, Robt A. Irion,[6] Chas. S. Taylor John Durst George Aldridge, Ranford Berry G. W. Tips, Joseph Rowe & myself, to
appear before the Committee on Public Lands at the City of Austin
on the 10th of December next, all I believe agreed to do,[7] paid
Daniel Lacy $22. par monay on a/c of the $50 he let me have
when I went to Grand Cane last year. I owe him yet $16. good
money and $60 Texas, he having now no claim on the Land I
then purchased

Tuesday Novr the 24th Cold, cloudy, windy weather, Jeremie[8]
is starting for Natchitochez this morning, gave him $15 Silver send
all my despatches by him gave F. T. Philips. the Sale I received
from Jose de los Santos Coy, to convey to me the Half of it as
agreed on and stipulated on the 7th inst. Benigno Santos was
married last night to Jose Ma Procela's Daughter, Hart. Taylor,
Roberts, and all the Elite of our Town were at the wedding.

Wednesday the 25th very cold weather today it rumored in
Town that Gel Sam Houston is dead— not sure— nothing new
otherwise translated a French Document for Vital Flores, and
gave him also a copy of his contract with Gel Rusk drank a good
Egg nog and went to bed—

Thursday the 26th Cold—cold—cold weather this morning—
moderated in the afternoon, many wagons with Emigrants passed
to day bound for Houston County, and the far west, jhon Thorn
is to be married next Tuesday, regret that I can not be at the
wedding.

Fryday the 27th fine weather, Emigrants literally, pouring

---

[1]Charles Chevallier was a wealthy merchant and landowner in Nacogdoches. The Nacogdoches County tax roll for 1837 lists 2,800 acres at an
evaluation of $4 518 in his possession. He was a member of Milam
Lodge No. 2, A. F. & A. M., and was a close friend of Sterne's. He died
on December 30, 1852.
[5]Moses Wood was the doorkeeper of the House of Representatives for the
Fourth Congress.
[6]Robert Anderson Irion was born on July 7, 1806 in Paris, Tennessee. His
doctorate in medicine was from Transylvania University. Irion abandoned his practice in Vicksburg, Mississippi, in 1831 to migrate to the
Ayish Bayou community near San Augustine, became a surveyor and
trader in partnership with George Aldrich, and also practiced medicine
in Nacogdoches. On September 14, 1835 he was elected to the Committee
of Safety and Vigilance for Nacogdoches, represented that place as a
senator in the First Congress, and on June 13, 1837 was appointed by
Houston as Secretary of State. He was married to Anna Raguet. Irion
died on March 2, 1861.
[7]For this testimony, see supplement to the House Journal of the Fifth
Congress. 329-71.
[8]Jeremy Ruff was Mrs. Sterne's brother. He lived in the Sterne house-
hold until his death on January 15, 1841.

in,— Capt Hooper[9] returned from Austin brought some Papers & a Letter from Muse[10] & Kaufman, Mr Woodward returned from San Augustin

Saturday the 28th very fine weather— preparing to go to Austin. Mr Silvester a merchant from New Orleans arrived was introduced to him, J. D. Clary also arrived, Francis Ramsdale gave me a Power of attorney to collect several debts due him by govnt. received a letter from S. A. Belden New Orleans & one from Ben Clark *Irish Ben Clark* as good a fellow as ever lived I belive he is an Honest man en toto

Sunday 29th November very fine weather today Mr Mitchel of N. Orleans left, western mail arrived, brought me several letters from the Post Master General, one of [them] orders me to change the departure of the mail to San Augustin. received also a full Power of attorney from the Daughter of Patricio de Torres from Bexar to attend to her Land affairs and to the her affairs as an Heir of Patricio de Torres generally. filed the Power of attorney for record in the office of the county Clerk of this county, received several other Documents respecting same claim filed away in their respective places— had an arrangement between Mr Blake & myself and John S. Roberts, Mr. Blake as the lessee of the Lower part of the Stone House under me, as agent of Mrs Mora, and Mr Roberts representing himself *to be the representative* of Mrs Finley, it was agreed, that from the time the House (or half of it was sold to Mrs Finley) the Rent of the Grocery Room is to be paid half to widow Finley and the other half to the Widow Mora, the Expence of repairing said Room to be taken out first, also that the west end room is to be to the benefit of Mrs Finley and the Eastern End Room below to the benefitt of Mrs Mora, and that Mr Blake shall keep the same Rooms he now occupies for the next twelve months from the 14th of January next at two hundred and fourty dollars a year; the rent of the West End Room to be deceided on when I return it is understood that the west end Room is to be in offset against the East end room at present occupied by me, and the ballance of the Rent from the day the said sale took place to be divided between them (Mrs Mora and Mrs Findley) after paying Blake for the floor he laid in the middle Room

Monday 30th Novr left home to John Durst's. left Mr J. H. Holland in charge of the Post office

Tuesday December 1th 1840 left early in the morning, fine weather, to jacob master's 35 miles

wednesday 2d very fine weather—left early, passed trough

---

[9]Richard Hooper, from Shelby County, was a member of the House of Representatives in the First Congress.
[10]Kindred H. Muse represented Nacogdoches in the House of Representatives in the First, Third, and Fourth Congresses, and in the Senate in the Fifth through the Seventh Congresses.

Croket, went to Judge Aldridge's[11] to dinner, went to Robin's on the west bank of Trinity 35 miles

Thursday the 3d Rained last night, Doctor Irion one of our company got very Sick and by unanimous advice of the Company returned home, at 10 A.M. Stopped Raining, but cloudy—went the old (upper) San Antonio Road to Rodger's 30 miles . . .

Fryday the 4th wind from the north very cold, almost too Severe to travel, passed the Nava Soto at tinnersville to Nashville on the Brassos 50 miles, Stopped at Beal's[12] good House,

Saturday December the 5th very fine weather, went to Jones's 15 miles passed in our journey a mountain (the sugar load[13] 400 feet high. wild country stopped at Jones's all day to recruit our force, for the purpose of going trough the (Strech) 75 miles indian country without a house. 5 persons arrived from Nashville Brassos to go on with us, (Capt Reed,[14] Col wheelock[15] Major Porter Mr Murray and Mr Wilson

Sunday December 6th fine weather—left early this morning, some fine, country Saw many herds of Buffalo but did not Stop to kill any stopped near night at a place called the Hole in the Rock from a peculiar Basin of water formed in a solid Rock, in the Bed of a Bayou here we took our Supper, but our Horses were very uneasy, and we supposed that indians were in the neighbourhood, at 8 oclock we saddled up and went 15 miles further to the Post Oak Grove and campt for the night

Monday the 7th left early, Prairie all the way to Austin 30 miles. arrived at 3 P.M. was met by all my friends, and some old acquaintances, was invited by my friend Kaufman to a Ball which was given in honor of the French & american ministers,— put up—at Bullock's[16] Austin is (as a Town Site) a fine place— went to the Ball, was introduced to Mons de Saligné[17] the French minister, to Mr Flood[18] the Chargé D' affairs from the u. States, and his Lady, a fine woman, danced two cotillions and retired

Tuesday the 8th December at the House of representatives to

---

[11]George Aldrich.
[12]Possibly Peter Hansborough Bell.
[13]Sugarloaf Mountain. At least four elevations in Texas bear this same title. Considering the route, this is probably the Sugarloaf Mountain located in the northwestern part of present-day Bell County near the Coryell County line.
[14]Captain Henry Reed.
[15]Eleazer Louis Ripley Wheelock.
[16]The Bullock House, constructed in 1839, was the first hotel in Austin. It was located at the northwest corner of present Sixth Street and Congress Avenue. Later it also bore the name of Swisher's and Smith's Hotel.
[17]Count Alphorso de Saligny. was secretary of the French legation in Washington in 1838, and was dispatched to Texas to further the interests of his country in the Republic. He was involved in the so-called "Pig War" with his landlord, Richard Bullock, and this and other trouble caused his withdrawal from Texas. He was instrumental in gaining French recognition of Texas.
[18]George H. Flood

day, cherokee Bill discussed, several members Spoke in favor & contra—

Wed:.esday the 9th Kaufman had the floor to day made an Eloquent Speach against the Cherokee Bill,[19] he occupied the floor all day—

Thursday the 10th Cherokee Bill— Mayfield had the floor to day, I very seldom have heard a better argument on any Subject—in the evening I was examined, by the Committee on Public Lands, had my interrogatories in writing, answered them in writing—have a copy of part of them N. B. on this Evening Gel Houston was attacked by Col Jordan of the late Federal army and had it not been for my interference Jordan would have killed him with an axe[20]—

Fryday the 11th Cherokee Bill—Gen Houston had the floor today, House crowded, with men, women and childern, got trough with our Testimony to day

Saturday the 12th December 1840 Cherokee Bill still under discussion, Mayfield—van Sant[21] of Harrison Spoke against the Bill, House adjourned till Monday next—

Sunday the 13th paid 100 dollars Texas monay for Tavern Bill, and cleared out. received an order from Col Hockley[22] to sell all Public Property in my possession except the drums. Order dated 12th Decemr in my possession, amongst "Letters on Business" went to Bastrop 38 miles—put up at Mr Moessel's a german, Mr Taylor lost his Saddle bags at this House.

Monday 14th— left early this morning went 45 miles and campt out, got some Buffalo meat from some Hunters to day which served us for our Supper, bought a Tonge to take Home with me, slept well under the trees

Tuesday the 15th left at 4 oclock this morning passed trough San Antonio Prairie a Beutiful Settlement, passed trough Tenoxtitlan,[23] cross the Brazos River to Mr Moss 40 miles

Wednesday the 16th left early this morning went 4 miles to Mrs Walkers, here a man in Spectacles from Houston took us out

---

[19]The Cherokee Bill was unsuccessful legislation that would have confirmed the title of lands awarded to the Cherokee Nation by the Treaty of 1836. Sam Houston was its principal supporter, but it was defeated.

[20]Samuel W. Jordan. This incident is not mentioned in Houston's best-known biographies.

[21]Isaac Van Zant was born in Franklin County, Tennessee on July 10, 1813. Business reverses in Mississippi forced his removal to Texas in 1838. He settled in Panola County, and in 1839 moved to Marshall. He represented Harrison County in the Fifth and Sixth Legislatures, and in 1842 Sam Houston made him **charge d'affairs** to the United States. He died on October 11, 1847.

[22]George Washington Hockley was an intimate of Houston, who appointed him his chief of staff when he commanded the Texas Army, colonel of ordnance on December 22, 1836, and secretary of war on November 13, 1838 and again on December 23, 1841. Hockley lived in Galveston.

[23]Tenoxtitlán, Texas was originally Fort Tenoxtitlán. When it was abandoned in 1832 by Mexican troops, some of the inhabitants remained near the Indian trading post. It gradually declined and ceased to be of importance by 1860.

of our Road, and on our discovering the fact we tried to regain our Road by going trough the woods, in attempting which, we got lost, and found ourselves in the Evening at a Mr Head's 10 miles from the place we had Started from in the morning

Thursday the 17th left early this morning passed trough Tinnersville 10 miles the Nava Soto was Swimming—Swam our Horses across, had our Baggage packet across a Log which was under water, and which we had to pass over, at our eminent risk of being drownded, finally we got over safe, and went to Robt Rodgers 25 miles—

Fryday the 18th left early crossed the River Trinity, to Judge Aldridges 45 miles, we crossed at a new place, (Boseman's Ferry) which is a much better, and nearer Road than by Robins's Ferry

Saturday the 19the Decembr Rained very much last night, keeps on this morning, left in the rain, and passed trough Crockett to Master's in the rain 20 miles, got wet outside, and got something to wet the inside, on our arrival,—

Sunday the 20th left in the Rain, rode all day in the rain to John Durst's 36 miles—

Monday the 21st arrived at Home found all well, John Thorn got married during my absence, to the widow Leander Smith,

Tuesday the 22d took charge of the post office again, found everything all Straight Capt English[24] has opened a mercantile Establishment in the old Tavern, every thing else is as it used to be

Wednesday the 23d paid charles chevallier $330.00 Texas Monay I had borrowed of him to pay Taxes for Rueg & John Norriss, an Election took place to day for Justice of the Peace, and B. Blake was reelected, without oposition, Jeremie informs me, that he has paid S. B. True Town of Natchitochez $3. to pay for some goods I expect up from New Orleans, Madame P. Bossier, has named our little girl, her name is "Laura." (a classic name!) was also informed of the death of my friend Victor Bossier

Thursday the 24th cloudy & cold, mail from galveston & Houston, no news; finding that george Wiede is not returning & hearing nothing from him sued him for $1650.00 and attached 640 acres of Land he bought from J. C. Hill John Walling Jr married one of John Dorsetts Daughters, A Ball this Evening, went off tolerable well, but none of our *Old Balls* like we had in 1833, 4. & 5.

Fryday the 25 Christmas fine weather Major Kimbro[25] of San Augustin, who left Austin 4 days after I did, reports that it is generally belived that the Mexicans are about to invade Texas,

---

[24]William K. English.

[25]William Kimbro of San Augustine raised the Eighth Company, Second Regiment for the Texas Army and commanded it at San Jacinto. He served as sheriff of San Augustine County from 1837 to 1843. He died on September 14, 1856.

young Van Ness[26] brought such news from San Antonio, it has also been ascertained that Seguin[27] has not joined the Enemy. L Meyers returned from New Orleans, says he has Letters for me, which he left in his trunk on a wagon, made friends with Mrs. Raguet, who had not Spoken to me since the marriage of her Daughter to Doctor Irion

Saturday the 26th December very fine weather Major Kimbro left a letter for from Kaufman at Blake's being of a public nature. left it at the office for general inspection—Mr Milam[28] a Brother of Col Benjamin Milam arrived, invited him to my House, accepted, received a letter from my Brother Isaac, he informs me that my half Sister Nancy is married to a man by the name of Steevens, received a Letter from Wiede, did not deter me from proceeding in my Suit against him, Wm. K. English receiving many goods to day (5 wagon loads)

Sunday the 27th Saint Johns Day. Fair weather Robt Patton Esq. came up, with the intention to get subscribers to clear out the Angelina River, he thinks that he will succeed in having the River in order for Keel Boats by next season[29]— Milam Lodge met to day for the first time in a year, got the late residence of Genl Douglass as Lodge Room, many strangers in town to day

Monday the 28th Hazy and cold weather Probate Court, my case about the Loco Land came on to day, posponed til next term of the Court at the request of A. Hotchkiss, the administrator on Emanuel Santo's Estate, many country people in Town, Mr witlesey[30] and Familie arrived last night, to open the old Tavern, Nacogdochez appears to be reviving—

Tuesday the 29th December cold hazy weather Commenced suit against Nat Noriss on account the debt he ows Ogilvy, John Norriss acknowledged the Deed from old Santos and wife to F. T. Philipps, and I received my deed from Philipps for half the Land— Sold my old Saddle Horse to B. Blake for $100.00 would not have sold that faithfull servant, but knowing he gets as good, or better

---

[26]This is either Cornelius or George Van Ness, two brothers who practiced law in San Antonio. They were the sons of Cornelius P. Van Ness, United States Minister to Spain from 1829 to 1837. Young Cornelius represented Bexar County in the Third, Fourth, Fifth and Sixth Congresses of the Republic, 1838-1842, and died on May 2, 1842. George Van Ness' death date cannot be determined.

[27]Juan Nepomucena Seguin was born in San Fernando de Bexar on October 27, 1806. Seguin befriended the Anglo settlers and was an early opponent of Santa Anna. He served with Austin near San Antonio in 1835, with Bowie at the Battle of Concepcion, and with William B. Travis shortly before the Alamo siege. He was then a captain in the regular Texas Army, and later rose to lieutenant-colonel, served in the Texas Senate, and was Mayor of San Antonio. He died in Nuevo Laredo in 1889.

[28]James Milam, who was associated with Benjamin Rush Milam in a colony between the Colorado and Guadalupe Rivers.

[29]For an excellent account of Robert S. Patton's efforts to navigate the Angelina River, see Lois Fitzhugh Foster Blount. "The Story of Old Pattonia," **East Texas Historical Journal**, V (March, 1967), 13-28.

[30]Probably the Ralph Whittlesey who operated a tavern in San Augustine.

master I parted with him—send several advertisements to the San Augustin Paper.

Wednesday the 30th. Cold rainy day   loaned myers ten dollars good monay   nothing of consequence transpired to day   W. K. English gave a Ball, in the Evening   *quite a Business transaction* the Ladies God bless them—looked as lovely as ever but it requires the pencil of Hogart to give a correct description of the Heterogenous Set of men, who were there congregated,

Thursday the 31t   Sleet, Snow, cold, ugly weather   Mr Hoya who came last night from Houston reports that his Holiness the Pope has acknowledged the independence of Texas, a Steam Boat Smagged in the River Trinity, on which Hoya had some goods, no Business transacted in Town to day, all hands on a frolic my Son Charles took Sick yesterday, not better to day— send for Doctor Starr, who gave him Some medicines

Fryday January the 1st 1841   the first day of the year, a cold but a beutifull cloudless Sky and the Sun rose in all its Splendor I hope that it is a good omen, and that our Country may during the coming year be disenthraled from all her difficulties, and every one be happy.   Subscribed to Benayah Thompson's School to send three Scholars at $50.00 par monay a year—advanced Mr Thompson twelve dollars good monay—mail from East, a letter from Sam Norriss nothing particular News from the west—mexicans 7000 East of the Rio Grande 13000 behind— Bedershin— hang the Banner eta well let them come— charles is getting better thank God.—

Saturday January 2d 1841   Beutifull weather, but it is very cold,   Sold public Stores to day Exepting the Powder, which at the Suggestion of general James Smith I posponed— we may want it before long— the Lodge met in the Evening, rented Douglass House for two months at $15 pr month

Sunday the 3d 1841   very fine weather made an engagement with a Mr Blair to bring me a Saddle Horse, from Tennessee, which he will bring next October or November   nothing transpired to day worth Speaking of   no further [news] from the west

Monday January the 4th 1841   Cloudy—warm weather nothing of consequence passed, saw an old acquaintance a Mr Stamps from Mississippi, a Ball in the Evening at Chevalliers, was well attended, and went off O. K.[31]

Tuesday the 5th. fine mild weather— *Sale day,* to day much Land was offered for sale by the Sheriff but none brought 2/3ds of its valuation, so they are to be sold on a 12 months credit—settled and paid my account to Chevallier up to date— (thank god)

---

[31] The use of the slang "O.K." at this early date and this far west is remarkable. Daniel Borstin in The Americans: The National Experience (Vintage Books: New York, 1967), 287) states that the term was formerly believed to have been derived from the reference to Martin Van Buren as "Old Kinderhook," but that now the weight of evidence leans to an assumed but improbable misspelling by Andrew Jackson as "oll Korrect" for "all correct." In either case it could scarcely be but five years old.

Joseph S. Cook, was accused, and brought up before me for Larceny, gave Bail to appear for Examination of Fryday the 15th inst—Town full of People

Wednesday the 6th Clowdy and warm in the morning, Rain (very heavy) about 10 A. M. North wind at 12. Clear in the Evening—made out my quarterly returns to Post Master genl—revenue in the Department, decreased since last year.

Thursday the 7th cold & clowdy in the morning, fine in the afternoon rode out with general Cleveland[32] to my Moral, place to sell it to him, asket $3.50 per acre, offered me $600. for the place—could not agree— Bought a Poney of Arnold Evans, a german for $25.00 paid him $17.50 on account, hired said Evans one month at $20 pr month to work on farm

Fryday the 8th— Cold during the day, Moderated at night Jeremie is very Sick of Plurisy, Doctor Starr attends on him. Emigrants are still coming in, Col Pierpont[33] and Son passed, to Shebyville— Lodge met in the Evening Conferred 3d on Doctor Hyde. anniversary of Battle of Orleans.[34]

Saturday the 9th Cold & rainy, rained nearly all night Kept at [it] all day— nobody Stirring, had a meeting of the Lodge— m. g. whitaker 3d 3. Jeremy continous to have fever—

Sunday January 10 1841 rain & cold in the morning clear in the afternoon. mr John Durst was in Town to day asked him if he would pay the $200. for Nat Norriss— was answered, no—so that the suit I had commenced but Stayed. the regular process will be carried on to morrow— Several Persons from the west, did not gather any news— wrote several Letters one to Kaufman one to S. Norriss, and others— Jeremy still very Sick

Monday the 11th very fine weather felt unwell last night effects of Cold. County Court to day adjourned till to morrow without doing any business, Road Commissioners met, more new Roads were Ordered to be Surveyed— bad business if the Public Roads we now have would be kept in good order we would do much better than to make more new bar Roads, I declined being a candidate for ass[o]ciate Justice. J. M. Watkins & B. Blake were elected. a large meeting was held by the Citizens of this County for the purpose of taking into consideration a proposition Robert S. Patton has made for clearing out the Angelina from Travis to the Sabine Bay for $10000. the Citizens being present John H Hyde Esq St was called to the Chair and myself appointed Secretary, general Rusk addressed the Meeting in a forcible and Eloquent manner pointing out the advantages that would arise

---

[32]Possibly Horotio N. Cleveland.

[33]William Pierpoint was born in Connecticut about 1797. He came to Texas shortly after the Revolution and represented Shelby County in the Second Congress. He later operated a mercantile business in Houston. The date of his death is not established.

[34]On January 8, 1815, United States forces under the command of Andrew Jackson repulsed an attack of British troops under Edward Packenham near New Orleans. For the United States, this represented the capstone of military efforts in the War of 1812.

from the opening of Navigation of that River. near $3400 were subscribed. Lodge met this Evening. Jeremy Still very Sick

Tuesday the 12th January Cold, rainy day— County Court in Session— Judge Hart indisposed. did not attend the County Court. the man I had hired got beastly drunk, discharged him! dishonorably—! —rained all day, and most part of the night—till

Wednesday the 13th Cold, damp, weather. County Court went trough their business— held Justices Court today, not many suits to decide. Placide sick to day — Jeremiah still sick getting worse, paid Palmer,[35] for Schooling $10.00 good money

Thursday the 14th very cold, frost (heavy) last night Splendid sun this morning, Counselor Hyde, Munroe Hyde & Mr Henderson set up last night with Jeremy, he is getting worse— in my opinion he will not get over it—

Fryday 15th Poor Jeremy is gone, to that Bourne from whence no traveler returns— he died at 12 Oclock last night, under intense suffering, had his Senses to the last moment, the last words he Spoke were Mama, Sister. two names dear to him he requested nothing before his Death, though concious he was dying. he only requested me to be present *in time to tell him good by—* poor fellow—! He was an honest industrious, and virtuous young man Peace be with thee, my dear Jeremy— Funeral took place at ½ past four P. M. attended by all the Citizens of the Place— J. H. Holland Esqr. made a Short but feeling address, wrote to Oliver Rouquir—

Saturday 16th Rained all night— rains still at 10. A.M. Placide very sick last night, I do not feel well this morning. Kept raining all day, feel better this Evening. Placide a little better—

Sunday the 17 January 1841 Tremendous frost and Snow last night, the Coldest weather I have experienced in Texas, sun came out, but did not melt the ice nor even the Snow, continued freezing in the Shade all day tremendously cold this afternoon, Kept close to the fire all day, and done more writing then I have done at any day during the last month. Placide is better to day, the Cold is so intense that some young Piggs froze to death—

Monday 18th very Cold weather, but not so disagreeable as yesterday. saw some skating to day no business doing. received some San Augustin Papers and a Letter from Mr Gould

Tuesday the 19th las night rained and froze as soon as it fell on the grownd, so that all the grownd is covered with a cake of ice, at the eminent risk, of falling I succeeded in getting to the office— weather moderated near noon and towards Evening all the ice off the grownd, notwithstanding the inclement weather several waggons came in

Wednesday 20th weather still moderating ice disappearing very fast— held an Examining Cou[r]t to day in the Case of Republic vs J. T. Cook for Cow Stealing— engaged all day in

---

[35] Henderson D. Palmer.

hearing evidence and listening to speaches of attorneys— bound
Cook over in $2500 to appear at next district Court—

Thursday 21st ice me[l]ting, but weather is still cold, wet,
unpleasant, held an examing Court Joseph & Steward Meredith
for Cow Stealing bound over to the District Court, in $1000 each
with good security, received a Letter from Chas H. Clarke respecting Ogilvy's Estate

Fryday the 22d January 1841 Cloudy & Cold in the morning—
the glorious Sun shone at noon— a perfect Stranger!— Sold several articles belonging to James Latham at auction. amount about
75$. posponed the Sale their being no monay!!!!!!

Saturday the 23d fine weather to day several persons from
the Country in Town— nothing particular happened up to 12
oclock noon— rented the upper part of the Stone House to J. H.
Holland Esqr. for twenty dollars pr month, one half of said sum
to go to the widow Findley and the other half to the Heirs of
Juan mora

Sunday 24th fine weather in the morning. cloudy towards
noon but no rain, a mail arrived from Red river the first this
year! wrote to Gould

Monday the 25th fine weather not too Cold nor too warm.
Probate Court in Session to day, my Suit about the Loco Land
Claim came up, which was decided in my favor— obtained also
an Order of Court to sell the Land Certificates of Conrad Eigenauer. Lodge met in the Evening, gave Judge Hart the 1st degree

Tuesday the 26th Cloudy, [occasional] rain, all day a gentleman from Mississippi a Mr [blank] was introduced to me, as a
gentleman wanting to purchase Land, made an arrangement with
him to go and show him the Loco Land next Sunday settled with
Mr Payne formerly of Natchitochez gave him my note for $36=00
send all Letters I had lately written by him to Natchitochez

Wednesday the 27th very warm, Sometimes cloudy and sometime we could see the sun, wrote to the Editor of the San Augustin
Paper determined to send for a mail towards the East, nothing
from the west yet— settled with Doctor Starr, gave him my note
for Seventy one dollars

Thursday January the 28th rainy weather till near night
when the sun came out a little time, wrote to muse, and send him
a certificate of the time his contract for carrying the mail was
efected— which was 10 January 1840 Send the letter by a Mr
McGree, wrote several Letters, to the members of the Lodge, on
Business concerning that institution

Fryday the 29th weather mild, Sun appeared occasionally
Genl Rusk went to Crocket, send a letter to B. A. Vanzicle by
him, no news yet from the west—no—nor East

Saturday the 30th fair during the day rain after Sun down—
Court day, disposed of several Cases many People in Town, The
Pope's Legate I understand arrived late this Evening, put up at
the tavern, too late to see him after the Lodge Closed, which Con-

vened to night as a regular meeting, raining hard at ½ past 9 oclock

Sunday the 31th rain! rain!! rain!!! was introduced to the rt reverend Mr Timan and the rt revd Mr Odin, the first Vicar general of the Pope in Texas, the second the Bishop (that will be of Texas).[36] two most learned men, they said Mass at the Stone House this morning, and notwithstanding the bad weather there was the largest, and most respectable congregation present that I have ever seen, during the performance of the Service, Mr Timan preached from [blank] and gave an Explanation of the service then performing in such a Chaste and eloquent language as perhaps never has been used by any Divine in Nacogdochez before; service again in the afternoon, Mr Timan was more eloquent than in the morning, the rain was pouring down in torrents, yet the House was crowded with Ladies, and gentlemen.

Monday the 1st February Cool but no rain, & sometime had a little Sunshine— Election day for Sheriff, County Clerk, and Coroner, result not known as yet 9 P.m. saw a Mr. Price from a large Landholder promised to go with him to John Norriss on Attoyac to morrow if the Bayous are not all Swimming, the rd Mrssrs. Timon & Odin, Judge Hart & Taylor dined with us to day, was still more charmed with the Conversational Powers of those gentlemen, then with the Preaching yesterday

Tuesday February the 2d fine weather to day bought a Piece of Land to day for my wife situated between the two bayous Lanana & Banito, all the Land between said Bayous, is now mine which lies East of the Street which passes in front of my House, it is payable in one year. the price $[blank]. sold some goods at auction for L. Myers ($63.93¾). posponed going with Mr Price til to morrow, dined with Mr Taylor the Red Messrs Timan & Mr Odin an arrangement was made to build a Roman Catholic Church, got Authority from the above very revd divines, Chas Chevallier, C. S. Taylor & myself appointed the Principal Committee. Mr Augustin member of Congress from San Augustin returned to day had no time to speak much to him Congress will adjourn to day, brought a paper from Kaufman, had preaching in the Evening—

Wednesday February the 3d— good weather— left after Breakfast with Mr price to go to Mr Garrisson Greenwoods's. road not very good— passed by John Norriss's stopped all night at Greenwoods good supper, good Bed, eta

Thursday the 4th the finest day since the 1st day of January returned to Nacogdochez by a different route, passed a deserted village of Choctaws—, passed Norriss old place on the Nacamihi, trough Sparks's Settlement, home. a letter mail was brought from

[36]Father John Timon and Father Jean Marie Odin were active in Roman Catholic activities. both within Texas and between Texas and Rome. For an account of their efforts. see Carlos E. Castaneda, **The Church in Texas Since Independence. 1836-1850**. volume VII in **Our Catholic Heritage in Texas**, 1519-1950 (5 Vols.; Von Boechmann-Jones: Austin, 1936-1958).

Crocket during my absence, old— brought a Letter from Pinede wants me to attend to vincents business. letter dated 22d November, also a Letter from Kaufman dated 12th, January— heard of the death of Mrs Floyd— Bautista chirino brought me a Cow & Calf he owed me

Fryday February the 5th Cool Clear weather Mr Price paid me $30.00 T. M. Duffield from San Augustin arrived here, had a conversation with him about the prospect of getting a Press established here, thinks it an easy matter to get Reese of the Natchitochez Herald to come over here with his Press if about $500 could be subscribed, which in my opinion can very easily be had

Saturday the 6th Cloudy, *nearly* raining,—at length a mail from the East, brought many Letters, no particular news—Texas monay is getting a little better since England has acknowledged our independence, many People in town, but little business doing

Sunday the 7th Feb. 1841. Cloudy hazy weather—Capt Skerrett passed trough here from Red River he states that Col Cook passed yesterday by Joseph Dursts[37] not coming by this place— cause unknown—Lodge met to day, nothing done, wrote to the Editor of the Journal & Advertiser about mails eta

Monday the 8th Cold, Hazy, ugly, weather, Col Pierpoint arrived to day, left his Son in Shelby County, nothing of consequence transpired to day— except a large Emigration of negroes from Missi. passed trough, glad of the late Law exempting negroes from Execution for debt contracted in the U. S.

Tuesday the 9th good weather Send of Eastern mail— Col Pierpoint left early this morning, rode with him to my place on the Aylitos, received some goods to be sold at Auction next Saturday—

Wednesday the 10th good weather, but cold, paid Chambers[38] $16 par monay for Shingling a part of the House, the Revd. Mr Odin returned from Augustin, Mr Gould arrived, goes to Crocket, Settled with Doctor Irion. Struck off even

Thursday the 11th. very Cold, hard frost last night nobody Stirring, Shops nearly all closed. James Durst in Town, a Show of wax figures in Town, *Showed* last night *go, go,* show again to night a real catch penny Concern.

Fryday February the 12th tremendous Frost last night, sun shines out glorious this morning Capt A. Hotchkiss staid with me last night

Saturday the 13th hard frost last night, very fine weather today, sold about $180.00 at action for Myers, Mail arrived from the East, received a Letter from Sheldon Shreveport, also pr

---

[37]Joseph Durst, or Darst, was born about 1790. He and his brothers came to Texas from Natchitoches, Louisiana in the early 1800's. In 1826 he served as Alcalde of Nacogdoches, and later was on the Committee of Safety and Correspondence. He died prior to April 1, 1843.
[38]Asa Chambers.

Gel. Henderson a Letter from Alanson Canfield[39] Editor San Augustin paper, news arrived today that our District Judge Terrill[40] is appointed Secretary of State, Doctor Chalmers,[41] Secretary of the Treasury, Treaty between Holland & Texas arrived, many People in Town, Show in the Evening

Sunday the 14th Cold, Clear, bracing weather. Mr Barnett,[42] the member of Congress from Sabine passed through to day, says that Judge Terrill has not accepted the place of Secretary of State, but that Mayfield[43] is appointed, and has accepted, however I did not see the gentleman myself—so do not know the real truth, Mr Lussan arrived from New Orleans, Mr Bondies from Houston, Mr Touvenin from Liberty, and Mr Blake from Natchitochez, by the latter I received some papers which I have as yet not perused, by Mr Lussan, I received a Letter from Alexander Philipps New Orleans, and an invoice of some goods he send me, which are in Natchitochez,

Monday the 15th white frost last night good weather today, no news from the west yet—

Tuesday the 16th fine weather, worked in the garden nothing else to do— nothing from the west, yet send of mail to San Augustin & Sabine Town, Ned Roberts arrived in Town. Confirms the news that Mayfield is appointed Secretary of State and that he has accepted the appointment, however we are left so completely in the dark as regards mails, we can not believe anything, untill we get it officially or trough such a Chanell as can not be doubted. Our infant child Laura was taken sick yesterday, continues to have fever to day God knows we have not been intierly without Sickness in the familie Since last July—

Wednesday the 17th very fine weather, worked in the garden one hour in the morning— went up Town, done some law business in the office. no news Stirring— our Boy Placide Rusk is three years old today, the infant not better.

Thursday the 18th very fine weather, worked in the garden 2 hours— went to the Office. Copied a Spanish Document for J. Durst. was introduced to Mr Wm Nixon of New Orleans, took

---

[39]Alanson Wyllys Canfield was born in New Milford, Connecticut. He came to Texas in 1836, lived for a time at Milam, and moved to San Augustine in 1840. Here he published the **Journal and Advertizer**, which was renamed the **Red-Lander**, until 1846. During the Civil War he was engaged in blockade running, and may be the Major Canfield who was killed at the battle of Mansfield on April 9, 1864.

[40]George Whitfield Terrill was born in Nelson County, Kentucky in 1803. He moved to Tennessee in 1827 and rose to the attorney-generalship under Governor Sam Houston. Financial reverses caused his removal to Texas in 1837. He served as Secretary of State in 1841, and in December became Attorney-General. Active in Indian and foreign affairs, he opposed annexation to the United States. He died on May 13, 1846.

[41]John G. Chalmers served briefly as Secretary of the Treasury under M. B. Lamar.

[42]S. Slade Barnett.

[43]James S. Mayfield filled the office of Secretary of State under M. B. Lamar from February 8 to April 30, 1841.

Tea with me. went to Judge Hart's and chatted till 10 oclock. our little girl is getting better

Fryday the 19th February fine weather continues working in the garden, no news from the west. Tom Simmes came in and gave himself up saying he Killed a Son of Bluford Mitchel. nothing of the Circumstance is yet Known. Mr Nixon has not left here today, but will leave to morrow, Mr Greenwood and wife came in to day to make Deeds to John Price for Lands purchased by Price of Greenwood.

Saturday the 20th weather continues very fine our infant is better— Auction all day at the Store of L. Myers, Mr Vanzant the Representative from Harrison County arrived, confirms the news of Mayfield being appointed Secretary of State, also the *Secret* Convention between Texas & England, respecting the Mediation of that Power, between us & Mexico, the thing is not quite so bad as I had anticipated, Texas will only agree to pay England five million dollars as part of the Debt Mexico owes to England, and England is to guarantee that Mexico will *Keep the Peace* for twenty years with us— all the Lawyers returned from Croket— no Court, no judge, term for holding our District Court changed from March to May,—Lodge met this Evening in a *case of emergency* gave Judge hart the 2d & 3d degs, passed a congenial and convivial Evening, went to bed at 2 A. M.

Sunday February 21st weather continues very fine. in my yesterdays Journal I omitted to State that I purchased of Louis Velard the ballance of his Head right for a third of a League of Land having purchased the other half previously— the price is One Hundred Dollars, payable in a Horse and Saddle at $50 the Ballance in cash—

Monday the 22d. weather *dito* as yesterday. Probate Court, vanzant started for home, has formed a copartnership with R. Potter Exqr nothing new—

Tuesday the 23d weather as yesterday— Judge Terrill passed trough here today. young Scurry[44] is appointed District attorney *bad appointment*, I respect the young man but will not do, for that very, very, very, responsible office— Major Kaufman arrived, the general news he brings is as yet not known to me as I had very little time to Converse with him. Tom Sims tried for Shooting Wm Mittchel not decided till to morrow—

Wednesday the 24th weather very fine, cool mornings a Bag full of news papers came from Crockett in a Waggon, received an Old Letter from Felix Houston[45] also one from Pineda, L. Myers

[44]William Reid Scurry was later a brigadier general in the Confederate Army.
[45]Felix Huston was born in Kentucky in 1800, moved to Natchez. Mississippi and became a lawyer. He was a promoter of the Texas cause in the United States, and migrated in May, 1836. He was made a brigadier-general in the Texas Army, briefly served as its principal officer, but because his attitudes toward Mexico were not in keeping with official policy he was replaced by Albert Sidney Johnston. Huston wound-

— 29 —

left for Natchitochez, left all his business with me, some accounts to collect, eta

Thursday the 25th weather dito as yesterday, no news worked in the garden nearly all day, tired of course, went to roost early—

Fryday the 26th fair weather, South wind. arranged my office received several Documents I had recorded from the late Clerk of the County Court Mr Corbin, also a Package of Documents recorded belonging to the Estate of Ogilvy decd. gave the County Clerk a Deed from F. T. Philipp to record. wrote a Letter to D. Lacy about the Division of the Land on the Loco, general Rusk who leaves here to day for Harrison County left me the nomination of Commissioners to divide said Land. Joshua J. Hall arrived from new Orleans, where he has been a resident of a *nameless place on Suspicion of Debt*, brought me a package of Papers from San Augustin— no news

Saturday the 27th the whole Country is on fire so much so, that the Sun has not, nor could not, make her appearance for several days past, and Contrary to Espy notwithstanding there has been so much Smoke, yet it will not rain, and I seriously belive it is going to end in Smoke alltogether, my little Son Placide had a very high Fever to day. Doctor Irion prescribed for him, the Smoke this Evening is so thick as to obscure the Sun completely, and is becoming very disagreable to the Eyes

Sunday the 28th fine weather, smoke in abundance. wrote several Letters to the General Post office. One to J. S. Mayfield of a private nature, answered two Letters received from Pineda, one 22 9br 1840, and one 20 Xbr 1840 entered a Suit of Trespass against G. W. McGowan and against Jose Maria Mora, for violently taking possession of Lands, belonging to Patricio de Torress

Monday March the 1st fine weather— cloudy in the afternoon—received a letter from S. B. True who send me a Barrill Potatoes, hired Michael Snider to work at 10 bits a day—no mail Placide is better

Tuesday the 2d March rain last night towards noon it began to grow dark, so that we eat our diner *by candle light*, I was writing after dinner when a Thunder clapp struck somewhere near the House and stupefied me for a few moments, but the whole House appeared to [be] in a flame— this is the Aniversary of our independence, hardly is it recollected by any one, at least it is no more noticed than any other day. the reason is not, that the People whish to be again as they were previous to this day 1836—but our Law givers—!!—!!!—

This is also the birth day of our oldest child Eugenia. she is 12 years old to day, she gave a party to her little Friends, and they enjoyed themselves no doubt much better than the Patriots of Texas. news was received that the mail rider between this

ed Johnston in a duel which followed. He remained in Texas until 1840, then opened law offices in New Orleans. He later returned to Natchez, and died in 1857.

— 30 —

place and Cincinnatti was under arrest at Crockett on an accusation of having stolen Judge Hart's monay, and that, a large mail is now at Douglass, brought there in a waggon, all this is rumor— however something must be wrong, or else the mail would have been here before this time, a mr Blount was tried to day for Stealing a waggon eta from B. A. Philipp— bound to appear at the District Court in the amount of $1000.00. Doctor Allen was security.

Wednesday the 3d march very foggy in the morning, but very fine weather the rest of the day received a large mail from the west, no news for me, Doctor Irion in Town informs me that General Henderson is very sick, Mrs Millard is very sick, expected to die

Thursday the 4th very fine weather to day was introduced to Judge Cummings of Rapide he is the owner of a League of Land granted to Domingo Cervantes, he is gone out to Mr Dursts to return to morrow, J. F. Lewis Esqr arrived in company with Judge Cummings, Mr. Lewis is authorized to settle the business between J. Ogilvy & Robert Chew of Alexandria, he also is to return to morrow to see about that business

Fryday the 5th rain last night, Cloudy & occasional Showers this morning, but commenced to rain Steadily after 12 oclock, and kept at [it] all day, send a petition for an injunction to the District Judge at San Augustin, against J. M. Mora. & G. W. Mc-Gowan, who have trespassed on Patricio de Torres's Land, send also all the Letter mail in this office for San Augustin, both by Mr W. W. Taylor of this County, Judge Cummings did not return on account of the rain, I suppose— Doctor Starr and Moses L. Patton received some goods to day from Galveston, all winter goods with a few exeptions

Saturday the 6th March beutifull weather, anniversary of the fall of the Alamo, Judge Cummings returned, showed him all the Documents respecting the League of Land he claims, I was disposed to give them all up to him, but he was not willing to pay me the small amount, due me individually, monay advanced for Taxes, nor the small amt due to Ogilvy's Estate, for monay advanced, for recording Titles eta. J. F. Lewes Esq also willing to receive Mr Robert Chew's Papers, but would not pay the monay advanced by Ogilvy for Copies had from the genl Land Office says that Chew has a claim of $560. Texas monay on the Estate, which I believe to be true, but he has not sufficient vouchers, for me to acknowledge the debt as just,

Sunday March the 7th beutifull Clear Skey; but a very cold north wind, which makes a good fire very agreable, Judge Cummings left here to day without making any arrangements about his Land, Mr Lewis on second thought, paid me fourty two 50/100 dollars in Texas monay which amount was expended by James Ogilvy for R. Chew— Lewis also took the Papers belonging to chew, I gave him also some notes & accounts belonging to Mr Hazard, for which Mr Lewis has to bring me Ogilvy's receipt, also the receipt Mr ogilvy gave Mr Chew for his Papers &c, trimmed trees nearly all day, oh! beg pardon did not know it was Sunday till I was done,

Monday the 8th March   very cold, frost last night, did not do any damage, rain towards night, paid over to B. Blake Treasurer of Milam Lodge $110.00 one Hundred & Ten dollars Texas monay which I have collected for the Lodge as monthly dues—for which he gave me his receipt

Tuesday the 9th   rain last night, rain to day A—M. and a very hard rain P. M. consequently no Business of any kind was transacted during the day, made an arrangement with Mr [blank] Wilson to cultivate part of my field which ought to have been cultivated last year by a Mr Easely, who did not do so, I give to Mr Wilson the rent free, provided he cultivates the Land, and if the Crop does not turn out well to make him a reasonable recompence—

Wednesday the 10th   rain! rain! rain! Cold! Cold! Cold! in the Evening made a large fire in the Peach Orchard expecting it would freeze, did not do so to day very cold with strong north wind, & looks like it was going to Clear up, I am making preperations for a heavy frost to night by having wood hawled and placed in heaps to set on fire to night—

Thursday the 11th   weather same as yesterday only more cold, determined to safe the fruit in the Orchard by preparing large wood piles to be set on fire again to night. no mail—no news—no business, yet a new Merchant named Byers is opened at the Tavern—

Friday the 12th march   cleared up last night, and had a *glorious Frost* every thing in the garden is destroyed, my large fires I made may have saved some of the Peaches—not sure— this afternoon Martin Rumpff an old friend of mine arrived from Houston, lives—pro tem—with me, very fine weather the ballance of the day—

Saturday the 13th   frost again, last night; a little before day Mrs Millard died after a severe, but very protracted illness. was burried at 4 P. M. received a Box and some few dry goods send to me by Alexander Philipps of New Orleans as pr Letter received sometime ago, received also some goods of Mr Myers's and agreably to his instructions sold them at Auction, exepting 8 caps which are unsold, the Ballance brough $18.06¼. Lodge met this Evening

Sunday the 14th   near night yesterday wind changed to the South, beutifull day, to day—wrote to the Clerk of the County court of Jasper to send me back my Title inclosed the letter in an envelop directed to C. M. Gould to be forwarded by him. Nathan Wade[46] (my second Liutenant) was joined in the Holy bonds of

[46]Nathan Wade was born in New Jersey on May 10, 1810. He moved to Nacogdoches in September, 1835, and shortly enlisted in Thomas J. Rusk's Company. His wife's correct name was Lucetta Wilburn. Wade was a tailor, and claimed to have made the buckskin suit worn by Houston in the Senate. He died on February 16, 1896.

matrimony to Miss urania willbourne, wrote out all my appeal cases to have them ready to hand to the District Clerk, which Court, now, alone has jurisdiction over appeals taken from a magistrate's Court—elegant—

Monday the 15th beutifull weather—mail arrived from the west—a miracle— nothing new. saw McGowan who lives on Patricio's place, is perfectly willing to hold the field he is working under me, or my agent;— Col S. Tipps one of the Commissioners to run the lines between the Heirs of Manuel Santos and myself & D. Lacy, came in Town, and went out to Mr Sharps' on the Loco, where the general rendevous is to take place to morrow at noon

Tuesday the 16th March fine weather, went to Mr Sharps's House on the Loco; accompanied by Mr C. S. Taylor & one of the Comrs M. R. Whitaker, the other Comrs had been at Sharps before me, and had went up to the N. W. part of the Land we tried to fine them but were unsuccessfull returned, and stayed all night at Sharps—

Wednesday the 17th very fine weather— at 8 A. M. all the Commissioners were assembled, commenced the Business of dividing the Land, Dolores Cortinas was also present, and it was on all Hands agreed to divide the Land North and South by running a Line trough the middle from west to East, which was done by starting at the N. W. Corner, running South 4375 vs then East, making an offsett to exclude the Land of Dolores Cortinas, stopped the survey on the west bank of the East Loco, to be finished some other time, went home, Mr S. B. True arrived from Natchitochez brought me a Letter from Kaufman, J. S. Roberts arrived from Galvezton, received by him a Letter from Sa[mue]l Banks[47] respecting Business he had with Ogilvy

Thursday the 18th March very fine weather saw Mr J. S. Roberts, nothing new from Galvezton many goods & no money to pay for them! confirms the report of the total wreck of the San Jacinto,[48] saw Mr True, who went to Douglass on Business, returned in the Evening, heard from the Comrs who are dividing the Loco Land, intend to finish the Survey to day, (if it is so, alls

---

[47]Samuel Bangs probably was born in Boston about 1797. He was engaged as a printer with the Mina Expedition, and on February 22, 1817 issued a **Manifesto** from Francisco Xavier Mina printed on Galveston Island. In 1839 he established the **Galvestonian** and may have also been associated with the **San Luis Advocate**. He published the **Musquito** from Houston in 1841 and 1842. Other Texas newspapers with which he was associated include the Galveston **Commercial Chronicle** (later **Independent Chronicle**), Galveston **News**, Galveston **Daily Globe**, Corpus Christi **Gazette** and Matamoros **Reveille**. He died somewhere in Kentucky in the 1850's.

[48]The 170-ton schooner **San Jacinto,** originally christened **Viper of Baltimore,** was the first ship in the Texas Navy. She was lost at the naval base at the Arcas Islands off the coast of Yucatan on October 31, 1840. She was driven against rocks by a storm.

right) Felix Grundy Roberts a Son of Elisha Roberts[49] stopped with me this Evening, he is returning from the Trinity, knew him as a little Boy— Major George A. Nixon in Town to day with Mr Tom Garner, tried to get a negro, who Nixon claims as his own, but who has been for the last year in possession of J. S. Mayfield Esqr negro run away Garner after him but no go— no Catch em—

Fryday the 19th weather continues very good— last night a *Select Party of good fellows played cards all night* the result was no Sleep, much drinking, and a little fighting, Ben Miller got innocently shot, how it will result god only knows—wrote to the general Post office Department, wrote also a private Letter to Mayfield about his Negro Joe, eta. McFarland and Mr Davison are going on to Austin who will take the Letters, heard from the Commissioners who run the Line between Santos's Heirs & myself say they have finished the Survey, did not go up to the Line formerly established in 1827, no matter, I am satisfied as long as the division is had, saw William Simpson, who wanted to make a Compromise about the Patricio Land, told him that I could not do so as that would lay me liable as administrator, but advised him to present his claim in due form of Law, and, in that way only can I do any thing

Saturday the 20th March 1841. weather fine Miller not very dangerous, set up with him till 12 P. M.

Sunday the 21st weather continues fine— Judge Hart returned from Houston & galvezton Muse our Senator returned from Austin yesterday. nothing new, heard it rumored to day that Gel Rusk[50] Shot a man in Harrisson county, (not ascertained) received a Letter pr Mr Nathan Wade from N. B. Thompson requesting me to go down to attend the District Court as interpreter and translator in a Suit between himself & Elisha Roberts. I have no Horse as yet, wrote to Thompson to send me one, however I'll go any how if I possibly can get off—

Monday the 22d Clowdy Sultry weather— wrote to Mr Bangs galvezton, in answer to a letter received pr J. S. Roberts, last night, or early this morning Louis Velard, an old Canadian an inhabitant of this Country for upwards of twenty years, died of Mania a Potu; Commenced raining very hard about 8 oclock A. M. stopped at 12. Mail from the west arrived in the rain brought many news Papers, but no Letters— a Mr Snively twinn Brother of old Jake arrived, and a most amusing Scene occurred every one ran to see the Colonel (old Jake) and much was the merriment occasioned by the mistake, wrote to Col Snively by his

[49]Elisha Roberts was born in 1774 at Watauga Settlement in Tennessee. Before coming to Texas he lived in Kentucky, South Carolina, and Washington Parish, Louisiana. Pursuing a runaway slave from the latter place, he came to the San Augustine area in 1818, liked it, and later moved there permanently. He built one of the first cotton gins in Texas (1825). He was Alcalde of the Ayish Bayou District (1831), and attended the Convention of 1833. He died on October 3, 1844.
[50]Sterne here refers to David Rusk.

Brother, send him a receipt of J. S. Roberts as quarter master in 1838 for $65.00 in favor of J. Ogilvy decd. to collect, send also a copy of my letters of administration—

Tuesday the 23d March fine weather rather cool— Burried Louis Velard, at 2 P. m. translated field notes from the Jose ygnacio ybarbo grant, for Duffield, no Horse yet from San Augustin, I suppose they dont want me very much

Wednesday the 24th very fine weather, cool, clear Sky nothing new send the mail to milam Sabine County pr Mr Pastuer, Ben miller getting worse no news from Rusk,

Thursday the 25th Cloudy weather—F. montgomery returned last night from the U. S. dull times there. A probability of war between England and the U. S. vel vot of it—so much the better for Texas, Whigs in the U. S. say times will now get better since Harrison is president— doubt it—some—Mr Pastuer did not leave till late to day, send a Letter by him to Burrill Thompson to send me a Horse *if he wants me,* Lussan Sick— Doctor Brown dito Ben miller no better,

Friday the 26th Cloudy, Sultry, looks like, but don't rain, David Rusk returned from the northern Counties report of Rusk having any difficulty all false—Mr Houston of the firm of Houston & McCreary of Natchitochez in town, brought San Augustin Papers—no news—Dull times & getting duller,

Saturday the 27th very hard rain last night continues raining this morning, plays the old scratch with my prospects of ploughing my bottom field. wrote to Gould respecting alexander Philipps business. the rain fell in torrents all day, near night, the little Creek west of Town was a stream deep and large enough to admit the largest Steamboat. 8 oclock P. m. the Bayou Lanana East of Town is higher than I have ever seen it, my lower Field is at least 4 to 6 feet under water and still rising, I fear to look at the devastation to morrow morning, not less than 100 dollars loss will let me off, I am sure, I have lived here since 1826 but never seen such a deluge before; a Mr Caldwell from Fannin County came from Austin last night he has all the mail Contracts East of the Trinity, he let out to day the Cincinatti contra[c]t to Mr Davison, the Epperson ferry Contract to [blank] and the Sabine or McLanahans's to Mrs. Hubert, all to commence running after the 1st April next

Sunday the 28th rained nearly all night keep still at it, and no prospect of its clearing up, the overflow of the Lanana was tremendous, the Bridge is gone, and a many Pannels of fence is swept away such of the field as was planted is completely ruined, rained very hard at 8 a.m. so much so that both Bayous which were falling have swollen again as high as before, however one consolation is, that the weather changed at noon, and had a beutifull afternoon. Capt English & Mr Holland dined with us. went down into the field to look at the havoc not quite so bad as I imagined at first, however it will take four days to repair all the damage

Monday the 29th very fine weather, repaired the damages done by the overflow of the Bayou. Mr Houston left for Natchitochez, wrote by him to Oliver Rouquiet, & to A. W. Canfield, a man by the name of Beauchamp who passed by trough here a few days ago, and for whom a reward of $500— was offered, he having murdered a man in indiana, was pursued and overtaken, and brought back, passed here to day on his way to the U. S. received a letter from Daniel Lacy—

Tuesday the 30th very fine weather still repairing fences eta. Caldwell *the mail contractor* left here to day

Wednesday the 31st weather Cloudy, felt unwell this morning, at 11— had a most excrutiating Headache, which continued all day, send for Doctor Hyde, prescribed calomel—ekeshow—dont catch old birds with chaff—

Thursday the 1st April. weather good, a little cloudy took magnesia, a warm foot bath, and plenty sage Tea, last night, feel much better this morning at 10 oclock felt well enough to go to the Office, made lists of Letters on hand for last quarter, put up dead Letters made out my quarterly return, Mr Wilson got married, the [affair] is to be to morrow, had an invitation, and will go if I feel well enough

Friday the 2d cloudy this morning wrote last Night a long Letter to the Post office Depart— respecting the sending all the Documents fo[r] quarter eta also respecting the small amount received last 4r about not getting mail bags made, no good stuff to and the making here worth twice the worth of the one purchased in the U.S., also about sending Mrs Huberts Boy 4 times to McLanahan, myself 3 times once gratis to the govt to San Augustin, Durst 5 times to cincinnatti eta.

April the 3d Cloudy some, little, rain, last night Mr Wilson gave a Ball to the Community in general, all hands were well satisfied—read the novel of Chrichton last night—good—

Sunday the 4th rain last night, rain this morning, and from the looks of the Clouds, it is uncertain if we shal see the Sun again in a week,— unexpectedly the Sun shown out in splendor after twelve, Mr Daukwerth arrived from Houston, no news from that place the indians have Shot a negro in the field of Mr Burton at the forks of the Road, near nechaz, stole two mules, & two Horses, they were pursued but could not get up with them— at Dark the weather was quite calm and pleasant—Mr Bondies returned from Masters's near the Town of Crockett. Mr Ned Roberts dito—Mail from red river failed again—

CHAPTER III

" . . . we all went home in the morning . . ."

Monday the 5th April my fourtieth birth day!!!!! beutifull weather—send off the mails East, and west, many persons in Town nothing new—Lodge met this Evening,

Tuesday the 6th Cold, nearly a frost last night very fine weather this morning, continued all day, sold Conrad Eigenauer's Certificates for 1920 and 1475 acres Land to day, one to C. S. Taylor for $233.3/3 and the other to Judge Hart for $200.00— much electioneering going on in Town to day

Wednesday the 7th April 1841 beutifull weather the Sheriff of Houston County having in charge Mr McKeever (who killed Joe Shanks) taking him on to San Augustin, to appear before Judge Terrill, on a writ of Habeas Corpus, genl Houston has arrived at San Augustin, Murray Orton returned from there last Evening, a Royal Arch Chapter[1] has been organized at that place; was appointed by Major Arnold the County Clerk, deputy Clerk of the Board of Land Comrs to receive one half of his fees, was Sworn into office by the Chief Justice— Major Reyly[2] & Lady & 2 children arrived to day, to spend the Summer with us, Committee on Accounts of the Lodge met at the Lodge Room to night, kept me up till 11 oclock

Friday—GOOD FRIDAY—the 9th April— fine weather Saw Mr & Mrs Wilson & Mr and Mrs Harry—all well— mail arrived from the U. States, brought many Letters, some directed to me as Post Master no interest— Collin Aldridge brought in a Load of drinkables for Mr J. S. Roberts, issued orders for the Company to muster on the 21st of this month to celebrate the Aniversary of the Battle of San Jacinto

Saturday the 10th April very heavy dew, fine weather during the day — Judge Aldridge brought a load of groceries from Alabama for Roberts, mail arrived from the west nothing new

Sunday the 11th Cloudy, warm weather Easter Sunday, nothing new of consequence

Monday the 12th weather cleared off cool, fine meeting of the Board of Road Commissioners met to day, County & Probate Court, send of mails to the East & west, send a *Communication* to

---

[1]The Royal Arch Chapter is a York Rite Masonic body of advanced or superimposed degrees. This is one of the oldest chapters of Royal Arch Masonry in Texas.
[2]Probably James Reily.

the Editor of the Journal & Advertiser San Augustin, engaged an Irishman to dig a ditch for me, at 6 bits pr Rod or 16 feet. removed our Lodge to the House of Nat Noriss, lately occupied by Murrey Orton, I placed Martin Rumpff in possession of it, having an attachment levied on it for a debt due Ogilvy's Estate.

Tuesday the 13th fine weather, sold to Mr Banayah Thompson 836 acres, of the Certificate of ⅓ of a League of Conrad Eigenauers got his note for $200.00 for the same, he is to locate the whole of the Certificate, and let me take choice of 640 acres, my paying an equal part of the Expence eta, the Schooling of my children is to be credited on said note every quarter

Wednesday the 14th april 1841 fine weather set up last night with a Sick B.[rother] M.[ason] Ben Miller, he is better this morning, a Mr Flats from San Augustin, is in Town, to purchase Texas Treasury notes, offers 17 cents— rumor says gel Hamilton[3] effected the Loan of 5 millions others say that Mexico has acknowledged our Independence, nous verrons—

Thursday the 15th fine weather; most finished planting corn, the 3d League of Land bid off by Judge Hart was not taken by him but by Mr. M. Rumpff, who transferred it to me (This is the same Certificate I sold 836 acres off to B. Thompson) —Hived some Bees to day & got stung— most beutifully —translated some field notes for Mr Ben E. Philipps

Friday the 16th Cloudy— no rain— the mail arrived to day from East— Loan effected Laffith & Co of Paris[4] —have not seen par.iculars— Col Ransom arrived, to recruit men for a Santafee[5] Expedition—have not seen him as yet—send off Casimiro Garcia to vicente micheli jimios, with Documents— to get the property belonging to the Daughter of Patricio de Torress decd, wrote Micheli a Long Letter on the subject,— saw Ransom, McLeod[6] at the head of the Expedition— *quin Sabe*— General Rusk returned from Red River County this Evening Col Bob Smith dito— Bob—got clear— good— very good— Rusk much improved in appearance— good again—

Saturday April 17th 1841 looks like rain Saw Rusk this morning all well, Chas. S. Taylor Sick— Sallivated— bad— can not attend a trial between Brown & Philipps, no matter, all will

---

[3] James Hamilton, one of Texas' ablest diplomats, was born on May 8, 1796 at Charleston, South Carolina. He served the Republic in many capacities, but is best known for the treaties which he negotiated with the Netherlands and England, and for his efforts to arrange for the loan to which Sterne refers. His service was in the Lamar administration, and when Houston returned to office he negated Hamilton's efforts and repudiated the loan. Hamilton drowned in the Gulf of Mexico in a shipwreck on November 15, 1857.

[4] The financial house of Lafitte and Company was one of the sources of capital from which Hamilton attempted to secure assistance for Texas.

[5] For a recent account of the Santa Fe Expedition and related items, see Joseph Milton Nance, **After San Jacinto, The Texas-Mexican Frontier, 1836-1841** (The University of Texas Press: Austin, 1963), 504-545.

[6] Brigadier General Hugh McLeod was the commander of the Santa Fe Expedition.

be agreably to Law & Justice— Col Ransom has *Stuck up* his Proclamation about the Santa fee Expedition— but the name of McLeod, will just lay the whole matter here as flat as a Pan Cake— the trial came on jury could not agree misstrial, to come on again 1st may next—

Sunday the 18th had a very fine rain last night, came in good time, Creation is dressed out in her best robe this morning, mail arrived from the west, no news of consequence

Monday the 19th the finest morning this Spring Send off mails to East, west, & north— gel Rusk left for San Augustin— Mrs. Reyley Mrs Lewis & miss Sims dined with Mrs Sterne to day—

Tuesday the 20th rain, very hard rain last night— cleared this morning—busy in the office all day, Mr May from Matamoras, and Mr. Generis from San Antonio arrived this Evening had not time to gather any news from them

Wednesday the 21st beutifull weather— aniversary of the Battle of San Jacinto—ordered the militia to fire a Salute at daylight, and sun down, a Mr Butler, at noon delivered an Eloquent address in the Stone House, Genl Sam Houston arrived in the afternoon— held a meeting to call a meeting of the People of the County on this day two weeks, for the purpose of nominating suitable candidates for President & vice President, and for two suitable Persons to represent us in Congress—

Thursday the 22d april 1841 beutifull day— genl Houston left here for Home— gel Jim Smith in town, much talk about candidates for Congress have a notion to run? myself. *quien Sabe* [who knows] Texas Monay getting better in New Orleans mail arrived from the U. S. brought nothing for me.

Fryday the 23d very fine weather, worked one hour A.M. & one Hour P.M. in the garden— much electioneering going on, many persons tell me they will Support me for Congress—*quien Sabe, the taste of the pudding eta*—Col Raguet[7] returned from John Durst's do not know if a reconciliation has taken place— hope it has

Saturday the 24th very fine weather—went to Douglass, to attend a Political meeting, made a few remarks— I found that a deep game is playing in regards to the division of the County, the East & West want to divide the County so as to make the divisionary Line near this Town not— as I belive, for any particular good to result from it— but especially to take away the County seat from this place— to kill—(as the click term it) Nacogdochez, the fact is I feel so disgusted at all things, that I am sorry that I have

---

[7] Henry Raguet was born on February 11, 1796 in Bucks County, Pennsylvania. After serving in the War of 1812 he entered business and became a director of the Bank of the United States. In 1833 he pled bankruptcy and traveled to New Orleans, from whence Sam Houston and John Durst persuaded him to move on to Texas. He and William G. Logan. whom he had met on the journey, entered the mercantile trade in Nacogdoches. After Logan's death, Raguet continued the business until 1852. Raguet died on December 8, 1877.

spent so much monay, in aiding to free (?) this Country from the Mexicans for I belive before 3 years, the new Setlers will deprive the Old ones, of every acre of Land which the[y] have honestly obtained under the Mexican Government— I dread to think of the future

Sunday the 25th fine weather, mail arrived, brought news of Texas Treasury notes being 27¢ per dollar— good— have not perused my news papers— rumor says Gel Harrison the President of the U.S. is dead also that Henry Clay is killed by King of Alabama in a duel— hope it is not so— received a Letter from Jose Pineda of Bexar, and a new Power of attorney from Ma. Josefa Pio de Torres and her *new* Husband.

monday the 26th very fine weather a little cloudy towards Evening. send of mails eta a most disgraceful drunken frolic took place to day John Noblett and Rinaldo Hotchkiss are the Principal Actors, the part the latter performed I feel too much delicacy, to write, ordered to Arrest Noblitt till 10 A.M. to morrow morning, Doctor Starr will be the Prosecutor if such conduct is to be tolerated I'll be one who will not sanction it, nous verrons—

Tuesday the 27th april 1841 fine weather (a little cloudy Doctor Starr has commenced suit against Noblett for assault & intend to kill, the trial is to be to morrow morning at 10 oclock Noblett is repentant, but it is too late, a Robbery was Committed last night at Mr Brichta's an attempt was also made at B. Blakes's grocery, but did not succeed, in Consequence I took all my valuable Papers out of the Office to my House— send a draft on Mrs Kesler at Houston for 30$ Texas monay, in favor of R. W. Smith, wrote a Letter to Wm. Daukwerth—

Wednesday the 28th windy, cloudy, weather, but no rain of which we are much in want,— John Noblett was examined to day, bound over in the Sum of $500.00 to appear at the District Court, wrote to Isaac Parker[8] mustang Prairie, about some Land P. has in his Possession of Pecks Estate.

Thursday the 29th a tremendous gust of wind blew about dark last night, continued all night and all day to day, blew down a beutifull arbour of mine, glad it did not blow down the House— my little Son Placide and infant daughter Laura very sick, the latter I am fearfull dangerously so—hope not, C. M. Gould came from San Augustin Court there has adjourned, was a *Boisterous Court*— Dick Scurry dying at Houston, *whiskey*—We will have Court next Monday— Judge Hart who had been sick for several days— is better—came *out* to day— Texas monay getting better 4 for one, the Shavers of this place do not take it at that—but the Honest men do. how it will be in 6 months hence—nous verrons

---

[8]Isaac Parker was born in Elbert County. Georgia on April 7, 1793. He lived in Tennessee, Virginia, and Illinois before coming to Texas in 1833. He represented Houston County in the Senate of the Eighth and Ninth Congresses and in the Convention of 1845. He represented Ellis and Tarrant Counties in the first four legislatures of the State of Texas. He died on April 14, 1883.

Fryday the 30th april fine weather— the court House is put in such a situation as to be in a state to hold Court in it, the next week, C. M. Gould Esqr gave me the Papers of Madame Despalliers Land north of P. de Torress Land, nothing new occurred this day— wrote an answer to a letter of Mr Brewer's respecting Madame Despalliers Business.

Saturday the 1st of may. may day weather— all fair held Court to day, a jury case came up, Philips vs Brown verdict of jury for Philips, many other cases disposed of. Mr Mitchell returned from New Orleans, also our old acquaintance Mr Pomeroy who used to visit here 7 and 8 years ago, nothing new stirring Lodge met to night, did not go— I can't say I have an excuse— yet I did not go—

Sunday the 2d May weather fair, was introduced to a Mr White from Tennessee, mail arrived, red a Letter from Mayfield, will be here in a day or two, expects there will be a call Session of Congress in June, I suppose to quarrel about the Loan, the whole five millions having been obtained; our frontier Spies from San Antonio have had a fight with some Mexicans near Laredo Killed four of them and took the rest 25 Prisoners 4 escaped— good—

Monday the 3d May fine weather, District Court met in the New Court House, Several Cases were *rolled off*, gained the case of Jose Santos Coy and wife vs Lemual P. Cook for $450.00 and 5% interest from 1838. —good— the Board of Land Commissioners met at my office this day, Commenced my duties as Clerk, went home and worked till 10 o'clock P.M. to get all in order, and to be ready for to morrow John Norriss staying with me to night. send of all the mails this morning— a busy day—

Tuesday the 4th Cloudy Sultry weather— my case of widow Beuford vs A. Sterne came up and a non suit was taken by the Plaintiff arranged that matter with Mr Simpson to satisfaction of all parties— land Comrs. met again, did not do much business— the Case of Bayley vs Sterne will come up to morrow is going to be argued as a forneign debt, like to hear the argument—had a fine rain—and a bad hail storm near dark to night, some good— some bad—

Wednesday the 5th Cloudy a little rain. not enough—Court in Session, argument on my Bayley Case posponed till next Monday

Thursday the 6th Weather same as yesterday gave the justices of the Peace—Jissy—for not sending up the Copy—instead of the Origl Bond— nimporte—mail from the East arrived to day no news—rumored general Jackson is dead— not sure. translated Pedro Telurio Padillas Tittle to an old Spanish grant

Fryday the 7th weather very oppressively warm, rain all round, except here, Court going it—nothing very particular— negro woman tried to run away—no go—gave her Jissy—besides good advise—all's well

Saturday the 8th May 1841 fine rain last night everything

looks flourishing to day, nature is decked out in her hollyday garment. District court adjourned to day at noon till 10 oclock A.M. next Monday, nothing extraordinary occurred to day, Lodge meets to night, I dont go—

Sunday, the 9th most tremendous Storm last night this morning after daylight, continued lightning & Thunder. Struck near major arnold's[9] House, nearly killed a little negro Boy. Knocked down Mr arnold, and Stunned several of the Family— do no other mischief rained till noon to day— mail at 4 P. M. dont know the news as yet—

Monday the 10th fair but cool weather, Court is still in Session, decided, a very important Land Case in favor of James Reily Esqr, Mr Snively. the Cols Brother in Town, nothing particular doing

Tuesday the 11 fine weather —Court— my case—Bayly vs Sterne, came up, was passed over, A. B. Canfield and Lady, N. B. Thompson & Lady arrived from San Augustin, also Judge Johnson, he is to take the Bench the day after to morrow—

Wednesday the 12th fine weather—Court—Mr Nickelson, the Agent for the Telegraph (Houston) arrived, on a Collecting Expedition, bad chance—Burrell Thompson in Town, nothing new.

Thursday the 13th Criminal Dockett came up to day Judge Johnson presiding—nothing of great consequence done—mail from the East arrived, no Letters from the U.S.— received by private conveyance, a few papers, send to me by J. P. Kay,

Fryday the 14th weather fine— Cool— Court going it nothing particular doing— a dance in the Evening at Mr Chevallier's, went with the Children—amused them, and myself, came home 12 oclock—

Saturday the 15th weather continues fine, but cool—A. W. Canfield appointed me Agent for the San Augustin Journal & Advertiser—got him about 40 subscribers—a clever fellow—

Sunday the 16th fine cool weather—mail arrived from west & north— no news

Monday the 17th fine, but cool weather Dispatched mails— Court nothing new—Judge Terrill gone, to Houston.

Tuesday the 18th fine weather—Court in session my Bayley case it seems has died a natural death—several cases were disposed of to day, in a summary manner—to wit—being quashed— a Mr Perault and a Mr Lauve arrived from Natchitochez to day the latter was raised in the same family with Mrs. Sterne, invited them to dine with me to morrow

Wednesday the 19th fine weather— Court adjourned to day. all the Lawyers got drunk except C. M. Gould Esqr. had company to dinner—

---

[9]Hayden S. Arnold was born in Tennessee in 1805 and migrated to Texas in December 1835. On March 6, 1836 he became a Captain of the Nacogdoches Volunteers, later the First Company. Second Regiment of Texas Volunteers, and served at San Jacinto. He died on July 3, 1839.

Thursday the 20th fine weather—nothing new, mail arrived, brought no news Texas monay appears to be advancing—

Fryday the 21st may very fine weather, rather too dry—every body left here to day. Mr. Lauve & Pirault Mr Caldwell for Galvezton, Capt English & Gould for the East—a general clearing out— One arrival our old Townsman Mr Mortimer Thorn, drove off from amongst the indians in arkansas—send a long Communication Signed—S. to San Augustin headed— "Eleven Leagues & Leagues & Labors,—send a draft pr Capt. English on John Prat of Campte for $25.00 requested him to get me a barrill of sugar & some Sperm candles for it—the draft was given me by Mr A. Thouvenin for services rendered to Said Prat in a case w[h]ere said Pratt is Plaintiff for a Lot of ground in this Town and Juan Jose Mariano Acosta is defendant—

Saturday the 22d fine weather, a little cloudy went fishing in the forenoon—good luck. Judge Terrell returned from Crockett having understood that there is no Court in Houston Mr May from Galvezton arrived to day with Mr Terrell, has land business to attend to — gave in the Tax of Louis Rueg, amounting to 16:605 acres deeded Land. Jose Ma Mora acknowledged the Deed he had made to Mrs Despallier for a Section of Land— on the Atascosa Law Suits—plenty to day—disposed of them all

Sunday the 23 may weather very fine, was unwell Kept the House all day, till 4 P. m. when the western mail arrived, it is officially announced by the Secretary of State that the whole Loan is negotiated in Paris, and will be at the disposal of the Congress by the 1st July next no further news.

Monday the 24th Sultry oppressive warm weather Dispatched mails. agreeably to an appointment of the Probate Court. went to Vital Flores's to make a division of the Land granted to Jose Flores decd arrived late at the House. rained hard, head ache, went to bed without supper

Tuesday the 25th Cloudy — sick all night Swore in John Reid. J. noblett & N. Wade as Commrs and [blank] Ham[10] as Surveyor. Started them off, to survey the whole tract of Land previous to our commencing the repartition of Land, was too sick to go with them, passed a disagreeable day at the House.

Wednesday the 26th rain all night rains still this morning—feel a little better. at 9 A.M. left for home, to return next fryday, arrived home at one P.M. A.H. Scott in Town, made me a present of a Sword

Thursday the 27th fine weather, Mr George Allen and his wife in Town, Mr Brown a Lawyer from galvezton & Mr Raglin[11] from Austin, settled up with Ferriss Montgomery, got a note on J. H. Wilson for $52.10 payable one day after date dated 25th inst promised to pay Montgomery $12.00 out of it, when collected, rented the garden opposite Whitlesey's to said Whitlesey for $12.00

[10]J. F. Ham.
[11]H. W. Raglin.

— 43 —

to be at my disposal whenever I want it, (the garden) rented the Bakers's House to Robert F. Milland at $12.50 per month, with the understanding that I can take and make use of the Frame House in the yard any time I please, but as long as I do not want it, to be at the disposition of said Millard; sold to Thomas H. Rodgers 400 acres of Land out of the Loco Tract for $600.00 payable half 1st March 1842 & half 1st January 1843 got two notes to that effect, said 400 Acres are to be taken out of the North East Corner in a Square, but not to cross the Loco to the west, gave Rodgers my Bond to make him a bona fide Title for the Land after Payments are all made, mail from East arrived, no news—

Fryday the 28th Cloudy weather— started back again to Flores's found they had not finished the running of the 4 Leagues, will finish to morrow if weather permits— the division will take place on Wednesday the 16th June next, made a Contract with maria del Carmel Mora, Maximilian, and Theresa Mora, to have their Share of said tract laid off (they being heirs of Cleta Flores) I am to have the Land separated for them, for which I am to receive one third part, which will be 504 acres. gave in Mrs Mora's Tax— on this day as follows [blank]—

Saturday the 29th May left Flores's after Breakfast cloudy, did not rain on the Road, but in Town had a bountiful Rain— Genel Henderson, Judge Terrill and others went on towards Crockett to day, George Allen and his wife left for Houston, Mayfield returned home last night, in good health, had no chance of conversing with him much,

Sunday the 30th fine weather— mail arrived from the west— failed, from Red River nothing new— received a communication from Jas. Izod, answered it to day to go in to morrows mail

Monday the 31st fine weather, send off all the mails received a list of about 120 defaulters of Taxes from the Sheriff, to issue Execution on, paid an order of $20.00 drawn by Post Master general J. S. Mayfield in favor of Mrs Hubert, got ready to start to Crockett

Tuesday the 1st June fine weather, left home for Crockett, to Col Bean's[12] 28 miles— good fare, an old friend of 15 years standing— spend a pleasant Evening with him, talked over Auld Lang sine—

Wednesday June 2d fine weather, left Col Bean's early in the morning traveled slow to Jacob Master's, an other old friend of 13 years standing, this day is the 13th anniversary of my marriage with my dear wife

---

[12]Peter Ellis Bean was a member of the Philip Nolan Expedition, and was held captive in Mexico from 1801 until 1807. Revolutionary tensions secured his release in return for service with the Royalists, but he deserted and joined the Rebels, rising to the rank of colonel. He was sent to the United States to secure aid. but had only moderate success. He served under Andrew Jackson at the Battle of New Orleans. January 8, 1815, but returned to Mexico shortly afterward. In 1873 he settled a land grant at Mount Prairie in East Texas. He died on October 3, 1846.

June 3d left Masters's 10 miles to Crocket, Court in Session, grand jury found a true Bill against Marchall B. McKeever for killing Joseph Shanks (which I sincerely belive he was justifiable in doing, met general J. P. Henderson gel Rusk, and Col Watrous[13] at the House of McKeever, these three gentlemen are to defend Mck.

Fryday the 4th very hot weather, visited Mrs. Jowers and some other Ladies— very much pleased with the place, good People. Judge Johnson left for Houston, at 8 P.m. a jury was empanelled to try McKeever—

Saturday the 5th very hot— examination of witnesses in McK Case, was examined myself as regards Joseph Shank's (the man killed) character— good when sober foolish, crazy, bad, insulting and dangerous when drunk— was present at an affray which took place between Mr Teague Mr Givens— and a Mr Key, who in trying to Shoot Givens, came within an inch of killing me. left at dark to Masters—

Sunday the 6th left very early this morning dined at Debards, supped at McKnights— and went home during the night, in consequence of the Board of Land Commissioners meeting to morrow arrived at Home

on this day the 7th June fine hot weather Fahrenheits' Thermometer at 83 at 10 A.M. & at dark— Board of Land Commissioners met dispatched much Business, had a long Conversation with the secretary of State Major Mayfield, got much information respecting the affair with Saligne the french Chargé D'affairs, and I am satisfied his (Mayfields) course was Correct,[14]

Tuesday the 8th Hot weather Thermometer at 86 on an average during the day— some Business in the Land Office, nothing of consequence transpired—, but many prespired—

Wednesday the 9th Thermometer at 86 in the Shade a tremendous rain at 5 P. m. air Cool at dark saw a Mr von Wrede[15] and his Son. although never Citizens of Texas (to do any good) a League & Labor of Land was adjudicated to the old man, who has no other Familie exept his Son, and he got a head right—all right perhaps— I am getting mighty tired of matters and things generally— may God send us better times

Thursday the 10th June Thermometer highest during the day

---

[13]John Charles Watrous, who in 1838 had served briefly as Attorney General of Texas.

[14]Sterne apparently refers to the celebrated feud between De Saligny and Richard Bullock. Although a personal matter. it had grave consequences for the financial affairs of the Republic. Mayfield's role is not explained.

[15]Frederick Wilhelm von Wrede was born near Cassel, Germany about 1788, and came to the United States in January 1836. He and his son traveled extensively in eastern Texas. as well as in the central and eastern parts of the United States. They returned briefly to Germany in 1843, then returned to Texas with Carl Prince zu Solms-Braunfels. Von Wrede was killed by Indians on October 24, 1845.

at 83. a little rain, mail arrived from San Augustin and the U.S. no news—

Fryday the 11th Therr same— no news— was relieved of my duties of Deputy Clerk of the County Court, good relieved from an ardous duty— nous verrons Gel Rusk, Terrell, & Henderson returned from Crockett a mistrial in McKeever's Case gave my note for $53.00 to B. Blake who will leave here to morrow morning—

Saturday the 12th Therr at 85 at 12 oclock—a refreshing little shower in the Evening, Justice Court, did much Business, Bennett Blake left here for to home, way down in vermont, I regret his absence, but allmost begrudge him the pleasure of meeting a *Father & Mother* after an absence of Six years— mail arrived from the west, not much news. our County Rangers fell in with some 15 indians about 80 miles above Fort Houston,[16] killed 7 of them, not one of our men hurt, heard also from Red River, gel Torrence[17] had a fight with the indians in that quarter Capt Denton (formerly a Preacher) was Killed one man wounded, they killed 12 indians known besides many not known, and wounded,

Sunday June the 13th Thermometer 85, at noon 84 at dark— made an offer to C. S. Taylor Esq. attorney for Plant about two notes I owe for $1200 each— to wit 3 ten acre lots on Galvezton Island, 800 acres on the Bernard near San felipe & 1107 acres on the Attoyac being part of Jose de los Santos Coy's League. I know this is on my part a very liberal offer, & if they do not accept of it my concience is clear as regards my duty towards them, and I will pay them when I'll get it—

Monday the 14th weather same as yesterday saw a Mr West from Woodville Miss. coming to Texas— Send of the mails West and East a Campaign is to be made against the indians high up on the Trinity, I espect this Company will Succeed, in as much as gage[18] had the fight with the indians on Trinity, orders to all the Colonels of the Regiment to one Company each in their respective counties, left in the Eastern mail to day

Tuesday the 15th Therr at 87½ at noon 86 at dark, nothing doing, no news— W. m. Cox very sick

Wednesday the 16th no news, weather same as yesterday. prepared to go to the attoyac to finish dividing vital Florres's Land.

Thursday the 17th Started at 3 a.m. arrived at Flores's at 9 a.m. met gel Rusk at Skellens's. Started to the woods, surveyed till dark very hot weather—

Fryday the 18th warm weather, in the woods all day surveying, saw some very fine land in the Evening had a refreshing Shower, cool during the night—

Saturday the 19th weather very Sultry— in the woods all

---

[16]Fort Houston was located two miles west of Palestine in Anderson County. and was built in 1835. It was an important Texas outpost for a decade.

[17]Probably General Edward H. Tarrant.

[18]David Gage.

day, trough Briars, canebreaks and Swamps of the Attoyac—
came to Flores's at dark very much fatigued

Sunday the 20— a refreshing breze is blowing finished surveying at 12 at noon entered into a Contract with the Heirs of
Clita Flores— to wit— Ma del Carmel— Theresa—& Maximiano—
to have their share of their mother's Land set apart for them for
which I am to receive their share of their Father's farm 2 leagues
East of this place on the old Road to Natchitochez consisting of 634
acres of Land, signed the Contract between us, and left it, in the
hands of vital Flores, for safe Keeping, took dinner, and Started
for home. arrived at home at 5 P.m. found all well, mails had
arrived during my absence, but nothing new,

Monday the 21st weather moderate— Therr. 84, 10 A.M.
Send off mails, saw Moses L. Patton, agreed to let him have the
Land I bargained for on the 20th inst. at $450.00. provided I get
$100. down in cash, Mr Vansant of Harrison County passed trough
here to go to Austin

Tuesday the 22 rained a little last night & again during the
day, not enough— crops suffering nothing new.

Wednesday the 23d cool Breze all day. Elisha Roberts passed
trough here on his way home from Austin, heard of the Death of
Mrs Debard, Jas Hall from crockett passed trough.

Thursday the 24th Saint John's day. moderate weather Therr
not above 78. mail from the East no news— a Ball in the Evening
at Col Thorn's

Fryday the 25th Cool weather, *no news* nothing doing, dull
times—

Saturday the 26th times as yesterday, mail from west brought
Nothing— Mr Short[19] & Quirk from Crockett arrived going to
New Orleans stopped with me till to morrow. made a Bond to
M. L. Patton for the Land purchased of Mrs Mora & her Brother
& Sister, received one hundred Dollars Cash, and he is to pay me
$325.00 in good notes when I'll make him the Title

Sunday the 27th weather dry. not good— want of rain mail
from Red River no news— as usual my Visitors left early this
morning

Monday the 28 June— weather same— send off mails— wrote
to Isaac my brother pr Mr Campbell, from Natchitochez—send Ten
dollars Texas monay by him to purchase me some shoes— Settled my accounts with him as agent for J. F. Cortes, gave my note
for $94.25. general Rusk started for vital Flores where I am to
meet him to go to Shelbyville on Wednesday—

Tuesday the 29— made out my quarterly returns, Mr Eakins[20]
the blacksmith died last night at 2 A.M. of Congestive fever,
after a sickness of 4 days he was a very industrious man— he
was burried at 4 P.M. to day— David Burney the Brother of
Bob Burney from Alexandria arrived to see something about his

---

[19]G. L. Short.
[20]E. M. Eakin.

late Brothers land concerns, had a long chatt with him— left me his agent— also for Bonner— the Documents of their Lands to be send to me or else the names of the original grantees to get Copies out of the gel Land office— had a Splendid Rain this afternoon at 5 P.M. made lots of corn all around this place at least— good. Mr Rumpff no come

Wednesday the 30th Cool pleasant weather, left home to join genl Rusk at vital Flores's, took dinner at Flores's and left for Shelby County. Styd all night at a widow Moore's—

Thursday the 1st July left for Shelbyville accompanied by young Mr Moore and an other man overtook about 15 persons on the Road, who are waiting for gel Rusk, to defend them in a suit brought against them by one west, to Keep the peace— warrant for informality was dismissed. rained very hard in the afternoon met a young man who is merchandizing here named Caspary a nephew of McDaniels from New Orleans, passed the Evening with Caspary at a game of whist—

Fryday the 2d left for San Augustin passed many fine farms crops look very fine, arrived at San Augustin at 12 a.m. purchased some provisions for my family send them in a wagon pr Hawkins Sparks, got acquainted with Mr DeYoung and his family, also with genl Henderson's Lady who to my surprise addressed me in german which language She speaks elegant, went to see Canfield, who gave a little Party in the Evening was introduced to some very handsome and very amiable Ladies, danced till 2 A.M. never enjoyed myself more at a little Party like I did at this, San Augustin has improved in every respect. Population improving the City, and more then all in morals.

Saturday the 3d July very warm weather genl Rusk goes to Sabine County to defend means for Killing Mulholland,[21] trial next monday, left San Augustin at 11 a.m. promised gel Darnell[22] to come down with Mr Holland on the 1st Saturday in August next to install the **Chapter**, arrived at home about 12 oclock at night very much exhausted— found all *well*.

Sunday the 4th Therr ranging from 85 to 88 in the shade too fatigued to go up town, send for my news papers which came by yesterdays mail heard that Mr Rumpff is sick went to see him not dangerous—

Monday the 5 send of Eastern mail send two dollars to P. W. Caspary in a letter for ink he sold me when I was at Shelbyville—

---

[21]Gifford White ('ed.). **The 1840 Census of the Republic of Texas** (The Pemberton Press: Austin, 1966), 167, lists a B. Mulholland, who owned a town lot in Sabine. one slave, and one gold watch. The Sabine County census does not list Means.

[22]Nicholas Henry Darnell. born on April 20, 1807 in Williamson County, Tennessee, moved to Texas in 1838 after serving in the Tennessee Legislature. He settled at San Augustine where he helped to found the Masonic Lodge, and was in 1844 Grand Master of the Grand Lodge of Texas. He served in the Texas Sixth and Seventh Legislatures, and he was the colonel commanding the 18th Texas Cavalry in the Confederate Army. He died in Fort Worth in July of 1885.

wrote to Michael de Young, many persons in Town to day, about the (hanging of Willis) came near a fuss but did not get into it— Judge Terrill presided at the Examination. many angry expressions escaped men on both sides— to wit regulators and Law abiding men— some call them the honest and some the Rogue party— god Knows how it is. I want to see the Rogues punished— but should like to see it done by Law if it can be done by law[23]

Tuesday the 6th July the hottest day this summer Thermometer near dark 90 degs. in the shade— the Examining Court Met & adjourned till thursday the 8th all hands went out to J. R. Clute's wedding

Wednesday the 7th weather same as yesterday, no news, all the persons said to be engaged in hanging willis are in Town, under the charge of Sheriff Rusk—

Thursday the 8th weather same as yesterday mail from East — means refused to be tried on account of the great exitement in milam. a man named Lewis Killed an other named [blank] the Court met here to day, and a kind of compromise was made. the accused party acknowledged that all the Dursts were innocent as regards the Knowledge of the Stealing in their neighbourhood, all entered into Bond to appear at the next District Court— Ex governor Runnels[24] arrived in Town from the west, has many friends here— (wonder what he came to Texas for?)

Fryday the 9th Excessively hot, broke my Thermometer, very sorry for it— Mrs Mangum died this morning after a very short illness, several persons sick— so far thank god none of my familie is Sick—I hope we may escape this year—wrote to Bennett Blake

Saturday the 10th July Weather as usual, looked like we would have a Shower in the Evening but no go— felt very unwell and did not go up to the Office all day, mails arrived & opened by my Deputy brought nothing from west nor north, Mrs. Mangum was burried this afternoon

Sunday the 11 weather warm stayed at home all day, felt not well—

Monday the 12th Send off mail, Mr Holland is sick, three of the Family of Col Raguet sick, as yet we are well except myself & I am not sick enough to keep the Bed

Tuesday the 13th weather very warm— Mrs Mora in Town, has played me a trick about the Land I contracted for sometime

---

[23]Much has been written about the Regulator-Moderator activity of San Augustine and contiguous counties, yet most of the story remains enshrouded in the mysteries of the piney woods. For representative treatments, see George L. Crocket, Two Centuries in East Texas, A History of San Augustine County and Surrounding Territory From 1685 to the Present Time (The Southwest Press: Dallas ,1932; facsimile reproduction, 1962), 194-202; John W. Middleton, History of the Regulators and Moderators and the Shelby County War in 1841 and 1842 in the Republic of Texas (Fort Worth, 1883).

[24]Hiram G. Runnels was governor of Mississippi, 1833-1835.

ago but nous verons— was up in the office and attended to Business regularly— got over my sickness—

Wednesday the 14 excessively hot— Mr Nelson[25] the County Surveyor Commenced to Board with me at $20.00 pr Month. I took him because he is a decent young man, and we allways have more on the Table then we want for the family, he lodges in his office— *Old* Crossman dined with me— Vital Flores who was Sick lately was in Town— old Marriano Mora the oldest Mexican in Town very sick this day a year ago I was taken sick

Thursday the 15th excessively hot near night it was allmost insupportable— mail from East—rd A Book from Mr Deyoung of San Augustin containing the Service of *Yom Kippur* in the Portuguese ritual, also $15.00 par funds to take 5 field notes out of the County Surveyors office— no news from the U.S.

Fryday the 16th— Thermometer at 97 in the Shade. too hot to breathe doing nothing, anniversary of the Battle of the nechaz,[26] [Neches] where Boweles[27] [Bowles] was killed

Saturday the 17th Thermr ½ degree higher than yesterday, mail arrived from the west, brought a large quantity of Papers— and left more then half behind at Cincinnatti, an old Publication against Sam Houston by Col Coleman, is republished,[28] received two Copies, recd a Letter from J. W. Smith[29] of Bexar, one from Roberts[30] the acting Secretary of War, dam him I owe him no good will— he is the chap who was very hospitably entertained by me about 6 years ago and gave me the *Devils thanks* to wit ingratitude in return— received also a Letter from Mr Butler of Galvezton, all have to be answered by next weeks mail

Sunday the 18th Therr at 98 in the Shade at 3 P. m. too hot that sure— read news-papers Books tried to be cool hunted the coolest place in the House to sleep the Siesta but it was all hot— everywhere, and at present 6½ P. m. the Therr is at 93½ degrees

Monday the 19th July 1841 a fine cool Breze, but yet where

[25]Albert Aldrich Nelson.

[26]The Battle of the Neches was fought on July 15 and 16, 1839, and was the principal engagement of the Cherokee War. The Texans were led by Thomas J. Rusk, the Indians by Chief Bowles. Sterne served as a Captain. The battle occurred a few miles west of Tyler near the Neches River, with Texan troops numbering 500 and the Indian warriors totaling 700 to 800. The Indians were routed, and this nearly ended Indian troubles in the eastern section of the state.

[27]Chief Bowles was the principal Cherokee Chief while his tribe lived in Texas. He was known to Mexican, Texas and United States agents as a leader of exceptional quality. He was killed at the Battle of the Neches on July 16, 1839.

[28]Sterne refers to **Houston Displayed, or Who Won the Battle of San Jacinto?** By a Farmer in the Army, published at Velasco, 1837.

[29]John William Smith was born in Virginia on March 4, 1792. He moved to Bexar in 1830 from Gonzales. his first Texas home. He fought in the siege of Bexar, and bore the last message from the Alamo. He was Mayor of San Antonio three times and also served in the Texas Senate. He died on January 13, 1845.

[30]Samuel A. Roberts was acting Secretary of State. On September 7, 1841 the post became his officially.

the wind does not have effect the Thermometer is 89 degrees (11 a. m) 92 at noon— send of mail to San Augustin and the United States wrote several letters to San Augustin— Send Mr Deyoung's field notes etc. no rain— yet it appears to be very healthy no one sick that I know of.

Tuesday the 20th weather rather a little more moderate than it was, paid miss M. Sims for a quarter Schooling for Eugenia, Mr W. F. Henderson who has been boarding with me for 3 months left by my particular request. I have been fooled enough in my life time,

Wednesday the 21st weather hot— every body in Town drunk, nothing doing, idleness Root of all evils, the whole Family of Hyde's got Poisoned this morning by having the seeds of Jameson weed trown into Coffee, supposed to be done by the negro woman Frances, she was arrested and the trial will come on to morrow at 10 oclock a. m. all the Poisoned, are better this Evening and none are fatal.

Thursday the 22d— very warm but not insupportable— the negro and goyens[31] negro man Jake were examined. confessed the crime voluntarily and were committed. mail from East no news— miss martha Sims very sick—

Fryday the 23 July 1841 weather warm— as yesterday—my son Charles a little Sick— not much danger, Staid at home all day— wrote Executions for Delinquent Tax payers all day— at 5 P. m. saw rain *in sight* but had none here

Saturday the 24th weather as yesterday— was sick again this forenoon— have a Sun pain, which leaves me at 12 oclock— went to the office in the afternoon western mail, not much news, except about 50 Cow Thieves have been overhawled by the mexicans and all Killed— good— the loan is positively effected.

Sunday the 25th had a fine rain yesterday afternoon cooled the air. fine weather this morning— got u[p] at day light translated a Title of Wm Chas Brookfields situated near Soda lake, for [which] he owes me $10.00 my sun pain came on again at Breakfeast the pain more intense, then yesterday but did not last so long

Monday the 26th Weather opressively hot— send of Eastern mail— send a couple of communications to the Red-lander, wrote to J. W. Smith of Bexar & to Jonas Butler Galvezton— in answer to letters received from them. Probate Court to day many People in Town. entered into an arrangement to Patrol in Town & Country to Keep the Negroes in Check who of late have grown quite too troublesome and consequential

July 27—Tuesday— very warm weather Therr at 97½ was at the office till noon, at home all the rest of the day, wrote an answer to Saml A. Roberts Acting Secretary of State to a letter received from him dated 5th inst send it by R. Parmalee[32] who goes on to Austin to morrow

---

[31] William Goyens, a free Negro, was a Nacogdoches blacksmith. Although himself a Negro, he owned some slaves.
[32] Richard Parmalee was Nacogdoches County District Court Clerk.

Wednesday the 28th hot— hot hot— allmost equal to the infernal Regions to go trough the Sunshine at 12 oclock— as usual nothing doing, Doctor Rowan left us to day— *whiskey* will *now* be cheaper. Parmalee & that Pink of .... Mr Wm. F. Henderson left for Austin to day— learnt for the first time to day that old Jimmy gaines Senator[33] Gaines from Sabine County has two living wives now in Texas— oh! dear!— he is the man who preaches morality, yes, and he is the man who made a Prisoner of me in february 1827 on the Attoyaque, for being opposed to said Gaines's *own* government mexico and now he is a Senator of the Republic of Texas— the greatest *Traitor* in that Body. the Correspondent of Almonte & Santana in 1834 & 1835 a Spy upon Texas!— & now— god save the mark— a grave Senator— he would change *coats* to morrow if circumstances would require it of him god save me from such *men*— paid Bridgit $10.00 on the Baker's Estate account

Thursday the 29th July 1841. weather continues hot Mr George H. Airy from Augusta La was here to day— has laid off a new Town!! wants cotton Shipped to the place— eta Texas first— then, La mail arrived a letter from Sheldon Shreeveport nothing particular in it—

Fryday the 30th weather same as yesterday, wrote from 6 till 10 A. m. impossible to do anything after that time— at 3 P. M. my wife complained of Head ache and pains in her side— had a hot fever near sun down—

Saturday the 31st July no change in the weather— Mrs. Sterne had fever all night— send for Doctor Starr at day light, prescribed, for her. took Blue mast and calomel, very sick all day— not much fever towards night fever intirely left— mail from the west brought me nothing but a Houston Telegraph— nothing in it expt Electioneering

Sunday the first of August 1841 weather changed a little cooler than it was before— Mrs Sterne better— thank god— send off western & northern mails— wrote to Jonas Butler of Galvezton & J. W. Smith of Bexar nothing else in the Political world— Mayfield was at Douglas yesterday made a favorable speach, a Mr Cox — a Confederate and confidant of that notorious scoundrel Juan Santos, wrote a letter to Douglas against mayfield, but the Man's rascality is so well established that he can not hurt Mayfield—

Monday August the 2d weather hot, but not so opresive as it has been, send of Eastern mail Mrs. Sterne better— missed her fever— no news from any where— aniversary of the Battle

---

[33]James Gaines was born about 1776 in Culpepper, Virginia. He came to Texas in 1812, and participated in filibustering activities. He was alcalde of the Sabine District (1823) and opposed Haden Edwards in the Fredonia Rebellion. He attended the Convention of 1836 and signed the Texas Declaration of Independence. He operated Gaines Ferry, now Pendleton Bridge, and was postmaster there. Gaines served in the Senate of the Fourth, Fifth, and Sixth Congresses. He joined the California gold rush, and died there in 1856.

with the troops under Col Piedrass in 1832—[34] which turned out in the expulsion of the mexican troops from this part of Texas—

Thursday the 3d the heat not so severe as yesterday— the People from the north Settlement and the Town of Nacogdoches held a meeting in the Court House for the purpose of organizing a Patrol, to keep in due check the negro Population who are getting rather too free— that is to say, they make too free with other Peoples property— particularly at night,—

Wednesday the 4th warm weather— Judge Terrill in Town came last Evening, was introduced by him to judge martin of Mississippi, nothing new

Thursday the 5th pleasant weather. sun obscured nearly all day—Doctor allen returned from the great Indian Expedition—saw no Indians. the men under gel James Smith are all returning, those under Gel. Tarrant are gone to the Brassos, to try to find them, M. B. McKeever who Killed Joe Shanks— was killed up at Fort King, in affray, mail from East. Texas Treasure notes at 15-17 & cotton 15-20 rumor that the loan is again *knocked in the head* I care not if it is— good—

Fryday the 6th August weather rather Hot— General Memucan Hunt[35] in Town, from San Augustin electioneering— quien Sabe— Several mexicans— who left here in 1838 are returning to this country very fast

Saturday the 7th fine weather went with Mayfield, Rusk, and Hunt, to the Town of Douglas, a large meeting of the People of that part of the County, were addressed by Mayfield, Hunt, John Brown Red, and Nath. Killough returned home at night, nothing new, in the mail, which arrived to day—

Sunday the 8th warm Sultry weather, looked very much like Rain, Thunder and lightning—but no rain—Gel—Judge Terrell & Capt wright an old acquaintance dined with me, Gel Hunt returned today from Jno Dursts, send off western mail. Wm. R. Scurry the District Attorney in Town

Monday the 9th very warm Judge Terrill organized a Special Term of the District Court for the trial of the two negroes in jail, grand jury found a true Bill— Court adjourned till to-morrow— Mayfield made a le[n]gthy and exelent Speach, spoke rather too much of Mr Cox— Brown & Killough also spoke, Town full full [sic] of People—

Tuesday the 10th weather as yesterday, the negro Jack tried

---

[34] Sterne refers to the Battle of Nacogdoches. The Mexican troops were commanded by Jose de las Piedras, who ordered the people to surrender their arms following the disturbances at Anahuac. Their resistance and Piedras' subsequent flight is known as the Battle of Nacogdoches.

[35] Memucan Hunt was born on August 7, 1807, in Vance County, North Carolina. He lived for a time in Mississippi before coming to Texas in 1836 to become a brigadier general. He worked for Texas annexation in Washington, and in 1837 was made Minister to the United States. In 1838 he became Secretary of the Texas Navy, and held other commissions and offices before his death on June 5, 1856.

& found guilty—patroled in the Evening till one A.M.— had a fine rain, but not near enough

Wednesday the 11th August weather is moderating last night a fellow named Peter Townsend Knowing that I was absent from home came to disturb my Family, gave him a severe cudgeling for his pains this morning; the negro who was found guilty yesterday was this day sentenced to be hung on the 20th this month a change of venue has been obtained for the negro girl— Rumpff and Brichta had a fight, Duffield[36] & W. M. Cox had *nearly* a fight, Henry Sublett in Town,

Thursday the 12th weather as yesterday— the Eastern mail, brought nothing— a Ball in the Evening at Mr Chevallier's was very much amused

Fryday the 13th weather in *Statu quo* dull, nothing doing, times getting worse every day— English made an other rise— very good— tried several cases in the Justices Court.—

Saturday the 14th—weather dito as yesterday— felt very unwell all day, went up Town to receive the western & northern mails, nothing new very particular, Electioneering is the order of the Day, abuses against the Candidates by the opposition papers, the order of the day

Sunday the 15th weather warm, more so then yesterday— took medecine last night Keep at home all day—James Arnold send off the mails—feel better this Evening

Monday August the 16th weather very warm, feel much better went up Town, the Election for Justice of the Peace was held, my time being out yesterday—was elected again unanimously Gave Orders for my company to muster next Fryday at 9 oclock, to preserve Order at the Execution of the negro Jack who was condemned to be hung next Fryday—

Tuesday the 17th weather same as yesterday—a dull day nothing doing, mail to East did not leave here untill to day, send a communication to the Red Lander

Wednesday the 18 warm & sultry— had a Storm in the afternoon but no rain— Town perfectly healthy, brought up my magistrate Dockett, wrote to Col. Bean

Thursday the 19th weather hot, and no rain renewed 75 Tax Executions, went to the jail to see the nego Jack, he is very repentant, appears very much in distress,— Doctor King and Judge Martin returned from Kingsborough, the latter is well pleased with the Country, and is to return with his Family in a short time

Fryday the 20th hot in the morning. a fine rain in the Evening— this day was set for the Execution, of the negro Jack—he was brough[t] to the gallows about ½ past 12 meridian, made a speach (religious) and stood it like a hero, he was swung of and died in one minute— the mail arrived from the East, brought me a Letter from General David B. Morgan of Madisonville La. about

---

[36]W. C. Duffield, a Nacogdoches attorney.

some Land Claims, heard the news of Capt Jackson[37] having been Killed in Shelby County & a german who was with him a good inoffensive man, who is much regretted by every body, Capt vandergiff arrived. an old acquaintance Capt Hotchkiss staid all night—

Saturday the 21 weather rather sulky wind but no rain— mail from North & West much Political News,—confound it— received a Letter from Mr Roberts the acting Secretary of State, also one from Senator Muse wrote an answer to gel Morgan's letter —dull times no rain—hot—uncomfortably so— whish winter was here—

Sunday the 22d Send of western mail, wrote to S. A. Roberts in answer to a letter received from him wrote to J. M. Dor also a communication to the Houston Telegraph, had a fine rain this afternoon a cool wind blows from the N.E. at dark

Monday the 23 very heavy rain from morning till near 12 oclock rained again very hard in the Evening, not many People in Town, and not much doing, Send off mail Eastward, wrote to Red Lander

Tuesday the 24th rain, rain, rain,— and yet the grownd is hardly wet ½ a foot, made arrangements to go to Belts (Teran) next Tuesday, and to divide some Land of P. de Torres next Thursday

Wednesday the 25th August More rain, Clear in the Evening, arranged all the Papers to obtain Patents on the League & Labor granted to the Heirs of J. E. Roof—Maria del Carmel (Widow Mora) George T. Walters, J. C. Cortes's Heirs (myself as assignee) & 1280 acres on account of ½ League granted to Louis Velard.

Thursday the 26th fair weather to day the eastern mail arrived no news, rd a Letter from Natchez of no consequence. Counsilor Hyde very sick at San Augustin, nearly made a trade with Wm K. English for a quarter of a League of Land my share left me out of a League & Labor granted to Ma del Carmel widow mora— but was no go he asked such an *infernal* high price for his goods he was to give me in payment, that I did not make the trade patroled in the Evening—Mrs Robt Patton & Mrs Berry are guests at our House to night

Fryday the 27th fine weather to day— gathered the little corn left in the field— Mrs Berry & Mrs Patton left for home, a suit was brought by Mrs Lazarin against ygnacio Sanchez for assault— Moses Patton told me that when he was at Galvezton last June, Gel S. Houston told him on taking leave to give his best respects, and kind remembrances to Doctor Irion and Mr Durst, and after a little reflection said, that's all I care any thing about down there *vel vot of it?* there is probably no love lost at all— Martin Lacy is in Town. young W. Lacy his son (the surveyor) dito—

---

[37]Charles W. Jackson was the organizer of the Regulators, and his death was a result of the Shelby County disturbances of the early 1840's.

Saturday the 28th August fair weather, Mr wingfield to whom I sold a third of a League of Land the Headright of Juan Prado Jr told me he had not my sale (having lost it). I got Juan Prado who fortunately was in the neighbourhood to come in and make a new sale, which was recorded— a certain Mr Lewis an old acquaintance arrived from the west—mail arrived from dito—received several Letters—None of importance all the news are of a political nature nothing worth to give a passing notice—

Sunday the 29th August weather fair— in the morning—rain in the afternoon— Patroled last night till 2 A.M. the Blackies had a dance. All was conducted in good order— went up town in the afternoon, W. A. Ferris returned from San Augustin. herd a hard Political Debate. old Sam got the worst of it—so it should be considering his *love?* for this County

Monday the 30th rain yesterday after dark, fair to day, Probate Court. send of mail to East— wrote to Louis Rueg about monay for Taxes—wrote to F. H. Hazard of Alexandria, Patrol Committee met to day appointed N. Wade Capt of the Town and Jas Charlton for the northern neighbourhood, for the ensuing month of September—made out Powers of Attorney to A. A. Nelson to get Patents— on the Headrights of Ma. del Carmel mora— Juan Clemente Cortes's Heirs—Louis Velard, Juan Prado Jr J. E. Rooff & G. T. Walters

Tuesday the 31st August delivered to A. A. Nelson the Powers of Attorneys and all the requisite and necessary documents, for the Lands mentioned yesterday, except the One of J. E. Roof. Mr Nelson left about noon to day, wrote to Jno A. Crutcher to assist N. in getting Patents to my lands, in the Evening was called out of my bed to commit to the jail two Negroes who ran away from their masters from San Augustin, the man says he belongs to Donald McDonald, and the woman to the widow H. Horton

Wednesday the 1st September 1841 weather Damp & Sultry nothing of consequence transpired this day, Mr Ham is County surveyor in the place of Nelson till N. return, Ham boards with me in place of Mr Nelson— in my yesterdays journal— I forgot— to put down that Mr A. A. Nelson gave me five dollars good monay on account of his Board, wrote a Deed for Isaac Lee— sold to Capt Wm K. English a note on J. H. Wilson for $52.00 for a sack of salt and a keg of lard—(better that, then nothing!!)

Thursday the 2d September weather same as yesterday received a Letter from Mr Deyoung San Augustin, nothing new going on, had a Ball in the evening at C. Chevaliers's given by Capt English—all good humored and well pleased, "we all went home in the morning"—

Fryday the 3d Hot sultry weather— a Mr Payne of *Magnolia* is in Town, wants to make a Town of Magnolia any how— Cant come it Judge—Politics, Politics—Politics—no monay, no Business, except the grog shops—oh! shade of 1831—!

Saturday the 4th September 1841 hot dry weather McDonald from San Augustin came after his negroes to day, mail arrived from the west brought no Papers nor letters from Austin, some few from Houston—received a letter from west Liberty from A. Thouvenin about business of Ogilvy's Estate filed among his papers also a letter from R. W. Woodward from Lagrange. Fayette County about a Certificate of 1280 acres Land he wants me to get out of the hands of the County surveyor. Muse returned from Austin have not spoke to him yet—

Sunday the 5th September very warm weather to day send of the northern & western mails, accepted a demand of 160 dollars good monay and $200.00 Texas monay in favor of Mr Chasseigne against the Estate of James Ogilvy, which receipt was given to Charles Chevalier and send on by him in to day's mail to West Liberty, to Mr Chassiagne's agent paid $300.00 Texas monay to the mail rider of A. C. Davidson on a/c of a Draft from the Gel Post Office, receipt in Post office Papers, Borrowed $40. Texas monay from Mr Charles Chevalier—was deceived in getting monay where I *ought* to have got it—Mr Oscar Engledow met with a misfortune by being trown of a Horse & seriously and perhaps dangerously injured many People came in Town to night preparatory to the Election to morrow— the Poor man's Christmas—! Greene of Harrison County!— author of the expression—good—

Monday the Sixth September 1841 very warm weather Election to day for President vice President & Representatives to Congress— genl Houston got 105 votes—Burnett 212—for vice Prest Burleson 183— Hunt 115, for Representatives— Mayfield 213— Watkins 204— Brown 127— Killough 28— Scattering 7— in all 333 votes were polled here— menneffee got 19 and Jones 1 for vice President[38] I was the Presiding Officer of the Election, and I do Belive that *one* man (?) voted twice, however I do not care who is elected exept Mayfield— I candidly belive we are in a state of *collapse* so that nothing in the shape of Legislation can save us from a general governmental as well as individual Bankruptcy— Mr Muse made a speach, saying that he is going to resign his Senatorship— pleading Poverty as his reasons for doing so— he is right;— our government is, like most of the People composing it— *not able to pay the Honest Labourer for his work*— I hope however that muse will not leave us now in such a critical situation, if he can do so without utter ruin to himself & family, for I belive he is a good, and faithfull servant of the Public— there were one or two *Drunken* fights in Town—but on the whole I have never seen an Election day so *Peacable* as this has been— send off mail to East. this morning wrote to Wm R. Scurry & to Canfield the Editor of the Red Lander I am tired exhausted and completely used up—

Tuesday the 7th very warm—unusually opresively Hot sev-

[38]Sam Houston was reelected President of Texas and took office on December 13. 1841 and served until December 9, 1844. Edward Burleson was elected Vice-President. Others referred to and not previously identified here include David G. Burnett. Memucan Hunt, James S. Mayfield, John "Red" Brown, William Menefee, and Anson Jones.

eral returns from the different districts have come in but no news of all—Mayfield watkins and Brown are running a hot race, nothing particular doing— Many People in Town, had a long Conversation with muse this Evening

Wednesday the 8th September warm cloudy in A.M. rain P.M. cleared of towards Evening, no definite News from the different Precincts two still to be heard from, understood to day that one of the Candidates presided as an officer or judge of the Election (Mr J. Brown Red) where he got all the votes—wont do Judge—!!! heard from San Augustin Houston far ahead Burnett only 48 votes, they will be sorry for it probably in less then *three years*— news of the death of Richard Fulgum arrived this Evening— he died of Congestive fever was a very fine promising young man—

Thursday the 9th very warm (too much so) the whole returns of the County have at last been received—Mayfield & Jno Brown (Red) are elected. B. by a majority of 10 over Watkins, Mayfield met Williston M. Cox to day at my office door and gave him a most tremendous thrashing— I really belive he deserved it— there was a Ball in the Evening at Jno Thorns went off well—came home at 12 oclock—

Fryday the 10th pleasant weather— not much business to day, went out to Julian Sanchez's to marry him— Mathew F. Sims —(a clever fellow) went with me also Mr Warren and J. S. Roberts, the bride and now her ligitimate Spouse have been (married) this last 15 years— but not exactly according to Law— danced till 12 oclock— Mr Roberts & warren went fire hunting & Sims & myself went home

Saturday the 11th weather same as yesterday— gel T. J. Rusk left for Red River, western mail, no news (of the Elections) recived Letter from Sec of State & 3 drafts against Raguet— Roberts—and J. Durst

Sunday the 12th Sept 1841 fine weather, send off mails wrote to nobody—dull monotonous times amused myself all day in reading *three Pages* of the 4ple Boston notion, hunted a little in the Evening

Monday the 13th cool night—warm day—my little Son Placide took sick with the fever— hope it is not dangerous. Send off mail to East— wrote to the Red Lander— in the Evening a party who had went down to the Angelina returned from a fishing expedition— Martin Rumpff who was one of them, complained of being sick all the time they were gone and at 8 P. m. Rumpff was found *dead* in his Bed without a Person being with him to see him die— the alarm was given by a friend who found him dead— we all went to see— he was dead— a coroner inquest was held over him—verdict— died a natural death by the visitation of god—

Tuesday the 14th weather dito—dito— I hired to day an old negro man and an old negro woman of Wm. K. English, out of a gang of negroes he hired from a person who brought them here

— 58 —

yesterday, how English made his arrangement I know not— but I hired the two negroes at 15 dollars fifteen dollars pr month for both, English is to make me any allowances for medicines or loss of time by sickness— we burried Martin Rumpff with *Masonic Honors* this afternoon— a large procession attended the funeral, Doctor Starr came to see Placide twice today, this Evening he is a little better— the infant Laura is quite recovered—

Wednesday the 15th September 1841 Cool night, warm day Placide is better this morning, had no fever all day negroes I hired of Mr English came here to day, the woman is very sick, attended on her as well as we could, her husband an african is very attentive and affectionate— nothing of consequence occurred to day was introduced by Mr Whitlesey to a Mr Tennille, a Brother of Mr Ben Tennille formerly a surveyor under Aldrete & Smith, Mr Tennille wants to Know about a Ten League grant his Brother had belonging to a certain Captain Medina— told him my mind about it— gave him no encouragement— and that is the trutht [sic] will cost him $5000.00 in par funds and then he will be just ready for a Law suit with the Persons residing on the Land— wont do—

Thursday the 16th Cool night— windy during the day— the negro woman hired of Capt English continues very sick the man attending on her— mail arrived to day from East. brought President Tylers veto message about the Bank Bill introduced into the Senate by Henry Clay— if I was a Citizen of the United States I would rejoice at the news, but as a Texien I am sorry for it for we would in less than 12 months have experienced the Benefits resulting from it— this may be selfish but it is nothing more than my candid opinion. Mr Caspary of Shelbyville arrived this afternoon in quest of news about a negro belonging to a Mr Rose who committed a Robbery in Shelbyville, found out that the negro passed trough here two days ago, and spend part of the monay which was identified— Mr C. obtained warrant to take him— I expect to go with Caspary to get the negro or at least the stolen property

Fryday the 17th September left with Mr Caspary towards the west in quest of the negro, stopped the first night at Bradshaws—

Saturday the 18th warm weather left early in the morning to Masters to Breakfast— went on to Crockett, got the warrant endorsed, got Col Mead[39] and Constable Spencer Townsend to go on with us went 10 miles to George Hollmarks near the Mustang prairie, where we found Mr Rose encamped— took the negro found part of the monay and a certain gold piece which is well identified as having been stolen—Mr Rose gave up the negro to the officer without a murmur, brought the negro on to crockett

Sunday the 19th left the negro in charge of the officer and came on to Macleans

---

[39] Eli Mead.

Monday the 20th sultry weather—was very sick all night, left sick this morning to Debards where I staid till 2 P.M. felt well enough to come on to Col Bean's where we staid all night—

Tuesday the 21st very sultry weather last night left early this morning to Jno Durst to Breakfeast, rained for about two Hours very hard, wind changed suddenly to the North arrived at home at 3 P.M. found all well; Mrs Davenports' child died during my absence, Hoya returned from Galvezton, received a load goods, brought in by a Mr wortman,[40] of Crockett a good friend of mine, Mr Leusch also came in Town

Wednesday the 22 September 1841 Cold weather a fire in the chimney last night & this morning was very comfortable, Mr Caspary who staid with me last night is here yet he is waiting for the negro Bob who at dark this Evening has not arrived, D. R. [David Rusk] whipt R. W[hitle]sy, to day perhaps he was right, quien sabe Mrs Davenport has a child very sick— took up a Debt of Genereux Benard of $69.00 paid with a note on Thos H. Rodgers—who owes me $300. payable 1st March 1842—paid $4.50 to Mcintire towards the funeral Expences of my Brother in Law Jeremy would have paid it long ago had I been asked for it

Thursday the 23d Cool nights— warm days— this day the mail arrived from East—brought nothing for me exept a Letter from Burrill Thomson wants me to go down to San Augustin Court—had a quarrell with Jno. R. Clute about his claiming my Land— was about cudgeling him if he had not denied his interference with my land, — Mr caspary is still here the negro has not yet come Greer[41] the Senator from San Augustin passed trough here to day from Crockett, renewed 83 Executions bad sign— the negro woman hired of English is still very sick her husband does not do much, being obliged to wait on her—

Fryday the 24th very cool nights, warm days— no news from the negro Bob— Doctor Irion had an altercation with mayfield— Irion is in the wrong— Sam Houston is expected here with his Lady— Elijah Lloyd arrived to day from San Augustin, Capt vanderveer returned from Trinity River—says it is navigable much better then Red River, Mr washington the Agent of Mrs Logan returned put up at Mr Whitlesey's nothing new particularly—

Saturday the 25th, September 1841 — Cool night warm days— Mr Caspary here yet, waiting for his negro got a Letter from the Officer— was not to leave till Thursday or Fryday—Judge Love[42] of San Augustin in Town to day brought a Subpoena for me to appear in San Augustin Court next Monday, several persons from the Country in Town to day, mail From the West arrived, brought

---

[40]Henry E. Wortman.

[41]John Alexander Greer represented San Augustine in eight of the nine Texas Congresses. He served as president **pro tempore** of the Senate during the Sixth, Seventh, and Eighth Congresses, Secretary of the Treasury following William B. Ochiltree, and in 1846, 1849, and 1851 served as Lieutenant Governor. He died on July 4, 1855.

[42]James Love.

a Letter from J. M. Dor of Galvezton, nothing particularly new from the west— exept a supposed fight with the indians by the Santa fee Pioneers, Burleson is Elected vice President— General Houston President by a large majority.

Sunday the 26th warm weather has set in again— it was very warm last night— dispached mails north & South this morning, wrote to Mr Woodward at Lagrange to the Editor of the Commonwealth at Frankfort Ky. Mr Caspary left here for home, dispairing to see the negro arrive here, however if he arrives here, we will see him send to Shelbyville, bought a load of hay for $5.50— the negro woman hired of English does not do any work yet— had a fever last night—

Monday the 27th weather warm—send off mail to West & East— made a Deed to Jas. S. Mayfield for 100 acres of Land as the Agent of Abram Frisby, who was in jail & gave it mayfield for a fee— Mr S. Townsend of Crockett brought in the negro Bob— send him of with Julian Sanchez to Shelbyville, am going myself to morrow, to see that the negro is safely delivered— Jno. Durst was in Town to day gave him a draft of $25.75 Texas monay to place to my credit, it being for his dues to the Post office Department which was drawn in my favor, County Court to day— Probate Court dito— obtained an Order to divide the Land of the Heirs of Clita Flores—

CHAPTER IV

"Now is this not a gallant speech for a man of 42."

Tuesday the 28th September One year since I commenced this journal— fine weather—left home for shelbyville, passed Vital Flores's overtook the negro Bob, about 10 miles beyond the atto-yacque, arrived at Shelbyville near night, delivered the negro to Alfred A. George, Sheriff of the County, also the gold Piece found upon the negro worth $8. the negro pointed out to the Sheriff a dry well into which he said he had trown the gold watch and Ring; he was immediately let down into the well, and brought both articles up—which is a full confirmation of his guilt, stopped at Dials's Tavern rested well after 40 miles riding.

Wednesday the 29th Cloudy warm weather left Shelbyville after early Breakfeast, arranged a difficulty between Mr P. W. Caspary & a Mr Jones. arrived at San Augustin at 2 P.M. found the Court in Session— general Houston and his Lady arrived last night, went with Genl Houston to J. D. Thomas's House introduced me to his Lady I find her very agreeable, and a very intelligent Countenance, though not a brilliant Beuty I believe the general has a *good* wife. spend the Evening at Mr Jennings's Office took a hand at a party of *Yuker* slept at the House of Jack Gillespie, whose Lady is a good woman, treated me with a great deal of kindness

Thursday the 30th September had a rain near day this morning raining still at 8 A. M. Cold— Overcoats put in requisition— Gel Houston left last Evening with his Lady for Subletts's— a verdict was had on yesterday against wm Goyens in favor of Elijah Loyd for a negro woman and some 6 or 7 children formerly the property of Susan Callier, a Step-Daughter of Mrs J. S. Roberts— Dined at the House of Mr Deyoung, he is a German Jew of the *old reverend class*, his wife and the eldest Daughter most amiable, Mrs D. Y. very much accomplished and deserves a better looking Husband, Court in full operation, many cases on the Dockett.—the Country arround San Augustin is improving— the City itself declining, was at a representation of Pizarro, performed by a Thespian Society, several young gentlemen showed a good deal of Talent in their parts the[y] had to perform, Mr Silvers & Col Ochiltree[1] particularly were much applauded, the first as Rolla

---

[1] William Stivers and William B. Ochiltree.

and the second as Pizarro, spend the night at the House of Doctor Fitzallan[2] a choice flock of choice fellows met here, and *we all went home in the morning—*

Fryday the 1st of October 1841 very fine weather left San Augustin about noon— in company with Mr Caspary who arrived last night from Shelbyville, stopped for the night at a Mr Thompsons's (Stedhams old place) good Bed—bad supper

Saturday the 2d October fine cool Bracing weather left at day light, breakfeast at Walter Murreys arrived at home at 2 P.M. found my wife & children well— the negro woman Susan Sick Doctor Starr attending on her— Mr Nelson arrived a few days ago from Austin brought me two Patents one for the Heirs of J. C. Cortez, and one for George T. Walters— they will not Patent Lands in the Cherokee nation—damd bad business— Mr W. A. Ferriss got married during his transit to Houston County— Mail arrived from west— Election for President and vice Presdt confirmed— Houston and Burleson are elected— receivd a Letter from Sl. A. Roberts acting Secretary of State, respecting some Land claims I sold him, and a man named Lee two or three years ago— at Houston—

Sunday the 3d October Cold night & morning wrote to S. A. Roberts, G. W. Sinks, and Daniel Lacy, all in answer to Letters received from them Paid off some notes I gave a few years ago to a Mr Rody— was introduced to Mrs Ferriss, find that my Friend Ferriss has a good taste, if her face is the mirror in which is reflected the Heart— she will no doubt make him a good wife— they spend the Evening at my house this is the birth day of our youngest Daughter Laura. Eugenia was a little unwell is better now—

Monday the 4th October weather same as yesterday. a fire in the Chimney very agreable— send off mail to the East, wrote to canfield— also to Rueg, and vicente Micheli— by Ygnacio Santos, to Micheli I wrote respecting Patricio de Torres's Estate; to Rueg about his Taxes on his Lands. C. M. Gould arrived from San Augustin. Court adjourned in that County—quien Sabe que hay— payd to Mr Hutton five dollars for which he is to let me have Beef next District court— also agreed to pay the Taxes of Maria del Carmel Mora for 31.60, for Ben Miller $10.20, J. H. Holland $10. Joe Polvador $2.00 to be taken out of mi fees as Justice who issued the Executions against the persons defau[l]ters for their Taxes—

Tuesday the 5th very fine weather, Sale day to Day much land was sold for Taxes to day, charles Chevallier was the principal purchaser, a meeting was held in the Tavern, for the purpose of paying due respect to the President Elect General Sam Houston but it was an intire failure. B. Blake Esqr returned

Wednesday October the 6th weather same as yesterday paid D. Rusk One Hundred & Twenty dollars I owed him. Taylor is

[2]The census of 1840 lists an O. Fitzallen as a resident of San Augustine County.

about Starting for Austin, send by him for a copy of my Headright, Judge Terrill of San Augustin arrived to day stayed at my House

Thursday the 7th muster day for the Officers composing the 2d Regiment T. M.—dito to morrow—and a big muster on Saturday— I am out of that Scrape but should it be necessary to fight the Enemies of our Country I shall like usual be ready—confound this thing Called drill, I never liked it, nor ever will like it, unless those who do drill know more than I *do*, about the matter— Judge Terrill left early this morning for San Augustin, mail from the East arrived brought many letters— none for me, translated a Spanish Document for Mr Moore the Son in Law of Mrs. Wollbourn's for which he owes me $2.50 par funds, news was received to day the Mexicans have destroyed San Patricio and two other Places on the Extreme western Frontier, burnt the Houses took what Property they could, and destroyed the ballance, and took all they did not kill as Prisoners to Matamoros, I hope this may not be true, but it is very probable, in asmuch as that Frontier, in fact like all the *rest of our Frontiers*, is intirely unprotected. what next?

Fryday the 8th October very warm weather— some little Sickness, my negro woman Susan Sick— the negro woman hired of Capt. English sick. my wife has to Cook— sorry for it, but we get clean well cooked dinners, eta, news was received that Doctor King[3] the founder of Kingsborough and Judge Martin, who lately visited this Country, died at Vicksbourgh, or on the River Mississippi of Yellow fever— this is a great loss to this Part of Texas. Doctor King was an interprising man and the Country near the three forks of Trinity will be trown back at least five years— unless some very strong effort is made by his Heirs or successors to carry on the work which he begun—wrote a long letter to the Editor of the Red Lander about the Houston meeting— wrote to the Editor of the Huntsville Alabama Democrat— Capt vail, and Mr Gibson of Natchitochez arrived in Town, I look upon them as two Sharks let loose amongst small fish—neither care a cent for Texas, nor would for a moment defend her from her Enemies, yet the first one obtained a Head right—when actualy a resident citizen of the United States. the other I do not Know very well but they deserve a notice in my diary

Saturday the 9th very warm weather—too much so—Battallion musters to day, a great many People in Town, mail from west arrived, nothing new.

Sunday 10th October very sultry warm weather send off mail to west and north, send to the Telegraph the Resolutions passed last Tuesday night in relation to an invitation to general Houston to a Public Dinner,—

Monday the 11th rain last night, a great deal to day—send off Eastern mail wrote to general David B. Morgan respecting his

---

[3]Doctor William P. King, president of the Holy Springs, Mississippi company that located on land grants in Kaufman County.

— 64 —

two Leagues of Land in this County, wrote to the Red Lander about matters and things in general especialy a piece signed *a regular Tax payer*— the Justices of the Peace of the County met to day as a Board of Roads & Revenues, Esquire Jno M Watkins's resignation was received and accepted, and I was unanimously elected associate Justice of the County Court in his place— made a trade with Captain English to day for a quarter of a League & Labor granted to Maria del Carmel Mora. being the interest I own in said Tract he is to pay me in all this week $300.00 Texas Treasury notes and $300.00 in good notes on solvent persons in this County for my share in said Land, and as the whole of the title is in my name I am to make him a Bona fide deed to the whole of the League & Labor, provided he can make an arrangement for James S. Mayfields quarter he owns in said Land, Capt Vail and Mr Gibson left— (no one wept at their leaving) several strangers in Town. Herriott the man who made a copy of the County map is in Town as drunk as usual— *bad wine in a good Barrill or visa versa*, he has a good Education but makes bad use of it a pity! and a pity tis a pity—

Tuesday the 12th of October very warm, showers of Rain— occasionally— this is the aniversary of the Patron Saint of this Town, and formarly Bull fights, feats of Horsemanship and many other Demonstrations of joy might be seen amongst these once enslaved, yet contented People, but all their glory like their race is gone to the Shades—to day Mr W. P. B. Gaines arrived from the United States, have not conversed with him much, Mr Payne of Magnolia left here today. my youngest chield Laura took sick this morning, better in the afternoon, Doctor Starr in attendance—Doctor Johnson of Melrose in Town to day, Mat Sims and myself have talked about getting the Contract to run the mail from this Place to Epperson's Ferry, more of this hereafter if we agree—(and get the Contract)—

Wednesday the 13th very warm weather last night rain— and cold weather before morning—meeting of the nightingale Clubb last night, Mat Sims *President!!*—three gentlemen who arrived last night at Mr Whitleseys's Tavern whose names I could not learn left for Austin this morning—Mr. J. F. Ham came in Town this Evening, got the order to Partition the land of Maria del Carmel Mora, Theresa Yabaro, & Maximano ybarbo, as parts of the Heirs of Clita Flores wife of ygnacio ybarbo & one of the Heirs of Jose Flores decd. agreed to meet at Vital Flores on Monday next, received 30 blls Corn part of my purchase of Adam James. brought up by John Dorsetts's wagon for one fourth of the articles received at the Plantation

Thursday the 14th October Cool morning— started at day break, with Richard Parmalee Esqr to Ruegs's old place, where the old negro Adam lives, of which I purchased Hoggs, corn eta— Charles my oldest son went with me, was very much delighted at the Trip, found the Place in tolerable good Order, a pity that Rueg ever left it, he would now have a Stock of 5000 head of cattle—

but we [do] not see all things *ahead,* passed Blufford Mitchels Place looked at Mr Brichtas's Place, *poor Business* arrived at the *Rancho* at 3 P. M. Set all hands to digging Potatoes, had a good supper, and the most desirable, a good Bed—slept soundly—

Fryday the 15th October Cool night, warm day. two waggons arrived which I had previously engaged One of Teodore Dorsett, and the other of Smith, a free man of Color, whom I pay the One fourth the Produce (Corn Potatoes eta) the Hawl— loaded One waggon, saw all the Hogg[s] 44 in number 9 Sows (big) 1 Boar (big) 6 Barrows (big) 20 Shoats about 30 o[r] 36 lb and the rest small Pigs—I am not sure if Mr Parmalee will take the half of them, which I bought of Adam James as his part. I do not care if he does, because the rest are Ruegs, and in my charge & I have as leave 44 as 22 to take care of—directed the Other waggon to be loaded, and left— dined at B. Mitchell's. very hospitable at his House— a fine old Lady is his wife. arrived at home at dark— Mr Jasper in Town— drunk Herriott dito— mail yesterday nothing for me.

Saturday the 16th October 1841 weather moderate— many Persons in Town to day—received Two waggons from Ruegs's Rancho loaded with corn Potatoes an Pumpkins, mail arrived from west & north, nothing new—no Letters for any body— received from Wm. K. English Three Hundred dollars in Texas Treasury notes agreably to our Contract for my fourth in the League and Labor of Land granted to Maria del Car[me]l Mora.

Sunday the 17th weather same as yesterday— dispatched mails paid $350.00 Texas monay to mail Boy north of this on a draft from the Secretary of State, on account of Postage due by me eta— the above amount makes up the sum of $650.00 of the whole amount of the draft filed in my office—

Monday the 18th weather in Statu quo. dispatched Eastern mail; after dinner Mr Generis returned; went out to vital Flores's accompanied by Mr F. J. Ham & John Noblett for the purpose of making the division between the lands of the Heirs of Clita Flores dcd, arrived after dark.

Tuesday the 19th weather same.—the Commissioners appointed to divide the Land, were Sworn in eta commenced the Survey agreed to run of 1000 acres being the Shares of two of the Heirs, to be divided afterwards— having seen the Surveyor fairly Started and my presence not being wanted, I returned Home, arrived at home at 4 P. M. in the Evening General Houston and his Lady arrived from San Augustin, Mrs Houston is unwell, Doctor Fosgate an eminent Phisician accompanies the general. Major Reily arrived— from Houston.

Wednesday the 20th weather turning cool— General Houston addressed the Citizens to day at 2 P. M. in the Court House—the House full of People— General Houston proved to the Satisfaction of *all* that the denunciations which were reported to have been made in a late Speach at Houston were false; and that Mr

Cruger[4] the Author is a *Liar*, it is my opinion that every thing in the Shape of an excitement against General Houston has intirely subsided—and there exists at present no difference between the People of this County, and General Houston exept the Cherokee question— amongst those who differ with the general upon that question I am One— and this is an *Honest* difference of opinion to which every free man *is* intitled—, had a Ball at Mr Whitlesey's came home at one A. M. on

Thursday the 21st October weather turned Cold during the night, the mail from the East came in to day. high political Exitements in the United States, the Beligerent Parties in Shelbyville have surrendered to Judge Terrill of this Judicial District, god Knows how long Peace may prevail amongst them—genl Houston still in Town— J. S. Roberts made his appearance to day— I believe his Sins were forgiven by the general!! was the Election to be run over again general Houston would get nearly all the votes in Town,

Friday the 22d last night a heavy white frost. omitted to state in my yesterdays journal— that I paid Mr Generiss of Bexar $150. Texas Monay on account of a note I collected against B. Chirino in favor of Juan Cortez of Natchitochez. there is now about Eleven dollars in par funds coming to the firm of Dangerfield & Generiss the Ballance of said debt—Mr Generiss left here this morning for New Orleans. General Rusk returned from the Red River Counties. Several of the gentlemen Delegates arrived on their way to Austin, had a very fine Party at Mr Charles Chevallier's. Mr and Mrs Mayfield Gels Rusk, & Houston and Lady eta all there—Doctor Irion and Lady,[5] dito—heard of the Death on one of Mr Jno Dursts Childern—a beutifull girl died yesterday, or the day before, I am sorry for it—Major Reyley returned in the Evening

Saturday the 23d a very heavy frost last night, destroyed all tender Summer plants purchased of Jno S. Roberts, (who purchased of Robin Casey) all the Land below my field between the two Bayous Lanana and Banito paid him One Hundred Dollars in Hoggs—which he has received—Placide my youngest son still Sick. Eugenia is sick with fever, hope it is not serious—Genl Houstons Horses—gone run away on yesterday—Doctor Johnson of the Town? of Melrose got married last night to Miss Amanda Engledowe. Hurrah. for us—

Sunday the 24th October 1841 last night weather moderated a little, send off western mail, Dined at Charles chevalliers, the Dinner was given to Gel Houston, Major Reyley was present

Monday the 25th frost last night, general Houston here yet— send off mail to U. S. wrote a communication to Canfield of the Red Lander— dined at Miss Anne Simmons, Genl Houston,—

---

[4]Jacob S. Cruger operated the **Texas Telegraph and Register** in partnership with Dr. Francis Moore, Jr.
[5]The wife of Robert A. Irion was Anna Raguet, whom Houston had once courted.

Reiley— Thorn eta passed a very pleasant afternoon, had the pleasure of Mrs. Houston's playing a *tune* on the Piano, She is a first rate musician, on the Piano forte & guitar— on which latter instrument she exells—

Genl Houston made a Deed to Eugenia of a square of ground in the Town situated East of Raguet's Lott, bounded South by Douglass, or Pilar Street north by Main Street, & East by the Street leading in front of my Dwelling House, and which is called after me.⁶ Sat as associate Judge in Probate Court, to settle Doctor Starrs administration Business— on Douglass's Estate.

Tuesday the 26th October frost, heavy frost last night general Houston got his Horses back, which he had lost; last night. This morning at 11 A. M. left here for Doctor Irion's House near the Angelina

Wednesday the 27th weather changed last night to a mild warm, a Company of gentlemen Serenaded last night. much gratified— major Reiley in Town yet— Capt Daniel, H. Vail & Lady arrived yesterday from Sabine Town

Thursday the 28th weather warm occasional Showers had a very fine Party a[t] Mayfields last night. a number of Ladies from the Country were present enjoyed myself very much—Major Reyley left here this morning early—Major Mayfield and family left here at about 11 A. M. Major and Mrs Mayfield were on Horseback, a large number of citizens accompanied them as far as the first little Brook where Judge Hart, in the name of The People of Nacogdochez bid farewell to Mayfield & Lady, in such a feeling and solem manner as drew Tears from all present. Major Mayfield answered in the same manner— they then proceeded on their journey, and the Citizens returned, to Town—translated a Title for John Chisum. Mail arrived from the East—no news—

Fryday the 29th October warm wet weather—not any business doing to day. heard from Red River County, am informed that the Persons living on the League of Land near Clarksville, are willing to enter upon a Compromise, expect to go up there with General Rusk next district court— Miss E. Sims at Tea to night played several fine marches on the Piano— Bill Simms arrived in Town this Evening

Saturday the 30th Rain, Rain, Rain,—Chas S. Taylor returned last night from Austin, obtained the Patent for my Father in Law's League & Labor of Land, brings no very particular News, the Santa feé Expedition has not been heard from. our Lodge met once more tonight, is to meet again next Saturday, to make a Strong effort to finish the Rooms over the Court House— received a letter from G. W. Sinks Chief Clerk of Post office Department, Drawing upon me for $470.00 I owe nothing to the department, which is acknowledged in the Letter, but poor Devils it was their only chance

⁶The site was later occupied by the Liberty Hotel and is presently used as a warehouse and office building. It was long claimed as the site of Sam Houston's first home in Texas.

Sunday the 31st October   very hard Rain with a considerable Storm last night after 11 oclock—Send of mail to west & north, wrote to the Post master of Clarksville respecting my League of Land—People commenced coming into town for Court— to morrow. Wrote a Letter directed to the Post master at Clarksville proposing to compromise with the Persons on my land

Monday the first November   rain, and Strong wind, in the fore part of the night, very cold towards morning— this is the day the District Court is to commence. the Sheriff opened Court, but no judge as yet. Mr. Gould the Only Lawyer as yet has arrived this Evening, the Town is full of People, made a proposition to Joseph Ables to go on to New York—not decided upon as yet— a draft of Eight Dollars in Silver was drawn on me which I rejected, having before this, agreably to a Letter to that effect received orders to sell the silver for Texas monay, which I did— Draft was drawn by chief Clerk of Post office Department[7]

Tuesday november the 2d   Cold nights—warm days—Judge Terrill arrived here to day in time to open Court at 10 A.M. organized, drafted grand jury, gave them an appropriate charge— adjourned till 3 P. M. immediately after Court, the sale of Douglass's Estate Commenced, negroes sold very high—I purchased in Copartnershipp with Judge Terrill a League of Land for $2000 situated above Joseph Dursts, on the west Bank of the angelina, originally granted to Helena Kemble being one of 4 Leagues granted to her—was appointed interpreter and Translator to the Court for the Present term, and took the Oath of office—

Wednesday the 3d November 1841   weather Same as yesterday—Lawyer Jennings, Scurry & Hyde[8] arrived from San Augustin, got final judgment, in a case in which the Estate of Ogilvy is plaintiff vs N. Norriss. Mr Border County Clerk of San Augustin in Town received a Bill of sale from Robin Casey for the Ballance of the Land below my field paid one Hundred Dollars in Hogs, which were received by John S. Roberts.

Thursday the 4th   Court in session, much business doing. Judge Terrill is a Business man— Judge Jack[9] arrived from Shelbyville, opened Court there but the grand jury *could not find any Bills*— Oh! dear what a moral County Shelbyville is—?

Fryday the 5th   cold nights warm days— Court going on *beutifully.* Judge Terrill the best judge ever presided here—Judge Jack left this morning for Spring Creek County, John Hall of Crockett still in Town, waiting to get hold of the man which kill McKeever at Kingsborough— Town full of People, an attempt was made to get the Piano Forte of Mrs Emanuel— but cant do it—

Saturday the 6th   weather beutifull court in Session, an im-

---

[7] A gloss identifying who had placed the draft was added by Sterne in the margin of his journal.

[8] James G. Hyde.

[9] Sterne possibly refers to Patrick Jack who was district attorney of the Sixth Judicial District.

portant case was decided by Judge Terrill to day, to wit— that if a Certificate issued to any Person as assignee it is evidence that the assignee must have shown before the original Board of Land Comrs that he was so— which I belive to be a just and equitable decision—General Henderson arrived Judge Terril went to Jno Dursts—Henderson & Jennings stayed at my House to night

Sunday the 7th November Cold night— warm day wrote to the Post master general, about the Draft paid Caldwell of $650.00 also $60 to Mrs. Hubert— the acceptance of a draft in favor of Mrs. Hubert for $470, the refusal of one for Eight Dollars par funds, having agreably to an order of the Department of 16th Octobr 1840 exchanged the Silver for Texas Treasury note, the western mail arrived last Evening late, brought no news of importance, exept a probable rupture between England & the U. States, but this has been the song so long as to be looked upon as mere talk—translated to day a deed to 2½ Leagues of Land sold to Sam Houston & P. Sublett by the grantee vicente Padilla—

Monday the 8th weather mild, South wind— dispatched Eastern mail, received a deed to the League of Land from Doctor Starr, purchased at the sale on the 2d inst gave a mortgage on the land and my note for $2000.00 gave Judge Terrell and Jno. M. Watkins as securities this League belongs half to Judge Terrill, and I am bound to make him a Deed for the same, and he is bound to pay one half of the purchase monay— Court still in session. the Land Case of Smith vs Watkins came up—was put off in consequence of an informality of the return of Ferriss who was ordered last court to survey the Tract,

Tuesday, the 9th weather warm & sultry— Court still in session Criminal Dockit— Col Pierpoint arrived from Shelbyville, paid him $9.50 par funds on account. Staid at my House.

Wednesday the 10th Warm, Cloudy, sultry weather Pierpoint started to day, court still in session, the criminal Docket goes off *easy* no body found guilty and if found guilty escapes punishment. I dont quite like the proceedings, yet there is no blame to be attached to the Judge, nor district Attorney, Wm Scurry who on this day made a very Eloquent Speach against Bigamy with which an individual named Bigham was accused, and aquitted,

Thursday the 11th Cloudy rainy weather— at 12 noon commenced Raining, Keeps at it at 3 P.m. court in Session, cases rattled off like lightning mail arrived from the East, brought nothing new. no mail from the U. States

Fryday the 12th rain. rain. rain. Court in Session. grand jury discharged, many indictments found against many individuals of this county, all fudge in my opinion, the Honble Mr. Dangerfield Senator from Bexar arrived to day, at my House to night, one of those who will guard the Ship from wreck or foe may be so.

Saturday the 13th fine weather. Dangerfield left this morning at 10 A.M. Court adjourned till next Wednesday, judge Terrill purchased young W. Lacy's Place on the upper San Antonio Road for 2300 dollars— him and genl Henderson left here after dinner, mail arrived from Austin. Congress in session K. L. Anderson[10] of San Augustin elected speaker— good choice— an Extra of the Austin City Gazette containing all the correspondence of the *new* Revolutionary Party in Mexico of which Santa ana is the head, the *Plan* which no doubt concocted at Mango de Clavo but *Pronunciado* in Jalisco. Texas ought to be on the look out, we will be either eternal friends or foes if the revolutionary party succeeds—

Sunday November the 14th fine weather—send of western & northern mails— wrote a long letter to K. H. Muse, our Senator about matters & things in general— read the [message] of President Lamar to Congress, an able well written document & if Congress carries out the wholesome advise given, Texas will be itself again—But I am fearful a *foul crowd* will veto *any* thing, coming from our worthy chief magistrate S...............s are so plenty that honesty will be in the back ground, Oh! tempora, or mores

Monday the 15th very fine weather—the Crowd of People who were in Town a Few days ago are all of for home—Silvester Bossier returned from the west with nine negroes run away from the State of Louisiana, the Ballance of the day is a perfect Blank—

Tuesday the 16th very fine weather, Jasper from Crockett arrived, purchased a grey Horse of Capt English gave him up T. H. Rodgers' note for 280$ and his own for $300—took the Horse and his note for $230.00 in good notes on solvent people in this County, also paid him the hire of the nego Jim and his wife untill the 25th December next sold F. v. d. Hoya T. H. Rodgers's note for 207$ received part in Texas Treasury notes, the ballance to be paid in goods, which I have as yet not received. the note I have delivered and endorsed, the Horse I have received, everybody in *high* Spirits!!!

Wednesday the 17th beutifull weather— Court Commenced again to day, Town full of People, the Trial of Burroughs for Killing McKeever was put off till next Court, Col Ochiltree in Town, he wants to purchase a piece of Land in this County paid Tax on Mrs. Sternes's property—did not pay mine, will do so probably— I am not sure till the government pays me 94 dollars they took from me wrongfully in George T. Walters and Juan Clemente Cortes's Head right— Judge Terrill, and general Henderson at my house

Thursday the 18th November fine weather Rawls[11] and others were put upon their trial to day, for hanging willis, the Horse thief. Duffield, Rusk, Burke, Jenning, and Wm K. Scurry made eloquent speachez. Court adjourned till to morrow

Fryday the 19th weather continues fine Trial of Rawls et all

[10]Kenneth Lewis Anderson was born on September 11, 1805 in North Carolina. He moved to Tennessee in 1829 and came to San Augustine in 1837, where he became Collector of Customs. He was Speaker of the House of Representatives in the **Sixth Congress,** and was elected Vice-President in September, **1844.** He died on July 3, 1845.
[11]Daniel Rawls.

was went into again this morning;— they were all acquitted— traded Horses to day with Col Raguet, got a Bay Poney and Two hundred Dollars in Notes for the grey I purchared a few days ago from Wm K. English—gave a Dancing Party at my House in the Evening— House crowded—every body was here, every body enjoyed themselves very much broke up at 3 A.M. on

Saturday the 20th Cloudy weather—Court adjourned—reced $75.00 as interpreter during the present term, loaned John Norriss $50.00 Texas Monay, a General Davis from Tennessee Arrived, says he is agent for a man named McLemore who claims Eleven Leagues of Land, granted to Dolores Martines; nous verons

Sunday the 21st November warm, Clowdy weather rained early in the morning; at 8 A.M. Started for Douglass in Company with the Masonic fraternity of this place, for the purpose of paying a tribute of respect to our deceased Brother Wm. Burton who died last summer, a large concourse of People attended, all joyned the Procession, and all were much gratified— Judge Terrill left for Burnett County Court—Jasper dito—Rusk do. Emile Sampeyrac arrived to day, was not here to see him, general Davis left for the west. about ten waggons with Emigrants passed our Town to day—

Monday the 22d very fine weather, send off the Eastern mail, at home nearly all day attending to repairing fences round the field,—Mrs Forbes very sick, Mrs Sterne sat up with her till 11 P.M.

Tuesday the 23rd very fine weather— Town very dull. Emigrants coming in fast. Charles Hall of Crockett passed trough to day with his Family for the U. S., wrote a long letter to Mrs Kessler the widow of H. Kessler of Houston respecting the land I sold to N. A. Bonzano her late Father, send the Letter and other Documents by Mr. George Bondies who is to receive $120.00 for me or return me the Papers intrusted to his Care, the land in question is on the angelina, and on the white Rock fork of the Trinity originally granted to Maria Josefa Sanchez I paid $120.00 (principal & interest) for an improvement on the Angelina part of Mr. Bonzano part, which must be refunded or the Claim to the white fork Land; given up to me as an equivalent, the Heirs of Bonzano have choice— Mr. Bondies is authorized to settle the matter as stated in my letter of to day directed to the widow Henry Kessler (Kept no Copy)

Wednesday the 24th November very fine weather nearly summer heat. Cloudy towards night—nothing doing in Town, Bondies started for Houston took my Papers eta for the widow Kessler,— busy repairing fences all day, Mrs. Forbes very sick—

Thursday the 25th very, very, very, Cold—mail arrived from East, brought nothing of any Consequence, a Ball this night at Wm Arnolds— . . .

Fryday the 26th Judge mason from Shelby County arrived from Austin, not much news of any importance, indians plenty on the frontier— Danger in going to Austin. Single—Sheriff of Shelby County deposited in my hands Texas monay Audited Claims, eta to the amount of upwards of $5000.00 to be delivered to the Secretary of the Treasury on my arrival at Austin—

Saturday the 27th Novr very cold. cold. Cold. making preparations to start for Austin. several Persons accompanying Ned Roberts started of for Crockett Court, Burke an eminent attorney and Counsilor, who lately defended Allison Lewis accused of Killing a man named [blank] in Sabine County was brutally attacket and bruised by three man on account of the Part Burke took— Oh! tempera oh! mores! Mail arrived from west, no news from Austin, no papers exept the Houstonian[12] from the City of Houston, something must be wrong sure—

Sunday the 28th very hard frost last night very cold all day— wrote nearly all day— Send of both mails (west and north) wrote to the County Surveyor of Austin County, to send me the field notes of Vital Flores, to Austin expecting to [pay?] all dues eta at that place, wrote a Communication to Canfield of the Red Lander, to be send in to morrows mail. still arranging Documents to go on to Austin went up town after supper, purchased a fine Horse of Wm K. English, gave his own note for $230 Charles Sims' note for $80, and on which there is $24 interest, the rest to make up $400.00 I am to do some Business for English for [sic] at Austin, and in case I do not succeed in doing his Business (collecting from Government) he is to pay me at all events something for my trouble, and the rest is payable in some note on a good man.

Monday the 29th November very, [very cold] fine day to day, send of mail to the East, [received] the Horse of Wm. K. English and paid him [as] stated in my yesterdays Journal, arranged my Justices of the Peace matters so that any person can at a glimps see all that is necessary. sat with Judge Hart in Probate Court to day— four Horse waggons two Carriages & 42 negroes passed trough to day— towards the west, genl Pinkney Henderson passed trough to day—Mr Nelson went towards Crockett to day—

Tuesday the 30th November very hard frost last night— weather moderated to day at 2 P.M. South wind blowing, but not very warm this Evening at 6 P.M. got all my Papers which I am to take on to Austin, getting ready to Start four waggons, 2 Carriages and fourty three negroes passed to day for the west—

Wednesday December the 1st 1841 Cloudy—left home for Austin received $5 par monay from Mr Millard $30 Texas Treasury notes from David Muckleroy to get out a patent for him. $1.50 par—from J. C. Morrisson for a Patent of Jack Hyde Jr. also $25.00 par funds from F. T. Phillipps to get Patents, went to John Durst's stopped for the night, 16 miles—

Thursday December 2d rainy rough weather left Dursts in

[12]The **Houstonian** was published at Houston by D. E. and John N. O. Smith. Its prospectus listed Joshua Burr as owner and Joseph Baker as editor.

the rain accompanied by John Durst, his Son Lewis, Esqr Ewing, Mr Jimpsey from Red River, and three Mexicans passed by Joseph Dursts. where James Durst joined us & one Mexican—went to Bradshaws, and campt for the night 23 miles

Fryday December 3d fair Cold weather left very early in the morning, passed by Master's & Crockett. Ned Roberts trial going on for Murder—Mistrial—went to Collin Alldridges Staid all night 40 miles.

Saturday December 4th left very early weather very fine borrowed a doubbled Barrelled gun of C. Alldridge, to go trough the upper Route. Arrived on the Banks of the Trinity opposite Boseman's Ferry at 12 noon Camped here to wait for Judge G. W. Terrill and Col Leonard Williams who will go on with us—Mr Jimpsey left us to go the lower Route— 17 miles

Sunday the 5th very fine weather, many Thousands of Thousands wild Pidgeons flew over Our Encampment last Evening & this Morning, two of the Pack mules got away last night, did not get them till Late this afternoon, Judge Terrill and Col Williams joined us this afternoon, several gentleman from Red River Counties passed to day to go on to Austin, We crossed the River and camped for the night on the west Bank having only traveled *One* mile

Monday the 6th very fine weather had a good nights rest left at 7 A.M. dined at Bob Rodgers's and camped for the night on the west Bank of the Nava Soto 39 miles

Tuesday the 7th left at 7 A.M. passed trough Tinnensville to Cedar Creek 8 miles. Crossed the Brassos at Nashville, and camped a mile below Town—39 miles—

Wednesday December the 8th fair weather left at 7 A.M. passed the Sugar loaf Peak Breakfeasted at Jones's a Mr A. C. Dood of Fort Bend County joined us here to go with us, we Camped all night at a Small Stream (which I shall call Deer Creek Mr John Durst having killed a Fine Deer at this place) traveled to day 34 miles

Thursday the 9th Cloudy in the morning, cleared off by 10 A.M. passed the lone and solitary dwelling of Mr Wells the Mail Contractor for that Route (from Austin to Crockett) at the Post Oak grove saw a large drove of Buffalo, our folks one and all went to shoot one, but being too eager. and the Prairy being deceptive as to distance they all Shot and killed—nothing—found no water on the whole route, did not join in the Buffalo Chase, and being very thirsty, Mr Dodd & myself went on to get to water but we had to wait till we got within 8 miles of Austin before we reached water Met Mr Wells the Mail Contractor who had the Eastern mail. Send the doubble Barrelled gun back by him to Judge Alldridge. Stopped all night at Boyce's 45 *long* miles

Friday the 10th December very fine weather—left after an early Breakfeast rode slow into Austin arrived at 11 a.m. Stopped at Mrs Eberly's formerly Mrs Peyton of San Philipe boarded with her during the Convention of 1833. after dinner went to the

Gel Land Office, deposited Morrissons & Killoughs field notes, Deposited F. S. Philipp's field notes and Certificates to wit Wm Skinner, 1 Labor and several others, was refused Patents, in Consequence of the Chain of Title, as the Commissioner of the General Land Office said was incomplete,

Saturday the 11th very fine weather, went to the office of the Commissioner of Revenue, paid on Bluford Mitchels Certificates & Field notes. *Texas* $16.00 paid Philipp's Ma Josefa Sanchez (being my own) deposited Louis Velards Headright (my own) also John C. Morrisons. B. Mitchel two separate surveys of 640 Acre each, also J. C. Hill ass[ignee] of O. W. Randall ass[ignee] of L. F. Carter, met a Special Committee of the Grand Lodge of the Republic of Texas to amend the constitution,

After the 11th I Kept no regular Journal, was informed that in Consequence of the accumulations of Business in the Gel Land Office I would not get Patents on the field notes I had deposited till May next, the inauguration took place on Monday the 13th the President and vice President Elect wore Hunting Shirts during the august Ceremony! *too much Indian that*—a splendid Ball in the Evening, tired next day, went to Barton's Spring, a most splendid affair, fish to be seen at the depth of 18 feet. Moses F. Roberts of Shelbyville got married, Congress very Busy—doing nothing good—got a Petition introduced into the House of Representatives to Audit my Claim of $950.00 for transporting Troops in 1835, passed all round and has become a Law— but have no money, nor no chance to get any—[13] Splendid Ball to Gel Lamar Brilliant Affair—All hands gone to San Antonio to Spend Christmass—Mail rider from San Antonio killed near this City—fine Capital!!!—Aniversary of Saint John the Evangelist Celebrated by the Masonic Fraternity, Splendid Procession, Splendid audience in the Senate Chamber to see the Instalation, Splendid Speaches by Major Reily and Judge Hutchinson[14] Splendid vocal music by Mrs Barker and her assistance, and to finish all, we had a Splendid Ball in the Evening, passed my time in not very agreable feelings, Cant get Patents, no monay owe my Board, Horse feed eta fine Pickle indeed. Finaly Borrowed monay to pay my debts, and have enough left with Judge Terrill to pay for the Patents if they are ever ready, and on the,

Thursday, the 6th of January 1842 left Austin in Company with James Durst & William F. Sparks familiarly Known as wild Bill—Stopt all night at the widow Rodgers's 22 miles

Fryday the 7th fine weather—passed trough Bastrop, and went to a Mr Miller's to pass the night 39 miles—

Saturday the 8th fine weather— left early in the morning, and went to a Capt Fullers, a very exelent House 37 miles—

---

[13]This claim grew out of Sterne's subsidation of the New Orleans Greys, under the command of Captain T. H. Breece, who came to assist in the Texas Revolution. Various measures for Sterne's relief were passed by Texas Congresses.

[14]Anderson Hutchinson was magistrate of the Fourth, or Western District.

Sunday the 9th January 1842 warm cloudy weather, left after Breakfeast passed trough Independence a beutifull little place 18 m. passed trough Washington (where the Declaration of Independence was made) a fine Place, but all the fine Stores and dwelling Houses most all deserted, 12 m. Crossed the Brassos and Mouth of the Nava Soto to Whitesides's, 34 miles—

Monday the 10th rain nearly all night, rains a little this morning, but notwithstanding, we left, passed by Fernthorps P. O. to Mr Roone's the place formerly occupied by Mr Kennard 25 miles—

Tuesday the 11th Cold but fair weather left after Breakfeast passed trough Cincinnatti Crossed the Trinity to Mr Thompkin's 40 miles

Wednesday the 12th left early passed trough Crockett to Masters's 35 miles—

Thursday the 13th left Masters early Crossed Nechaz saw Mrs Terrill who has mooved during my absence to Young Lacy's Place, delivered a Letter from her Husband the late Judge—but now Attorney General—[15] Stopt all night at Joseph Durst's 34 miles—

Fryday the 14th left very early this morning passed trough Douglass and arrived at home at 2 P. M. 20 miles found my wife very Sick of an inflamatory fever, her breast inflamed and very painfull, Doctor Starr in attendance, Children all well, Wm Arnold, our County Clerk, Doctor L. B. Brown the Coroner, and Major Harry have died since I left, Jackson Todd killed Tom Sims, found the Post office in Order, but no quarterly returns have been made, Commenced making them in the Evening sat up nearly all night, nursing the infant Laura who has to be weaned in Consequence of my wife's sickness

Saturday the 15th fine Cold weather, Mrs Sterne not much better, yet she has not grown any worse. finished my quarterly Post office returns. Answered all the Letters which were received for me during my absence—to wit— Rueg, Madame Lacombe, Genl Morgan of New Orleans Cockerille of Natchitochez, and Nixon[16] of New Orleans—

Sunday the 16th January 1842 fine weather. Mrs. Sterne much better this morning, the first time she spoke in any rational manner to me, Mr Wm R. Scurry has commenced boarding with us a few days after I left for Austin, and consequently has been here over a month—Send of western mail also Red River—the rider of the Red River Mail boards with me every Saturday nights at $1.00 per night.

Monday the 17th fine Cold weather, Mrs Stern is still getting better, arranged my Office to day, Emigrants still coming in, business very dull

Tuesday the 18 Cold weather . Commenced to work in the

---

[15]George W. Terrill was confirmed as Attorney General on December 24, 1841.
[16]George Antonio Nixon, formerly of Nacogdoches.

new garden opposite my House. Mrs Stern getting better very fast, the infant a little troublesome, —fatigued to death

Wednesday the 19th weather as usual Mrs Sterne recovering very fast. work all day in my new garden, find much more pleasure in it then to [go] up Town.

Thursday the 20th fine weather—work in garden, received Eastern mail nothing very particularly new

Fryday the 21st Made an arrangement with J. M. Watkins to let him have 300 acres of Land out of a League I have in my Charge having been granted to Domingo Cervantes

Saturday the 22d Mrs Stern has so far recovered from her Sickness that she can sit up, the infant is more easy. Made an arrangement to send my three children Eugenie, Charles & Joseph [to] School to Miss Martha Sims. Eugenia is taking lessons from Miss Elizabeth Sims on the Piano at 15$ pr quarter—Wm Jones was ini[ti]atted into the Masonic fraternity to night— wrote several letters tonight, directed to New Orleans, Galvezton & Austin

Sunday the 23d fine weather. had nine negroes hired to day to put up fences and put the field in a fit situation for Cultivation

Monday the 24th Sold a Horse to Wm Scurry being the Same Horse I last purchased from Wm. K. English, Mr Scurry is to pay me $350.00 in good notes on good solvent men in this County

Tuesday January the 25th 1842 Working in the garden & transplanting trees, Mrs Stern quite recovered.

Wednesday the 26th received the Horse for which I made an arrangement with J. M. Watkins for, for the 300 Acres of Land, sold a little Horse I got from Raguet to Solomon Wolfe for $50.00 $30 payable in Corn or Cash next fall and a note on John Durst for $20.00

Thursday the 27th Mild fair weather, transplanting trees and working in the garden Eastern Mail arrived brought me a letter from Mrs Sarah Silverberg not answered yet

Fryday the 28 Mild weather loaned R. F. Floyd my Blue Cloath Cloack, he is going to the State of Georgia and South Carolina, wrote by him to Gel Morgan of New Orleans— received 4 Hoggs weighing alltogether 400 lb from the Stock of Parmalee & myself for which I am to allow him payment in Sows or the Same quantity in Hoggs weighing the same number of Pounds

Saturday the 29th fine, very fine, weather—held Court to day not much business of any kind Stirring, Moses L. Patton was in Town, gave me a note on Madame Mora for $90.00 on account of the notes he has to pay me for the place he now lives on, Miss Elizabeth Culp took dinner with us to day, very fine young Lady, very [blank]

Sunday the 30th rather warm Sultry weather, dispatched western mail, wrote to Judge Terrell, to A. Macdonald to the Commissioner of the General Land Office, and the Chief Clerk of the Post office Department, in answer to a Letter received pr last mail from that Depart

Monday the 31st rain last night, cloudy this morning Col

Thorn's Lady was blessed with a little Daughter yesterday, Child well Mother not very well, send off Eastern Mail wrote to Canfield, about matters and things in general, and about not being able to Collect any money for him in particular.

Tuesday the 1st of February 1842 warm last night, Cool but Clear fine weather to day, Mrs Stern has Completely recovered from her Sickness. we have heard of the Sickness of Mr[s]. P. Bossier, Mrs. Stern's Foster mother, we dont attent Balls in consequence of it—Sam Sackett was to be hung last friday

Wednesday the 2d February 1842 very hard Rain last night. Keeps on raining to day— wrote a very long letter this morning to Mrs Silverberg of Canton, very severe Showers of Rain and gusts of wind during the day had to mend Fences eta. Bennett Blake Commenced Boarding with me at $20 per month.

Thursday the 3d rain during the night, Clar this morning, Settled to day with (the widow) Carmel Mora the Owner of the Stone House paid her nine Dollars which is the Ballance I owed her up to this day, gave up my Power of attorney, I retain the lower end Room of the Stone House till I see Juna Mora who is now the agent. Eastern mail arrived but brought nothing from beyond San Augustin,

Friday the 4th February 1842 weather cleared of last night Cold north wind this morning. planted trees before breakfeast went up to the Office . . Juan Mora the Husband of Maria del Carmel Mora who in presence yesterday of Bennett Blake gave up all her power and interest to the said Juan Mora to the half of the Stone House, this day in the presence of James Smith Bennett Blake, J. H. Holland, and Mr Hollingsworth[17] made a bargain with me to let me have the East small Room on the lower ground of the Stone House at two dollars & fifty cents per month untill the first of January 1843 next ensuing. I, having paid up till the 1st of February *presento.* Mr Bennett Blake at the same time rented the half of the Middle Room at $5.00 pr month till the 1st of January 1843.

Saturday the 5th Cold last night, bright day to day— nothing of interest occurred. Grog Shops all Shutt up *no Cash* Credit very Sick, held Court to day on a very intricate case, not decided yet— Lodge met tonight affiliated Taliafero made my report to the [Lodge] as its representative in the Grand Lodge of The Republic

Sunday the 6th February 1842 Cloudy warm weather. the mail from the west arrived, Mr Hall the Subcontractor informed me he would not carry said mail any longer, and went away without the mail, I wrote immidiatly to John G. Berry to send some one to take the mail to Cincinnatti next week, he (Mr. Berry) and a Mr Mason being the *real* contractors, and my not Knowing the residence of Mason, wrote to Berry only. wrote to Davison of Panola County, Contractor of Route No 5 about the difficulty

---

[17]S. P. Hollingsworth.

between the arrival and Departure of the mails on route No 3 & 5 and urging the great necessity I am under to go in Strict Conformity with the Law on the Subject, Communicated the actual distracted situation of our mail routes (as above stated) to the general Post office Department, send (or had ready to send) a Petition recommending the establishment of a Post office at Shawnee Town on the Road to Marshall crossing at John Wallings's on the Sabine

Monday the 7th of February cold fair weather wrote a letter to J. P. Border & to A. A. George of Shelby County before daylight this morning, send off Eastern mail at the usual Hour. did not decide the Case of Reddin vs Ferriss & Durst not being satisfied about the law. on next Saturday will make my decision, rented the Part belonging to Ma del Carmel Mora of the upper part of the Stone House being the one half, as chairman of a committee of Milam Lodge till the first of January 1843 for 24 twenty four dollars pr year payable quarterly commencing on the 1st of January last; all the repairs we (the masonic fraternity make on said Rooms are at our own expense Nathan wade & John Noblitt were present and called upon to witness the contract between said Mora & myself, Reddin[18] commenced to fix the front gallery of my House to day,

Tuesday the 8th Cold weather, frost last night, nothing of consequence happened during the day, a rumor is afloat that Gel Houston is dead, hope it is not so as we surely would be in a much wors fix than we are now (so far as *a President* is concerned)

Wednesday the 9th Cold, frost last night, ninety negroes passed trough to day belonging to a Mr Runnels of Mississippi probably the Ex governor—Mr Gibson arrived from Natchitochez

Thursday the 10th Weather moderate, many People in Town to day. held an Election for County Clerk & Coroner. Orton got the most votes here (55) 144 votes given in here, mail arrived from East received a Letter from J. P. Border in answer to one of mine of 7th inst. also one from Mason & Berry mail contractors for route No 3, Nacogo, & Cincinnatti, to get a rider offering to let the ballance of this year for $500, the Letter received from Border informs me that I can not get a negro by the way of hiring one, nor will Garner let Mr Scurry have one, he (Garner) having purchased a farm which he is going to cultivate

Fryday the 11th of February 1842 rain last night, north wind and Rain all day. Capt English & myself entered into an arrangement to collect a debt due by Henry Rueg to Marvin & Trask New York, all the profits arising from that arrangement to be equally divided between us, (I would not [have] had anything to do in this affair, but I know Rueg owes the monay about $3000 honestly and the Land he has in this Country he has in a manner abandoned so if the debt is paid with his Lands, he will no doubt con-

---

[18]C. W. Reddin.

sider it a good come of) therefore all I can make in this transaction is honest gain—

Saturday the 12th Rain last night, Continues Raining with very Cold north wind, cleared at 12, in the afternoon Jackson Grayson was Committed to jail for Killing John Cayson, Mr Gibson left here, Mr Scurry is also gone to San Augustin— Northern mail, nothing new in it.

Sunday the 13th fair weather frost last night send off northern mail nothing new. a Mr Dupree from Georgia Passed trough to day with 96 negroes,—hurrah for Texas!

Monday the 14th Cold Clear weather, all hands on the *plantation* have bad colds, owing to the sudden change of the weather. send off the western mail by Thomas Hubert on account of Berry & Mason, became personaly responsible for the payment of his Bill at the different places he stops at, for which Col John G. Berry & Mr Mason are responsible to me. Jackson Grayson was brought before Judge Hart Justice Blake & myself on a writ of Habeas Corpus, was released but immidiately recommitted to the Custody of the Sheriff for Examination, took down the Statements of the Witnesses. adjourned till 6 P. M. Met in the upper part of the Stone House gave my decision to permit the accused to be bailed 1000$, went home left *them* hammering away at it. *quien sabe.*

Tuesday the 15th mild fair weather in the morning with wind in the Evening. Jackson Grayson was admitted to Bail in the Sum of $1500 news from Austin by Judge Hansford[19] who is here to day, the whole court is removed to Washington, a Holland minister arrived at Austin with Mr. Hamilton, the late loan Commissioner. Holmes[20] is elected Clerk of the County Court—

Wednesday the 16 February 1842 Cold weather last night, was very sick all night with Sore troath, very sick to day ,was obliged to [go] up Town, and this Evening my pains are augmented. genl Henderson of San Augustin arrived, brought a Letter to me from W. R. Scurry Esqr. he informs me he can not get a negro for me, if he does not, I shall be in a bad fix for planting this year.

Thursday the 17 Cold, with a strong East wind, very sick last night, much better this Evening, did not leave my Room all day, our Son Placide Rusk's is four years old to day

Fryday the 18th Cloudy and a little rain early this morning, cleared with a very strong S. W. Wind all day, N. wind at dark, went to the office Eastern mail arrived brought nothing from the U. S. the Red lander of to day gives a description of a tremendous large meeting which took place at the arcade in New Orleans urging upon the government of the U. S. to commence Hostilities at once against Mexico for the outrages committed and insults heaped upon american citizens who were in the Santa fe expedition as amateur travelers. and the treatment of the American

---

[19]John M. Hansford was judge of the Seventh Judicial District from January 31, 1840 until January 19, 1842. He was killed in 1844 as a consequence of the Regulator-Moderator War.

[20]Probably O. L. Holmes.

Consul and murder of American Citizens at Santa fe— translated the account Book of Martin Rumpff decd at the request of Oscar Engledow the administrator—for which he owes me $4.00

Saturday the 19th fair cold weather, Brown our Representative to Congress returned, did not see him, Mail from galvezton & Austin, not much news, no more than we Knew before. we are however in my opinion near a Crisis, should Mexico persevere in her outrageous career towards us, and some of the Citizens of the U. S. who were with the Santa fee Expedition a war with Mexico must be inevitable, which no doubt will result in the anexation of Texas to the U. S. bought 15 Blls Corn from a Mr Thos. J. Moore at $3.00 per Bll! and glad to get it at that! received also 3 Blls and one Bushel of Corn from B. Blake at $12.00

Sunday the 20th cold clear weather, every thing in Town looks dead, hired 4 negroes to make a fence around the School House, Ricd Parmalee arrived from Natchitochez to day, have not seen him yet.

Monday february 21st 1842 weather same as yesterday—Send off western and Eastern mails, wrote to the P. M. at Douglass, and Cincinatti Col Potter Senator from Red River, Col Smith[21] the Representative from Fannin, general Hunt, & Mr De Morse arrived from Austin, Mr Demorse is going to publish a Paper at Clarksville Red River County,[22] judging of the man as I have heard those who know him well speak of him, I am satisfied the Paper, will be a very respectable one, Judge Mills[23]—the Judge elect of the 7th Judicial District, and General Henderson, also arrived—Judge Mills & Col Potter took Tea with me Mr Worthman arrived from Crockett brought a Bag!!! full of newspapers, which could not be brought in the mail—

Tuesday the 22d Cold this morning, moderated in the Evening Messrs Potter, Demorse & Smith still here, Judge Mills left for San Augustin, nothing transpired of consequence to day

Wednesday the 23d Cold morning, warm day, moderate with South wind in the Evening. Wm. R. Scurry returned from San

---

[21]Thomas F. Smith was born in South Carolina in 1812, and came to Texas in 1837. He represented Fannin County in the Sixth Congress. He was still alive in 1855, and the date of his death is unknown.

[22]Charles DeMorse or Charles D. Morse had a long career of service to Texas. He was born on January 21, 1816 in Leicester, Massachusetts, and was trained for the law. In 1835 he joined Major Edwin Morehouse's volunteers and came to assist Texas. In 1836 he was commissioned an officer in the Texas Navy, but shortly resigned to serve as a major under Albert Sidney Johnston. He practiced law in Matagorda. and became a reporter for the Texas House of Representatives. In 1842 he founded the **Northern Standard** at Clarksville and continued as its publisher until he died on October 25, 1887. Additional services and honors included his selection as colonel of the 29th Texas Cavalry during the Civil War, founder of the Texas Veterans' Association, a director of the Agricultural & Mechanical College of Texas, and the honorarium "Father of Texas Journalism."

[23]John T. Mills, who was magistrate of the Third. Seventh, and Eighth Judicial Districts, respectively, between 1839 and 1846.

Augustin *without a negro* as he promised!!! Bluford Mitchel has to give Security in the Sum of $1500.00 to keep the Peace towards James Sims. the Judge of Probate granted me temporary Letters of administration on the Estate of Wm. B. Cabble decd till a regular Administrator can be appointed, got by this—two Stout negroes in my possession, till the next probate Court, gave Bond & Security for $3000.00 for the Keeping said Property as I would my own— after all this, it is very lucky inasmuch as I have been *so much disappointed by Mr Scurry,* Patter, Demorse & Smith left for Red River, Worthman left for Crockett—More Bustle in Town to day then usual worket in the garden four Hours to day, gave my contract with J. ygnacio ybarbo's Heirs to be recorded in the Clerk's office—

Thursday the 24th weather moderate—worked hard in the garden till 11 A. M. planted Corn eta let Roberts have Douglass field for next year for the purpose of cultivating it, Eastern mail to day, nothing new. Col Berry[24] of San Augustin came in Town this Evening & went out to Col Tipp's dont know his business—received the field notes of the Santos Tract of Land from Hill. Plat making out by Mr Nelson

Fryday the 25 February 1842 Cold nights warm days— settled with Gel Rusk, for postage paid me $12.00 in an Order on John Durst, Leander E. Tipps was nominated Deputy collector for this County. Houston, & Burnett, went his Security in a Bond of $5000.00 I know he is honest—

Saturday the 26th weather moderate, J. R. Clute in town, told him that I considered our trade about the exchanging land on the Moral as null and void, because his land is mortgaged to Joseph F. Lewis, Clute says he will make me a clear Title to it— nous verrons—Justice Court, mail from the west nothing very particularly new.

Saturday the 27th Send off Red River mail, an arrangement making to have a Ball at my House the 2d March 1842 being the Sixth aniversary of Texas Independence,— very warm weather to day, got my Petition against Wm & J. J. Simpson ready to send to San Augustin to morrow, to obtain the District Judges Order eta Send the Papers to J. P. Border to attend to for me

Monday the 28th fine pleasant weather—send off Eastern & western mails, wrote to P. Maste at Cincinnatti respecting the arrival of mail on Route No. 2. Send the Petition & Documents for an Injunction to prevent Wm Simson & John J. Simpson from working on a Tract of Land granted to Jose Ygnacio Ybarbo 2 Leagues East of this place at present occupied by M. L. Patton my Tenant—an Hour after having send the Papers eta was informed that an amicable arrangement had taken place between Patton & Simpson—good—Probate Court met, obtained longer time (at the discretion of the Court) to settle the Estate of James Ogilvy & Patricio de Torres decd also handed in the Reports of

---

[24]John G. Berry.

the Commissioners who were nominated to divide the Land between the Heirs of Jose Flores (or Clita Flores) and the division of the Land on the Loco between Manuel Santos Coy's Heirs & D. Lacy & myself as Assignees of Ygnacio de los Santos Coy which were ordered to be placed upon the Records of the Court—gave a Power of attorney to J. B. Reed, to collect all the property belonging to the Estate of Wm. B. Cable decd and report the same to me, in conformity with the Law—

Tuesday March the 1st very warm Sultry weather, looks like Rain— first day of Spring. Peach Trees all in Blossom vegetation very forward, preparing for Ball to morrow night, all day the House was full of Beutifull Ladies helping to make Cakes. All right, if it was not for the sight of the Divine part of Creation all would be a [blank] in the History of the life of man— Now is this not a gallant Speach for a man of 42.[25] purchased a House & two lots the former property of Nat Norriss for a debt due the Estate of James Ogilvy of $550.00 property sold for $133.⅔ Cash the money is not near enough to pay me for what monay I have advanced and what is due me for Boarding eta

Wednesday the 2d March Warm, Cloudy weather, Eugenia is 13 years old, had the Ball Contemplated, was well attended a Mrs. Shaw (a Widow) a fine looking woman, Mr, and Mrs Berry stopped with us all night, the day passed off very, very! very! very! dull! !! the general derangement of the financial affairs of the Country are such as to trow a damper on all things,—Ball was a fine one broke up at day break— on

Thursday the 3d warm Cloudy but no rain—got up early in the morning, worket in the garden all day, Sold my double barrelled gun to Radford Berry, for a note of 30$ on J. S. Roberts, and twenty Barrills of Corn to be delivered here, next October, the Eastern Mail arrived but nothing new.

Fryday the 4th a little rain last night, beutifull warm weather all day, worked nearly all day in the garden planting Corn eta went up Town in the afternoon late, saw Mr Gould from San Augustin, Mr. Wm R. Scurry who has boarded with us, for about three months left for the Red River Counties without telling any of the family good bye. dont know the Reason, unless he was not well pleased with his Landlord, or probably the bad fare he got—I like the young man, but if such are his ways, I am sure that I shall not like them. Poverty is no shame, and does not lower a man in my estimation but promises a man *Knows he can not perform* do lower him sure.

Saturday the 5th March Cold night, & very warm day—all day at work in the garden, Corn planting eta feel much fatigued, C. M. Gould dined with us to day, Red River & western mails arrived—western mails arrived so late & was so large that I posponed opening it till to morrow morning

---

[25]Sterne errs in his age. Born on April 5, 1801, he would on this date be but 41 years of age.

Sunday the 6th warm cloudy weather—opened mail at day light this morning nothing new of a very particular nature received a Letter from Mrs. Silverberg [of] canton miss. about some land eta Also one from Madame Lacombe a ligitimate Daughter of J. B. Casenave, whishing me to attend to her part of the Estate of her Father, to enter into an amicable arrangement with Tyler who has possession of all the Estate, no news yet from Gel morgan

Monday the 7th fine cool weather send off western & Eastern mail wrote to gel Post office Department how I am to do after the 1st April next, respecting the collecting of Postage in Silver on Letters remaining on hand or received after date of 1st April, which may have been mailed in March—Worket nearly all day in the gardens negro woman Sick— Doctor Starr seen her, gave Pills, & Castor Oil,—news was received pr Mr. Wilder, from the North that Col Bob. Potter & Mat Sims are killed by a man called *Old Rose*—[26] not ascertained possitively, but generally belived, wrote to John P. Border about Mr DeMorse, the Editor of the Northern Standard to be printed at Clarksville or Napoleon to advocate the interest of the People on Red River

Tuesday the 8th weather same as yesterday— Mr Blake left for Montgomery County & Probably to Houston & galveston expects to overtake Charles chevallier who left here a few days ago, send by Mr Bl[a]ke (or Chevallier) in case Blake dont go to Galveston) an Order on Wm Pierpoint for a note of $500,00 on S. R. Eves. Capt of the Steam Boat Ned Burleson, given to me in 1837 for land, gave either of said gentlemen plenary power to act in the matter as if the note was their own property—*Father Mat*— the old Priest 103 years old, died to day, he was a resident of this place since 1772 his real name is juan jose Medina— he was the oldest Mexican in this part of Texas— I know his History of which something shall appear hereafter in the Redlander—

[26]Robert Potter was killed by Captain William Pinkney Rose on March 2, 1842. For a vivid, eye-witness account of the affair, see Kemp, Signers, 269-274.

CHAPTER V

"Oh . . . dear Texas have I worn chains for thee . . ."

Wednesday March the 9th 1842   warm dry weather, are very much in want of rain, Times getting worse & worse every day. Ten dollars now is as much an object as one Hundred were some few years ago, how the People of this County can get the nescessaries of life till next fall god only Knows, a perfect Barrier is placed now between the introduction of even the Staff of Life (Bacon & flour because those who have the fortune to raise monay enough to purchase a little at Natchitochez, have not the means to pay the duties on them, (glorious change! hurrah for Texas, and its Independence and *god* take to his *holy* Keeping its Law givers—

Thursday the 10th March   warm, still no rain—nothing new— mail arrived from East, worked nearly all day in the garden. feel well after the days fatigue, Mr. Woodruff of the firm of Turner & Woodruff of New Orleans and Michael Colgan passed trough here to day in a hurry, did not stop but a very short time

Fryday the 11th   warm in the morning. after noon a sudden north wind blowing very cold, with a little rain, god Knows which way the wind will turn before morning, as it is we stand a fair chance to loose all our early labor in the garden. gave to Simon Wiess my Headright League Title to have it recorded in Liberty County, the *Original* County in which said Land was Originaly Located I send previously a Certified Copy of my Headright Title to Jasper thinking it in that County. I never heard any thing from it since I send it down & am afraid some rascality has been done by someone, at least my not hearing of my Title makes me belive so at least.

Saturday the 12th   Cold no rain, no frost— but cold enough to freese—mail from Red River corroborates the news that Col Bob Potter is killed, mail from west brings news of Bexar being taken by the Mexican forces under general Vasques[1] all hands are in a hub bub about it, the news is to be belived, but I would not go to much trouble to raise the militia, was I general untill

---

[1] Rafael Vasquez occupied San Antonio on March 5, 1842 with several hundred men, forcing the Texans to flee. Vasquez, though regarded as a partisan, raised the Mexican flag and declared that nation to be the lawful authority there until he left on March 7.

further news—gel Jas Smith has been send for, gave the despatches to be copied by Nelson & [blank]

Sunday the 13th March 1842 last night wind turned Eastward very fine rain all day, send off northern mail, send the despatches received yesterday to gel Rusk Clarksville genl Smith is in Town, he send Orders to the different Cols of Regiments to be in readiness for any emergency. we are on the *qui vive* expecting every minute to hear from the west pr Express if any thing realy serious is going on

Monday the 14th Cleared up warm, send off western & Eastern mails, Probate Court to day, the Case respecting the Estate of Wm Cabble was not decided, the two negroes therefore remain in my possession till the next regular session of the Probate Court— gel Rusk arrived, confirms the news of Col Potter having been killed, Wm Scurry is gone to Clarksville & will not be back in 5 weeks— we have not had any further news from the west up to this time 8 ½ P. M.

Tuesday the 15th very cold *nearly frost* last night, very fine weather to day, worked in the garden some time, went up Town. no more news from the west, then what we had before, hope it all may be false alarm—Judge Davis[2] of San Augustin County arrived

Wednesday the 16th a little frost last night, did not as much damage to vegetation as I anticipated, wind changed to S.E. this afternoon— was not much in Town to day, nothing further from the west, Mr Joost the former Clerk of Charles chevallier received an assortment of Materials and Tools for Shoe making visited him and his workshop— it looks something like the workshop of *an old country artiste* good luck to him—

Thursday the 17th warm weather in the morning, rain and a strong S.E. wind towards sundown—Saint Patrick's day— mail from East no news. A Mr Lewis from Alabama who passed trough here for the west sometime ago with 60 Slaves— returned to day wanting to hire the most of them till October next & cultivate a small farm, provided he can get Provisions eta —Land and inclosed Plantations plenty but no provisions— times have never been so hard in Texas, like they are now, *I* have never Known the *want* of two bits untill now.—!!!!!!

Fryday the 18th March 1842 fine weather— vegetation looks Splendid a man came from the guadalupe (Mr Strong) reports that 800 Mexicans took peaceable possession of Bexar, The Texians leaving with all their Arms Cannons ammunition eta— Prisoners let go, on parol not to fight against Mexico— gel Burleson on the 10th inst was on his way from Austin towards Bexar (24 miles from Austin) with 600 men and receiving reinforcements Hourly, gel Houston has issued a proclamation that every man in the Republic be ready at a minutes notice to march with arms, 48 rounds of Carthridges 8 days provisions and an expectation to

---

[2]Probably Samuel S. Davis, who had been a member of the Fourth Legislature from San Augustine, and was later sheriff of that place.

serve 3 months—this is the report of Mr Strong how true it is; we will certainly Know very shortly—

Saturday March 19 very fair & warm weather, finished planting corn to day, Mr Blake returned from Montgomery County brought intelligence, (& an Extra of Austin city gazette[3] of the 7th inst) that the Mexicans have taken San Antonio & Goliad, that 3000 men (Texians) are now in the field— 1200 were at Seguin (between Bexar & Austin) under Col Moore[4] Gel Burleson with 350 was to join them on the 10th inst. and leave the Capital protected— Col Jacob Snively wrote to the same effect to Raguet Rusk, Muse & Starr, Austin seems to be in Danger of being attacked by the Mexicans, or Indians— *Splendid Capital* there has as yet no stirr taken place here nor East of this, but every body is on the *qui vice*—

Sunday the 20th weather very fine— send off northern mail— News was received to day that Col John G. Berry the Collector of impost dues was Killed in Shelby County, hope—it is not so— J. F. Cortez of Natchitochez Killed a Lawyer named Giles it is said—for diving too deep into Family secrets— well I can form no Opinion of the Subject as I am ignorant of facts— D. S. Kaufman arrived late this Evening, he reports that the Mexicans have evacuated San Antonio and that—that devoted City is again in possession of the Texians, he gave not any particulars, but vouches for the truth of the fact, the original Letter directed by the Col Commanding the Washington Militia to the Post M. at Independence I have read, which confirms the news—Hurrah

Monday March the 21st 1842 _Splendid weather—send off Western & Eastern mails— Judge Ochiltree, Gel Henderson & a Mr Allen from San Augustin arrived ready to go to the army they are rather doubtful wether to go on, or not,— they contradict the report of Col Berry's death— very good— the war party from San Augustin have returned home till further Orders— to day we are without Sugar, flour and nearly out of Coffee, and no monay to purchase those articles they may, to be sure be considered articles of Luxury, but having had them ever since I have been in Texas and since I have had a family, they have become rather necessaries, these Luxuries of life— If I had the money I expended in 1835 to recruit troops in New Orleans to bring me and my family to the glorious State of Liberty? in which we now are, I would at least keep a *little* to purchase the necessaries of life with I am not friendly to a change at present, and would sacrifice my life in sustaining the government which I assisted in rearing, but Knowing what I Know if the same thing had to be gone over Again god Knows I would not spend *one cent to bring my family to want* and to make *great men out of Trash*

---

[3]The Austin City Gazette, a weekly and one of the first newspapers in Austin, was begun on October 30, 1839. Samuel Whiting was the publisher, but after 1840 it was edited by George K. Teulon. Its publication was suspended in 1842 because of a threatened Mexican invasion.
[4]Probably John Henry Moore.

Tuesday the 22d weather same as yesterday, nothing new to morrow a meeting of the Citizens of this County is to take place to take into Consideration our affairs as regards the impending war with Mexico— eta eta— Mr Nelson went to the Nechaz in quest of a Horse to go to the wars— agreed to go with Bondies to the Angelina to morrow—.

Wednesday the 23d fine weather a meeting was held at the court House in Consequence of the Mexican invasion; Judge Hart chairman Judge Taylor Secretary, general Rusk addressed the meeting merely to state the object, when a Committee of 5 was appointed to draft resolutions expressive of the feelings of the People of this County in regard to the present Crisis, said Committee to report on Saturday next, when a general meeting of the People of this County is expected— After dinner left for Mr Hills's on the Loco met an Express on the Road, bringing dispatches from the Secretary of war, and Proclamations of the President, went as far as Mr Hills plantation left Mr Bondies there and returned to Town;— learned that the Mexicans have left the City of Bexar after a general Pillage, took with them every thing that was portable— General Burleson with upwards of 400 men was in pursuit, and within 40 miles of them the last news from him, nothing in particular from the war Department, exept to have the militia divided into three classes, and have all ready to march at a moments warning

Thursday the 24th March weather extreemly fine— this afternoon the Eastern mail arrived brought nothing new by private conveyance we have positive news that one half of the Banks— the Mechanics & Traders Exchange Atchafalaya, Bank of Orleans, Citizens, and some more are broke besides half the merchants in New Orleans, a gentleman who presented me a Letter of introduction (Count de Narbonne)[5] from genl Houston arrived in the Evening. He bears with him a commission from the President to treat with all the Indians on our Northern & Northwestern frontier, he is a very intelligent man, but I would preferr any other mission to his—

Fryday the 25 beutifull weather the Count left this afternoon for Lewis Sanchez's. sold him my Patent bridge gun, out of accomodation (he having lost his) gave me a draft for the amount on McKinney & Williams galvezton— I do not Know what to think. taken things alltogether, in regard to this Count—he certainly has a Commission from the President, and his Letter of introduction from the President to myself is genuine— but the rest is rather a mixed up concern the Count having Contradicted himself in a great many instan[c]es— if he can do us any good at all— he can do us much good; and again if he is the man he represents himself to be, he has it in his power to do us much harm, Houston is

[5]For a brief explanation of the Count de Narbonne's activities and his relations with Houston, see Smither, "Diary of Adolphus Sterne," Southwestern Historical Journal, XXXIII (January, 1930), 234. Sterne's own estimate of the Count and his uneasiness about his character and mission follows.

very easy to be gulled by any one who will undertake it— any man who is vain, and *loves flattery* is easy to be made a dupe of— for a specimen I would refer to Santa Ana, who *did* gull Houston abominaly

Saturday the 26th March very fine weather, had a refreshing shower in the Evening, a meeting at the Court House took place to day, a great many persons present, general Rusk addressed the meeting in a very Eloquent Manner, a set of Resolutions drafted by Gel R. were adopted— Mail from Red River arrived, no news from west, brought nothing from Austin, and the news from Houston we have had in advance of the mail—rcd a Letter from my Sister Nancy, which gratified me very much & wrote her an answer of 4 pages—

Sunday the 27th weather as usual fine— send off Red River mail, wrote to Wm Nixon of New Orleans inclosing one to Nancy which I wrote yesterday, wrote to C. H. Gibson Natchitochez— we received news of a large meeting whitch was held in New Orleans & Natchitochez, by Col Thorn, all are in the very humor of fighting Mexico—$500. has been subscribed towards ammunition eta for Texas, in Natchitoches, wrote to McKinney williams & Co Galvezton, inclosed a draft of $15.00 drawn in my favor by the Count Leontio de Narbonne being for a gun I let him have

Monday the 28th weather as yesterday, Judge Mason one of the Contractors of mail rout No 3 made an arrangement for George Clevenger to carry said mail from and after the 1st April next and to receive *all* the pay pr quarter for which said route was contracted gave bond & security & will carry the mail next trip— Send off Eastern mail wrote to C. H. Gibson Natchitochez, to McKinney williams & Co— send a communication to Canfield the Editor of the Red Lander respecting the *Count de Narbonne*— Probate Court to day a Stormy day for the Probate Judge as respects the Estate of Wm Cabble, and the two negroes I have in my possession, much talking on the subject, the judge will give his decision on to morrow at 9 oclock

Tuesday the 29th weather same. rain wanted very much— the Probate Court met and gave the administration of Cabb[l]es Estate to J. M. Watkins, Scott appealed & I went his Security, the two negroes remaining in my possession till the decision of the District Court gave Power of Attorney to L. A. Gilbert to take charge of the effects of Wm Cable, revoket the Power of attorney I had given to B. Reed for that purpose

Wednesday the 30th March 1842 a little Rain last night⁶ but not enough, cloudy, nothing whatever transpired to day, stayed at home most of the day working in the gardens

Thursday the 31st March Cloudy but no rain, which is very

---

⁶In the edition of the Sterne diary published by Smithers, the entry for Wednesday, March 30 is omitted and the entry for Thursday, March 31 is printed erroneously under the earlier date. See Smither. "Diary of Adolphus Sterne," Southwestern Historical Quarterly, XXXIII (January, 1930), 235-36.

much wanting. Mail from the West but not a Single Letter nor any news. times most abominably dull, if it was not for my o[r]chard and gardens I would be hippoed to death— last day of the quarter of the Post office establishment, the Specie Sistem takes place to morrow the 1st of April *nous verrons*—

Fryday the 1st April 1842 Cold dry weather, rain very much wanted no news from the west— nothing stirring except *April fools*

Saturday April 2d a fine day, had a very fine Rain in the afternoon, which we wanted realy very much— the Red River Mail arrived no news— Davison has changed his Stand—good— the mail Boy no[w] comes in on Sunday and leaves same day— western mail came & brought no news further than we Know, Charles Chevallier arrived from Houston have not had much conversation with him, brings Houstons Letter to Santana and such a Scouring the Dictator gets from Gel H. is a perfect Caution— Major Burton[7] & W. A. Ferriss in Town

Sunday the 3d rain last night, looks like we would have some more, made out my quarterly returns of the Post office for the 1st quarter of this year & wrote to the Post Master Gel about the Situation of the mail routes A.S.F. generally

Monday the 4th weather Cloudy and very warm— Mr Generiss from San Antonio arrived, reports that the Mexican Troops took nothing away from that place on their retreat but that the Citizens of Bexar who had joined and went away with the Mexicans robbed and plundered the Houses of those Texans who had abandoned them—that only 200 men are now in Bexar, and an equal number in goliad, and that two Speis had been Schott by Clark Owen at goliad, Mrs Sims widow of Tom Sims in Town to day at my house, Major Burton dined with us gleaned much information from him about our future prospects—that is to say so far as our President is concerned— the wife of Ned Tolliver (Taliafero) arrived from the U. S. came in Doctor Jousts's Carriage, Send off Eastern & Western mail, wrote to the Editor of the Red Lander about matters & things in general, send off my quarterly returns to the General Post Office. gave One of my Horses—the sorrell I got from J. M. Watkins Esqr to Mathew Arnold, to plough, to Keep the Horse in good Order and deliver him to me fat—between the 1st and 15th October next, he being answerable for the Horse—beside which he is to let me have a good milch Cow to milk this season untill fall, he (arnold) being responsible to me for any accident which may befall the Horse— witnesses James R. Arnold, Ed Sims, John G. Green & others—

Tuesday the 5th April 1842 my forty first birth day a fine morning a sligh[t] Shower about 11 a.m. fine weather afternoon Mr Generiss dined with us— Doctor Jous[t] a resident of Natchitochez formerly of Texas who brought Mrs Taliafero out in his

---

[7]Isaac Watts Burton, a former resident of Nacogdoches, who in partnership with Charles D. Ferris, published the **Texas Chronicle** there. In 1841 he moved to Crockett and died there in 1843.

Carriage Stopped here this morning to take a Letter from me, and a Message from Mrs Sterne to Madame Placide Bossier the Foster Mother of my wife, worket in the garden the best part of the day 41 YEARS OLD! OH! DEAR!!—

Wednesday the 6th warm & Cloudy, Gould, Beckton, & vanbibber arrived from San Augustin, Mr. and Mrs Berry and many other Persons came in from the Country to Judge Harts wedding— which took place at Col Thorn's this Evening— married Mrs Davenport, a very sp[l]endid party, danced, during a tremendous rain till very late.

Thursday the 7th Still Clowdy but no rain— every thing perfectly Calm—the gentlemen who are going to join the army left here to day— H. H. Edwards,[8] Rinaldo Hotchkiss— G. Bondis James Carter, James H. Dursts Nei Taliafero Pen Luckett & others, Eastern mail arrived, no news—

Fryday the 8th Weather fair, cool morning, had a drop in at the House of Col Jennings[9] in the Evening, came Home at 12 oclock

Saturday the 9th very fine weather, at daylight this morning went with R, Parmalee & Edwin Sims below the junctions of the Alazane & Moral a fishing (12 miles) Caught some Fish, our Horses got away, did not get them again till nearly dark, had to camp in the Swamp and was nearly eat up with Black gnats & musquitoes, never passed a more wretched night— so much for pleasure—

Sunday April the 10th 1842 Beutifull weather arrived home from the fishing Scrape at 10 A.M. Mail arrived last night from west, without the least news, mail beyond Cincinnatti failed, and no mail from Austin

Monday the 11 fine weather— Board of Commissioners on Roads & Revenues met to day, was elected together with Bennett Blake associate Justice of the County Court to serve untill the 1st of January next— County Court met did not do much Business—gave my note to A. A. Nelson for $53.55 [paid 18 October 1842 in Settlement][10] and settled with him till the 14 inst took up my note given 19 October 1842 for Locating and surveying Mrs Sternes and Mrs Taylor's League & Labor of Land, for $200.00 also a note given to Nelson for $95.00 in Texas Monay, received a quarter of Beef from Joseph Polvador in payment of all he owes me up to this day, Mrs Jno Durst dined with us, worked in the garden in the afternoon, and feel a little fatigued—

Tuesday the 12th weather in Statu quo—no news, no body in

---

[8]Haden Harrison Edwards should not be confused with his father, Haden Edwards, who is noted for his activity in the Fredonia Rebellion.

[9]Thomas Jefferson Jennings, who arrived in Nacogdoches from Virginia via Kentucky and San Augustine in the fall of 1840. In 1852 he became attorney general of Texas, later served as a member of the secession convention (1861), and briefly held a commission in the Confederate Army. He died September 23, 1881.

[10]The phrase "paid 18 October 1842" was added in a marginal gloss, and was indicated to be included here by an "X."

Town every body at work on their Farms, hard at work in my gardens for 4 hours to day not that I am so very industrious but every body else is at work and I can do no less than follow Suit. Arnaux Lauve a creole of Louisiana an old acquaintance of mine was here, and dined with us to day— Mr Nelson gone west on his own Business

Wednesday the 13th rain last night, did not stop till 12 oclock to day, tock advantage of the rainy time and made a Pigeon house, went up Town, but all was dreary, stale, and unprofitable—

Thursday the 14th very cold this morning,— too wet to plough— planted Sweet Potatoe slips, worked in the garden, interpreted between General Rusk & Jose Ma Mora respecting a Suit Mora is about to institute against J. J. Simpson & Wm Simpson. Gel Rusk promised me half of the fee if he gains the suit— which is one fourth of the Land, Judge Hart in Town, much pleased with his new wife god Knows I hope he may allways be pleased— Col Frost Thorn has gone to Natchitochez. no mail to day from the East — something the matter—

Fryday the 15th fine weather in the morning, rain in the Evening received a private mail from Houston, the Contractors have given up the chase, no monay to pay them, — mail from east — no news— reced two Letters, one from Canfield, and one from A. R. George Sheriff of Shelby County, acknowledgeing receipt of my letter Sending receipts eta Mr Lauve supped here to night, going away to morrow, — rains at 8 P. M.

Saturday the 16th April 1842 Rain Cold, and Rain, Cleared off this morning at 11 A.M. Mr Lauve left, wrote by him to my Sister Nancy, and my Daughter Eugenia wrote to Madame Placide Bossier who is in New Orleans— western mail arrived but brought no news whatever, gave Doctor James H. Starr two notes one on Radford Berry & one on Solomon Wolfe for 50 Barrills Corn payable in October next— for Ten Barrills Corn which I received to day— *hurrah for Texas* Lodge met in the Evening gave the 2d d. to Jno F. graham— mail arrived from west nothing new as usual

Sunday the 17th rain & cloudy— alternatively, from day light till now 12 noon —it is as cold as if we were in the month of December!— winter Coats & gloves are in requisition, the Red River Mail arrived brought no news (of course) send it off as dry as it came 1 P.M. a drisly rain, dont Know how it [is] going to end. if it clears up & have a frost tonight— it will nearly ruin the County

Monday the 18th Cold a fire in the Chimney most desirable, it is said that there was frost last night and injured the Cotton. but not to any extend. Sun made its beautiful appearance at 9 a.m. but still it is cold, send off western & Eastern mails wrote to *Red Lander*, the Board of Land Commissioners met to day but could not agree as to the legal time of meeting so postponed it to meet on the 1st Monday of May next, loaned David Rusk $100 00 Texas Treasury notes

Tuesday the 19th very fine weather, but a fire in the Chimney, is not a disagreeable thing, worked all day in the gardens, nothing happened in Town worth noticing— three fourths of the time a cannon with grape might be shot through the Streets, and not hit any body, oh! bless us what times— this Evening Mr Clevenger brought 10 kegs of Powder and several Kegs of Lead from Natchitochez, Subscribed by the Citizens of that Town for the use of Texas against Mexico—

Wednesday the 20th very fine weather, aniversary of the meeting of the Texians under Houston and the Mexicans under Santaana at San Jacinto, Town more dull, for every body who had a Horse is gone out to Mr John Durst's to Reinhardt's wedding, would have gone myself but all the Horses I have are ploughing, — and now a days making Corn comes before going to weddings— yet I whish the new pair every success and happiness in life—made a Contract with Mrs L. B. Brown troug[h] S. M. Orton, to live in the House I lately purchased until next January when she is to deliver it up to me paying no rent, nor am I to pay her any thing for such improvements she may make.

Thursday the 21st fine weather, aniversary of the Battle of San Jacinto, every thing still & Dead as a quaker meeting, mail from East the news from the United States sound warlike, if the U. S. go to war with England no doubt Mexico will commence with us—

Fryday the 22d weather as usual, nights rather cold—nothing of Consequence transpired—a german— the County Surveyor of Bowie County passed trough from Austin, reports that the General Land Office has been closed since the 6th March last a great féte is to be given by the Germans on Mill Creek on Palm Sunday and Succeeding days, to celebrate the aniversary of the formation of the Teutonic Order Of Texas[11] — have a great mind to go

Saturday the 23 April 1842 weather most beutifull, the western mail arrived and brought *no news* nothing from Galvezton or Houston nor from austin— nothing from beyond Crockett General Darnell from San Augustin in Town— an Election for Constable of this Beat was held and Edwin P. Sims was elected by a majority of Sixteen. Judge Hart and his Lady took Dinner with us to day

Sunday the 24th warm weather— Cloudy—Red River mail no news— send it off as it came, without news—

Monday the 25th Cloudy, severe Storm with hail at noon, Keeps on raining, and is very Cold wind N.w. the Probate Court sat to day was a member of the same (entitled to three dollars) many persons in Town several important cases disposed of.

Tuesday the 26th Cold Clear weather, as cold as December— wrote a Letter to Messrs Cruger & Moore reminding Mr Cruger

---

[11]The **Teutonia Orden** was founded in 1841 by Fredrich Ernst, and was one of several groups formed among German immigrants to preserve their national heritage. The **Teutonia Orden**, or Teutonic Society of Texas, was completely loyal to the Republic, and gave proof of this by celebrating Independence Day and other occasions.

about a conversation in Austin last winter respecting his sending me some volumes of the Laws of Texas to sell, requested him to send them by Mr Richards, a nephew of Albert Long, was engaged to go to Vital Flores's to marry P. Flores to Miss Merchant on the next Thursday—County Court & Corporation met to day, Did every thing in their Power to satisfy Mr John Read. but could not do so, he has received more for the Building of the court House (and it is not finished) than would build a Splendid Brick House

Wednesday the 27th very Cold night & morning a fire is highly necessary in chimney— a Mr Rose his son & Son in law, were brought here to day in the Coustody of the Sheriff of Red River County and Several guards to be put in Our Jail to await their trial for the Killing of Bob Potter late Senator from Red River County;— the sheriff of this County will not receive them, as the jail is too insecure— Bill Scurry send the Horse I let him have— dead poor I am every day less disappointed in Mr Scurry!

Thursday 28th April weather nearly same as yesterday. agreable to appointment & promise to vital Flores at 2. P.M. left home for vital Flores's for the Purpose of Celebrating the rites of Matrimony between a Son of Flores & a Miss. Merchant—arrived at J. D. Merchants House at 6 P.M. performed the ceremony in presence of a very large assembly of as mixed a concern as very seldom can be seen, for the Bride, her Sister and many other Ladies are very beutifull women whose beutifull Skin is as white as Snow and also there were Mexicans—particularly men, who if their Hair would be a little curly would be taken any where for Negroes— however their being no accommodation for Lodgings we had to Stand up, sit up, or dance all night, I prefered the latter, and realy amused myself very much— at day light left and returned home by 10 A.M. on

Fryday the 29th weather fine a little Cloudy Slept nearly all day went up to the office mail from East had arrived during my absense brought nothing at all, at all—

Saturday the 30th very fine weather, Capt Berryman formerly of the United States army Stationed at cantonement Jessup[12] who knew my wife when a little girl—arrived here to day, he is going to Mrs Nelson's on the Angelina who is his mother in Law, Captain Wheeler arrived, brought me a Letter from Pierre Roblo respecting his affairs in this Country, Texas, Annexation, war with England and the U. States Mexico invasion, failing of the best Houses in New Orleans, resignation as Senator of Henry Clay of Kentucky, and an anticipated general hubbub in Embryo; the Order of the day. Mr Wm Scurry send the Horse I sold him, which he was to have paid me this Court $350. in good notes for. was send back as before stated on the 27th seing no one would receive the Horse, and I not having any thing to give him to eat,

---

[12]Fort Jesup, located a few miles northeast of present-day Many, Louisiana, was built in 1823 by the United States. Its purpose was to bring law and order to the Sabine Strip. It remained an important military installation until the 1840's.

or any way to Keep him, sold him to Mr Jno. F. Graham for $200. 100 in groceries as follows—300 lb of Bacon (received)—at 60 dollars 12 lb Coffee at 3$—25 lb Sugar & 16 lb Coffee also 10$ worth of some other articles in his Store and $100.00 in good Cash notes or such things as we can agree upon which shall be worth the Amount— this day our Son Joseph Amador is Ten years old—A Mr Thomasin of the large Shoe Establishment of H. R. Lee & Co— N. Orleans arrived to day in quest of that which he will not get from Roberts Allen & Co—monay—

Sunday May the 1st 1842 Cool weather for the Season— windy Northern mail & no news—George wiede arrived, Horatio Nelson dito—the latter took Supper with us—F Anthony dined with us for the first time since 1837

Monday the 2d weather moderate, many persons in Town for the Court, the judge did not arrive, in Settling up with the officers of the Court, there is only $95.05 cents left to the Estate of J. Ogilvy out of the proceeds of the Sale of Nat Norriss's House & Lott, Mr Canfield the Editor of the Red Lander in Town—several Ladies & gentlemen spend the Evening with us, passed of very pleasant

Tuesday the 3d Cold, very Cold weather, Cloaks, and over-coats, fires in the Chimney are all things devoutly to be wished for—Judge Ochiltree arrived opened Court at 9. dispatched several Jury Cases. *A Business man* Board of Land Commissioners met to day agreed to take 10 bits per Certificate in par funds—had an understanding with Joseph F. Lewis to day about making him a Deed to a League of Land as administrator of Ogilvey's Estate he is to pay me $50.00 for Ogilvy—last night my friend Taliafero got a most allmighty—flogging—sorry for it but can't help it—he has electioneered much for this event —hope he may take a lesson—a good fellow—but too too— too— never mind—

Wednesday May the 4th very cold morning—no rain, Court in session tried several Cases. Board of Land Commissioners met, busy times

Thursday the 5th weather same as yesterday—Court in session petition to the Judge to adjourn—no go—right—Mr Thomasin left for New Orleans, wrote by him to my sister Nancy, Eastern mail arrived brought a Letter from Thos Ogilvy a Brother of James Ogilvy who died at my House in 1840, wrote a long answer to it—

Fryday the 6th weather same as yesterday— the Habeas Corpus Case in the Case of the Republic vs Rose came up and was very eloquently argued on both sides, all the reports and cases Known were brought forward for & against the Prisoners. the Judge will decide to morrow wither he ought, or ought not to hear testimony in the Case—

Saturday the 7th weather dry, cold, and like January Judge Ochiltree decided this morning to hear testimony in Rose's Case— I belive he will be bailed— the Battallion of Jack Tod mustered to day. was on the Staff of Brigadier General Smith; preparing to receive Company to night to a dancing Party—the Party assembled at 7 every thing went on in harmony, untill about 10 oclock some wretch set my stable on fire, and with much difficulty the House was saved, the young men in a trice were on the House, after the Stable was burnt the Dance was resumed, as though nothing had happened—I do not Know how this happened, it certainly was not an accident, as no One was down at the Stable with fire, nor was there anything which could have produced fire had a cigar been trown down, so it must have been an incendiary, and that he was one who *was not invited to the Party*, probably time will show

Sunday the 8th fine weather no news of who set my Stable on fire I have several men and One Boy under suspicions but can not come at a correct conclusion, I whish I Knew the truth no matter how it happened it would relieve me— no news by the Northern mail, Mr Davison the Contractor on route no 5 passed to day to Austin wrote by him to the P. O. Department

Monday the 9th May 1842 fine weather rather dry—rain wanting— no news yet of the Incendiary—the Judge of the District Court deceided to day that Rose, his Son, and Son in Law might be admitted to bail the former in $25000.00 and the two latter in $10000.00—I went security for One of them Rose's Son for $5000.00—he looks so honest & I belive him to be so else I would not have went his Security—send of Eastern & western mails— send off my Letter to Mr Thomas Ogilvy in the Eastern mail, attended on the grand jury as a witness & interpreter, Set as an associate on the Board of Land Commissioners—was rather busy all day repairing fences and preparing a new Stable—

Tuesday the 10th May fine fair weather—On this day 14 years ago I got license to marry, and now I am here an old gray headed man; *nimporte*— alls right— our District Court in Session —the case of the Republic vs Borroughs came up for the Killing of McKeever of Crockett hard work to get a jury—at 1 P. M. got a jury, the Case took up all day and most of the Bar made Speeches, gel Rusk concluding against the Prisioner, but his argument was more of a Cast, to aquit, then to bring in the man guilty, I belive it is the first time he has taken the part of the Prosecution in a Criminal offence where death would be the Penalty if the Accused would be found guilty—he merely expounded the Law but did not appeal to the feelings of the Jury which he is so cabable [sic] of doing & which no doubt he would have done on the other side of the question—he done his duty and no more— the jury retired at 8 ½ P. M. returned at 10 P. M. verdict not guilty, a thing most devoutly hoped for by every one

Wednesday the 11th fine weather, rather dry. want rain very much. Court in Session cases dispatched rapidly—the Missess Simms and Miss Culp, and several gentlemen spend the Evening with us—music and Song was the Order of the night, went to bed at 10 at Peace with the whole world.

Thursday the 12th fine weather—a little rain wanting—Court in session—Jackson Todd's case—for Killing Tom Sims came up—got only four jurors out of Sixty—Mr De Young his Daughter Mr Canfield, his Lady, a Miss M. Edwards & several gentlemen arrived from San Augustin, had a Dancing Party at Charles Chevallier danced till near morning— fine party—

Fryday May 13th weather getting to be very warm—rebuilding Stable, Court adjourned till Monday, every thing dull

Saturday the 14th weather same as yesterday, rain wanting very much, Mr Moore, Jones & McIntire assisted me in arranging my new Corn House & Stable, lodge met this Evening—Mail arrived from the West, and brought nothing

Sunday the 15th weather same—nothing Stirring every body gone home to return to morrow when Jackson Todd's trial is to come on

Monday the 16 weather in Status quo, many Persons coming in town got a Jury to try Jackson Todd for Killing Sims Testimony on behalf of the Republic gone trouhg [sic] with—the Lodge met—gave J. F. Graham the 3d degree, went from the lodge to Miss Sim's to a dancing Party, enjoyed myself very much till 1½ P. M. tired to death—

Tuesday the 17th Cloudy—had a very fine rain worth at least One hundred dollars to me alone, and must be of immense value to the County generaly—Jackson Todd's Trial going on, got trough with the Testimony— Governor Runnels and a Col Ross of Mississippi arrived yesterday, was introduced to them to day, the Ex-Governor a very intelligent man, the other a warrior of the real Jackson School, Party given by Mrs Frost Thorn, our visitors invited of Course, Stable nearly finished, Col Crane[13] offered me 1000 feet Lumber towards building a new Stable, I thank him Kindly for his disinterrested generosity, but having allready a new Corn Crib and Stable, shall no accept of his Kind offer

Wednesday the 18th fine weather Court in session Jackson Todd's case going on very intricate several fine speaches made by Rusk, Burke, & wheeler the District attorny, the Jury retired at Dark and in 15 minutes brought in a verdict of not guilty, every body gratified—Mr J. S. Roberts gave a Party, went off first rate, did not go, but my San Augustin guests went, Came home at 2 P.m.—

Thursday May the 19th fine weather—Court in Session, Jackson Grayson for Killing—Cayson is on his trial Rusk, Holland & Grammage for Defendant—Jury out one Hour—verdict *not guilty* time goes of heavily no news from any quarter. Eastern mail arrived but brought (as usual) nothing.

Fryday the 20th the Court dismissed all Jurors, motion day to day—did not reach the negro Case of Cabbles's Estate—do not Know how it will go hereafter, the negroes however remain in my possession till they are legaly are [sic] taken out of it—Judge

---

[13]Probably Ambros Crain.

Hart & Lady give a Ball eta to night at their residence 6 miles from here, my wife & Eugenia and *all* hands from Town gone, stay at home to mind the Children—Consider myself a *good Boy* of Course

Saturday the 21st very warm weather, all hands came home from the Ball before 7 A. M. at 3 P. M. Mr Deyoung Canfield and the Ladies left for San Augustin. Court having adjourned, the Town looks very Blank. towards Evening wrote to Thos Ogilvy, send the Letter by Col Gammage who goes to Alabama, after his Family, the western mail arrived, but brought nothing new no—nor old either—a thing realy to be deplored, we are now Six weeks without a mail from Galvezton & Houston

Sunday May the 22d weather in Status quo, Town very dull nothing doing, Red River Mail Boy & his mule arrived, & as usual *empty* mail Bags, send him as he Came—empty. D. S. Kaufman dined with us, and in the afternoon left for home A Child (the oldest) of the late Doctor Brown died to day

Monday the 23d weather in Status quo things dito dito no body in Town, no one Stirring, a celebrated gambler a Doctor Bennett from Shreveport and his Campion arrived in quest of a Stolen Horse?, very eager to get off yet remained all day and all night too—

Tuesday the 24th May Cloudy a little rain in the forenoon, not enough to do any good, Doctor Bennett in Town yet, and is likely to remain to recover his Horse Oh! dear! worked all day in arranging the Papers of James Ogilvy to have them in readiness to be delivered to his Brother in case he comes here

Wednesday the 25th Cloudy in the morning, and a very bright sun in the afternoon— a Sure sign of dry weather—nothing at all doing, all's as silent as the grave

Thursday the 26th very hot no sign of rain, though much wanting in the County—mail from the East no news as usual, was thinking about accepting the place of assessor for this County for three years—dont Know yet

Fryday the 27th warm dry weather, a Mr Patton arrived last night from Houston in 6 days, reports that an other Mexican force of about 800 Cavalry have been at Bexar, for the purpose of mooving away the Mexican Families, which they accomplished—Col Seguin has joined them, and as is usually the Case, when our warm Friends turn against us, they became the most inveterate foes, I am satisfied, that it will be so in this case, before next October we will see—received a Letter from Danl Lacy inclosing orders for $25.00 each on M. F. Sims & J. Wilson—*bad chance* also an Order on B. Blake to hand me all monies he may collect for Lacy—*an other bad chance*— a waggon arrived from Houston loaded for C. Chevallier

Saturday the 28th weather very warm & dry —rain wanting very much indeed—done some business in the Office, but generally times are—Stale, flat, and unprofitable.

Sunday the 29th weather warmer & dryer, and rain more

wanting than ever, Red River Mail arrived, and brought nothing—wrote to Levy Jordan respecting the Claim of $1017.55 the Estate of James Ogilvy has against him also respecting the League of Land of Kinching Odom, requesting him to give me a full history of the transaction respecting that land, between him (Jordan) John Ricord and James Ogilvy—of one thing I am certain Ogilvy has either a Claim upon Livy Jordan for $1017.55 or he has a claim for that amount upon the above mentioned League of Land—

Monday the 30th translated a Land Title for Capt. English, for which he owes me Eight Dollars, also paid him five dollars at graham's on a/c/ of $70.00 I owe him—sat as associate Justice in Probate Court. H. H. Edwards & James Carter returned from the west last night—

Tuesday the 31st had a fine rain this morning, a Mr Holland brought the Presidents Proclamation for an Extra Session of Congress to convene at Houston on the 27th June next, also a call for this county to furnish 194 men; in all 3614 men are ordered out of the militia of the Republic—General Memucan Hunt is appointed Inspector general

Wednesday the 1st of June 1842 fine dry *rainwanting* weather—nothing of note transpired to day

Thursday the 2d Cloudy looks like—but no—rain—this is the fourteenth anniversary of our Marriage—and but few Clouds, have darkened our nuptial Hemisphere—my wife is *now* as *dear* and as *lovely* in my sight and my Heart thrills with as much enthusiasme as when I first called her mine—may the great ruler of the Universe vouchsave to end our union with as much harmony as it has begun and is now—

Fryday the 3d June very dry weather rain wanting very much Judge Terrill arrived, dined with us and went on towards San Augustin, informs me that the mail now goes again between Cincinnatti & Houston, our mail to Cincinnatti will start next Monday Morning. Mrs Taylor my Sister in Law was delivered of a fine Boy this morning, and about 9 or ten girls were born in this Town & vicinity within the last week—*hurrah for Texas*

Saturday the 4th weather in Statue quo. wrote a Bill of Sale for Maximiliano & Theresa Ybarbo to sign gave it to Vital Flores to have it arranged for me—Lodge met this Evening, had a *Stormy Session*

Sunday the 5th weather same—Red River mail brought nothing send it away as it came—wrote Letters to Mrs J. W. Adam's widow respecting Ogilvy's Land, wrote D. S. Kaufman in answer to a Letter of his dated 1st June, wrote to Canfield & Mr Deyoung San Augustin—Made arrangements to send my two Boys Charles and Joseph to School to Mr Farmer[14]

Monday the 6th very dry weather rain is now wanting very much, and if none falls soon, it will ruin many crops who had a very fine appearance a week ago—Send off Eastern mail and once

[14]James A. Farmer.

more Started the Western Mail Court of probates to day, sat as one of the Judges, agreed to make out Z L. Stringers account current on Wm Johnson's Estate, Board of Land Commissioners met transacted some Business—alltogether has this been a more busy day then many previous ones—

Tuesday June the 7th 1842 weather same, went with Mr Clevenger to show him some Land belonging to J. S. Mayfield near the Door place, returned at 12 sold 1284 acres of Land of the Headright League of Patricio de Torres. H. H. Edwards bought it at 33⅓ cents pr acre but he is to take only enough of it to pay his demand against the Estate, the rest is all Coming to me, exept $25.00 to C. S. Taylor, so that I shall make some Disposition of it to suit all round

Wednesday the 8th no rain yet—made out a Power of attorney, gave to Hoya to get out Patents for Maria Josepha Sanchez's Headright League & Labor of Land half of which belongs to the Heirs of N. A. Bonzano of Houston Mr Gould from San Augustin here, dined with me to day

Thursday the 9th no rain. Crops suffering very much—Judge Terrill passed trough for home to day, — did not mention any thing to him about the Texas Treasury notes he owes me, but he is coming back next week—Eastern mail arrived brought nothing but the Rad Lander

Fryday the 10 Crops suffering very much indeed it looks like rain but wont come

Saturday the 11th Western mail arrived, brought me a Letter from Messrs McKinney & williams that the draft of Count Narbonne is no a-Count—that the fellow is an Imposter, received a Letter from a Mr Burke to inquire about a box of Books & Plate belonging to the widow Dart left 2 years ago by her Husband with C. H. Sims—Sims is not at home so can not do any thing in the matter at present, reced a letter from the Post office Bureaus at Houston—abt Mrs Huberts drafts letter filed, not yet answered—received a letter from Wm Nixon New Orleans—does not want an answer Eugenie received her music send by my adopted Sister Nancy Stephens pr Mail she is much pleased with it received several Papers—busy reading them all the Evening

Sunday the 12th looks very much, but does not rain—the Red River mail came, and went—Wm Scurry gone to the U. S. adieu my $50.00 for Boarding— wrote to my Sister Nancy to Wm Daukerwerth of Houston, to Canfield, and the General Post office department

Monday June the 13th 1842 nearly had a rain but not *quite* send off Eastern & western mails, took the Papers of the Estate of A. Richman to put in Order for John Leusch the Administrator, nothing particular stirring in Town, finished getting in my oats to day—set the two negroes to Split Rails to fence in the Lot General Houston gave to my Daughter Eugenie

Tuesday the 14th dry, dry, dry, burning up nothing astir made out for Mr Leusch an account current in the Estate of A.

Richman decd, gave it to C. S. Taylor Esqr to get an order to Sell the Headright 640 acres of the decd to pay the debts of the Estate, —made arrangement to go and spend some two or three days in the woods fishing, hunting eta late supper Judge Terrill & His Lady arrived.

Wednesday the 15 no rain no news nothing doing nothing of any interest whatever, the sun did not shine all day, yet it was infernaly hot, and as dry as a Powderhouse, take all in all it was certainly a day—oh yes—I belive it is the birthday of Napoleon, (If I am not mistaken—)[15] flat, stale & unprofitable

Thursday the 16 nothing new, Judge Terrill and Family left for home, Eastern mail arrived and as usual brought nothing looks more like rain this evening then any other previous time.

Fryday the 17 nothing new cloudy all day, a rain in the Evening looks like we would have a plenty of rain, if so, the benefit to this County will be incalculable, provided the rain is general

Saturday the 18 had a very fine rain last night, every thing looks refreshed, went into my Corn field, could *allmost hear it* grow. Keeps Cloudy and occasional showers up to 12 noon western mail arrived but brought nothing for this place

Sunday the 19 mild weather mail from north, send it off again. wrote to the Editor of the Sabine Advocate, to the General Post office department about Mrs Huberts claim, to James Burke of Galvezton in answer to a letter of his about a Box of Books eta in the possession of Charles Sims, wrote to Judge Ochiltree about Jones House, he wants to purchase to Mr Deyoung, a he[l]l of a Letter, nothing new

Monday the 20th June 1842 fine morning—Send off Eastern mail did not send western mail there being a change in the arrival at Cincinnatti, a Splendid rain fell this afternoon—Keeps on raining at dark—worth more than 10000 dollars to this County. our Son Joseph took sick this afternoon feels a little better at dark—Susan the negro woman, her Boy Tom, and the old negro man Charles are all sick—very bad sign for the Season—Mrs Israel P. Reinhardt died a few days ago after an illness of four days, her Husband was absent at the time to Houston—poor fellow!! he was married only a few weeks ago, —gave F. von der Hoya an order on Wm Pierpoint for a note in my favor drawn by Capt Sam. B. Ybes (or Eves) commands the Steamer Ned Burleson running between Houston & Galvezton, that is provided the note has not been heretofore been delivered J. Kleberg. gave Mr Hoya full power to get any thing he can for the note he is also to collect $150.00 from Bonzano's Heirs for me, if he does he must account to me for it.

Tuesday the 21st Cloudy, and a Shower after 12—Joseph is sick yet, the old negro man and negro woman the same, got Doctor Starr to attend on all, Tom is better

---

[15]Sterne is in error. Napoleon Bonaparte states in his **Memoirs** that he was born on August 15, 1769.

Wednesday the 22 rain, made out Deed to F. Thorn for 1287 acres of Land of the Patricio de Torres League sold by Order of Probate Court—Thorn made me a Deed for 753 Acres out of the Same back again, send off western mail, Mr Taliafero returned from Corpus Christy reports only 400 men at that place, nothing new—all my Sick appear to be on the mend this Evening

Thursday 23 Cloudy and a little rain in the Evening—Mr A. McDonald of Austin, arrived with his Lady, the youngest Daughter of E[l]isha Roberts Esqr of San Augustin County—only married on the 15th inst—Eastern mail arrived in the afternoon brought nothing at all at all

Fryday the 24th fine weather, all my sick convalescend. Eugenie took sick this afternoon, not very serious—this is St Johns day, and the masonic fraternity does—nothing —I am apprehensive our Lodge will fall to nothing— hope not

Saturday June 25th very fine weather—our young couple left here early this morning at 12 a good many People had assembled in Town, a meeting was called, Col Thorn presiding, several speaches were made, Mr Muse our Senator being on the eve of leaving for Houston made a speach, from which I conclude that he is not in favor of invading Mexico, he may be right.

Sunday the 26th fine weather, the Red River mail failed Bennett Blake Esqr left to day for Houston—wrote to Mrs J. W. Adams about the claim the Estate of Ogilvy has on her late Husbands League of Land. Wrote to J. A. Walton of Galvezton, & to general Houston, & Jeff Wright. Muse Left for Houston. Joseph F. Lewis arrived from Alexandria, gave me $20.00 on account of $50.00 which he was to pay me on account of Ogilvy's Estate, for Francis Hazard of Alexandria. Eugenia is still unwell all the other sick better— Col John Forbes, and his Daughter Mrs Wells and Children arrived in Town this afternoon, Mr Wells is with the volunteers at Corpus Christy—gaining—?glory—probably—

Monday the 27 weather fine Probate Court met sat as one of the associate Justices, Board of Land Commissioners met also dispatched several cases. Red River mail came in, was detained by high waters above Shawneetown, very singular, yet true for the Contents of the Mail Bags showed either much rain, or much Swimming.

Tuesday the 28th very warm weather at an early hour People commenced coming into Town, at 11 A. m. Speaches were made in the Court House by general Rusk & Others, at 1 P. m. all those belonging to the 1st Class of militia paraded, for the purpose of getting volunteers to fill the number required by Secretary of war in this County, more then the requisite number of Cavalry, and a whole Company of Infantry volunteered, to morrow the troops muster again, and it is supposed the whole number of men will be obtained. Mail from west, brought nothing new—all hands drunk this Evening yet not one fight occurred during the day

Wednesday the 29th June hot weather. am very unwell, yet am obliged to be in the office all day. Town full of people all the

Companies required from this County made up without being drafted; General Hunt the Inspector General arrived last night inspected them to day, the cavalry company is commanded by R. W. Winn, the other two companies ,the one by Capt Caddell,[16] and the other by *Old Col Hayden Edwards* who was one of the first to volunteer if the old man had only about 40 years stricken of the 4 score of years, it would do very well. near dark left very sick, went home allmost exhausted found my son Charles sick, Eugeny a little better, took a doze of medecine & went to bed— send off Eastern mail this morning

Thursday the 30th weather moderately warm had a restless night took more medicine in the morning, was relieved near noon Eugenie is also better, Charles dito, had a fine shower of rain in the afternoon accompanied with thunder & lightning hope it may so refresh the air, that we may not have any more sickness.— James Arnold send off the western mail.

Fryday the 1st of July 1842 Cold rainy morning, remained so till towards Evening when it cleared up— loaned Joseph F. Lewis my Sorrell Horse to send an Express to San Augustin. feel much better to day so much so, that I wrote nearly all day and towards Evening went to the office, there are none Sick thank god in the Family to day—nothing stirring in Town, paid Miss Martha Sims $7.70 on a/c of Schooling.

Saturday the 2d dry weather, but so cold, that a fire in the Chimney before Breakfast was indispensible, the day however was very fine, the Eastern mail brought not much news, received a Letter from Mrs Cabbell the Mistress of the two Slaves in my possession, she is very well satisfied, and begs me to treat them well. took a Bee hive to day containing upwards of fifty lb of very fine Honey, but got myself well Stung in committing the Robbery, poor Creatures, how Industrious, they are all at work again this Evening, to make *more* for the —destroyer—man!

Sunday the 3d July 1842 fine weather all hands in Town gone out to Preaching, hope they all got Religion for God Knows the[y] have none— the Red River mail oh!! Bar! why talk about nothing—wrote to Mrs Cabble the Mistress of the two Slaves in my possession, in answer to a letter received dated may the 20th last

Monday the 4th July Splendid day, the Aniversary of the Independence of the United States, passed off without being even noticed—when the Mexican Troops were here, that day was celebrated in some way—but now—it was not even talked of. not a Soul in Town, not even any one drunk exept John Dorsett, & he has 4th July all the year round—the Board of Land Commissioners met to day and singular enough the first applicants name was Darling *Washington*

Tuesday the 5th weather as yesterday. everything in Statue quo the western mail arrived, brought nothing exept the Presi-

16Probably Andres Caddell.

— 103 —

dents Message—it is a *mixed up* Document, the President from what I can understand of the Language—wants more monay more Power, and a perfect Controul over the dearly beloved and never to be forgotten Cherokee Lands— (cherokees) to look at the Document divested of all prejudices—it is a *non-commital-anti-Austin-City—* and *go-it-Houston-City-Cherokee-Land-and King-Sam Houston-* Document— Oh— dear Texas have I worn chains for thee, to see such fellows try to fatten on thy ruin! Confound all demagogues— all Political gamblers, god grant that Texas may belong to the great union of the Land of Washington,—if it does not soon I'll give up all hopes, of ever seeing this a happy Country!

Wednesday the 6th nothing new send off eastern mail and after that all's said

Thursday the 7th warm sultry weather, send off western mail wrote by Mr Johnson the Mail rider to A. C. Hyde the Chief Clerk of the Post office Department, send also a letter to Mrs Cabble of Alabamer— respecting the two negroes in my possession— Mr Jones is *recovering* my kitchen to day—

Fryday the 8th July 1842 very hot day, news was received in Town that Jim Sims has run off with Tom Sim's negroes—it is dog eat Hog— or Hog eat Dog— I allways believed that James Sims was the greatest rascal of the two Brothers. send monay pr James M. Draper for 100 lbs Flour to the City of Houston—Nothing particularly new to day

Saturday the 9th very hot untill 3 P. m. had a Thunder Storm and a very hard rain for an Hour, we were in want of just such a rain, the Crops of every description troughout this County will be very large, thank god that's something these hard times. The three companies of volunteers mustered in Town to day. mail from East, nothing from beyond San Augustin, reced a Letter from A. McDonald inclosing one for Miss Culp, to be send to her immediately

Sunday the 10th weather moderately warm, the Red River mail failed nothing new in Town, spend the day in reading Bulwers last Novel Zemoni good—VERY GOOD—

Monday the 11th very warm in the morning— had an other fine Shower of rain in the afternoon—the Probate, and County Courts met, nothing transacted particularly— the Justices of the County as Commissioners of Roads and revenue met made three new Roads— one from here by Capt Hotchkiss's to the Nechaz— one by the Lananna Mills to Shawnee prairie, and one from here to meet the public road of Shelby County at Caro's Crossing on the Attoyac

Tuesday the 12th everything dull. mail from Houston in the Evening, Congress has done nothing as yet, but quarrelling, rd a Letter from Muse.

Wednesday the 13th Send off Eastern Mail, Mr. A. McDonald his Lady, and Mr & Miss Edwards, a niece and nephew of Mrs Elisha Roberts arrived, spend the day very agreably,—made a Sale to Moses L. Patton of the Land I purchased from Jose Ygnacio Ybarbo's Heirs, got my note for $71.00 I gave Doctor Starr, also a receipt I gave Patton for $90.00—spoke to Ned Taliafero respecting some Land, he wants to purchase of me on the Loco, but it is no go, as he wants it on a credit—

Thursday the 14 July 1842 fine weather, done some business at the Office, gave Mr McDonald a Ball in the Evening was well attended, and every body enjoyed themselves—

Fryday the 15th Aniversary of the first fight with the Cherokees, did not celebrate it much being so tired from the last nights dancing. Slept half the day—

Saturday the 16th aniversary of the Battle of the Nechaz and Death of Bowls, spend the day a *little merry*— Mr Edwards and his Sister from San Augustin went home, mail arrived from Sabine Town, received a letter from Mr Demorse, also One from Canfield

Sunday the 17th Mr McDonald left for the west. Col Thorn & myself accompanied him a few miles on the Road; the Red River Mail brought me a letter from Mr Levi Jordan respecting the Claim Ogilvy has on a League of Land, granted to Kinching Odom, Letter filed—

Monday the 18th weather rather Cloudy, commenced pulling fodder in the Big field, hope it wont rain much, nothing stirring of Consequence, Mr Engledowe went to San Augustin, Send a Pistol by him to be mended by a Mr Jackson at San Augustin—

Tuesday the 19th nothing stirring. a Thunderstorm, but not any rain here—good— for my fodder mail from west, no news

Wednesday the 20 weather Cloudy but no rain, good again for my fodder. Bennett Blake Esqr Arrived from Houston brought me a letter from Walton the Post Master at that place and one from J. M. Dor. Congress not doing much— no nor that isnt all they are not going to do any thing. send off the Eastern mail wrote to Canfield—

Thursday the 21st Send off Western mail, took up a runaway negro belonging to a Mr Todd of Crockett gave him to George Clevenger to Keep till his Owner can come for him, Mr F. v. d. Hoya arrived from Houston, brings news that Sam B. Eves is dead. he owes me $500.00 my old luck. May be his Estate is sufficient to pay the Debts— but I doubt it most damnably, my confounded luck—

Fryday the 22d Cloudy every day in the afternoon yet it does not rain, dont care if it holds on a day longer, so I'll get all my fodder I have down, Stacked

Saturday the 23d weather same as before—some Business in the office to day, the Eastern mail arrived but did not bring any news

Sunday the 24th an other sultry, cloudy, rainy day—R. Scurry Esqr from San Augustin arrived, says the War Bill has passed the Lower House by a majority of three 15 against and 18 in favor. all, look forward with the greatest anxiety to know what will be its result in the Senate— Wrote to my Sister, and to Capt Thos.

Ogilvy pr Mr Thos Barrett who leaves for New Orleans to morrow

Monday the 25th weather just the same— (that is to say) fine bright sun in the morning and a thunderstorm in the afternoon yet did not rain, want rain very much— nothing particularly happened. Probate Court met done some some [sic] Business gave Dolores Cortinas the old Spanish Title to the Locco Lands and agreed to take a copy from the Records myself he (Dolores) paying for it—

Tuesday the 26th weather same, mail from west—the War Bill has passed — 200 volunteers under general Davis had a Skirmish on the west side of the Nueces opposite San Patricio, with 200 regular Mexican Troops and 500 Rancheros under Gel Canales,[17] the Texians whipt them killed and wounded about 30 and put the rest to flight

Wednesday the 27th weather very hot nothing astirr at all.

Thursday the 28th weather if any, more hot then yesterday, went to Jesse Wallings, upwards of 300 persons present, the Candidates for Congress made Speaches promising *of Course* to do great things if elected, a good deal of the queens English was murdered, much roast Beaf and Pork was devoured, and lots of dancing, left near dark, met with Judge Ochiltree, Lansing, Capt Wheeler of San Augustin and Mr Gibson of Natchitochez

Fryday the 29th had a settlement with Lansing as administrator of the Estate of W. W. Parker the late Editor of the Red Lander,[18] fell $25.00 in debt for which I gave my note dated it 1st January 1842 made payable 12 months after that date bearing 10 per cent interest pr Annum till paid. Col Anderson and Greer[19] from San Augustin, the first Speaker of the House of Representatives and the other the Senator of that County, passed trough here. Congress had adjourned the War Bill has been vetoed by the President; I belive that the veto message reflects more luster on Houston's name then even the Battle of San Jacinto.

Saturday 30 June[20] 1842 fine weather felt unwell and Kept at home till 3 P. m. went up Town attended to some Business in the office, Eastern mail—nothing but Red Landers. no news from the United States. Red River Mail arrived and brought . . . as usual— glad it came to day send it off again, so I am not disturbed to morrow. Doctor James Starr presented the greatest part of the Business of K. H. Douglass to the Probate Court, felt too unwell to attend, but B. Blake Esquire being with Judge Hart my presence was dispenced with. made an offer to day to Doctor

[17]Antonio Canales, whose expedition west of the Nueces was defeated. Later he commanded at Mier, in December, 1842, when the Mier Expedition attacked.

[18]W. W. Parker established the **Red-Lander** in San Augustine in September, 1838, after he bought out Isaac W. Burton's **Texas Chronicle**, published in Nacogdoches. Later, Alanson W. Canfield established the **Journal and Advertiser**, and in 1841 the two papers merged under the name of **Red-Lander**, with Canfield as editor.

[19]Kenneth Lewis Anderson and John Alexander Greer.

[20]The correct date is Saturday, July 30, 1842.

Starr to pay my debt due Douglass's Estate in Land in this County, and all within half a days ride of this place, gave him choice of five different tracts, at most reasonable prices and if he is not satisfied at my offer, I authorize him to leave it to two impartial men, and that I will abide by what they say—Doctor Starr acts as an Agent for New Orleans Creditors of Douglass Estate one half *of them broke* and if he does not accept my offer he does not do Justice to his Employers, I could not have made a more liberal offer if all I owe the Estate was coming to Douglass wife and children, which alas it is not—if it is accepted—! well, if not, it will be sometime before I make an other such a one, and pay at the end of the rope—

Sunday July 31st very warm in the forenoon, had a Thunder Storm and rain in the afternoon, the negro Boy Joe very sick. Doctor Starr attending on him—Capt wheeler Gibson & an other gentleman from Natchitochez left in the Evening

Monday August the 1st 1842 rainy Cloudy Cold weather— the Negro Boy Joe very sick, Probate Court met to act on the Business of James H. Starr admr of K. H. Douglass— Succession not closed, but passed so far— Board of Land Commissioners met in the afternoon transacted some Business—have a serious Idea of resigning my Postmastership. it is a loss to me, every day, and the government is so destitute of means that the Establishment can not be Kept up as it ought to be—it is the beginning of the End—God grant it may not be— but!!!

Tuesday August the 2d fine weather this is the tenth aniversary of the Battle fought here against the Mexican Troops—Capt Vandergriff arrived from Natchitochez stays at my House. brings no very particular news from the United States— the western mail arrived in the Evening brought nothing new the negro Boy Joe very sick, of Congestive fever—

Wednesday the 3d Cold weather, unusually so for this season. The negro Boy Joe still very sick. no hopes of his recovering. Town allmost evacuated—nothing doing. Capt Vandergriff is still here, Col Snively a late Prisoner of the Santa Fee Expedition supped with us, after supper the Misses Sims came down and we had music on the Piano till 10 P.M.

Thursday the 4th weather still Cold— several cases of sickness in Town. negro Boy not better, dito as yesterday. Mrs Mason very sick.

Fryday the 5th weather as yesterday, Mr Vandergriff left for Natchitochez—negro Boy not expe[c]ted to live—do everything for him we can, Doctor Starr had to go to the mill to day Judge hart and three children sick there— 8 P.m. negro Boy a little better—have to stimulate him with Toddy—Snively and his party left here to day for Red River eta eta

Saturday the 6th August 1842 Weather a little warmer then the 3 or 4 previous days. Negro Boy pronounced out of danger by Doctor Starr. Mrs Roberts, Mrs Edwards and the Old Colonel Sick;— our Representative Judge Brown returned to day from

Houston—did not see him, mail arrived from the East— belive it to be the last one for some time to come there being no monay to pay the contractors—fine—very— the news of the release of the Santa fee Prisoners is ascertained as a fact beyond a doubt, they were released on the 13th July Santa Ana's Birth day—!!!!!

Sunday the 7th weather as it usually is this time of the year. there was Preaching in the Court House to day, and yesterday in the Evening, by the Revd Milton Moore—Col Forbes went west to day taking Mrs Wells his oldest Daughter home to her Husband, who was lately an Aid de camp to Gel Davis & no doubt in the *Battle of the Blankets* on the Nueces—Red River Mail came, and went, as usual, brought One, and carried away *One* Letter, negro Boy Joe getting better—received a Paper from Major Riley our Minister to the United States, Containing his Letter to Senator King respecting Texas (Eastern & Northern Texas particularly) understand he has asked to be recalled which, has been done by the President, and the Honble Isaac Van Zant of Harrisson County has been nominated to fill the vacancy, Van. is a clever fellow but he never Can, & never will, fill that high Station as it was by his Predecessor Major R., Col Anderson the late Speaker of the House has declined being a candidate for Representative for San Augustin County in the next Congress—

Monday the 8th very hot weather, in the forenoon, cloudy & sultry not a breath of air in the latter part of the afternoon. negro boy still getting better—we must be in the Dog days if the *extra Shines* and *didos* kicked up this afternoon in Town by Jack Graham are indicative signs—he is a very good neighbour, and exelent Citizen when Sober, but the Lord Keep me out of his Company when Drunk—every thing else to day was Stale, flat and unprofitable

Tuesday the 9th August fine fresh breese blowing all day (4 P. m) yesterday Evening took a hot Fever, had it all night, took Medecine this morning, feel a little better, negro much better understand that Mr Patten has Succeeded in Clearing out the River Angelina from a point 12 miles from here to the mouth of the Iish Bayou, this will bring navigation only twelve miles from this Town, above the mouth of the Carriso is situated the Town of Travis laid out in 1838 by Mr Chevallier, Dor, myself & others— who Knows but that it may become a valuable Speculation, after having been laught at by every body

Wednesday the 10th)
Thursday the 11th)
Fryday the 12th)   very Sick
Saturday the 13th)
Sunday the 14th

Monday the 15th had no fever of any consequence last night am exessively weak, but made out to get to my writing Table to write this; Exessive heavy Rains have fallen during my sickness, to day the wind is north, and the air is as pure and as invigorating as if it was in winter,—Our little infant Laura was taken very

Sick yesterday Evening and the Fever has not been off yet 4 ½ P. m

Tuesday the 16th Splendid weather, am recovering of my Sickness sat up nearly all day, had several visits—Mr Parmalee came to see me in the Evening just returned with Gel Rusk from Crockett; informs me that there has been a most tremendous Flood in that County; little branchez which have seldom been Known to be Swimming were so for 300 to 400 yards, whole corn fields, fences Corn and Cotton completely covered with water, the Cotton where it was any way adjacent to a Branch or even hollow is literally ruined, Stacks of fodder intirely gone and not many a fence standing; such a flood as this I never have heard of during my life-time;—five of the U S. Corpus Christy volunteers arrived here, report says all fine young men, they are out of Clothing and every other thing—going to stop to try to get work

Wednesday the 17th August 1842 very fine weather—am recovering very fast from my Sickness, rode up to the office this Evening and transacted some business, my little Daughter Laura is better to day, hope to god she may remain so—"the last Link is Broken"—the Eastern mail has stopped, for want of pay—Mrs Hubert has been a very faithfull Servant of the Public she has carried the mail since last January without any pay whatsoever, it is realy too much—how long will we last longer? *nous verrons*

Thursday the 18th weather rather hot—nothing Stirring felt strong enough to walk up to the Office to day wrote several Letters to different persons—Little girl well

Friday the 19th weather fair in the forenoon, went to the Office, allmost entierly recovered from my illness at 1 P. M. commenced raining 3 P. m. looks like it was going to set in again in earnest—Mr Chevallier received a Letter from Mr Barrett reports that the yellow Fever is in New Orleans & in Alexandria, La

Saturday the 20th fair weather in the Morning, rain in the afternoon, Canfield send the Red landers up by his Servant, received a long Letter from him, answered it, by the Boy. Blake & Parmalee left for Alexandria Red River in quest of a Horse that was stolen from Parmalee sometime ago, no news of consequence

Sunday the 21st Rain. Rain. Rain. Red River mail arrived, said, could not cross the waters last trip no other reason for the failure—recd a Letter from Levi Jordan of not much importance, Madame Lacombe, a Daughter of the late J. B. Cazenaue arrived in quest of her Father's Property. a Mr Pemberton and Mr McKinchney a partner of the House of Robinson from Natchitochez arrived in the afternoon, bring no news, the latter is a great friend of the Late James Ogilvy. he promises to call on me on his return from the west to get a Sinopsis of the Affairs of the Decd and he promised to try and get me the amount which is due me by the Estate

Monday the 22d August still raining—went up to Mr Lee's to see Mrs Lacomb, found her one of those little vivacious French women, who amidst all their troubles show their nationality by a light and gay air so peculiar to that nation—, I hope she may meet with full success in getting her property, which I belive legitimately belongs to her—she came to spend nearly all day with Mrs Sterne, who [was] much pleased with her; how could that Brute of a Father of hers abandon his children? —received a Letter from Mr Eugene Michamps—respecting his Property here—at present worth nothing— was at the Office, but done no Business whatever—

Tuesday the 23d Cloudy but no rain, in the afternoon a Stranger, in the shape of the Sun appeared looks like it was going to clear up—hope so— a new Candidate for County Surveyor is out. Mr Ben Vansicle[21]—I do not think he will be elected, he is a very fine, good valuable, Citizen, and a tolorable good surveyor, but he has not the requisite qualifications for that office all the Candidates for Congress are doing their d............ts to be elected. Just as if the office was worth having or if they could do any good to the Country generaly or to this County in paritcular, ha! ha! ha. ha!

Wednesday the 24th rainy, Cloudy, wet weather—if this weather Continues ten days longer, the whole Cotton Crop will be ruined, and at least one third of the Corn Crops—I send into the field to day to gather such ears as were on and near the ground, all of which were either rotton or sprouted, it looks this Evening as if it would Clear up—god grant it may—

Mrs Hubert did not have the mail carried to Sabine Town as I anticipated—She is right, the Labourer is worthy of his hire, but she does not get that—there was a Political meeting at James Wallings's to day. all the Candidates in attendance, including Mr Nelson and Ben Vansickle candidates for County surveyor—

Thursday the 25th August still Cloudy & rain, went up Town. Started a Subscription to have the Eastern mail transported again, made arrangements to have it carried for $12.00 pr Month, by getting a horse furnished eta. have $32.00 subscribed, want 18 more to carry it from now, till first January next; the first 7 bales of Cotton of this years Crop came into Town yesterday, five of which were send off by H. H. Edwards to day. Cotton is from the Plantation of Mr Fulgam,[22] one of the first Farmers in this County

Fryday the 26th Once more fair weather, thank god, hard at work from early in the morning till 12 oclock I have been trying for the last year to get repair part of a Brick chimney and Hearth. despairing of getting it done by a *workman* I *took hold* of it myself this morning & with the assistance of a hand to bring materials I finished the job as neat, and I belive, more substantial than a real mason would have done it— not alone that this little matter has saved me some ten dollars but it has taught me this Lesson— that a man *can do* a great many things, if he will only try, determination a little Knowledge of the matter and perseverance will

---

[21]Benjamin Van Sickle.
[22]Arthur Fulgham.

accomplish many things, and eventually will erase the word *impossible* out of our Dictionary. This afternoon was invited to go to the School House to hear an Examination of Mr. Farmer's Pupils, was much gratified, think he is a very exelent Teacher and that the Children advance, *not* rapidly, but S[t]eadily, under his Tuition, Isaac W. Burton in Town gave him a note drawn by Ben Vansickle in favor of himself for $25.00 payable in Cotton left with me by Mr Mick Teague to whom I gave a receipt for it— which Mr Burton has promised to send to me or to destroy it— my wife my Son Joseph, and the little mulatto Boy are unwell, hope it is nothing serious—

Saturday August the 27th fine weather, some threatening Clouds but no rain— was called upon to issue a capias against the Williams Simons, for shooting Wm Goyens with intend to murder, heard nothing up to this Evening from Goyens nor the Shooting man— Several People in Town all very merry— Capt Wm K. English made me an offer for my Loco Land, but I belive it will be no go exept I can have something *tangible* wrote a letter to Capt Vandergriff to send me some Coffee & Sugar by Walter Murray or D. Muckleroy— promising to pay him within two months, and if he sends it I'll be as good as my promise.

Sunday the 28th fine weather the Red River mail failed again to day, nothing stirring, Goyens who was shot by Wm Simons is but slightly wounded not enought to [do?] any good. wrote pr Madame Lazarin to Canfield advising him of the arrangement made for carrying the Eastern mail eta, Mrs Lacomb spend the day with us *devilish smart Woman* improves upon acquaintance eta

Monday the 29th very fine weather Probate Court in session sat as one of the Judges to settle several estates, in the afternoon had a little *flare up* in Town, Judge Taylor and gel Rusk fell out, and made friends again, the Cause of the quarrell was— *whiskey* & Taylor was in the wrong. Miss E. Culp arrived accompanied by a Mr Crump lately from Houston,

Tuesday the 30th very fair & very hot was up town nearly all day but done not much Business. Closed the Eastern Mail this Evening to be ready to send off early to morrow—

Wednesday the 31st August very hot weather, send off Eastern Mail on my Sorrell Horse— up Town in the morning, no Business Miss Culp and Mr Crump left— Mr Crump a Clever fellow— after dinner done some *carpenters work* which no Carpenter would have done for less then at least $5.00 if these hard times last much longer I expect to be a Jack of all trades— getting ready to go to morrow to Shawnee Prairie to marry Mr John K. Carsons to a Miss McDonald

Thursday the first of September 1842 very Hot— weather at 8 A.M. left for Shawnee prairie. arrived at the House of Mr McDonnall at about 4 P.M. found all ready the Bride waiting eta performed the Ceremony, supped, and went to bed, gave Doctor Starr my note for $48.75 medical Bill

Friday the 2d after an Early Breakfast left— passed Rueg's old Rancho, all in ruins, stopped at the widow Sims to rest and feed Horses— arrived home at ½ pas[t] 4 P.m Mr Blake & Parmalee arrived to day, did not get Parmalee's Horse, Blake brought the S[t]ray Letter written to me by Thos Ogilvy two days previous to writing the one I received from him—Mr Barrett returned yesterday from New Orleans, he brought me a letter from my Sister Nancy Stevens, also One from J. W. Collins the Son in Law of Alexander Philipps Esqr. I have written to him about his own Business in this Country for the last three years—and this is the first time I have received any Letter from him, he owns half of old Ramsdale's Headright, I have strove hard to have it for Collins, but his Own neglect to attend to it will I am afraid Cause him to loose it after all my Care

Saturday the 3d fine weather Showers in the afternoon Cooled the Air Considerably, settled with Doctor Starr for Medical Attendance, and medicines from 1st January last up to this day $48.75 gave my due Bill for it—and agreed to board Mr Engledown on account of it at $20.00 pr Month to commence on next Tuesday received also an account of $32.50 for Medical attendance on two negroes Joe & Charlie & have in my possession to be Collected from the Owener or Oweners whoever they are— Mr Engledow informs me that Hoe Durst the Commissioner together with the rest have returned from their Mission, they have seen the Indians, made treaty with four tribes, the rest of the tribes are to meet them at Comanche Peak on the Brassos sometime this fall— hope it may all turn out for our Benefit— Eastern mail arrived brought some few letters, no, news of any note—

Sunday the 4th September 1842 warm Cloudy and a few Showers of rain Red River mail arrived, brough[t] the first number of the Northern Standard— Edited, and owned, by Charles de Morse Esqr it is printed at Clarksville the County seat of Red River County, and is in appearance a much *better looking* Sheet, then the *Friend of the Laws* printed in New Orleans in 1821 when I first arrived in that City, and is a far better looking Sheet then half the Country Papers of our Sister Republic the United States, success attend the Standard, and its Editor, as good a fellow as ever lived— Mr Lubbock, and Mr Monroe who lately passed trough here with Mr Snively (Jacks Brother) for the North returned to day, seen them but had no Conversion with them stopped with Doctor Starr

Monday the 5th beutifull weather— Nelson paid me a Cow worth Twelve dollars on account of his Boarding this was the great day for the Sovereigns, Election day for members to Congress & a County Surveyor—277 votes were polled in Town, out of which Jesse Walling got 130— W. W. Wingfield 109. Wm F, Sparks 115 TJ Jennings 91 & James Smith 62—for Surveyor A.A. Nelson received 238, and B. A. Vansickle 32 votes

Tuesday the 6th very fine weather, small (very small) shower in the afternoon, most all the returns came in from the different

Precincts. belive walling & Sparks to be elected Nelson is elected sure— the western mail arrived brought by a Mr Davis, Kept him & mule at my house this time—must get an other stand next time, the mail brought Nothing New— My wife sick, hope to god it is not serious. the Infant is better, my Son Joseph the same, he is going to School to day

Wednesday the 7th one of the hottests days we have had this Summer—western mail send off, no returns from Williams's Settlement, the only one lacking— Mr Raymond[23] the new Secretary of Legation to the U.S. passed trough here, to go to his place of destination (Washington City) Amory, the former Secr is promoted to Texas Consul at Boston

Thursday the 8th of Sepr 1842 very hot weather to day Eastern mail arrived nothing new except that the former Senator A. Greer is elected 40 votes over his opponent Campbell[24] — Mr Snively (Jack's Brother) arrived this Evening, stops with me— did not Succeed in their undertaking — eta— tells me that Bill Scurry is at Clarksville, located permanently. no (certain) returns of the Election from William's settlement yet— rumor says that Walling & Sparks are elected, the first beyond doubt of being overtaken and the second by two or three votes over Wingfield. Oscar Engledow comenced Boarding to day

Friday the 9th very hot all day near dark had a Small Shower looks rainy but no prospect—nothing of any thing notable happened to day, the rest of Mr Snively's Companions arrived to day, done all I could to make them Comfortable—Oscar Engledow who commenced Boarding on Yesterday is to Board with me untill the return of Doctor Starr at whose expence he Boards — at the rate of Twenty dollars a month

Saturday the 10th very hot for this season of the year, had a Shower in the afternoon which cooled the air a little— all the Houston *Boys* who came with Snively left here this Morning, all Breakfeasted with me —a fine Set of young men—Snively went to Col Raguets's to return in a few days— done some Business in the Justice of the Peace way— no returns as yet from Williams's Settlement.

Sunday the 11th fine weather—the Red River mail arrived, brought a letter from Wm R. Scurry to A.A. Nelson, Mr Scurry having returned to Clarksville and as he writes to Mr Nelson that he has a plenty of the Rhino, I send up the account of Mr S. Board he owes requesting him to send it by mail, it is rumored that we will soon be invaded by Mexico, probably to have three different divisions to attack us at the same time, Sabine, Galvezton, and by land from Matamoros. General Rusk returned this Evening from Harrison County Court adjourned on last Friday, did not

---

[23]Charles H. Raymond was sent to Washington, D. C., with legation dispatches, and succeeded Isaac Van Zandt as charge d'affaires in 1843. In 1844 he served as legation secretary.
[24]Probably Isaac Campbell, who had served as San Augustine's representative in the Fourth Congress.

do much business. Esqr Hamilton returned with his waggon from Natchitochez, Cotton only 6 cents sales dull even at that. every thing cheap in proportion exept Coffee which is 15c.

Monday the 12th Sepr fine warm (rather hot) weather had a cloudy afternoon but not much rain— Mrs Hubert took it into her head to run the mail again to Sabine Town, I hope she will not change her mind again, as a good arrangement for carrying the mail was made after she had positively declined running it, the never mind it I can not quarrell with a woman—poor John Johnson was sadly disappointed at hearing the news of his being superceeded by Thomas Hubert.— this afternoon received all the returns of the Election — Sparks (fool Bill) and Walling (the Dismal of Darien) are elected— I voted for Walling but bless my Soul what a set they will make in a Congress—a Mr Porter from Mississippi arived here in a gig to day—lookes much like *a man of the world* but is realy a Preacher of the Gospel of the very first Class— he preached at the Court House this Evening after Candle light; and a better discourse never has been delivered upon religion since Bishop Timon preached here, after the Discourse an old man a Mr [blank] said a few foolish things about the Citizens of Nacogdochez not hearing or going to hear Preachers of the Gospel—well he may say Brayers of the Gospel— let the Presbitery send men like Porter, who can *teach* us, and *explain* to us about matters of *Christianity* we do not understand, and all will gladly embrace the opportunity to go and hear, and perhaps to be convinced— but if *ignoramuses* are send amongst us they will meet with the encouragement they deserve. a meeting was held of the citizens generaly to request Mr Porter to remain to morrow, to preach a Sermon to morrow Evening. Holland chairman of Committee

CHAPTER VI

"I whish to god we had a good Phisician here . . ."

Tuesday the 13th September 1842 fine weather in the morning clouds & showers in the Afternoon—commenced pulling corn, but had to stop on account of rain—Mr nelson paid One Barrill of Flour for his Board for one month paid him $1.50 ¢ to booth [sic]. Dorsetts (John) waggon hawled rails for me yesterday & to day and is to hawl again to morrow for a debt I hold against him in favor of Joe Polvadore— Commenced gathering Corn to day got in a considerable quantity but this afternoons rain prevented me from hawling any more, a Captain Allen who commanded a Company of volunteers from Mississippi arrived from Judge Terrell's, came up from Houston with the Judge. mail from the West & Galvezton arrived, but had nothing in it the mail from Houston having failed to arrive in due time at Cincinnatti

Wednesday the 14th Commenced raining early in the morning and Continued all day; interferes very much with my arrangements about gathering Corn, Dorsetts waggon here all day but did not do more than half a days work in consequence of the rain Send off western mail, wrote to Walton[1] Post Master at Galvezton, respecting the Boxes of Books & Silver plate left at Charles H. Sims by C. Dart[2] Decd, Capt Allen here yet could not get off on account of the rain— am very much pleased with him,

Thursday the 15th Sept 1842 Cloudy but not any rain very busy to day in making a new fence between Douglass field and ours, was called upon to give testimony by interregotary in a land suit where the question will be which is the old Kings high way. the Eastern mail arrived, but brought nothing new. Mr McKechney & Mr Pemberton arrived here late this Evening, stops with me all night, Mr Reinhart also stopped all night.

Friday the 16th a little cloudy, but not rain & occasional sunshine—, made out a Statement for Mr McKechney respecting Ogilvy's Estate, about the land the decd is intitled to, also made out an account of the debts due to the Estate, and what is due me

[1]John H. Walton.
[2]Christopher Dart was an old acquaintance of Sterne's, both having been charter members of the Grand Lodge of Texas, A. F. & A. M. In the first roster of officers of the Grand Lodge Sterne was Deputy Grand Master and Dart was Junior Grand Warden. Dart was from the settlements along the Red River.

by the Estate about $272.00. Mr. Pemberton took sick to day which prevented him and Mr Kechney from Starting on their Journey—Mr P. not better at 6 P.m—nothing of any consequence stirring to day.

Saturday the 17th Sepr fine, Clear, but cold weather— Mr Pemberton better to day, left after Breakfast, Eugenia wrote a Letter pr Mr Pemberton to her grand mother widow P. Bossier, gave to mr McKechney two notes drawn in favor of James Ogilvy, by John Waddell one for $50.00 & one for $125.00 dated 27 March 1838 payable in 30 days after said day. took his receipt for the same. he is to try to Collect these notes or part of them, which is to be remitted to me as a part of what the Estate of Ogilvy owes me— Mr McKechney is also to see Captain Thos Ogilvy when he returns to New Orleans from Schottland, for the purpose of obtaining from him the Amount due me by the Estate of his Brother James Mr Morse of Natchitochez arrived here this afternoon (or morning) stops at Col Thorn's— he is a Son in Law of Ambrose Sompeyrac of Natchitochez, he is a Clever fellow (so are they Natchitochez gents all, when over here, in Texas,—but when you see them in their own *diggins,* unless they can make something out of you, they see you d........d first before they would [do] for you, what we do for them, when they come amongst us—

Sunday the 18th very Cold weather fire in the Chimney very agreable cloudy in the afternoon. Red River mail failed—went to the residence of the Brothers Ham, to celebrate the Rites of Matrimony between J. C. Eaton & Miss C. C. Melton, returned home by nine P, M. nothing of any consequence happened, nor transpired, to my neighbours my friends, Enemies (if I have any) nor myself to day—

Monday Sept the 19th Commenced raining about daylight and continued all day, at dark it rained harder then at any time during the day,—send off Eastern mail this morning, was up Town but Short time, a daughter of B. F. whitaker died to day. nothing of any thing worth noticing happened to day disappointed me very much in gathering corn however those who have cotton to pick are worse of then those who have corn only to gather

Tuesday the 20th More rain, more rain, if it rains much more the cotton crops will be ruined— the western mail arrived. brought nothing new of any importance, exept that Old Sam Whiting who trough the Austin City Gazette assisted in no small degree to get Houston elected President,—has in Consequence of Houstons opposition (I suppose) to the Archives remaining at Austin, turned against H. saying *that what little means are left him shall be expended in showing Houston in his true character*— nous verróns—

Wednesday the 21st the *ugly* rain Keeps still on, nothing can be done in the cotton fields nor Corn fields, send off Western mail —wrote a long Letter to J. H. Walton the former Postmaster of galvezton, was invited to go to a wedding to morrow— the Widow

Wm Arnold and Mr Carroll Reddin are to be married, Hurrah for Texas,

Thursday the 22d as usual for this week—Rain—some little business in the office—my wife sick, unfortunately Doctor Starr is absent, hope it will not be serious, did not go to the wedding in Consequence of my wife's illness—mail from East came in brought nothing of consequence, as usual—

Fryday the 23d rain and Sunshine alternatively went to the Office after Breakfeast, but had to return home, with a hot fever on me, lasted till nearly dark, Mrs Sterne much better to day, not being dry enough to pull corn, made use of the time in getting fire wood for winter

Saturday September the 24th 1842 Cloudy this morning, but about 10 A.M. the sun shone out again in 6 days in its full glory & went down perfectly Clear— so that we may expect fair weather to morrow and then for Corn gathering next monday with a rush! —Mrs Sterne had fever again to day—She has got the every other days fever, which if I have a fever again to morrow I think both of us have, one thing good about it is, we take it turn about, that is to say my well day is her sick day & vice versa— too bad to make a joke of— some Cotton came into Town to day and was sold here—many persons in Town. a family moving west name Caldwell—Jack Gillespie passed for the west, had a talk with J. R. Clute about my place. going to take possession of it again so soon as he gets his crop off, Yankee (new york) as he is Cant— Swindle me out [of] that place

Sunday the 25th some Clouds, but upon the whole it was a fine day— but it was not fine for myself for I had a hot fever again as on friday last went of at dark— signed a Certificate in favor of Mrs Hubert to draw pay (if she can) for carrying the mail from this place to Sabine Town, wrote a letter to the Chief Clerk of the Department giving him the (Fatherly) advice not to draw on this Office as he would draw upon nothing

Monday the 26th very fine weather, commenced again to gather Corn, done a good days work at it, but worked too hard for a Sick man, probate Court in Session made an arrangement of an amicable nature (final) between the Brothers von der Hoya, think it a meritorious act to Keep *Brothers* from fighting when their difficulties can be settled Brotherly, Mr John Durst & Mr Chevallier had a falling out and *nearly* came to blows—bad that— dont like it—had a quarrel with my old african negro, but made up friends before we stopped—send off the Eastern mail early in the morning —feel perfectly exhausted and shall go to bed in- stanter, taking Dr Champions Pills to morrow morning—that is— if I am in existence

Tuesday the 27th fine weather, gathering Corn all day, took Champions Pills & escaped my fever to day, the mail arrived to day, brought the news confirmed about the Mexicans having taken

— 117 —

Bexar 1300 men under the command of general Adrien Wall,[3] the District Court was in Session, so that all the Court, Lawyers Jury Plaintiffs & defendants are prisoners, they write however that they are well treated as Prisoners of war, the Western Counties are Marching towards the *rescue* of the Prisoners a requisition is also made on the East & no doubt will be answered— Major Burrill Thompson arrived this Evening on some business with myself respecting an old spanish deed, one of the witnesses names I can prove to be genuine eta. Sat as Probate Judge to day

Wednesday the 28th weather fine, continue to gather Corn. the floor of the Corn House broke down but did not do as much damage as I at first expected—sat as associate Judge of Probate Court again to day to settle the Estate of Alexander Jurdan decd Send off western mail, send a Sinopsis of the news received from the west to Canfield San Augustin. Mr Carson[4] mooved into Douglass' House yesterday

Thursday the 29th fine weather still continues, got in all my Corn, made a calculation, have about 200 Barrills. my wife took sick to day again, she is in much pain, the result of having caught cold, Eugenia had a fever to day, missed mine clear— intend to give Eugenia same kind of Pills I took—good remedy—Eastern mail with the following new wit..—....—....—

Friday the 30th September 1842 fine weather— Commenced Housing my fodder & Pumpkins to day, have a very large quantity of Pumpkins, more then I Know what to do with, Mrs. S. Better to day, Eugenia also better. no more news from the west, a Mr Baillieu passed trough here to day on his way west, has camped on the Bayou Banito waiting for news— Major Cessna[5] Lady and the young-uns in Town stopped at Mr J. S. Roberts's. Camp meeting going on flourishing at Douglass

Saturday October the 1st 1842 fine weather—got trough with Housing my crop—to wit—corn, fodder, and Pumpkins—all my Sick, thank god, are better—nothing more from the west—a Ball to be given to Mr & Mrs Cessna to night by Col Thorn, Family sick did not go.

Sunday October the 2d Weather same as yesterday, nothing new to day, Red River mail arrived having failed twice, brought the Clarksville Northern Standard, nothing else, received a letter from C. De Morse dated Marshall, authorizing me to take notes payable next January for Subscriptions for the Northern Standard wont do— time too short— commenced to make my quarterly Post office returns for 3d qr 1842— not much revenue to the government—anxiously waiting for news from the west—

Monday October the 3d fine, very fine, weather—send off

---

[3]Adrian Woll commanded the second Mexican army to seize San Antonio within six months. His one thousand-man force occupied the city on September 11, 1842 and held it for several days before retreating. Although a native of France, Woll was a friend of Santa Anna and had served as an officer in the Mexican army since the 1830's.
[4]Probably H. H. Carson, a Nacogdoches blacksmith.
[5]G. K. Cessna, a local farmer.

Eastern mail, wrote to Canfield, send list of Letters on hand at the end of the quarter, many People in Town. done Considerable business in the Land Office, in granting Certificates, made an arrangement with a Mexican named Jose Maria Montes to work for me a month for a double barrelled gun I have, he is to make Boards & Shingles—sowed a small piece of ground in Reye to day for a pasture

Tuesday the 4th weather same as yesterday— mail from the west arrived, Gel woll has left Bexar and retreated to the medina, Caldwell[6] with 600 men is between them and the Rio Grande, all hands from west of Brassos & most of Trinity are a *going it.* no doubt a general fight has taken place before this—the result of which we will hear no doubt in a few days, mayfield is with the army—good, good, Mrs Terrill and Sister Miss E. Culp on their way to San Augustin stopped with us to night, —had quite a frolic here, in the shape of dancing eta. all hands in this county waiting to be called to go and try their hand. some of them never have had a chance. I hope they may have their curiosity satisfied now, I like fighting—but confound them bullits

Wednesday October the 5th 1842 fine, very fine, weather Mrs Terrill, sister, and sons left early this morning for San Augustin—. Send off western mail— nothing new— at work on my Farm in Town all day fixing fences, and placing it in a situation to prevent cattle of all descriptions from entering and doing harm —a mr Vaughan from Harrisson County arrived, has business with Mr Nelson, as County surveyor, wants to file certificates to secure a Certain portion of Land, Mr N. not being at home designs leaving the Certificates with me,

Thursday the 6th weather fine, settled up with O. L. Holmes as my Constable—he falls in my debt $1.75 up to date, Mr Payne from Fort Houston Dined with me to day—brings nothing new— wants to engage Cotton to take down the Trinity—Eastern mail arrived, nothing new particularly—exept that Press Loggins was Killed at San Augustin a few days ago—*so much for a perfect Desperado*

Friday the 7th fine weather, busy in the forenoon fixing fences afternoon sawing blocks for Boards to cover House, surveyor of Harrison County Mr Hill gave me eleven certificates to locate Land on the Sabine, to be handed to A. A. Nelson the

[6]Mathew ("Old Paint") Caldwell, a native of Kentucky, had long been in the service of Texas. Following his immigration in 1831, he represented Gonzales at the Convention of 1836 and was a signer of the Declaration of Independence. In 1839 he commanded a company of rangers in the defense of Goliad, and a company in the First Infantry Regiment. He was involved in various actions against Mexican raiders, and was captured with the Santa Fe Expedition in 1841 and imprisoned in Mexico. He was released in 1842 and was elected to the command of the volunteer unit charged with the relief of San Antonio following its occupation by Woll. This unit, composed of two hundred men, defeated the Mexican forces on September 18, 1842 at the Battle of Salado. Caldwell died December 28, 1842.

County Surveyor on his return, received a letter from G. W. Reese Editor of the Nachitochez Democratic Herald accompanied by a Package of the first number of said Paper, appointing me agent eta, no go—for there is no monay.—news was received to day, that a person named Johnson employed by Mr Carson was drowned in the Angelina in attempting to Cross said stream, it being swollen very much, the Coroner Mr Jones[7] has summoned a Jury to go and have a post mortem examination—to morrow morning

Saturday the 8th Cloudy, with a little rain, in the morning cloudy all day but did not rain much, very cold north wind blowing at dark—it is rumored that a Battle has been fought between the Mexicans and our Troops under Burleson & Caldwell, in whic[h] 600 Mexicans and 50 Texians were Killed, the Mexicans flying towards the Rio Grande this report has as yet not been confirmed, Mr Nelson returned from San Augustin; delivered to him all the certificates received, during his absence

Sunday October 9th 1842 Clear dry day, but so cold that Cloaks and a good fire in the chimney are indispensable. no Northern mail to day, no further news from the west, all hands gone out to Douglass to a Camp meeting,

Monday the 10 fine, but very Cold weather, frost last night send off Eastern Mail, wrote to G. W. Reese, advising him to take notes for $5.00 payable in one year, in place of demanding $3 in advance in monay for the Democratic Herald, nothing more new from the west Camp meeting at Douglass came off gloriously, nine poor Sinners, amongst them Mary Dill, professed Religion last night, this tells good in favor of Religious advocates when such old Sinners as her get Religion— County Court met to day— done not much business of course, as it is scowed into nothing, (by Law), the Board of Roads and Revenue were to meet, but as several were at Camp Meeting with their families—of course they could not attend—so all the important business respecting the financial affairs of the County Could not be settled to day in consequence of there not being a quorum of Justices present

Tuesday the 11th fair cold weather—western mail arrived all the news we heard are false—the Mexicans are gone again and in place of having had a battle with them they have recrossed the Rio Grande again in safety and as luck would have it Capt Hays[8] of the Spy Company overtook the Enemy's rear guard and Killed 6, took a cannon, but Kept it only 10 minutes, five Texians wounded—only—several Baggage waggons were taken by our Troops— there is now a full determination to carry on the war into the Enemies Country—right—if the government will only Sanction such a measure it is the only safety for Texas—for as I predicted, it was only an *annoying force* and not a *regular invading army,* and so it will be every Six months till Texas crosses the Rio Grande—

---

[7]Probably William Jones, whose name appears in the earliest Bond Records for Nacogdoches County as a constable.
[8]John Coffee ("Jack") Hays.

Wednesday the 12th October 1842. fine cool weather—a fire now can be dispe[n]sed with during the day—send off Western Mail, busily at work all day in making improvements about the place, which five years ago I thought I could not have done—but bad times have a great influence on man, he finds he can do things which once was thought to be impossible, and *do with out* things he once thought it impossible to do without. received a Letter from Mr Pierre Roblo, the same old song. wants me to attend to his business— but dont send me the requisite Power of attorney,—to day was the Patron Saints day of Nacogdochez, at One time a day celebrated by the Natives, with great pomp and splendour, and no doubt looked upon by the few remaining Mexicans as a day that has been, and to them, at least—in Texas, never to return. was appointed agent by Madame Lazarin to take char[g]e of some Buildings situated on Main Street, the property of the widow or Heirs of Pedro ybarbo

Thursday the 13th fine weather—work in the garden a little before Breakfeast, went to the Office, many suits before me as magistrate to day, not much difficulty in dispatching them. Eastern Mail arrived nothing new in it—a Colorado man passed trough here to day, Confirms the new[s] of the Mexicans having succeeded in making their retreat across the Rio Grande with all our Fellow Citizens in their Power—. god help the poor fellows— they have 17 of the fayette Company *prisoners of war?*

Friday the 14th weather cool, very dry & Smoky, does not look like it would rain soon, but that we are going to have the *Indian Summer*—Mrs Terrell & familie returned from San Augustin, remains here to day till to morrow all hands preparing to go to—(and some are allready gone) to Melrose Campmeeting, feel very unwell this Evening had a fever to day, hope it is not going to continue. Mrs Sterne better thank god, Joseph is sick, allways some one Sick about the House—

Saturday the 15th October—cool, dry weather, white frost last night, wind from the South in the afternoon—Mrs Terrell and Sister left after Breakfast—there is a rumour afloat that the President has by proclamation closed the Land Offices and thereby suspending all, surveying, and so far as I am concerned as associate Commissioner of the Board of Land Comrs "Othell's Occupations gone"—Nelson is gone to the camp meeting at Melrose, Blake is going, Engledow's going, Thorn's going, Hart's going, every body's going, so I'll be all alone, well if I can not go after Religion I hope Religion will come after me—but we are going to have a camp meeting of our own two miles from here, next we[e]k and I'll be even with all the rest of the folks—If I am alive—

Sunday October the 16th warmer weather, wind South, Town nearly des[er]ted, all gone to Camp meeting to Melrose, Red River Mail arrived to day, but sans any thing exept the Standard of 16th September last—Jack Gillespie returned from Montgomery County. 560 men gone from Montgomery County to invade the valley of the Rio Grande, it generally supposed that 3000 men will start from San Antonio—and if so there no doubt will be many more that will follow them—Mr David Snively arrived stopped with me, is sick this Evening, so was I all day, took medecine this morning and feel a little better at 8 P. M.

Monday the 17th weather same—feel very weak, and unwell went up to the office several times to day, send of the Eastern Mail, nothing new to day. my son Joseph getting better

Tuesday the 18th weather getting warmer—Summer heat at noon not much cooler at dark—did miss my fever to day for the first time in ten days, Col Snively not better—our late Representative in Congress James S. Mayfield Esqr. arrived this afternoon from the Army, in quest of volunteers to cross the Rio Grande, a thing by the bye which should have been done long ago, God grant he may succeed in raising many—Major Mayfield was in the fight at the Salado near Bexar, reports that the Notorious Vicente Cordova,[9] one of the Bodens,[10] and 10 or 11 Cherokee indians were Killed, confirms the news of 33 men under Dawson[11] were Killed, the rest (which did not escape were taken Prisoner and send immidately off towards the Rio Grande where those taken at San Antonio had been send previously, Mayfield contradicts many stories we had here before, such as the records of the Court and Archives of Bexar had been taken away, he says that the Mexican troops behaved well, paid for all they got, and that the wounded Texian prisoners who fell into their hands were well treated—mail from west arrived after Supper nothing of consequence in it, received a long letter from Alexander McDonald dated at Huntsville October 15th; McDonald is going to establish himself at that place, wrote him an answer to be send by to morrow's mail,

Wednesday the 19th October 1842 turned cold during last night very Cold this morning, send off western mail. Bennett Blake Esqr send his waggon to Natchitochez to day wrote a letter to Mr McKechney pr Mr Lawrence, requesting McK. to write to me if Capt Ogilvy has arrived at New Orleans or not, and if he wants me to carry his Papers to Sabine Town or not—I also wrote to him to send me a Bll sugar a sack Coffee and some lard, on a/c of my claim on Ogilvy's Estate, Agreed to go to Crockett next week with Hoya—and May perhaps go to Huntsville

Thursday the 20th weather moderate, Mayfield was to address the People to day but it was postponed till Saturday, when it is to take place at the Camp ground—Mr Snively left for Col Raguets's to night, A Mr Hopfelt arrived from the City of Hous-

[9]Vincente Cordova led a Mexican-Indian uprising against the Texas government in the area around Naccgdoches in the summer of 1838. The Texas Army under Thomas J. Rusk successfully routed Cordova and 600 effectives, and he made his escape to Mexico.

[10]The 1837 Tax Roll for Nacogdoches County lists a Juan Pier Boden.

[11]Nicholas Mosby Dawson led the volunteer company from Fayette County that came to assist in the relief of San Antonio. Finding the battle of Salado already taking place they attempted to effect a union with Caldwell and were all felled in "Dawson's Massacre" by Mexican forces.

ton, reports that (8 days ago) when he left that place a rumor was afloat that Gel Woll had not retreated any further than the Nueces, and that a reinforcement had arrived from Mexico of 5000 men, if this is true some fine sport in the way of fighting may be expected shortly—Eastern mail arrived, did not bring any thing exept the Red Lander, and few Natchitochez Papers—paid $80.00 towards Post office concern—old negro charles sick—gave him medicines—hard at work improving the place, no matter what comes, hope, hope, for peace

Friday the 21st October 1842 warm cloudy weather—nothing new to day camp meeting in full blast—all hand going—going, and gone, expect to go to morrow,—maybe—the preachers refused to let Mayfield address the People on the war question to morrow, he is to deliver an address to the Citizens in Town to morrow at 12 oclock, Mr Engledow returned from San Augustin, Parties the Order of the day & *night too.* bad times—the cause, of course:

Saturday the 22d rain last night, Showers occasionally during the day, clear at dark—Major Mayfield who was to have addressed the People to day at the Court house, did so, when the meeting was adjourned to the Camp meeting, where Mr M. delivered a splendid discourse showing the great necessity to Carry the war into the Enemy's Country, it was well received by most all present, and I am in hopes will have a great result, Col Thorn & the rest of the San Augustin Party returned to day

Sunday the 23 rain last night a little showery this morning— Cleared up about 12 oclock, went with the Children to Camp meeting, a Mr Rhodes preached, that is to say, he made noise, rather productive of scaring babys than to convert men to christianity, when a man undertakes to teach others that which he does not, understand himself he must make it up in Bawling, or ranting, or talking, right down nonsense, O! allmighty Father! Creator of the universe! how those children of theine cut up Shines in they holy name—they realy do—"play such fantastic tricks before thee, as to make even they holy angels weep"—Red River mail came & went M. T.

Monday the 24th fine weather, send off Eastern mail—held magistrates Court—went with my wife to Camp meeting, a Mr Cawley from Red River preached or gave a Lecture—a Lecture on Brotherly love—his Text was a very appropriate one "how good & how pleasant it is for Brethren to dwell together in amity" he gave also a moral Lecture to the youth of our country, I am very much pleased with this Man's Discourse, whish all Preachers would be like him

Tuesday the 25th fair cool weather, gel Rusk returned from Red River County on yesterday, mail from west arrived P[r]esident Houston has issued his proclamation convening Congress at Washington on the 14th of next month, received the official communications for the different members of the Northern & Eastern Counties for distribution. delivered & send all off this Evening— Capt English who got Religious last night was Babtised this Evening the Revd Mr Cawley preached at the Court House, of Course every body was there, if not to see a good Christian made out of an old Sinner, but to hear Mr Cawly preach—it is useless to say that everybody was well pleased—Made a contract to day with Mr James Eakin to let him have the Patricio de Torress place till 1st October 1843 for $15.00 better this then nothing, as the place was going to ruin fast

Wednesday the 26 very cold weather last night, white frost this morning busy getting wood for winter—have three men employed send off western mail, wrote to A. McDonald of Huntsville after B[r]eakfeast went to J. M. Acosta's to marry a couple of Mexicans, man named Candelario Perez, very cold this Evening 8 P. M.

Thursday the 27th weather same—busy all day making a Room, by dividing the Store house (or Smoke house) also building a shed to South end of Corn crib for Stable—did not go up to the Office but for a short time at noon—Eastern mail came in at Supper did not open it, not feeling well enough, to go to the office—send Bautista Chirino's Cart home at noon, to day has worked 4 days last week and 2½ days this week in all 6½ days at $1.00 pr day in goods—paid him on account 50¢ in Silver

Friday the 28th weather same, only a much heavier frost last night then before, nothing of consequence came in the Eastern mail we see in the Red Lander an extract from a New Orleans paper accounting the death of Midshipman Culp, Brother to Mrs Terrell, the death was the result of a duel—felt sick all day—feel a little better this Evening—gave my Business of Ma Josefa Sanchez to Col Holland to attend to, on account of no pay—well,!—

Saturday the 29th weather very fine, though a heavy white frost last night—Mr Sandford Holman, and Lady arrived from Home—is at my House—Know not his Business—did not go up Town much to day, busy arranging matters for the coming winter such as firewood eta—no news from the west,

Sunday the 30th weather continues the same—the mail from the North arrived, the old thing—nothing new—Mr Holman left here after dinner, appointed Oscar Engledow Deputy Collector of this place, learned to day that all the waggons which went to Natchitochez came back empty, there not being any groceries whatever in the place, and the River very low for my own part I am not sorry for it, because it will and must turn the attention of our Farmers & Merchants to some place in Texas where such things as the[y] want can be had at all seasons—

Monday the 31st weather same—send off Eastern mail, Probate Court sat as one of the Judges, all the waggons returned from Natchitochez, did bring a Bll Sugar for B. Blake, he let me have fifty Pounds of it, have not agreed on the price, but will go on account of his Board—at work about the place all day, tired

Tuesday the 1st November 1842 weather still fine but not so cold as it has been—Commenced taking up my Sweet Potatoes, a very fair crop—western mail arrived without any thing whatsoever—no news from the west—Mr. Chevallier has a party at his House to night, my folks are going of course. I must see them safely there & back, again. Capt Vail of Natchitochez, and his Cara Sposa arrived to day

Wednesday the 2d fine warm weather, continued all day to take up potatoes, laid a floor in the Boys's Room, this morning send off western mail, send it off nearly as empty as it came—the party last night came off well for the first time in my life I did not dance all night.

Thursday the 3d weather still same, continue taking up Potatoes—papered up the little Room I made—felt very unwell all day—Eastern Mail arrived, brougth, [sic] the intelligence, that Gel Henderson has killed N. P. Garner of San Augustin, send Gel Rusk to go & defend him

Friday the 4th November 1842 fine weather, cloudy towards Evening & looks like Rain—got trough taking up Potatoes at noon —been hard at work plastering in my new Room all day—the Mexican Jose whom I had hired left, his time being out, gave him my double barrell gun according to agreement, nothing more from San Augustin about the Killing of Garner, Gel Rusk left late last night, to be there at the examining trial—Col Mayfield, Muse & Noblett[12] went with him

Saturday the 5th very hard rain last night, cloudy all day but did not rain any more—received from Mr Nelson, *pr Massingal*[13] 200 lb Beef for $7.00 on a/c of Board workt a little, but feel extreemly weak, and getting more so every day, have no appetite, I am almost prostrate yet have no fever, I whish to god we had a good Phisician here—arranged the Papers between Madame Lafleur & Mr C. Chevallier, and am ready for a final Settlement between the parties

Sunday the 6th Cool fair weather, feel much better this Morning made a settlement with Chevallier this morning went up to the Office to send off the Red River mail—a Mr Phipps who has been in Town several days, and who brought a Letter of Introduction to me from A. McDonald Esqr, which he left at my house during my absence at the Office, intend to see him to morrow if I am well enough. Judge Scurry arrived this Evening from San Augustin, Gel Henderson has not yet been examined, the reason is—an Examination is now going on of some persons who are accused of having attempted to steal some negroes from Garner who who [sic] was Killed a few days ago by Henderson

Monday the 7th fair Cold weather, Called on Mr Phipps, find him an agreable gentleman, Doctor Chalmers arrived from the west, Mr Phipps, Doctor Chalmers & Judge Scurry Dined with me, District Court in Session, but a motion was made by Col Mayfield to continue all the Cases, in consequence of the invasion,— not decided till to morrow 10 A.M. Wrote a letter to my Sister

---

[12] John Noblitt.
[13] The 1837 Tax Roll for Nacogdoches County lists an Isaac, George, John and Henry Massingill, probably a family of local farmers.

Nancy, and instruction to Mr Barrett respecting Ogilvy's estate & Capt Thos Ogilvy

Tuesday the 8th November 1842 very cold weather, am nearly entirely recovered from my Sickness—Court met this morning, it was agreed by the Bar that all Civil Cases should be continued, which was done accordingly, the Petit Jury was dismissed the grand jury were empannelled and charged by the Judge as usual, Criminal or State Dockett will be taken up on Monday next, general Rusk returned this afternoon from San Augustin also D. S. Kaufman Gel Henderson is still in charge of the Sheriff— all hands gone to the mill (judge Hart's) this Evening.

Wednesday the 9th very heavy frost last night, very fine weather during the day, the case of the Administration of Cabbells Estate has been laid over for next Court, which gives me the Control of the two Negroes 6 months longer good— Genl Henderson is in Town to day, Judge Ochiltree and Mr Hall of Crockett dined with us to day, Mr Joseph F. Lewis of Rapide arrived to day Robt Mitchell dito, Court adjourned till next Monday, when the Criminal Docket *only,* will be taken up, the grand Jury will only have a Single case to attend to, and that is the Shooting business between the Mexican Jose M. Montes and F. Lazarin,—this tells well for Nacogdochez County— Mr Barrett left this morning for New Orleans wrote an other letter last night to Capt Ogilvy, send by Barrett

Thursday the 10th Cold in the morning, moderated a little during the day with occasionally a little rain, Cloudy & Cold east wind blowing at dark—Court sat only a few minutes to day, decided the Case of Joseph F. Lewis vs A. Sterne Admr of J. Ogilvy to make a title to a league of Land by a Decree from Court I signed the Deed to the Land L. paid me all the money ($50.00) coming to the Estate for Services rendered in that Business exept $15.00 which Mr Lewis promises to pay me next Monday—Judge Ochiltree & genl Henderson dined with us to day—the Judge will no doubt become a Citizen of our Town he is about trading with K. H. Muse for his residence on the Hill,

Friday the 11th November 1842—Cloudy and hard S.E. wind in the morning, cleared up and a Strong Northerner is blowing at dark,--very Cold— nothing of consequence transpired to day, Doctor Kirchoffer dined with us to day,

Saturday 12th November Clear & Cold, Jessy Walling passed trough to Washington—Doctor Starr arrived at home night before last Sick—Muse our Senator will leave this Evening or to Morrow Morning, it is reported in town to day that the army which was going to cross the Rio Grande to chastise the Mexicans, are returning home, don't Know the particulars—rumor says Galvezton is Blockaded. Bedershin—[14]

Sunday the 13th weather same till noon, moderate toward evening, Cloudy, at dark—the red river mail arrived but nothing

---

[14] Sterne here uses a combination of Yiddish and German to express astonishment. A close translation is "if you please."

in it exept, Standards Muse not left yet, James Arnold went to San Augustin, wrote by him to Col J. Z. Berry requesting him to send me $13.00 which I went Security for last Spring, at the different Stands. their (Berry & Mason's) mail rider put up between this place & Cincinnatti

Monday the 14th very mild weather cloudy towards Evening send off Eastern mail, Court in session trying nothing but Criminal Cases, tried three—two not guilty one mistrial

Tuesday the 15th rain at day break this morning, rained till about 2 P.M. wind S.E. at dark—no western mail at 7 P.M. the Court in session to day tried a few petty Larceny cases, and a few assault & Battery cases, none guilty, exept those who plead guilty of assault eta. fined from One to ten dollars Court adjourned till next friday

Wednesday the 16th misty & Cloudy all day, Mail from west arrived, brought a Houston mail but nothing very particularly new, nothing from Mexico, nothing of the Blockade, preparing to go to a party at Mr Chevalliers

Thursday the 17th allmighty Cold this morning, the wind is N.W. and nearly blowing trough a body, had a very fine Party last night at Chevallier's did not send off the western mail, was afraid the little mail rider would freeze—however the Eastern mail came in but did not bring any thing exept the Redlanders

Friday the 18th hard frost last night, very cold day, Court in session tried to get a jury in the Case of Mitchel, Davis and others for Killing Tiger Willis, very difficult matter to get a Jury, adjourned Court till to morrow—send off the western Mail, wrote to George Allen, Houston to inquire into the affairs of Sam B. Eves's Estate which owes me $500. Doctor Kirchoffer left for Crockett.

Saturday the 19th the Cold weather Continues. Court in session those accused of Killing willis not found guilty—Court adjourned till May next, nothing doing, a Mr Cook from Natchitochez arrived, reported that the Steam boat Odessa is sunk above Grand Ecore,

Sunday the 20th very cold day, the sun shone bright yet it froze all day in the shade, Red River mail failed. had preaching by wholesale, during the day and at night

Monday the 21st Cold continues—Sleet in the morning and noon, moderated near dark—raining—send off Eastern Mail this morning, Mr Millard the Overseer on the Road within the Corporation limits, had his Boys out at work to make a new Bridge across the Lanana, and to repair the Road had to quit at 3 P. m. on account of rain & Sleet—Mr Bondies returned to day from Houston, says that (when) he left there were no goods at Houston, nor Galvezton, coffee was not to be had at any price when he left—so that Mr Nations to whom I gave $5.00 to purchase Coffee with, will not bring any—A Mr Rayner (rainer) passed trough here to day from the west, he left Washington on Wednesday last, says the latest news from the west is that Gel Woll is on the Rio Grande, & the Texians returning home destitute of clothing & provisions, there was no quorum when Mr R. left Washington in either House, Seven were wanting to have a quorum in the House of Representatives. does not Know how many were wanting in the Senate—the best thing our Folks can do is to agree to come back home, for I can not see that they can do any thing to make things different from what they at present are exept they make some new Shin plasters to pay themselves!!!

Tuesday november the 22d Weather moderated, and sun shone out a little, quite pleasant out of doors at dark—went to the Office— James Eakin administrator of E. M. Eakin instituted upwards of 30 suits,—bad Business— no monay—J. Nations returned to day from Houston without any thing. there was no Coffee in the City—glorious commercial Emporium of Texas ! ! !—got my monay back, I send for the coffee, took a certificate for 320 acres of Land out of the office issued in favor of James Ogilvy' Heirs,

Wednesday the 23d fine weather, wind N. blew fresh all day, Cold toward night—western mail failed Town extremely dull, several families mooved towards the west to day

Thursday the 24th very fine weather—at 9 A. M. left for San Augustin, in company with gel Rusk. Col Jennings Mr Noblett and gel Smith, at 4 P. m. arrived at Stedham's place where there had been a race of 2 year old untried Colts, Mr Kimbro's Colt won—separated here with my Company, and went home with Sandford Holman Esqr where I staid all night—

Friday the 25th Cloudy in the morning, fair towards noon arrived at San Augustin at 10 A. M. purchased some Coffee and other Articles of Deyoung—after dinner went to see Canfield, Mr Flateau Deyoungs Partner (with whom he has fallen out) returned from Natchitochez expect he will settle his Business amicably with Deyoung—he does well, and let the ge........l go to Heaven— Gel Henderson's Examination before magistrated for the Killing of Garner took place to day, and contrary to my Expectations there was not the least commotion about it in the place, hope all will go well with Henderson for he is a good Citizen *a good man* left San Augustin at 3 P. M. in company with S. H. Hamil Esq Stopped all night at Milton Garretts—he was not at home but [we] were extremely well treated by his Servants who Knew me, had a fine Supper and a fine Bed to Sleep on—

Saturday the 26th November 1842 very fine weather—left at day light, passed over the Attoyaque Bridge, and saw several fine Plantations which have been made since I was here before—arrived at home at 12 oclock—after dinner went to the office tried two cases which came on to day the mail arrived during my absence from the west brought nothing, the last news from Washington (Texas) there was no quorum, and not likely to be one, as the western members are all against, the Congress's meeting in Washington

Sunday the 27th a little rain, Kept up a drisly rain all day. no northern mail. most outrageous dull day. Mr Holland dined with us to day. the Misses Sims are packing up to moove to Washington

Monday the 28th rain all night last, and all day to day, Cold weather wind N. E., send off Eastern mail wrote to C. M. Gould, Flatau and Canfield, Probate Court not much Business—Gel Rusk returned from San Augustin. Henderson got discharged honorably, good, very good,— the Miss Sim's are packing up to leave here for washington, am very sorry for it. will Create quite a void in our little Society not easy to be filled up

Tuesday the 29th Cloudy all day, weather moderated towards Evening and looks like it would clear off, wrote Summonses all the morning, went up to the office, but found all blank—

Wednesday the 30th beutifull weather to day—the Estate of L. B. Brown has not been administered on, was appointed temporary administrator—dont like it at all, for the widow dont understand the Laws,—and will blame me as intermedling which is [far] from me—went to Lee's but have not taken any Property in my possession, hope the widow will take the Administration into her own hands—which will enable her to pay of all debts the Estate owes in one year out of the hire of the negroes—no business was done in the Office to day exept a few Suits instituted, worked a little to day making an alteration in the smoke house. set the negroes at work today to clear the field for ploughing—the Misses Sims, Miss Hotchkiss, Miss Forbes Col Mayfield, Nelson, and Edwards spend the Evening with us

Thursday December the 1st 1842 very cold weather, a hard white frost last night,—Mr Francis von der Hoya and his Clerk Commenced to Board with us to day at $32.00 pr month the two— nothing doing in Town—Eastern & western mails arrived but brought nothing—as usual— David Snively who returned as far as John Dursts from Washington on his way back to the United States. he brought me a letter from Judge Scurry dated 18th ult— no quorum, and not likely to be one so no Congress will meet at Washington;—wrote an answer to Scurry to be send in to morrows mail.

Friday the 2d not quite so cold this morning as yesterday send off western mail—a Mr Butler from Galvezton arrived, enquired about two Leagues of Land granted to Pedro Bermea one which is located on Pine Island Bayou which was sold by a Mr John Ricord to a Gentleman in New York. questionable if Ricord has full power to sell it, and if he had if part of it dont belong to the Estate of Jas Ogilvy,— Col Thorn returned to day from Natchitochez brings nothing new, weather moderated and wind South quite warm after dark.

Saturday the 3d weather moderate, rather warm towards Evening. paid Chas Chevallier my account and note of $72.00 up to the 1st of this month, also a $45.00 note I gave Thos J. Moore on the 19th February last for 15 Blls Corn, in the following way the claim I have on Ogilvy's Estate is $250.00, which if collected within 3 months from date Mr Chevallier gets the amounts above mentioned out of it, but if it is not paid then I give him my whole Claim on said Estate, Swapt Horses with Mr Chevallier got $30.00 to booth [sic] which I paid over to the Misses Sims for Schooling I owed them, paid them all now exept $8.00 which I must pay them shortly, Swapt the Horse I got from Chevallier for a Horse of S. M. Orton's. got my own note for $22.00 the shooing of a Horse all round and half a Hog to boot,—at all events I paid up nearly $200.00 of my debts to day—good days work any how— Mr Buttler left fo[r] home. Judge Ochiltree, wheeler, Roberts and gel Henderson of San Augustin passed trough here on to Crockett Court, Gel Rusk, and Col Jennings are also gone to the same place, saw Col Thorn to day but has no news from the U S.— bought a Beef of Banigno Santos for $8.00—there is a ventriloquist in Town to night. received a Letter from Benayah Thompson, informing me he has Surveyed the Land belonging to him and my son Charles (the Head right of Conrad Eigenauer) Letter filed with "Letters on Business"

Sunday the 4th Weather same as yesterday, Red River mail arrived latest news from Clarksville 5th ult—David Snively was in Town to day, dull day—

Monday the 5th Very warm Sultry weather, send off Eastern mail, received a letter from Jessy Walling dated Washington 26th ult, the House had a quorum, Senate had not yet a quorum but expected to have one monday last. sold my Moral land to Wm Smith a free man of Color for $400.00 payable half in 12 and the other half in 24 months, no interest on the first note, and 10 pr cent int pr annum on the last note from date till final payment, with mortgage on the land till final payment. in the afternoon Smith who was going to take possession of the place to day, came and told me, that John R. Clute prevented him from taking possion (that arch Scoundrel who wanted to swindle me out of that land several times) I went out accompanied by David Rusk Esqr, and put Smith in possession of the House and premises, without seeing that Coward Clute, returned home near dark—I owed John S. Roberts forty two Dollars & 6½ bits, for the $12.82½ I translate a Spanish Title for him, and $30.00 I am to settle after Mr J. C. Morrisson in his and my land trade

Tuesday the 6th this morning rain wind S.E.—E.N. and S.E. again this Evening, had a very fine Party last night at Col Thorns, nothing doing, all day rain— Mr D. Snively Dined with us—

Wednesday the 7th rain, rain, rain, done some business at the office arranging a new Stable at home—two waggons loaded with Cotton, went trough from Crockett bound for Natchitochez, something new this—a ventriloquist named Hervey amused the People this Evening with his rare powers notwithstanding the mud

Thursday the 8th December Clear weather, Wind north but not too Cold—the western mail arrived last night, did not see it till this morning, nothing but a few Letters (apparently such) were put in but the Boy having rode two days in the rain so that the whole Contents were so mangled, and mixed up that it looked more like mush then anything else, so that nothing can be read, to find out to whom the documents belong or where they came from — Eastern mail came in the Evening without bringing any thing exept the Redlanders for subscribers in this County— Smith, to whom I sold some land a few days ago was in to day and said that Mr Clute has not interrupted him since he has remooved to the place—

Friday the 9th very cold, white frost this morning, nothing of Consequence happened to day, it is ascertained that several more of the New Orleans Banks have resumed Specie Payment, good. the Red River is up—so that several Boats have been at Natchitochez, good again—done some Business in the Office to day

Saturday the 10th white frost again this morning, beutifull weather during the day, several People from the country in Town, to day, Mr Hamilton arrived from Natchitochez, Col Thorn & Family left here for Natchitochez, Mr Man, Cousin of the Misses Sims, arrived from Washington to take the Sims Family away. Mr Flatau arrived from San Augustin, stops with us— the Bill of sale and mortgage made out on yesterday between Wm Smith and myself about my Moral land we signed to day, and gave them to be recorded in the proper office. wrote a Letter to my Brother Isaac, send it by Wm Smith who is going to Natchitochez, to morrow

Sunday the 11th weather same as yesterday, the Red river mail arrived, carrier said that, he has not been to Marshall (his destination) in consequence of the Bayous, and River Sabine being so Swollen by late rains, that they are impassible, was introduced to Mr Mann[15] of Washington, Texas. David Snively left for Clarksville, and Mr Gardner to New Orleans—

Monday December the 12th 1842 weather still same as yesterday and the previous days—send off Eastern mail, (for the first time since I have been post master) without the least thing in them, not one single Letter or paper— the Misses Sims,—Ann—Maria & Elizbeth—left here to day, the old Lady and Miss Martha remain to go in a week or ten days—Mrs Durst and Mrs Terrill in Town. nothing new. Mr Flatau has made an arrangement to take Mr Graham's Store house at 15 dollars per month, I am glad some one will establish a Store here, so that we can get supplied and not have to be without Shoes for weeks together—Nacogdochez will come out yet, if we can only get peace from Mexico,

Tuesday the 13th weather still same—many persons in Town Mrs Terrill and Mrs Durst dined with us to day, nothing of consequence transpired.

Wednesday the 14th weather same—Mr Flatau left here—wrote by him to my Sister in New Orleans—to Capt Peter Delmore & C. M. Gould, to the latter about getting a lot from him which he has in this place, to Capt Delmore about sending me the articles I wrote to him about in a former Letter, and to my sister a letter of introduction—the western mail arrived, everything wet,

[15]The 1840 Census for Washington lists a William Mann.

— 131 —

nothing however for this place, congress it appears in session, I presume doing what they have allways done—nothing—

Thursday the 15th weather same as yesterday—weather moderated about noon, and turned Cold again near dark—Mr Davidson the contractor of mail route No 5 arrived from Washington—he says that nothing is doing, that there is just a quorum to do Business, but nothing is done, nor is anything intended to be done (by the western members) for if any thing is intended of any consequence and it comes to the focus—one of the western members makes himself scarce, or absquatulates, to defeat the Bill, in order to *devil* the Eastern members to go to the City of the Mountains Austin—route no 5 will be discontinued on the 1st January next—good—no use no how—send off western mail this morning—received Eastern mail this Evening, and brought nothing exept the Red Lander from San Augustin

Friday the 16th weather a little moderate, not so very cold, yet cloaks and *Blankett Coats* are not disagreeable things. paid Doctor Starr $170.80 on account of what I am indebted to K. H. Douglass's Estate, remain Still in debt about $83.00 which I hope to settle soon, issued some dozen or more Executions in favor of Starr as administrator of Douglass, been rather busy all day in the Office, Mr Wheeler from Crockett Court passed trough here, the Court at Crockett is adjourned, the Judge (Ochiltree) gone to Washington, no other news of importance

Saturday the 17 December 1842 weather moderate, held an Election for Justice of the Peace to day. Bennett Blake Esqr was reelected, done some business in the office, many people from the Country were in Town—nothing new of consequence wrote a letter to Madame Pedro Ybarbo respecting her Houses & lots in this place send the letter pr Policarpio Flores—

Sunday the 18th weather same, rather cloudy—Red River Mail failed—Lodge met and held the annual Election for Officers Charles S. Taylor elected master, Blake Sr Warden Judge Hart Jr warden, Parmalee Secretary and C. Chevallier Treasurer, a Mr Burton from San Augustin arrived from washington brought some Papers, nothing new

Monday the 19th weather same send off Eastern mail—wrote to J. P. Border, not on important Business, did not go to the office till after dinner, busy all morning pruning Trees in the Orchard, had some Rey sowed in the Orchard,—

Tuesday the 20th fair weather North wind, but not very cold, Doctor Greer from San Augustin passed trough here, brings no news from washington exept that nothing is doing nor any thing likely to be done by this Congress— Mr B. E. Phillips who returned to day last from the west says there have been two expresses received by government that our *Boys* have gone across the Rio Grande,—and in my opinion a grande flogging they will get—I hope it may not be so—Mr Jno. W. Burton and Henry Crutcher in Town, Mr Wm Scurry arrived after an absence since the last 4th of March. received a letter from C. M. Gould giving

— 132 —

Adolphus Sterne Home

EVA ROSINE STERNE
WIFE OF ADOLPHUS STERNE.

Mrs. Adolphus Sterne

A shoe buckle belonging to the Sterne family.
— Courtesy the Sterne House Museum

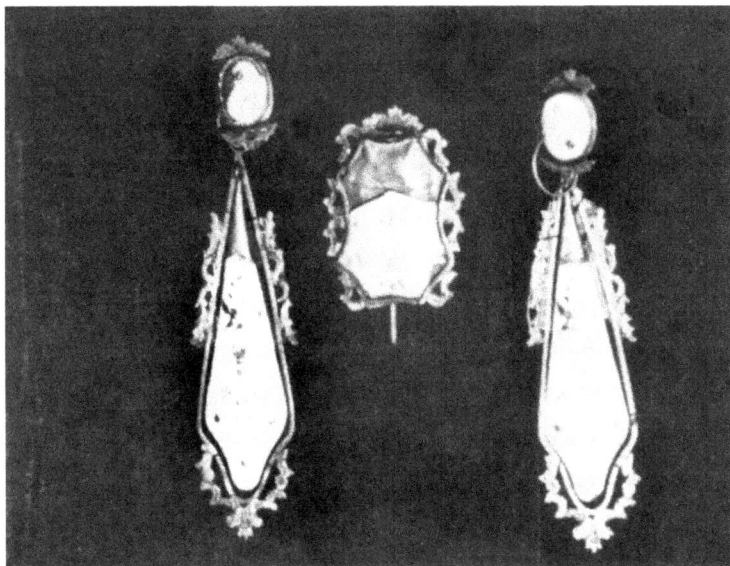

Jewelry of the Sterne family.
— Courtesy the Sterne House Museum

Old Stone Fort

me permission to take possession of the Lot fronting the square, at a ground rent of—see the Letter which is filed—

Wednesday December the 21st white frost this morning—Mr Wm K. Scurry gave me an order for fifty dollars payable in goods in any Store in San Augustin, Send it down by Mr A. A. Nelson who went to the Red lands to day—to see if the Order is good—wrote to C. M. Gould— if the Order above mentioned is good it will be payment in full for Mr Scurry's Board he owes me, he is also to pay me fifty dollars in Exchequer Bills on his return from Washington, Mr Nelson paid me four dollars in Silver, which I paid to Miss Martha Sims—said Four dollars were payment in full for Mr Nelsons Board up to the 15th of this month, from which time he is to pay $16. pr month cash or in such things as he can give me I may be in want of at Cash prices—

Thursday the 22d very cold—done some Business in the office—was introduced by gel Rusk to a Major Peters[16] from Bowie County, mail from the East arrived but brought nothing exept the Red Lander— gel Rusk is announced as a Candidate for the next Presidency—good—

Friday the 23d Cold, same as yesterday—rode out this morning with Mr F. Hoya to Capt English's Plantation where Mr C. E. Taliaferro lives—got acquainted with his Lady who is a very fine amiable woman fit to be an Ornament to any Society, but poor Ned her husband, unfortunately nature has cast him in One of her roughest moulds, *ned* amongst good fellows is a hail fellow well met—but how *such* a woman could marry *such a man* is certainly a puzzle to me—the trade I formerly made with H. K. Carson respecting the waggon & the Hogs at Ruegs place was rescinded to day—and he is to have the one half of my share for taking care of them, this may be a bad trade on my side but I consider the Hoggs as nearly lost any how—and any thing I get will be that much saved for had it not been for the much trouble I took last year to find out something about the Hoggs they would have all been lost before this time

Sunday the 25th December 1842 Christmas day, a rainy, nasty, mean, day it is and the poor fellows who take a drop on Christmas are to be pitied, not a single thing in the shape of Liquor in Town, no matter we had a most Splendid dinner (exept wine) Judge Hart, his Lady, Mrs Mason, Miss Martha Sims Miss Sarah Forbes, Mrs Lewis, and Major Burton from Crockett dined with us, and we passed the afternoon very agreeably, near Evening Judge Hansford[17] came in Town, but went out again soon after, and near Candle light Mr Barrett[18] returned from New Orleans brought no news for me—saw my Brother Issac at alexandria, was well.

Monday the 26th fair weather, South wind, send off Eastern

---

[16]Possibly W. S. Peters.
[17]John M. Hansford, magistrate of the Seventh Judicial District. Hansford was also a physician.
[18]Thomas C. Barrett.

mail, Probate Court in Session, but did not do much Business saw Mr Barrett but had little conversation with him. worked in the garden trimming trees all day nearly—

Tuesday the 27th Saint John's Day— Cloudy, and occasionaly drizley rain; Instalation of officers took place to day, had a very pleasant time of it, sat down to a very fine Cold Collation, at 3 P.M. had plenty to eat but nothing whatever to drink but water; I belive in temperance but a few bottles of good wine upon such an occasion is not very disagreeable. Mr Farmer, the Schoolmaster is staying with us at present till he can make arrangements to get monay for his passed Services—I do not charge Mr Farmer any Board—and he has volunteered to give my children a lesson or two dayly provided he has no other Business to attend to—

Wednesday the 28th December 1842 rain last night, fair to day. Western Mail arrived to day and as usual nearly empty. received a Letter from the Post Office Department, instructing me not to have Letters advertized which may remain on hand at the End of the quarters unless the publisher will take 3 cents each letter— received the Houstonian Containing Judge Scurry's Speach on the motion to adjourn to the City of Austin, if the argument is not a brilliant one, it is full of good sense, and truth; which is not often the Case now a days, on similar occasions,

Thursday the 29th fine weather— the ballance of the Sims family left to day for Washington, Eastern mail arrived brought a few Letters no Red landers, Boys took Christmass Hollidays—was at home all day at work

Friday the 30th very cold, but fair hard frost last night, made out my quarterly Post office returns, Judge Terrell passed trough here to day for San Augustin, nothing doing— gave my note for $39.64 to J. S. Roberts for my part of the payment of Mr Farmer for teaching my two Boys Charles & Joseph—also gave my note for $22.00 to Wm M. Moore for work done on my Cart—

Saturday the 31st last day of the [week], last day of the month and last day of the year—had a very heavy white frost last night, day very fine moderate towards Evening, moved out of my office in the Stone House into the Frame House in the rear of Millards grocery, the Bakers old residence, many Country people in Town to day

Sunday January the 1st 1843 New years day, very cold weather during the night, warm after 10 oclock A.M. and cloudy near dark—last night the Kitchen and Store room of Mr F. T. Phillips was burnt down and every thing in the Building Containing Sugar Coffee, and other articles. Mrs Taliafero Mother in law of C. E. Taliafero arrived to day. made an arrangement with Massingail to take charge of my Hoggs on the Other side of the Angelina. gave him half of all he saves, Parmalee made the same arrangement with him. —a very dull new years day, not a drop of anything to drink—Mr Beckton preached here

Monday the 2d Cloudy this morning, cleared up, and was very fine weather during the day, Mr Gibson from Natchitochez arrived in the Evening I went out to Bautisto chirino's House to marry a couple. Santiago Toscano to Ma. E. Ybarbo. returned home at ½ past 10 P.M.— the wind has changed to the North and a fine clear Sky

Tuesday the 3d fair Cold weather, moderate towards Evening several persons from the Country in Town, sale day--but nothing selling— done some business in the Office, worked the rest of the day with the Cart and Horse—Judge Ochiltree returned from washington says that Congress is doing business quietly, I hope they may do something to benefit the Country, for god Knows we are at a very low Ebb in every respect—Doctor Kirchhoffer returned from New Orleans, gives a gloomy description as regards the price of cotton, but every thing else is equally low as Cotton, Doctor K. says the Democratic party is gaining strength in the U.S. and it is expected that either Van Buren or Calhoun will be the next President; I hope the latter will be—because he is the most favorable to Texas

Wednesday the 4th fine weather, this is the Aniversary of a fight which took place between the Fredonians and Mexicans in 1827. settled to day with B. Blake. took up my notes amounting to $250.00 also an account of $74.34—remained in his debt $115.75 for which I gave my note, made an arrangement with Charles Chevallier to do all the Business he gives me as Justice of the peace and deduct 20 pr cent from my cost but I look only to Chevallier for it, and he to the Persons against whom judgement is rendered,—Judge Terrell returned from San Augustin, Doctor Kirchhoffer left for Crockett, Robert Patton Esqr arrived in town. near dark—

Thursday the 5th January 1843 Cloudy this morning, Clear at noon, very warm after dark. worked all day in the Office, issuing Execution, Judge Terrell left for home. Eastern mail from Sabine Town—brought nothing but Red landers—Sold to solomon Wolfe 100 Trees to day for $25.00. this is the first I have ever received for Trees having allways been in the habit of giving them away —I have *unfortunately* heretofore won many a time a thousand dollars at a game of chance, but it never has given me half the pleasure these twenty five dollars give me, *it is the reward of honest Industry*—received a Letter pr Capt English from A. McDonald of Huntsville, which I answered immediately by John Gillespy, who stays with me to night—

Friday the 6th very windy till 2 P.M. rain, very warm, was employed in transplating rosebushes, Mr Thouvenia[19] paid me a visit, Capt Wheeler from San Augustin arrived. no news

Saturday the 7th very cold, but fine weather, at 10 A.M. left for the Bayou Alazane to marry a couple of Mexicans, Antonio Padilla (alias Pelon) to a Daughter of Juan Isidro Acosta, at dark arrived at the House of J. M. Acosta where there was a dance. found nearly every one of the gentlemen from Town there, re-

---

[19]The Census of 1840 lists an A. Thouvenin as a resident of Liberty County.

mained myself till 10 P.M. and Came home at 11 nearly froze
to death

Sunday the 8th very heavy white frost this morning about 9
A.M. wind shifted to S.E. cloudy, cold wind, a little rain at dark—
Red River mail came in for the last time on that route, being dis-
continued. wrote a long Letter to the general Post office Depart-
ment, several waggons loaded with cotton passed trough towards
Natchitochez

Monday January the 9th 1843 Cold, damp, disagreeable
weather cleared off near night a strong north wind blowing—this
day the Commissioners of Roads and Revenues met. associate
Justices were elected Bennett Blake & myself were reelected, was
appointed on the reviewing out a Road to where Patton has landed with his Boat at the Angelina. Sam S. Flournoy returned from
Washington, brought me nothing but *news paper*. Holland Coffee
Tom Smith & Mr Caldwell came down from Red River, the two
last are going on to Washington, Settled with Mr Hoya remain
indebted to him $48.68

Tuesday the 10th very hard frost last night, wrote a long
letter to the gel Post office Department. send it and my quarterly
returns pr Mr Caldwell from Red River, done good deal of Business in the Justices office for C. Chevallier settled with Doctor
Starr took up my note which I gave him Sepr 1st 1842. Mr Engledow quit to board with me to day his month being out— I also
paid Doctor Starr $6.29 on a/c of Medical Services for the two
negroes I have in my charge

Wednesday the 11th very cold cold weather, Mr Gibson left
this morning send by him for some few Articles which He promised to send me, but he returned again this Evening with Mr
Wheeler of San Augustin, a Mr. Rose a Lawyer formerly of New
Orleans now of Galvezton passed trough here, reports that England has made Peace with China, and that Cotton had risen a Cent
pr pound, good—several waggon loads of Cotton left here to day
for Mr Hoya bound for Natchitochez

Thursday the 12th the Cold continues, wind blowing very
hard all day N.W. a little business doing now dayly in the office—
Eastern Mail came in no particular news. received a letter from
John V. Scott Son in law of my friend Mrs Silverberg. the letter
is dated Canton August the 6th last and by P. M. Flournoy who
neglected to deliver me the letter and only happened to think of
it to day, and send it by the mail Boy. was introduced to Mr Rose
from Galvezton, he is the Attorney of the New York Company,
and has Business with Mr Archibald Hotchkiss—

Friday January the 13th the intense Cold is still continuing
notwithstanding the Scarcity of monay, if a negro is for sale *cheap*
People *have* monay to purchase, Col Tipps whom no one *accused*
of having monay bought a negro woman to day of Mrs Wadlington
for $500.00 and paid all down, and I venture to say that if 50
negroes were brought into this County to sell for Cash purchasers
no doubt could be found with monay to give for them— Miss E.

Culp & Mr John Dursts little Daughter came in to day, My little Daughter and the rest of the younguns had a dance at my House to close the day. went to bed at 12 and left them dancing—agreed to go with F.v.d. Hoya across the Sabine to Stills's on some business

Saturday the 14 very cold, but not so much as yesterday— done some Business in the office, several Executions issued against Wilson (J. H.) he is gone poor devil he was badly *used up* here— bad place for Rogues to carry on their trade this Texas—Making ready to go with Hoya across the State, wrote a very long letter to J. W. Collins about his business with Ramsdale—send also pr Mr Hoya all Papers belonging to two Leagues of Land, claimed by Gel Morgan, and the Heirs of S. g. Clark, I send in the Claim for $100.00 which if Hoya dont get, he is to bring me back all the papers—

Sunday the 15th left home for San Augustin accompanied by Mr Mayfield & Mr F. v.d. Hoya, got to george Teal's stopped all night

Monday the 16 weather moderate left Teal's after an early Breakfast arrived at San Augustin at 10 A.M. Town improving, all the vacant Houses which were so only a few months ago now have Tenants, it is one of the sure signs that our Western Country is breaking up, San Augustin will rise by the downfall of the Western Country but if we have Peace with Mexico and People can live in Security on the western frontier—San Augustin will be an *indifferent sort* of a village, was introduced to Mrs Morange the Mother in Law of Mihael Deyoung, her Sons and Daughter, a very beutifull girl, dined with Canfield. went to Burrill Thompsons—to stay all night—

Tuesday the 17th January weather still moderate—Concluded not to go any further East, Sabine very high—Mr Hoya went on with C. H. Gibson to Natchitochez —and myself returned to San Augustin, Stopped on the Road to see my old friend and acquaintance Mrs Elisha Roberts also Mr and Mrs Sublett, arrived at San Augustin at 11 A.M. Dined with Deyoung. heard miss Morange perform on the Piano—herself and her Brother performed a Duet composed by Braham it was a treat indeed, such a one as I do not expect again in Texas—left San Augustin at 2 oclock P. M. and stopped all night at Walter Murrays

Wednesday the 18th Cloudy and looks very much like rain, left Murrays early before Breakfast, arrived at Home at 10 A.M. news from the west during my absence, our Troops appear to be in Hockelty surrounded by Woll's Troops—god grant them a safe delivery. nothing new up Town—Mrs John Durst and Daughter came into Town, Miss Maria Hotchkiss dito—all hands including Doctor Starr his lady Judge Taylor Miss Sarah Forbes, and a Gentleman from San Augustin spend the Evening here, passed the time very agreably till 10 P.M.

Thursday the 19th Cloudy warm weather. Occupied all the forenoon in planting Trees in my nursery, translated a land Title for Wm K. English, Mr Frizzell & Lady (a sister of Mrs Terrell's) arrived here on their way to to Martin Lacy's old place, west of the Angelina, Mr Gardner arrived from New Orleans, had not time to speak to him, heard of the Death of Isaac W. Burton of Crockett, Poor Burton, he had his faults like many of us, but he was a noble generous, man his bravery could not be doubted, and he has been some Service to his Country—I knew him since 1832 —*Resquiat in Pace.* Mail from east—some few letters, and Red landers, bare of news—Treaty between Texas & the U.S. ratified, Cotton Peltries Hides eta go into the united States free of duty— *good. Major Reily here are* my thanks

Friday the 20th January a rainy, bad, disagreable, weather— translated a land title for Wm. K. English—which makes our accounts square up to this day—traded my Horse I got from Murray Orton to Mr Joost, got a Poney, and a very fine Double Barrelled gun to booth — good trade — was housed up all the afternoon. continues raining as bad as ever at dark

Saturday the 21st Still cloudy and very warm, but no rain, looks clear at noon, all hands went down to Judge Harts Mill, sat down to a fine Supper, and afterwards danced till passed midnight

Sunday the 22d fine weather, yet it is very warm, rose early and came up Town with Judge Hart, left all the rest of Party at the mill, General Darnell and Col Hewett[20] arrived from Washington, received a Brief from the grand master of the g[rand] L[odge] of the Republic as Deputy District grand master for this, San Augustin, Sabine, Shelby, Jasper, and Houston Counties; they bring nothing more new from the west; about a dozen Ladies & Gentlemen passed the Evening at our House

Monday the 23d weather same as yesterday, worked in the garden till dinner, send off Eastern mail early this morning, had a very fine Party at the House in the Evening danced till 3 A.M.

Tuesday the 24th weather continues warm and cloudy, feel very much fatigued this morning from the effects of the last nights frolic

Wednesday the 25th weather in Statue quo. worked all day in the garden, went up Town near night, saw no body, was glad to return home again, Mr. Lussan[21] who has resided here since 1837, commenced with nothing and made a *Little fortune,* took into his head to get crazy, he left here yesterday never to return, he left Mr Joost in Charge of his Business Poor Fellow he took with him $4000.00 in cash—enough to turn any man crazy now a days, on an average this is a very unhealthy climate for frenchmen, three, within my knowledge within the last three years have committed Suicide, and no doubt Lussan will never reach France his few goods he left here will bother him so much as to make him drown himself, if he dont hang himself—

---

[20]Probably Henry M. Hewitt, who represented Shelby County in the Sixth Congress. He served in the army during the campaigns against Vasquez and Woll.

[21]John Lussan.

Thursday January the 26th weather very warm, worked all day in the garden, Mail from East came in, brought nothing but Redlanders, which however is more interresting this week than it has been for many previous weeks—David Rusk is to be married to night, all hands gone out to John Reids the Bride's Fathers House.

Friday the 27th fine weather a little Cloudy occasionally— not much news Stirring—Gel Rusk gives a Ball this Evening the whole world is invited—went with my wife & Eugenia *of course,* staid till one A.M. Mrs Philipps stops with us to night, went to bed tired to death, and tired of frolics

Saturday the 28th weather a little Colder, had a great Mass of Business in the office about 35 cases to try—went trough all them without difficulty, Wm F. Sparks our Representative in Congress was in Town to day, all hands round him, and so a body would—Bill has improved in every way, he speaks of Bills (not wild Bills), Committees, 1, 2 & 3d readings, vetoe's and so on, like an old veteran of the House so here goes for *Colonel William F. Sparks* and let wild Bill, Devil Bill, and fool Bill, be forever buried Amen.

Sunday the 29th a very disagreable day rained all night in torrents, Keeps on raining 10 A.M. finished translating a long Land Title for David Brown of San Augustin. stopped raining near dark. went to the office, all still and dreary, settled up with Mr H. K. Carson. struck off even up to date

Monday the 30th weather fine after such a boisterous day. as we had yesterday, it is quite exhilirating to look at a fine Clear Skye and feel the influence of a bright Sun—Probate Court to day, sat as one of the associates, examined M. G. Whitakers & Mrs Bigham's accounts will have an extra session of the Court on the 9th next month C. S. Taylor handed in my Petition to sell land in the Ogilvy Estate to pay the debts of said Estate, also to divide the League & Labor of Land belonging to his wife & mine obtained as the heirs of John Everhart Ruff from the Board of Land Commissioners of this County & for which a Patent has been obtained which is in the Posession of C. S. Taylor

Tuesday January the 31st 1843 the wind blowing a strong gale from the N. W. all day, and is very cold, yet the sun shone in great splendor, this day is one of the many blanks,—Major Cesna's Family passed trough here to reside on John Dursts Place on the Angelina, Parson Bacon in Town from San Augustin made out a Statement of James Ogilvy's Real Estate—it is as cold as the North Pole at 5 P. M.

Wednesday the 1st February 1843 very cold, cold, weather, however had a bright sun all day, a few waggons came in with a *few* things but no assortment of goods—what a fine Business a first rate Mercantile Establishment would do here, these little Concerns will not do well—Lafayette a Son of Mr Holland arrived to day from New Orleans.

Thursday the 2d weather this morning same—abating in its

asperity towards noon, wind changed, from the South, worked a little in the garden not much Business stirring

Friday the 3d weather moderate, rather warm, received a **Package of Papers** and Letters from Mr Flatau, he is no[t] coming here too much attraction in San Augustin, well—all right—Eastern Mail arrived nothing new particularly—

Saturday the 4th Weather as yesterday — decided several suits to day in the Justices Court—Capt Wheeler of San Augustin in Town no news from the west, nor any hopes of getting any soon. paid off some Mexicans for getting picketts to fence in the garden opposite the House, also for Posts and railings, gave orders on Charles Chevallier's Store for all the payment of the workmen and Laborers—Milam L. No 2 met this Evening at Richard Parmaly's House.

Sunday the 5th Cloudy in the morning—started for San Augustin—was very fine weather in the afternoon, arrived at San Augustin after sunset— put up at Mr Whitlesey's Tavern, was introduced to Mr Montrose, the President (or some such name) of the San Augustin University,[22] a Scotchman who is no doubt a very Clever fellow and has seen the world, but makes the *Natives* of San Augustin belive he is a perfect curiosity—!! go it my Montrose—gull the Augustin Classic Parents with your Greek, Latin, and Algebra, but you can not cram your learning down the .... of such Ignoramuses as we are in Nacogdochez

Monday February the 6th 1843 weather cold in the morning, changed at noon to nearly oppressively warm, and to a cold N.E. wind before 8 P.M. —rose early this morning, went to see Mr Flatau, who changed his mind about coming to reside here it is probably as well—we will no doubt have a fool less in our Burgh— saw Mr T. G. Brooks he has not received his goods as yet, but beliving him to be perfectly honest I gave him a due-Bill I had on him for $50.00 and told him to send me such goods as I want which he agreed to do, taking a memorandum of the articles I want. purchased several articles for my Family, left some Spanish Documents and the Translations of them I made with Mr S. T. Burnes at Mr Carthwrights to be delivered to Mr David Brown (when he pays $10.00)—an Election for Sheriff of the County going on. Sam Davies—the Brother of the Chief Justice is Elected—all hands appear satisfied—dined with J. D. Thomas—saw Mrs Deyoung and Family. made application for membership to the Royal Arch Chapter of San Augustin—and at 4 P. M. started for home—stopped all night with that amicable Family George Teal—

Tuesday the 7th Cold Cloudy weather left after early Breakfeast, overtook Wm Jones and general P. Pinckney Henderson on the Road. a drissly rain is falling during the afternoon, but not

[22]The University of San Augustine was founded by the people of that community and chartered on June 5. 1842. Marcus A. Montrose was its first president. and he served until 1845. James Russell served as president from 1845 until 1847, when the school closed.

enough to wet any one—arrived at home at dark—found all my family well

Wednesday the 8th very Cold damp, hazy, cloudy, *mean* weather, went up to the office attended to some suits, issued some more Summonses arranged the Papers of the office—purchased a horse from Mr Thos Barrett for $80.00 to be paid by boarding him at $16.00 pr month. send word by Esquire Ewing to Mr Reynolds who lives on the Pierre Boden place (as it is generaly know[n]) being the property of my wife & Mrs Mayfield—to come in and make some arrangement about his remaining on it for the next year or he will be sued and put off—that he may have all the benefitt of next years Crop for the improvements he has made and if he wants it after that, it will be an other arrangement, but I must have papers drawn on the subject—

Thursday the 9th February 1843 weather same as yesterday, moderated a little towards Evening, sold the grey Poney I purchased sometime ago from Joost to Anastacio Barela for $30.00 payable in peltry, Hides or Beef eta made also a compromise with James H. Starr about a note he holds of mine for a League of Land purchased at admr Sale of the Douglass Estate, and in which Judge Terrell was in copartnership with me, the note was for $2000.00 which would have taken the same land, and all I have besides to pay, by Judge Terrells verbal Instruction to me I made as good an arrangement as I could, which is I gave him the land back, and the matter is dropt, but Judge Terrell owes me now half of the amount of Land (¼ of a league) or its equivalent which if he is an honest man he will pay me, or in case of death to my Family; the Eastern Mail came in nothing but Redlanders, hardly worth while to read as all the news it contains has been Known here for several days past

Friday the 10th very hard rain last night, Cleared up, and a west wind at 8 A. M. which Changed during the day to a North wind, a fine clear Skey near dark. did not go up to the office all day was occupied in making a new fence around the garden in front of our House, tired to death.

Saturday the 11th white frost last night—fine weather during the day, was employed as yesterday, nothing new up Town

Sunday the 12th very heavy dew this morning, sun shone out out [sic] bright at 9 A.M. was left alone to Keep house, Mrs S. gone to Capt Hotchkiss's and part of the Childern gone to Mr Taylor's nothing doing, nor nothing done this day—

Monday the 13th warm & Cloudy, send off Eastern mail wrote a letter to S. T. Burnes, send him a certificate for the Heirs of John D. Lacy (Mr & Mrs Blount) which being in payment in full for a League of Land sold in New Orleans by me in 1837— that is to say said certificate and an other one like it was in payment of said head right, of said Lacy—also let Mr Burnes Know respecting a deed of Land made by Edmund Quirk in 1828 to John Bodine, —Mr Barrett left here for San Augustin—busy all day haling rails for the Enclosure of the field—Burrell Thompson in Town.

Tuesday the 14th February 1843 last night about 9 o'clock a hard north wind began to blow it rained a little, and this morning it is Sleeting and getting colder every moment, about noon it sleeted so much that it resembled more a Snow storm then any thing else. in the afternoon so cold that all out door work had to be suspended—Mr S. T. Burnes to whom I had written yesterday came up here last night. he had however received my letter and inclosed Documents, which he promised he would attend to, gave up to Doctor Starr, all the papers I had in my Possession respecting the League of Land and the House and Lot of K. H. Douglass Estate, which he also took back, so that I am released from that trouble also, thereby Killing $2600.00 worth of notes which had my name on them, by degrees I'll get them all in, and I'll be very carefull how I give out others again

Wednesday the 15th hard, very hard frost last night, a bright sun Saluted mortals Eyes this morning, yet it is Cold. the day passed without any particular *doings*

Thursday the 16 very hard frost last night, fine bright Sun this morning, Mr Burrill Thompson stayed with me last night early this morning continued to make my fence round the garden opposite the house, was very busy at work at it all day, Mr Holland spend the Evening with us—had some conversation with Gel Rusk about getting Mr A. A. Nelson to teach our children—hope he may accept for he is very capable—more so than any one I Know of now in this County—sold Sam Rodgers' note of $25.00 which I got from Solomon Wolf for apple trees—to Mr Joost for two Sacks Salt. had to endorse the note and become responsible for the payment next January. Eastern Mail arrived, brought nothing but Red landers—and *those* are nearly nothing—

Friday the 17th frost last night, but not very severe, moderated towards Evening, all hands on a frolic to day, made arrangement with Mr Joost to purchase an old negro woman of Mr Lussan, Constance to give him the note I hold against Wm Smith the Colored man who purchased my Plantation provided Lussan has not sold her to Mr Thouvenin or made her a present to Joost— Parson McDonald stays with us to night—

Saturday february the 18th 1843 weather moderated last Evening and have a South wind this morning, Cloudy and looks like bad weather again—worked in the garden—had a Log rolling in the afternoon, A Mr Newel[23] United States Consul for Matagorda Velasco & Galvezton arrived, stays with us tonight, received a letter from Mr Negrevernis from Bayor Sci, nothing of much interest occurred to day

---

[23]Stewart Newell.

"... let it be a warning to those who may read these pages ..."

Sunday february the 19th 1843 weather very warm, cloudy, and a strong South wind blowing at 7 a. m. fine weather the Ballance of the day, my Wife went on a visit to Judge Hart's Mill

Monday the 20th fine weather, send off Eastern mail nothing new. finished pailing in, my garden opposite the House, worked some in the garden—in the afternoon made an enclosure round my Brother in Law's grave (Jeremie). my wife planted all kinds of plants, and flowers. Mr Edrington[1] from washington arrd.

Tuesday the 21 very fine weather, sowed oats, and planted Irish Potatoes, Mr Newell & Edrington remain here to day. Mr Edrington brought me a letter from Mr Toler[2] the present chief clerk of the Post Office Bureau—he is a good old man an old friend of mine since 1829. I got aquainted with him in Matamoros,—he directs me to take possession of all the Effects of the Discontinued Post-offices,—that Scamp Joost flew from his trade about the negro woman; the rascal.—Mr A. A. Nelson paid me twenty dollars on account of his Board. Philipp A. Sublett in Town going on to Washington

Wednesday the 22d Washingtons Birthday—fine weather left home in company with Mr Edrington and Mr Newell for San Augustin, appointed R. F. Millard my Deputy and gave him up my Keys before starting,—went to George Teel's and staid all night— very tired—

Thursday the 23d February 1843 the weather is fine but all the whole country is on fire—to wit—every Farmer is burning Logs or Brush—left Teels after Breakfeast went to San Augustin —purchased a Barrill of Flour and some sperm candles of Mr Peck, paid him the $20. Exchequer Bills I received of Mr Nelson at Six bits in the Dollar, and for which amount Mr Nelson is hereby credited and not for $20.00 as stated in my note of the 21st instant. Mr Hoya returned from New Orleans, says that he has received for me and on my account from the Son in Law of David B. Morgan Eighty five Dollars in Cash, for which amount he is indebted to me, saw Canfield, he has remooved to a fine New Building on Columbia Street, got back my note for $3000.00 and my

---

[1]The Census of 1841 lists a J. F. Edrington from Travis County.
[2]Daniel J. Toler. In 1844 Toler became Post Master General for the Republic.

Bond for two Leagues & two Labors of Land which I gave to Mr John Lacy, the former Husband of Mrs Stephen Blount. I gave him all the requisite certificates to get the two leagues & labors of Land, to pay the Expenses on one of the Leagues and labors of Land, but afterwards on Examining the note of $3000.00 I find that Mr Lacy owed me $30.00 which must be rectified, and which I must attend to—put all my things purchased previously at San Augustin and those purchased to day on Board Caddell's waggon bound for this place—dined with Mr Nelson, Clerk or partner of Mr Wheeler, took a cup of Coffee with Madame Deyoung— and left Town—for home. went as far as George Teel's in company with Mr Hoya

Friday the 24th Cold during the night. Sleeting this morning—went away after Breakfeast, rode till 10 A. M. in the rain, cleared off at noon, dined at Maasts[3] —in company with James Gaines and his wife who is mooving to this County, after having lived 24 years on the Sabine, arrived at home at 3 P. M. all well. Mail from East arrived yesterday, brought me One Letter from Sabine Town from Mr D. S. Kaufman enquiring of me several matters concerning Lands and land titles, which I will answer when a fee is forthcoming.

Saturday the 25th very heavy white frost last night, am fearfull it has destroyed all the Peaches—worked in the garden in the forenoon—had a logg rolling in the afternoon, received my things pr Caddells waggon, which I had purchased in San Augustin

Sunday the 26th very fine weather—saw Martin Birds for the first time this Season—hope the Cold weather is over—wrote a letter to C. H. Gibson, Natchitoches, also, to Radford Berry nothing new to day

Monday the 27th Cloudy weather, haled Rails all day, planted Potatoes, sat as an associate Justice in the Probate Court disposed of several matters, and so closed this day—by the bey a north wind is blowing after Dark, and the whole world looks to be on fire—

Tuesday the 28th very Cold north wind blowing Sleet & frost at noon—nothing very particular happened to day, invited several persons to the Party I am to give on the 2d of March *proximo*

Wednesday March 1st 1843 most bitter cold weather, notwithstanding the intense Cold *made a Room* out of the front gallery for a supper room for the party on to morrow. Killed Pigs, Turkies. Chickens, and so forth, invited all hands—and gave Nelson *Authority to invite* the *rest*—

Thursday the 2d very cold in the morning. Cleared up at noon and a fine day after all—this is the 7th anniversary of the Declaration of Independence—and we are not so very Independent after all—Our Oldest Daughter Eugeny is fourteen years of age to day, gave her a Ball & supper which was a fine a party as

---

[3] Jacob Mast.

has been given in this place so says every body—of Course it must be so—the Dancing did not cease till after day light on the

Friday the 3d Cold still continues, Mr F. Hoya received several waggon loads of goods to day—received of him 200 lb sugar and 140 lb. Coffee, at Cost and charges, being on account of the monay recived for me in New Orleans, sold to Nathan Wade the House & Lot purchased at sheriffs sale Known as Nat Norriss's Lot for $25.00 and a land certificate for 320 acres

Saturday the 4th Rain last night, Keeps on raining this morning. wind north, had a Dinner Party at the House the wines furnished by Mr Hoya, all hands in good humour, saw Doctor Starr to day, did not say much about the trade for the Douglass Property, authorized Mr Taylor to settle the matter for god Knows I do not want a Law Suit, and allthough I Know I am right, yet the cheapest Law Suit is very dear in the long run—a great many Persons in Town. Mayfield left for the west—*I belive* as Major general Rusk's Aid de Camp, to see about matters & things in general

Sunday the 5th March 1843 weather rather fair but looks rather Suspicious—sun shone out at noon, but very Cold towards Evening—was introduced to a Brother of Thomas F. McKinney, of Galvezton, Mr Farmer returned from Red River County, stops at my House, but do not Know his determination about residing here again. the Company who was at the House for several days left for Capt Hotchkiss's. Mr Barrett left for San Augustin, the trade I made with him for the Horse was transferred to Mr Nelson—that is to say I Keep the Horse and Board Mr Nelson five months, which I agreed should commence on the 15th of last month up to which time he has to pay me

Monday the 6th rain last night, rains this morning, and all day and is very Cold, was up to the office but there is not much business stirring, Judge Hart dined with us

Tuesday the 7th tremendous rain last night the Bayou on the East of the Town is overflowing—Cleared up at noon and once more saw the glorious Sun shine with all its splendour. this was sale day. according to law part of Mr Wm Jones's Furniture was sold at sheriff's sale—the first time such a thing has happened since I have been in this Town—fine sign of the times!!!!! after Candle light, I was called out of the Room to see a Phenomenon in the Heavens—it was a very bright Straight reflection of some Starr, commonly called the tail of a Comet—I recollect it is just such a One as I saw when a Boy in (I belive) 1811, it is a very long Tail and going down towards the west—an old african negro in my employ says it is a sign of war—no matter what it is, it certainly is very Strange, and uncommon—[4]

Wednesday March the 8th 1843 very Cloudy this morning

[4]Sterne probably observed one of a number of small groups of comets that reappear along predictable orbits and at regular intervals. Both orbits and time intervals increase each revolution as the groups get further from the sun.

looks like Snow, hail, or rain, Cold enough for either—Cleared up at noon and the Sun went down clear, and it is not very cold, worked in the garden, and done several other small jobs about the House, nothing doing up Town. Bennett Blake who has been boarding with us for more than a year, quit to day, to keep Bachelor's Hall. we part as we met as friends—true friends—

Thursday the 9th Cloudy, hazy, weather, an unaccountable sort of weather—neither warm, nor, Cold, nor sunshine nor Cloudy —but a little of all combined—done some business in the office—at 2 P. M. was called upon by Mr Millard my Deputy P. M. to let me Know that Mr Goodman the new mail contractor has arrived from the west—received the western mail which contained but little news—Mr Goodman tells me that he has the contract for carrying the mail from Lagrange on the Colorado to Sabine Town, on the Sabine—and promises to have the mail carried regularly hereafter—*Ojalá* the arrangement is different from that which appeared in the proposals for carrying the mail inasmuch as Mount Ayry or hairy is made the middle point between the route of Cincinnatti and this place (Douglass ought to have been the *Place*) but the Powers that be—hem!!!—at all events I hope the mail will be carried regularly hereafter—nous verrons—

Friday the 10th March cold windy night, rainy this morning with very cold north wind—Clearned [sic] up at noon and very fine but cold weather this Evening— Mr Canfield of the Redlander, arived this morning, stops with me comes on a Collecting expedition, also to get some testimony about some Land cases in suit in Sabine County—wrote my answer to the Interrogatories, ready to sign tomorrow— settled with Mr Charles Chevallier, gave him my notes (2) for Seventy five dollars each, with a collateral Security on a note in my favor drawn by Wm Smith a free man of colour, got his due bill (chevallier's) for $29.58 payable in his Store, also for my account previous to December I gave him all my right title and Interest in and to the Estate of Ogilvy—

Saturday the 11th Cold, Cloudy, and Sleeting in the morning, but it Cleared of and moderated, Mr Hoya gave a dance at our House this Evening, Mr Canfield here yet, gave testimony in some Suits pending in Sabine County, Heirs of Russell, vs. Vickers, and Mason—done Some business in the Justices office, Hoya received some more goods—

Sunday the 12th fair but very cold weather, nothing Stirring to day.

Monday the 13th very hard black frost last night, fine weather to day, the Eastern & Red River mail arrived once more. hope it may continue, Canfield left for home, found one of our Cows with a young Calf to day—good-luck—

Tuesday March 14th 1843 frost again last night—all the Peaches gone certain—turned out to be a very fine day, wind blowing fresh from S. W., —Commenced to plough to day nothing new in Town—

Wednesday the 15th what not a day may bring forth may

well be said of this day—it was cloudy but warm in the morning, like the Climate of Italy, at 9 A.M. the wind suddenly changed to the north, a severe Storm Thunder and lightning, with a tremendous rain, growing colder and colder every second—rain continued till noon when it commenced Snowing, and at 4 P.M. what was Italy this morning is now changed to Seberia. snowing and freezing—the western mail was made up and I had determined to take it to Judge Terrells myself rather then there should be a failure, but, the sudden change of weather, tremendous rain, cold, and snow, I determined not alone not to go myself, but would not have turned a common curr dog out of Doors. I made up the mail at all events, for the first time in two months,

Thursday the 16 the hardest frost we had this winter was last night, the Sun Shone bright all day, yet in the shade the Snow and Ice did not melt—made an arrangement to day with ygnacio Mendes to Carry the mail from Judge Terrill's to Sabine Town for $250.00 pr annum payable quarterly

Friday the 17th March Saint Patricks day, hard frost last night, and all day a most piercing cold wind blew from the North, send off the Eastern mail by ygnacio Mendez after having administered to him the Oath prescribed by Law. in the afternoon I had an altercation with John Dorsett intierly seekt for on his own part (I belive he is part Irish and wanted to celebrate the day) and he got what he richly deserved, a good beating;—I do not Know if his son or son in Law will take it up—but they would be foolish if they do, Caution is the Mother of Prudence and in this case, I shall pay due regard to Mother and Daughter. and there is some rumor afloat that England will positively interfere between Mexico and Texas, that is that Mexico shall acknowledge our Independence, god grant it may be so,

Saturday March the 18th a hard frost again last night, wind Changed to the South, yet it is very Cold, saw Mr T. Dorsett and made up with him, he having inquired into the matter of the altercation yesterday between his Father and myself and found, that I done exactly right—a Mr Martin from Natchitochez, and Nelson from San Augustin stop with me to day—nothing doing in Town at all—

Sunday the 19th frost last night, fine day to day but a very hard wind blowing from the S. W. which is very cold nothing doing of any consequence—

Monday the 20th frost last night fine day today mail from Sabine Town arrived. no news—

Tuesday the 21st Cloudy last night the day commenced with rain and Kept raining till after Breakfeast, send of the western mail in the rain, it cleared up after dinner and we had a very fine, mild day after all the bad looking weather this morning, wrote to Miss Elizabeth and Miss Maria Sims, also to Mr Goodman informing him of an arrangement with ygnacio Mendez the mail rider—wrote to Post Master at Mount Airy, requesting him to send the mail at that place to morrow morning in place of Thursday Morning

Wednesday the 22d March fine Spring weather all day till near dark when it showed its cloven foot again—it c[h]anged from Spring to the middle of winter again— the western mail came in but did not bring the Galvezton or Houston Mails, and had in consequence nothing in it, exept the Laws of last congress. Col Jacob Snively who arrived here a few days ago bound for *up red River* he dined with us to day.

Thursday the 23d frost last night—a South wind, yet very Cold. nothing new

Friday the 24th frost last night very cold to day, rain Sleet, Snow, and most rascally weather, send of the Eastern mail, loaned my Horse to the mail rider his not being shod, was up Town, but all is dull, silent as the grave, Mr. Hoya started on yesterday to Crocket which I forgot to mention on yesterday, Mr. Parmalee went with him, wrote to George Aldrichto send me a copy of Jose Ma Mora's Survey of a League & Labor of Land, in which I have an interest

Saturday the 25th March 1843 very hard frost last night—sun shines brilliant to day, yet it is very cold, millions of Pidgeons flew over the Town to day . shot one only, some business in the office in the way of Justices court— Board of Land Commissioners met again to day under the new Law. issued only one certificate Spend the afternoon in shooting grouse—

Sunday the 26th weather still cold but no frost last night moderated during the day, day passed as monotonous as usual Jack Gillespy arrived from the west nothing new

Monday the 27th warm last night commenced raining at day light, rained very hard for more than one hour—at 9 A. M. Stopt raining but it grew colder and colder till Evening when a clear Sky and north wind was predominate. saw the comet at 8 P. M. apparently leaving us—cold as Greenland—OH. ho ho ho hum—

Tuesday the 28th frost last night a bright and beutifull Sky this morning, send off western mail wrote to the Gel Post Office Bureau recommending R. G. Hall as a fit man to be Post Master at Douglass—wrote to the Heirs of Bonzano at the City of Houston respecting the claim they have in and to a League & Labor granted to me as assignee of Maria Josefa Sanchez. telling them, that if they dont pay me $100.00 for an improvement made on their part of said Land and purchased by me, that I will bring suit— and so I will, for they have Bamboozled me long enough. Probate Court to day sat as an associate justice of said Court

Wednesday March 29th 1843 had a very little white frost last night— wind changed to the South after Breakfeast had a very fine day—commenced to Plough again, god Knows how long we will be able to continue or when we can plant corn—Met John Dorsett to day as friendly as if nothing had happened— mail arrived from the west, received two letters from Mayfield one from Lagrange and One from Bastrop, also one from Mr Goodman the mail contractor, ratifying the arrangement I made with Madame Procela, about her son riding the mail, received Circular from Gel Post Office Bureau, Major James Reily our late Minister to the U. S. arrived this Evening.

Thursday the 30th warm night, cloudy this morning, notwithstanding the looks of rain, commenced planting corn. it is cloudy, yet no rain at 4 P. M. saw Major Reily—he brings the news that the Yucatan commissioners amongst which young Zavala is—arrived lately in New Orleans and gave Commodre Moore[5] of the Texas Navy $7500.00 for the purpose of fitting out, —Col Wm G. Cook has gone on Board the Austin as Captain of Marines, and Major Howard[6] as Liutenant—well done say I—

Friday the 31st beutifull real Spring weather to day, the wind blew fresh from the north and N. W. yet it was not cold— Burnt Brush. ploughing, and planting corn going on all day. Major Reily dined with us—send off Eastern mail this morning. wrote to Kaufman on Business—concerning Alexander Philipp of New Orleans and others who had claims against George Pollitt,— Made out my quarterly Post office returns—

Saturday April the 1st fine weather—Planting corn working in the garden eta. Mr Hoya returned from Crockett. heard of the Death of Joseph Durst. he died from Plurisy in the Head— nothing new—Lodge met in the Evening

Sunday the 2d fine Spring weather, very dull day all hands gone away some to preaching and my wife and Daughter a visiting, had to Keep house all day—

Monday the 3d very fine weather, opened the office of Board of Land Commissioners. done no Business. heard the news of the grand jury of San Augustin County have found a true Bill against General Henderson, for the Killing of Garner—I am really very sorry for this, not that I fear the ultimate result, but the trouble it will give him, and his Lady. mail arrived from East nothing new—

Tuesday the 4th fine weather all hands busy in the Field and in the garden—send off western mail wrote to Judge Terrill requesting him to pay the Texas Treasury notes he owes me—to the Gel Post office Depart, wrote also to Mr Goodman the Mail Contractor, Sold Madame Louis Procela a Horse for $100.00 payable out of the pay She is to receive for carrying the mail. was introduced to a german named Adler who resides in Natchitochez who resided formerly in Bastrop—

Wednesday the 5th April 1843 a beutifull day, my Birthday —the mail arrived from the west, brought many Letters, none for me—worked all day in the garden, Mr F. Hoya received some more goods, nothing of consequence

---

[5]Edwin Ward Moore, commander of the Texas Navy. His most notable achievement lay in the Yucatan area and in troubling Mexican shipping. He fell out with the Houston administration, and at his own request was given a court martial. The verdict was substantially in Moore's favor, with only minor charges being confirmed.

[6]Probably George Thomas Howard.

Thursday the 6th weather continues very fine ploughing, planting Sweet Potatoes, and working in the garden goes on without intermission—nothing else stirring—

Friday the 7th fine weather, the warmest day this Spring send off Eastern mail. General Davies of Corpus Christy recollection, and a Col Washington arrived—

Saturday the 8th Splendid weather—many People in Town done some Business in the Office, in the afternoon went out to the Carrizo to marry a couple of Mexicans Francisco Cardenas to Thomasa Cordova—Mr Nelson returned from Mount Airy—heard of the Death of Mrs McFarland one of the Oldest Inhabitants in This Country

Sunday the 9th fine warm weather dull day—a Mr H. H. Sibley an old aquaintance of Mrs Sterne's passed trough here

Monday the 10th weather same—Genl Davis who holds my Papers for the Dolores Martinez grant of Eleven Leagues of Land and thereby released me from any further responsibility,—the Eastern Mail arrived full—brought many Letters but none for me & several Newspapers from Clarksville San Augustin and Natchitochez

Tuesday the 11th Spring weather—rather Cloudy in the afternoon. Thunder and lightning after dark, much sign of rain— send off the western mail this afternoon. Sat as one of the Board of Land Comrs passed only one Case—Wrote to the Commanding Officer of Canto[nmen]t Jessupp—send the letter pr Mr Ford— advising the officer that Liutenant Sibly has passed here in pursuit of the Deserter who stole the $2000.00 out of the Pay Masters Department advising him that a certain Mr A. .... was here in Company with the Thief, and Showed much gold Coin—they may take their own Course about this matter but if any one was to abscond from Texas with ever so many crimes on his Back, I doubt whether the Gents of Cantonement Jessupp would pay any attention to it, or assist us in capturing the Criminal—but we ought not to retaliate but act as honest Texians ought to do

Wednesday the 12th Thunder and lightning last night, and Cloudy, but no rain—fine day, the warmest we have had yet this Spring, surveyed the field to day. contains under fence nineteen acres and of that there is now in Cultivation 15 acres. wrote by Francisco Cardenas to Minchacca to let me Know about the land he sold to Douglass. if he sold mine in front of the House or if he only sold his own—Send also by Cardenas a Power of attorney to villegas he gave me in 1839—a note for 100 dollars on J. K. Allen and a Contract between said Villegas and J. M. Medrano. western mail came in brought nothing very particularly new

Thursday the 13th April fine weather, finished planting corn planted some Rice—a Mr Elliott from Louisville Kentucky arrived, brought a Letter of Introduction to me from Gel Henderson; Mr E. is bound for the upper Trinity to Explore that region of Country as an agent for the Company which has lately obtained a grant from our government,—a large company of Equestrians arrived here from the west going on to the United States, they have been in Mexico, times are so hard, and monay so scarce that I belive they will not perform here

Friday the 14th weather same as yesterday, looks like rain, but at noon sun shone out in all its splendour—to day the rest of the Circus Company passed trough here, they had a Baboon, which amused the children very much— Mr Elliott left here to day on his trip to *up the Trinity,* success attend him. send off the Eastern mail this morning crammed full

Saturday the 15th weather cloudy, no rain, yet it is wanting *now* Kept Cloudy all day, a Mr Hart the head Partner of the former Firm of Hart Labatt & Co. arrived here to day, on a Collecting Expedition, *quien sabe* he has a claim of Sixty odd dollars against me, but the firm is owing me $100.00 justly, he is not willing to make a Stand off, but it is just that I should be paid, the $100.00 were to be paid me in a Suit of Clothes for Securing to the Firm a debt of $1500.00 which they though[t] was lost, and which *I* secured to them and for which the aforesaid promise was made, I took some few things out of their Store, amounting as I thought to about half what was promised to me, intending to let them off—but if it is now insisted that I shall pay—they shall pay me—the debt I secured was due them by Doctor Hertz who had absconded

Sunday Easter April the 16th weather very warm — rain wanting, it looks like rain, but thats all—day passed off like all other Sundays. Judge Hart and Lady came in Town, stop with us—Miss Maria Hotchkiss to.

Monday the 17th weather *too* fine, rain wanting very much gardens, drying up, Mr Hart left for New Orleans, made an arrangement with S. M. Baird to bring suit on a League of Land situated near Clarksville, before the Limitation Law takes effect. mail from East arrived nothing new

Tuesday April 18th Weather same, send off Western Mail— nothing Stirring—

Wednesday the 19th rain last night Cloudy to day Mr Hoya left for Natchitochez. (done some business in the Justices office, mail from west, received a Letter from Capt Allen of Grand Gulf Mi nothing further new

Thursday the 20th about daylight it commenced raining and had a most tremendous fall of rain, Kept on till 9 oclock—Keeps Cloudy—a german who comes from Arkansas arrived to day says he has lost two Slaves for which he offers a Reward of Sixty dollars, he says there are seven German Families coming down from Arkansas to settle in Texas and that they will be here in a few days—he says his name is Reinhardt—it is my opinion there is something not all right about this man, I may be wrong in my opinion, but am certainly not to blame for it having been *taken in* since I am in Texas by Strangers and particularly by my own Countrymen.

Friday April the 21st rain, rain, rain, after Breakfeast this morning it appeared as if all the flood gates of Heaven were opened to let out the water, the Bayou Lanana is overflowing and rising very fast, I am afraid it will overflow my field and take away the fences, hope not—in all the rain the mail Boy came for his mail. send it off Eastward but am fearfull the little fellow can not get along on account of the high waters—Mr Reinhardt is still here, wrote several advertisements for him offering the $60 reward for the apprehension of his Slaves—Mail Boy returned after swimming one Creek—he could not get across the second. Dont blame him—

Saturday the 22d fair, fine weather — had a devil of a rompuss with the negro woman Susan, after giving her a sound beating which she well deserved—she absquatolated to furrin parts, dont trouble myself much about her, no news—exept every creek, Bayou & Branch is Swimming—

Sunday the 23 weather same looks a little Cloudy, but not any thing like the End of the World—gel Rusk returned from Harrisson County; the *German* who arrived here last Thursday absquatulated, and is all I had anticipated of him a take in—but he did not take me in much—

Monday the 24th fine weather, my negro woman Susan has not come back yet—work in garden all day—exept half an Hour I was on the Bench as one of the Probate Judges, Mrs Mason Miss Gray, Col Jennings and munroe Hyde spend the Evening with us

Tuesday the 25th[7] fine weather, it is very warm, but cloudy So that workin in the garden is not disagreable—nothing new—send off western mail—

Wednesday the 26th weather very sultry, Mr Black[8] the School master we engaged sometime ago, left off—paid him Six dollars for the Tuition of Charles & Joseph for one month. Western mail arrived, received a letter from Mr Goodman, says he will get drafts on me for all monays Collected in my office, received my Commission as Post Master, from Sam Houston President of the Republic of Texas,—*how we apples swim*

Thursday the 27th Cloudy, but no rain much cooler then it was yesterday, worked on the Roads all day made a good of a bad Crossing at the Lower corner of my Field across the Lanana, Mayfield returned from the west. Lewis P. Cook also arrived from the west—have not seen them but a very short time, so dont Know the News they bring—if any—Ira R. Lewis of Matagorda in Town, K. H. Muse dito—

Friday the 28th Cool weather even a fire in the chimney is not very disagreable, send off the Eastern mail, the negro woman

---

[7]The entry for Tuesday, April 25. 1843 was omitted from the Smither edition and the entry for Wednesday, April 2 , 1843, was printed as April 25. 'See Smithers. "The Diary of Adolphus Sterne," **Southwestern Historical Quarterly**. XXXV (January, 1932), 241.
[8]John S. Black, who was the First Junior Deacon of the Grand Lodge of the Republic of Texas.

being tired of her *rural excursion* returned home, feel very un-well this Evening

Saturday the 29th Cool weather, commenced raining early in the morning, cleared up at noon fine weather rest of the day. feel well today, wrote part of the day in my office. Nothing particular doing in Town, nor any where else

Sunday April the 30th 1843 fine weather, felt very sick after Breakfeast so much so that I had to send for a Phisician, took an Emetic, and feel much better this Evening,

Monday May the 1st 1843 fine but Cold weather—feel a little better this morning but feel very weak—Joseph, my son took the Fever to day, and has it on him yet. very high 6 P. m. I am fearfull we will have a very sickly Season of it— District Court met to day. many Lawyers in Town from San Augustin, and some from Red River County—did not leave my office all day for fear of being exposed to the Sun. made out my Post Office Bond, Sam M. Flournoy and Walter Murray went my Securities. Eastern Mail arrived brougth [sic] many Letters, none however for me— Concluded a trade with Mr Hayter[9] for part of my Loco Lands, all that part situated on the East side of the Loco for Six hundred Dollars—$100. in Cash down $50 payable next December One mule or Horse to be valued at Cash prices—the ballance of the Six hundred dollars to be divided the one half payable next fall in Horses mules or a waggon at their Cash valuation the other half payable in the Fall (say December) 1844 in monay which however the maker of the note may at his option pay in Cotton at the then market price. said last note to bear interest at the rate of ten pr cent pr annum from the first of January next till final payment, I am to give a guarantee Deed for the Land, witness to this contract was John Gillespy of San Augustin

Tuesday the 3d May Summer Days, and winter nights—District Court in Session, rattling off Business in Stile—Mr Rose who is to stand trial here for Killing Robert Potter, arrived to day, with all his friends, Town very lively—Mr Hoya returned from Natchitochez, nothing new—

Wednesday the 4th fine weather —Court in Session, Town full of People, western mail arrived, nothing new—

Thursday the 5th warm weather Court in session much business transacted, Mr Jones from Gonzales who was taken with the San Antonio Prisoners taken by Gel Woll last Summer, returned by way of New Orleans and Natchitochez he was released with Judge Hutchinson, a Mr Maverick, and a few others. the ballance are in the Castle of Perote, Mr J. addressed the Citizens to day at the Court House, giving a short narrative of his Capture and Captivity. also his views in regard to the present Political State of Mexico, and said it is all folly to think of Mexico acknowledging our Independence Mr L. P. Cook also spoke for half an Hour—and was very much applauded. *his was a war Speech—*

---

[9] J. J. Hayter.

Friday the 6th weather same—Mr Deyoung arrived yesterday Evening from San Augustin, with his Daughter put up at Judge Hart's. Send off Eastern mail, the Cabble Case was decided to day. Watkins gets the Administration, but Mr Holland has appealed. *verremos.* Debating Society met made my Speech and absquatulated for home—

Saturday the 6th May 1843 Summer weather—Court still in Session, a writ of sequestration was taken out for the two negroes in my possession, in favor of Mrs Ann Cable. I am going to Bond them, which will Keep them in my Posession for at least Six months longer. Mr J. J. Hayter came in Town to day, we put off our passing the Bill of sale till next Friday—

Sunday the 7th fine weather—dull day, all hands gone out to the Country—

Monday the 8th Cloudy this morning, rain in the afternoon, Court in Session, Criminal Docket came on, no cases of consequence came on— the Sheriff presented me the Order to take the two Negroes into his possession, told him that I would have my Bond ready by tomorrow morning nine Oclock— had a large Party at our House to night—rained very hard this afternoon. Mr and Mrs Canfield from San Augustin arrived—

Tuesday the 9th a tremendous rain last night—Clear to day, gave my Bond for the two negroes in my possession, a large meeting was held in the Court House to day, to nominate a Suitable Candidate for the Presidency. Gel Rusk was nominated; several gentlemen made Speaches, Muse and Parker the two Candidates for the Senate had a *tug* at one an other. Mr and Mrs Canfield here yet, all hands gone to Judge Harts—8 P. m. stay at home to mind the childern—

Wednesday the 10th very warm weather, court nearly trough with all the Business, Mr Canfield and Lady here yet—they had quite a Party at Judge Harts last night—Mr Greer the Senator from San Augustin County arrived from Galvezton, brings the news that Mexico has overcome the Yucatecos, and that the latter have surrendered to the former, and that we may look out for Squalls now. Mail arrived from the west, confirms Mr Greer's Statements Exchequer Monay had a *Sudden fall* at Galvezton from 80 to 40 cents in the Dollar, hurrah, for Texas—

Thursday the 11th weather very very warm—Court adjourned to day, Mr Chevallier gave a Party at his House in the Evening, and we all went home in the morning

Friday the 12th weather same, Deyoung, and Canfield went home, those who were here during Court are gone and Nacogdochez is as dead a looking place as I have seldom seen it before— Mr Bondies arrived from Crockett— Mr Hayter who was to have come in to day to get his Bill of sale for the Land, did not come according to his promise, and if I could possibly do, without selling him the Land, I would not sell it to him now, if he does not come in to morrow, I shall not consider that I am under any obligation to sell him the Land, under our former arrangement, Canfield left several accounts against Persons with me to sue on.

Saturday May the 13th weather very warm—Town a little more lively than usual—Hoya received a load of goods from Natchitochez. Mr Hayter came in, and I made out the Bill of sale for the Land, received the mule he contracted for, at $100.00 also $100.00 in Cash, his note for $50.00 payable next January, also one for $175.00 payable next January in a waggon, Horses or Mules at their Cash valuation, also one note for $175.00 payable January 1845, which he can pay if he choses in Cotton at the then market price— I must here state, that the last note we agreed should bear ten pr Cent interest pr annum from and after the first of January next, which trough mistake was not inserted in the body of the note, but which Mr Hayter will no doubt rectify so soon as I see him—sold the $50.00 note to Charles Whitaker for $30.00 in gold and five Bushels of Reye payable this fall or so soon as he can reap and thrash it out—he has the note, and is to send me in the monay to morrow

Sunday the 14th Commenced raining a little after day light and rained very hard, till nearly noon— whitaker send me in the monay for the note. nothing stirring but negroes

Monday the 15th Cloudy, Sultry weather in the morning Cleared up in the Evening, Eastern Mail arrived but did not bring any thing—James Durst took out Licence to get married to Miss E. R. Culp—got an invitation to the wedding but can not go—

Tuesday the 16th weather Keeps Cloudy—Mr Hayter came in and, I got a Horse, a fine watch and Chain and thirty dollars, $10 in Cash and his note for $20.00 payable next January in trade —and I returned him the note of $175.00 which was payable in trade next January—he corrected so far as he could the mistake he made in writing the other note—respecting the omitting of putting in the 10 pr Cent interest, Major Reiley returned.

Wednesday the 17th a little rain last night looks like rain to day, got $15.00 from Mr Wm R. Scurry on account of the Horse business he gave me also an Order on his Brother for ten dollars more which will when I get it set us even about the Horse, am now ready to start but it looks so much like rain I will defer it till tomorrow—Mr Touvenin arrived from Liberty County

Thursday the 18th Cloudy Cleared at noon—left home at 3 P. M. met Richardson Scurry paid me the ten dollars for his brother William, stopped all night at my old friend Radford Berry's

Friday the 19th left early—dined at Mr Ratlief's[10] arrived at San Augustin at 5½ P. M. stopped at Mr De Young's met some of my old Friends, saw Mr Barrett was also introduced to several strangers, passed the Evening agreably.

Saturday the 20th May fine weather for traveling—left after Breakfeast, called to see my old friends Elisha Roberts and his wife, arrived at Sabine Town at 5 P. m. stopped at the House of

---

[10]W. D. Ratliff.

Judge Hotchkiss, met with Mr Pemberton, Mr Peck, and Mr Austin, was introduced to Mr Clapp partner of Austin, they appear to do good Business. they have the only Store in the place, wrote a letter home to be send in the mail to morrow morning—

Sunday the 21st Cloudy looks like rain—left at 8 A. M. Crossed the Sabine and once more entered the United States, arrived at the Residence of W. R. D. Speight an old aquaintance of mine, who has lately been elected Parish Judge of the New Parish of Sabine, dined with Judge Speight and his amiable Daughters. left Speights at 3 P. M. with the intention of going to Clarks 17 miles from Natchitochez, but a tremendous Storm arrising we stopped at the House of Mr Phillipps who formerly resided and kept a Hotel at the garrisson, it rained very hard for one Hour

Monday the 22d left at 6 A. M. Roads very muddy passed the garrison as they were mounting guard, had the Benefit of some fine music, Breakfeasted at Clarks, and arrived at Natchitochez at 3⅓ P.M. found old Madame Placide Bossier, my wife's Foster Mother in rather bad health, met with many of my old aquaintances, who when last I saw them held their *Heads high,* now are Bankrupts and not worth a Shuck Cigar, the old Mansion of my late Friend and Father in Law, the same it appeared to me in 1828— Yet God Knows what changes have taken place since—purchased several Articles for the use of my Family—made a Settlement with F. Williams. gave him my note for $45.00 which I know is more then I honestly owe (having paid his Partner Wiley) yet to avoid a *fuss* I gave the note which I intend to pay—delivered all Letters, and mailed those I had to mail. saw Mr Eder a German whom I formed a liking for. belive him to be a Clever fellow—a Mr Oliver Rouquier who was a mere child when we were married —now is married himself, to a Miss Jonty a very Beutifull woman, spend the Evening at the old Mansion, talking over *Auld lang Sine*

Tuesday the 23d very fine weather went out shopping with Eugenia, and Madame Lestage, and Madame Felix Estrada, there is no use to say any thing about how my Poor Purse suffered. but if any one thinks he can keep the purse strings closed, just let him go out a Shopping with a Daughter just beginning to *grow up,* Eugenia was introduced to many of her Mother's old friends who were much pleased with her,—the Steam Boat Cote Joyeuse passed down the River on her way to New Orleans—

Wednesday the 24th fine weather—the Belle of Red River Came up from New Orleans and passed up to Shreve Port, nothing particularly new—*shipped* my goods I purchased on Board the good waggon of which my friend Joseph Nations Esq. is master in good Order to be delivered in like good Order at Nacogdochez Texas, the accidents of the Road and Custom House only exepted —weather very hot but lots of ice to cool a man—

Thursday the 25th very warm weather—passed the time as well as I could, among old aquaintances, ice Lemonade & a dined in Company with the Curé Justiniani, fine man

Friday the 26th weather same—time same—same—same—same—

Saturday the 27th left after Breakfeast in Company with Mr Olivier Rouquir, to go to Col Bludworth's who I understood has some old Spanish Land Papers in his possession, in which I am interested (about the Palo Gacho claim—) did not find the Col at home, however got a good Dinner, took a Siesta in a fine *Shady Bower* and came back to Town at about 3 P. M.

Sunday the 28th weather same, news reached Town that Daniel R. Hopkins died on *his?* Plantation yesterday and his Body was brought down this morning,—he was one of the oldest Merchants in Natchitochez and stood as high in Society as any man in Louisiana, but the hard times and over reaching himself in the Speculations of the day he went down, & took the benefitt of the Bankrupt Law, but as an honest man, gave up all to his Creditors, and died so poor that (as I was told) his body was interred at the Expence of one of the Banks—his Funeral, which would have been followed five years ago, by *all Natchitochez*—scarcely was followed by a dozen friends, and I am happy to say that I was one to show that respect to the Memory of an old friend, a *Brother Mason,* and an HONEST MAN, when those who had *eat his Bread,* & *drank his wine,* and lived upon the fat of *his* land, did not even follow him to his last residence upon Earth *sic transit gloria mundi—*

Monday May the 29th rain somewhere last night, for it is cool this morning, bade adieu to all my friends and left at 7 A. M. Mr Peck former Partner of Pemberton accompanied us—arrived at the garrison at 5 P. M. My Brother Isaac stops here he keeps a Billiard Table and Bar Room—(no good place for him) Eugenia stopped at Leutenant Sibley's to whose Lady and amiable Sister in Law I was introduced—I stopped at Isaac's Establishment, and Mr Peck at the Officers Mess house played Billiards till 2 oclock A. M. and went to bed to be waked up by the lively notes of the Kent Bugle, and sound of the Cannon at day light—

Tuesday the 30th fine weather, left the garrison at 7 A. M. Isaac rode out with us about 5 miles. arrived at Sabine Town at 5 P. M. stopped again at Judge Hotchkiss's

Wednesday the 31st fine Cool weather—left at 7 A. M. arrived at San Augustin at 3 P. M. did not stopp here but went to Mr George Teal's fatigued to death—

Thursday the 1st of June 1843 fine weather, left at 6 Oclock A. M. arrived at home at 2 P. M. found all well, there is a big Barbecue in Town given for the purpose of raising volunteers to make out a company for this Town, arrived in time to pick some of the Bones, and some of the address of Col Mayfield. found all my friends well and (of course) in good spirits

Friday the 2d Splendid weather, our 15th Aniversary of our Marriage, if the next 15 years will pass with as much harmony and love as those just finished I shall be contented—received the Articles purchased at Natchitochez pr Mr Nation's waggon. all O.K.

Saturday the 3d. weather still same, did not learn untill to day that Mrs Hyde has died during my absence. received again the Keys of my office, and it is now the old thing over again, Town dull as ever, loaned my mule to Mr Nelson to go to Mr Rawls's to survey some land

Sunday the 4th June very fine weather, the fall of a good Shower of rain is wanted—went with Mr Parmalee to Goyens's old mill a fishing, returned near sun down with a mess of Fish—

Monday the 5th Cloudy—a very heavy Shower of rain in the afternoon, worth several hundred Dollars to this neighborhood Mail from East arrived, Commodore Moore has had an Engagement with the Mexican Fleet both sides got badly cripled and made a draw game of it, no doubt both sides Claim a victory, B. Blake gone West—

Tuesday the 6th fine weather send off western mail. wrote to Judge Terrell respecting the monay he owes me also requesting him to look in the War Department about the Land and monay due to Herman Ehrenberg[11] sat on the Board of Land Commissioners issued two certificates Ned Roberts arrived last night from Crockett his trial is remooved to this place

wednesday the 7th fair weather, dull times during the day, had a large Party given by the young men of the Town all hands went to it, was rather *warm work* went home at 2 A. M. western mail arrived in the afternoon but had nothing in it

Thursday 8 weather same, made an agreement with J. H. Arnett and Wm Hensley to Shingle my House—they are to deliver the Shingles on the spot, and put them on the House and I am to furnish the Nails, they are also to remoove the old shingles and rotten Laths, and put on new Laths, or Rough edge plank wherever wanted, and raise the front gallery, for which I give them my mule, Hayter's note for $20. $25.00 in goods, and $25.00 in provisions, when the work is done, exept the provisions which are payable while at work—

Friday June the 9th 1843 this morning at 3 A. M. was suddenly attacked with a severe fit of Plurisey, send for Doctor Starr who gave me some Pills which Kept me most all day in a state of great agony, he having had at first some scruples to bleed me, which however at 7 P. M. he was compelled to do, and which gave me most instant relief I was then blistered, took some more medicine, and tried to get some sleep—

Saturday the 10th feel a little better, *more* medecines but feel sick pretty generally—

---

[11]Herman Ehrenberg was a native of Germany, who, like Sterne, came to the United States to make his fortune. In 1835 he came to New Orleans, and soon joined the New Orleans Greys. At seventeen, he was the group's youngest soldier. He fought in the action at San Jacinto, and served under James W. Fannin at Goliad, although he escaped the fate that befell most of this command. Ehrenberg returned to Germany after the Texas Revolution. but eventually returned to the American frontier, the last time to Arizona. Also like Sterne, he kept a diary of his Texas experiences. Ehrenberg died in 1866 in the Majove Desert.

Sunday the 11th more medecine, purging, and swallowing Tea—I feel however much better, there is no *hopes* of my dying this time—

Monday the 12th had rains for the last three days, can allmost *hear* the corn grow, rested tolerable well last night, no medecine to day exept a little nitric acid however cheated the Doctor by taking some fine Buttermilk at dinner, and it had such an effect upon me that now 5 P. M. I am well enough to set down and write my Journal—the Eastern mail arrived received a letter from Mr. H Cloppenburg formerly a merchant of New Orleans, more recently a clerk in the Treasury Department of Texas, and now allmost without Bread in New Orleans he writes me respecting a claim on Major K. which if [it] is a just one (& no doubt it is) ought certainly be paid by K.—a Redlander was received of to day—an other naval Engagement has taken place between Com Moore and the Mexican Fleet, it seems our little Ships had to haul off, no wonder these confounded large Steamers are an overmatch for our small Sailing Crafts, and there are the Paixhan guns—a man may be ever so chivalrous, ever so brave, yet it can not be expected he can fight against such odds as Com Moore had to contend with, I'll stake my Existence on it, give Com Moore one of the Steamers, and give the Mexicans both his vessels, and Moore would have had them long ago

Tuesday the 13th Weather rather cloudy, but no rain, feel much better, went into the garden, and all over the Premises, feel an appetite, and belive I am quite restored to health, the only thing I want is my usual strength, and if good nursing will restore that, I'll soon be Richard himself again—

Wednesday the 14th fine weather, am getting still better. my mouth however is sore—confound the calomel—put all my Papers in Order to day, went up to the Office near Sun down, Mrs Starr is very Sick she has the congestive fever, bad beginning that— for Summer

Thursday the 15th very hot, feel quite recovered from my sickness, went up to the office and attended to my Business. mail arrived from the west, recd a Letter from Gel Rusk dated at Montgomery June 5th. nothing new of any Consequence, took up a note for $97.87 I gave to R. F. Millard last June, rented him the shop he now lives in at 5 dollars pr month, no time fixed. he is to hold it for at that rate, Mrs Starr is better, wrote a long Letter to My sister Nancy to go by to morrow's mail

Friday the 16th June 1843 Weather very warm, improoving every day in health—however after sending off Eastern mail did not return to the Office all day, send off the Letter I wrote a few days ago to Mr Eder of Natchitochez

Saturday the 17th Cloudy, several Showers of rain during the day felt a little unwell this morning, took Seidlitz Powders— felt well enough to go up to the office and attend to Business. Judge Legrand, who for some time has been trying to get me to sell him some Land located in Harrisson County. I sold said Land to a certain Joel K. Mead as great a Rascal as ever went unhung, he promised to give me $2000.00 for the Land, which I agreed to, but no sooner had he the Papers, he said he could only give 1500, finding that I had fallen in the hands of a Sharper I thought better that, then nothing, so I agreed if he would give me that amount I would be satisfied, and say no more about it, but he only gave me $13.00 at last saying that if we would achieve our Independence or be annexed to the United States he would give me the other two hundred dollars—but to this day I have heard nothing from him, and if I did, it would be all the same, so that I consider that I had a just Claim on the Land till my $200.00 were paid, which Mr Legrand agreed to do provided I would give him all my right, title, claim, and interest to said Land— which I did to day, I received $50.00 down and a note for $150.00 signed by Legrand and a Mr Gill who I belive resides on or near the Land, and who is interrested, in my release of the same—I am thus particular for fear that it may hereafter be thought I sold the same land twice, I only wanted my monay justly due me and I got it— and it was the only way

Sunday the 18th June very warm, Kept the House all day, nothing stirring—

Monday the 19th very warm weather, commenced *laying by* my Corn, it is nearly all Silking, there will be extraordinary Corn crops if no unforeseen accident happens. Eastern mail arrived late in the Evening, nothing new

Tuesday the 20th weather dito as yesterday—was at the office nearly all day, there is however nothing doing at all

Wednesday the 21st very warm, settled with Doctor Starr the last of the judgement he held against me in favor of Douglass's Estate for 86.61 also $27.00 due him for attending on my Brother in law Jeremiah Roof, also $32.50 for attending on the two negroes Charles & Joe last summer, and a note he got against me for $25.00 given to Lansing of San Augustin as administrator of W. W. Parker's Estate, I gave Starr in payment of the above, the note for $175.00 given to me by the two Hayters and Charles Whitaker last month—the western mail arrived,—Nelson gone to San Augustin

Thursday the 22d Cloudy but no rain here, rained all around this place, nothing stirring—

Friday the 23d had rain somewhere near this, which is Known by the cool air—Madame Louis Procela announced to me that she shall discontinue to carry the mail. this is unfortunate at this time, as we look for news with much anxiety from the west, I must try and see if I can get an other carrier, have one in view, whom I shall see to morrow—

Saturday June the 24th Cloudy, rain occasionally during the day,—this is Saint John's day, nothing at all doing amongst the Masonic Fraternity, this is not as it should be—Mr Nelson returned from San Augustin Mr Peck arrived, from same place,

Sunday the 25th rain, rain, rain, sun set cloudy—wrote a letter to David F. Tabor, inclosing twenty dollars in gold to redeem my watch, intended to send it pr Mr Wood who took sick to day, it is unknown when I shall have an opportunity to send it now; wrote also to A. W. Canfield. Our little Laura is sick—hope to god it will not be dangerous

Monday the 26th fair weather, cut down my oats to day sat as one of the associate Justices of the Probate Court in Moore & Thorns cases—sold the Lot opposite Norris's south of Moreland's Lot to J. C. Morrison for fifty dollars, Deed not made yet—made arrangements with Lafayette Holland to carry the mail for a few trips to Sabine Town, my Son Charles will carry it to Mount Airy, till I can hear from Mr Goodman the contractor to whom I have written to night, informing him of the failure of Ignacio Mendez—the late mail rider, Mr Blake returned last night from Houston, and Montgomery no, news—

Tuesday the 27th fair weather, send off the western mail, by my son Charles, wrote to Mr Goodman eta. sued Madame Procela for $100.00 price of my Horse. send $20.00 by Mr John Adams to Mr Tabor of Natchitochez to redeem my watch,

Wednesday the 28th very warm, mail from west, no news— Joel wilbourne got married, to a Miss ward, Mr Peck left for San Augustin—

Thursday the 29th weather dito—Doctor Lewis commenced to board with us—Lodge met this Evening. nothing new—exept Joe Wilbourn was Serenaded last night

Friday the 30th Cloudy, but very Sultry—send off Eastern mail pr Lafayette A. Holland, wrote to the Lodge in San Augustin, respecting the dues to the Grand Lodge, also to N. H. Darnell, on same subject—received from B. J. H. Holland $800. and from B. Blake $176.00 in Texas Treasury notes as Deputy District Grand Master—being the amount due from Milam Lodge No. 2. to the Grand Lodge of the Republic of Texas up to 1st January 1841. gave Mr F. Hoya a note drawn in my favor by Benayah Thompson for $200.00 dated payable the 1st April 1842. upon which there is a credit of $21.43. he (Mr Hoya) is to collect said note from Thompson who I belive is at Galvezton.

Saturday the first of July 1843 rain this morning—noon, and all day— made out my quarterly Post Office returns. omitted in stating yesterday that I have received on account of dues by Milam Lodge No 2. to the Grand Lodge $32.50 in Exchequer Bills of this government in payment of the G. L. Dues for the year (1842) eighteen hundred and forty two. nothing new. Militia Company Classed to day into Six Classes, I am out of the Scrape

Sunday July 2 1843 Cloudy, rain, and some sunshine no news from any quarter—

Monday the 3d fair weather, all the officers of the County (militia) met for a Regimental drill, it is now ascertained that Jackson Todd is elected Colonel and Nathan wade Liutenant Col—the Eastern mail arrived. It is rumored that Commodore Moore has Captured one of the Mexican Steamers, Montezuma and so much crippled the Guadalupe that he will capture her also; (it may be a mistake in the names in place of the Montezuma it may be Guadalupe) for my part I hope it may be so for it will accelerate the Peace which I hope will be concluded between Mexico and Texas. received pr mail several notes in favor of A. W. Canfield, which are to be collected, or sued on Mr Bondies arrived from Crockett.

Tuesday the 4th fine day—the 3d Regiment of Texas militia in Town for muster—all went off well—exept a Small chunk of a fight between old friends—whiskey was the cause of the quarrell no doubt—Major Muse, and Mr Parker, (the two Candidates for the Senate) made Speaches in the Court House. if all is true they said against one an other they are both very bad men, but we must make some allowance for Electioneering eta eta

Wednesday July the 5th fine weather—send of my son Charles with the western mail, wrote to G. K. Teulon G. Secretary of the Grand Lodge, send also in the mail all the returns of Milam Lodge No 2. from its Commencement of working under the G. L. of Texas up to December 27th 1842 up to which time all dues are paid, agreable to the several Resolutions passed by the Grand Lodge—the funds are in my hands—Major James Durst as agent for Madame Procela alias Ma Dolores de Soto settled with me to the Satisfaction of all parties—made an arrangement with John Johnson to carry the mail between Mount Airy and Sabine Town at seven dollars Texas Exchequer bills pr each Trip—Johnson gets only five dollars for the first trip in consequence of having send my Son to Mt Airy—this arrangement is only to last till Mr Goodman arrives, or till I can hear from him.

Thursday the 6th very hot weather, hard at work in Building a House for fodder, oats eta, commonly called a Barn—western mail arrived, received a letter from Mr Burke about Mrs Darts Books and Plate left in possession of Charles Sims, nothing particularly new from the West, exept that General Rusk has declined to be a Candidate for the office of Major General in Consequence a Call by several citizens has been made on Col J. S. Mayfield to become a candidate for that office, send off Eastern mail pr John Johnson being his first trip to Sabine Town—

Friday the 7th fine weather, Settled with O. L. Holmes up to this day, owe him one dollar, which (if god willing) I'll pay him to morrow, after dinner went out to Mr Taliafero's place accompanied with my wife, Daughter, Mr Nelson & Lafayette Holland—found Capt Taliafero the Father in Law of friend Ned. very sick, Doctor Rains[12] in attendance, the older Mrs. Taliafero is as amiable a Lady as her Daughter, and I only regret that we paid this visit at a time so unpropitious; however my wife is much pleased with Taliafero's Family—old & young—got home at 8 P. M.

Saturday the 8th fine weather; Election to day for Justice of the Peace. received 32 out of 33 votes, gave my own to old man Hyde—an auction of the Effects of John Lussan who is an

[12]Possibly Charles Raines.

Idiot at New Orleans, Mr Joost sells his Effects sans ceremony—
the Probate court ought to notice this

Sunday the 9th—rain, nearly all day—transacted a Land Title
belonging to the widow Bethany Rogers—

Monday the 10th Cloudy; worked in the Garden till 9 a. m.
was called up Town, by Judge Hart, to hold a meeting in Consequence of the news having reached here that Commodore Moore
has taken, the Mexican War Steamer Guadalupe, and probably
the rest of the Fleet, the meeting was called to order, Col Thorn
Chairman, and myself Secretary, Col J. H. Holland addressed the
meeting in a very Eloquent manner—setting forth the difficulties
which surrounded Com. Moore, and persecutions of even his own
governt the immaginary dread of Steam Ships and Paixhan Guns
—the meeting adjourned till 5 P. M. a committee having been
previously been [sic] appointed— to draft Resolutions to show
the feelings of the People of Nacogdochez County in regard to the
Commodore—Doctor Starr the Chairman of said Committee at 5
P. M. presented Resolutions highly complimentary to Com. Moore
and Col Morgan,[13] the Commissioner who was send to New Orleans by our President to take charge of the Navy, eta, after the
adjournment of the meeting several kegs of Powder were made
use of in various manners, and the Citizens generally Serenaded
all the Ladies in Town, and the assembly broke up very harmoni-
ously at 3 Oclock A.M. on the— was reelected associate Justice
C. C.

Tuesday the 11th July near day it began to rain as if all the
f[l]ood gates of Heaven had been opened, send off the western
mail, (omitted to state on yesterday that Mr Bondies, and Mr Peck
arrived from San Augustin)

Wednesday the 12 fair weather, Mr Peck & Bondies left for
Crockett. western mail arrived no news, received letters from
Mr Goodman telling me to go on with mail contract eta at all
risks—very well—very busy building a Barn— Mr Chevallier who
returned from New Orleans brings no news—

Thursday July the 13 very hot weather, no business going
on, paid Madame Candida Delgado Ten Dollars on Account of a
larger sum I owe her for which she holds my note, upon which
the Ten Dollars ought to be credited, Col Thorn and Lady spend
the Evening with us—

Friday the 14th very very very hot—had however a fine
Shower of rain in the Evening to cool the air—John Adams the
old waggoner whom I had given twenty dollars to— to redeem my
watch at Natchitochez has returned. he has deceived me, spend
my monay and will probably be the cause of my loosing my watch
—here is an instance of the ways of the world, a man who for the
last ten years has borne a name for honesty, Industry and Integ-
rity—yet after my telling him that not alone I would loose my
watch if not redeemed at about the time he would reach Natchitochez that besides I would loose my reputation as a man of

---

[13]James Morgan.

veracity, having pledged my word that the watch should be redeemed, yet notwithstanding all this the fellow has acted bad, mean—infamous— so let it be a warning to those who may read these pages after I am gone, that *a man who will get beastly drunk* occasionally, no matter what reputation he may have for honesty— he should not be trusted with matters of this kind— Mr Hoya received some few things, Mr Chevallier dito, I am afraid both of them will not make up one Store, what a fine chance now for a good assortment of goods—

Saturday the 15th hot in the afternoon, a heavy fall of rain in the afternoon, Mr C. E. Taliafero and Lady paid us a visit, Mr Sanks a merchant from Natchitochez is here, gave him twenty Dollars to try and redeem my watch if possible—wrote to D. F. Tabor on the subject, received 22 Barrills of corn for the note I held against Mr Collins for $21.75. paid off the order for 19 Blls Corn of Arenda, let Smith the f.m.c. have Seven Blls for which he is to deliver me nine next october; held an Election to day for Eight Aldermen for this Corporation. this is the 4th Anniversary of the 1st Battle we had with the Indians on the Nechaz—

Sunday July 16th weather very hot—Mr Sanks left here for home. Beard, Muse, and J. F. Graham dined here to day. Wm Hensley one of the men who Contracted with me to cover the House returned to day,—hope they will go to work now—if not I shall claim my damages as pr Contract—

Monday the 17th Fahrenheit's Thermometer was at 100 in the Shade, fronting the north, nothing stirring—in the Evening had a *drop* in Mrs Phillipps Mrs Thorn and other Ladies, and several gents spend the Evening— Gel Rusk, Gel Hunt, Judge Ochiltree and a Brother of Gel Hendersons, arrived late in the Evening, an Election for Mayor, Treasurer and Secretary of the Corporation were elected—it resulted in C. S. Ta[y]lor for Mayor, J. H. Starr Treasurer and R. Parmalee for Secretary

Tuesday the 18th weather same as yesterday, only a *little more so.* Eastern mail arrived— no news— dispatched western mail, Gels Rusk & Hunt paid us a visit to day— I belive my men who were to get Shingles & Cover my House are gone to work once more,—Gel Rusk confirms the report that Gel Houston has an Heir[14]

Wednesday the 19th weather a little more cool—settled with Clevenger my account of Blacksmithing $15.88—and he gave me $2.00 on Hoya's Store for the $11.62½ Adams his waggoner spend of my monay, the western mail came in, nothing new—received from the War Department Certified Copies of my Muster Roll of the Company I Commanded in 1840 also the Orders from the Department ordering the ranging on the frontier directed to Genl Smith

Thursday the 20th weather same, translated a Land Title for

[14]Sam Houston, Jr., was born on May 25, 1843.

Hudson Hall, he owes me $5.00 for same lives on the other side of the Attoyacque, nothing else in the place stirring—

Friday the 21st Weather moderated, a fine brieze stirring all day, at work improving *the Farm* for so I must now call our residence as that name is much more appropriate then any thing else. no news in town, nothing from west East or South dull, dreary, dead, defunct—*poor old Nacogdochez.* N. B. Pigs, Poultry & Potatoes in a thriving condition

Saturday the 22d July very warm, but not so oppressive as it was a few days ago—made arrangements with Mr Moffitt[15] to send my two oldest Boys to school, to him, some business in the justices office—many country People in Town. A Soiré at judge Taylors—

Sunday the 23d fine weather in the morning—nothing Stirring got *hold* of Jack Hinton by the Author of Charles O'Mahley[16] —very good —but much more Sentimental than Charley, wife & Daughter went out ruralising with Mrs Phillipps— (Athala Hotchkiss) a rain and Thunder Storm in the afternoon prevented my folks from coming home—spend my Evening in taking both Paternal and Maternal care of the Childern, and went head and Ears into Jack Hinton till 2 oclock Past midnight—

Monday the 24th fine bracing morning—wife & Daughter came home after breakfeast, accompanied by Miss Maria Hotchkiss—sat on an Examining Court, Thos and Wesley Hanks—accused of assault and battery with intend to Kill Wm Caldwell (alias Georgia Caldwell)—heard, and wrote down the Testimony, Judge Hart and Blake sitting with me—bound both the Hanks's over in the sum of $500.00 for their appearance at the next district Court—Arendt and Hensley commenced to Shingle the House to day

Tuesday the 25th July fine weather, at work to day recovering (Shingling) the House— Miss Maria Hotchkiss & Miss Agusta Raguet paid us a visit— a deaf and dumb man named Jackson a printer by trade stopped with me to day— send off western mail made out a copy of the yesterdays proceedings, for which I received a note for Four Dollars and some cents—loaned Bautista chirino $50. Texas Treasury notes for which he is to pay me a young Cow, if not returned within a short time—

Wednesday the 26th this was one of the warmest days of this summer, to day I Payd up all my Taxes for 1841—to wit—my own $156.95—as Administrator of g. Benard's Estate $31.19 as Administrator of Patricio de Torres $27.67—as administrator of James Ogilvy $92.25, and as Agent for Jose de los Santos Coy $27.67— &

---

[15]John H. Moffett, who was a teacher in Nacogdoches in 1843. In 1844 he was elected to represent Nacogdoches in the Ninth, and last, Legislature of the Republic. He also served in the Third Legislature of the State of Texas. 1849-50.

[16]Jack Hinton, The Guardian was written by Charles Lever (1806-1872). It was published in London by G. Routledge in the 1830's or 1840's. **Charles O' Mabley, The Irish Dragoon** was published in Philadelphia in 1841 by Carey and Hart.

Joseph Polvador, $1.27— the mail came in from the west, Com Moore has arrived at Galvezton—no particulars— mail contractor Goodman's Brother wrote to me that he is very sick, but whishes me to go on with the mail at all events—done some business in the office

Thursday the 27th at 3 P. M. Fahrenheit's thermometer was 100—in the Shade—! nothing doing—some little Sickness about in the country, my wife complaining a little to day, hope to god she will not get Sick— the whooping Cough is in Town, Judge Hart's childern have got it, am afraid our little ones will get it

Friday the 28th very warm, there is however a little breeze stirring bought and paid for a cow at the Plantation of Bautista chirino, he is to deliver her to me in October next, or sooner if she has a calf, gave him (chirino) my Branding Iron to put it on the Cow—, at noon Mr A. McDonald and Lady arrived from Huntsville—received a Letter from Judge Terrell. he has not paid the monay (Texas Treasury notes) he owes me to the General Post Office Department as he ought to have done, but says he made all right— Col Jennings arrived from washington—

Saturday the 29th weather allmost too hot to breathe Mr McDonald & Lady remain here to day—a very dull hot, lazy, day— Col Thorn gave a Party in the Evening.

Sunday the 30th a cool Breeze in the morning, and a very heavy rain in the Evening—Mr Roberts arrived and his Son and Daughter all left at 4 P. M. to go as far as Jessy walling's. a Mr Collier traveling Agent for the Houston Telegraph arrived, stops at my House, Placide is a little unwell to day,

Monday the 31th had a settlement with Mr Collier for the Houston Telegraph—gave him my note for $48.00 this amount mostly was contracted under the old Law, but n'importe—I'll pay it—Mr Collier left at noon—for Jessy walling's—

Tuesday the 1th of August 1843 Cool bracing weather—it is as cool as it generally is in october— had a tremendous rain last Evening—paid Wm Jones $5.50 on a note he has of mine which he ought to credit me with, and which I Expect he will do—send off western mail, wrote to the mail contractor Mr goodman, that if he does not come on himself or send me on monay to Keep the mail going it will stop.— I have allready advanced upwards of Sixty dollars for him and can not go it any more— I also wrote to Judge Terrell about our Land affair, hope he will give me a favorable answer, or I shall be obliged to go after him to Crockett —and if I do we will, and must, have a Settlement

Wednesday the 2d weather still cool, mail from the west arrived, an officer from Matamoros arrived at Washington from Matamoros with Despatches from Gel Woll respecting the armistice, received a Letter from Judge Webb—grand master of Masons of Texas—respecting the funds in my hands, requesting me to send them on—received a Letter from Judge Terrell acknowledging that he is in Copartnership with me in the Land purchase of Douglass's Estate purchased at Probate sale, which I have settled with

Doctor Starr the Administrator. Judge T. promises to settle with me on his return from the Indian Treaty—received $325.00 Exchequer Bills from Mr Miller[17] Private Secretary of the President —to sell for Silver

Thursday August the 3d fine weather, it is cool in the Evening and morning, and a fine Breeze during the day— the whooping Cough is prevailing in Town allmost in our neighbourhood— not yet at the House but no doubt we will have it, no matter better now then at any other time, the childern are all healthy—

Friday the 4th weather continues the same had a Small Shower of rain at noon—felt unwell last night, took medicine this morning better this Evening—Kept the House all day—read Howitt's Germany[18] — very correct description of the People their manners and coustoms (at least so far as I am acquainted with them) read also Kate in Search of a Husband—good thing—

Saturday the 5th fine weather—Kept the House till 2 P. M. went to Town on Horseback to Blake's office to attend to some Law Suits of Canfield's—in the Evening received my watch from Natchitochez—but how did I receive it—the cristal broke & my gold K chain and gold Seal gone— how this is God only Knows as I have not received any Letter

Sunday the 6th fair, a refreshing Shower in the afternoon B. Blake gone to Rusk County, paid me $3.50 Texas Exchequer Bills, which he owes to the Lodge No 2. nothing particular doing, being Sunday spend the whole day in reading—

Monday the 7th August weather a little warmer than it has been for a few days past, Commenced to pull fodder to day, wrote to David F. Tabor respecting my watch chain, wrote to Mr Kechney, in no very flattering terms about how he has cheated me in the articles of Coffee, send him a Sample of it so that he may look and see that he has cheated me if he does not allready Know it, wrote to H. M. Eder—send off the Letters pr Mr wood of this place, opened the Land office to day but there was no business before us, it was adjour[ne]d

Tuesday the 8th weather very oppressive during the day till 2 P. M. had a fine Shower, Thunder & Lightning, did not rain enough however to injure my Fodder which is pulled—the mail did not arrive from the East, the Horse got Sick and could not travel, there will however not be any failure as an other Horse has been send on and will no doubt be here to meet the western Mail in due time—One of the Persons who left here for the Indian treaty returned—got sick—says gel Houston has gone on to the place where the treaty is to be held—and several that intended to go had returned to washington.

Wednesday the 9th fine August weather,—hard at work pulling fodder—the Eastern mail arrived (at last) brought no news,

[17]Washington Miller, a native of South Carolina, also served as Secretary to the Senate.
[18]Probably William Howitt's German Experiences, published by Longman, Brown, Green, and Longman, in London.

received a Letter from Mr Brooks P.M. San Augustin, respecting the non appearance of the mail Contractor, received an invitation to a Ball to be given at San Augustin to morrow Evening

Thursday the 10th weather still the same—the western mail arrived, but no monay—a young man by the name of Brown arrived, he is to carry the mail on the Eastern route from Mount Airy to Sabine Town he stops with me to night, and will go back to morrow to go where Mr goodman is, and get monay, or there will be no more mail carrying on this route sure—

Friday the 11th very warm, had a hard shower of rain in the Evening. had all the Fodder out, but none was much damaged— wrote a Letter to Mr goodman the mail Contractor, send it by Mr Brown, whom I expect back next wednesday Evening.

Saturday the 12th weather fine, a cool Breeze Blowing from the S.w. saved all my fodder which was pulled I shall have enough for all the year—a Mr Wm Cobb returned to day from Snively's expedition he reports, that Snively has had a fight with the Mexican Troops, which came from Santa Feé to escort the Mexican Merchants, half of Snively's men were disarmed by U. S. Dragoons, who escorted the Caravan to the Texas Line, an other Party of Snively's men happily were out so that he has at all events enough left to Capture the waggons who will not suspicion any thing of Snively's having any more men exept those which were disarmed.

I whish *old Jack* all the Success in the world. hope to see him arrive here at the head of all the waggons

Sunday the 13th August 1843 fair in the morning with a strong S. w. wind—hard rain in the afternoon, Mr McDonald and Lady arrived from San Augustin on their way home—having some business in Montgomery County, I have at the earnest solicitation of Mr McD. determined to go on with him

Monday the 14th fair weather—left directions respecting the farm eta left at 7 oclock A. M. and went to the widow McLean's Six miles beyond the Nechaz 42 miles—here I found Mr Peck of San Augustin very sick, he arrived thus far on his way back from galvezton and was taken Sick. also Mr Gil is here Sick, he paid me $25.00 in Exchequer monay in place of $20.00 good monay he owed me—

Tuesday the 15th fair weather—left at 6 oclock A.M. took Breakfeast at old Masters's arrived at Crockett at 2 P.M. rested an hour, saw Mr Kirchoffer[19] got a letter of Introduction from him to a Mr B. Hudnall, where we arrived (14 miles beyond Crockett on the Cincinnaitti Road) at 7 P.M. we found the gentleman of the Mansion. a gentleman in every sense of the word—his Lady is in the United States. made a conditional trade with him for his Barouch, he asks 18 Cows & Calves—or the Equivalent, which I intend to pay if I can—got a fine rural supper—dito Breakfeast, and on

---

[19]John H. Kirchoofer.

Wednesday the 16th at 6 A.M. Started, a lonely Road between this and Cincinnatti—arrived at that place at 1½ P.M., took dinner at Mr Hunter's a tolorable good Tavern for Texas—the Steamboat Vesta is here, River too low for her to go down—found John Hall Sick at this place, Cincinnatti has not much improved since I saw it last—left at 4 oclock P.M. arrived at Huntsville at dark—found Mr McDonald's Brother very Sick— was made acquainted with a Mr Hannah from Galvezton a Schotch gentleman with whom I am much pleased, saw old Schotch Robert formerly of this place— R. M. Williamson[20] commonly Called Three legged Wilie—he is a Candidate for the Senate for this (Montgomery) Washington & Brassos Counties, — also Doctor Barnett a Candidate for the same office, and Jessy Grimes, dito candidate— saw my old friend Mr Hayden with whom I got acquainted at Austin when there last—a clever fellow—Huntsville is much improved since last I saw it in 1838, it will no doubt be one of the most flourishing inland Towns in Texas. the Population arround it is dense—and of the most respectable and substantial farmers I am much pleased with the place and the Country arround it, and if I could meet with a Purchaser of my House here— would moove there

Thursday the 17th a very fine day—the people from the Country arrived in great numbers early in the morning at 11 A.M. about 800 persons were assembled. they done ample Justice to the Babacue, and to my surprise (not having seen it afore) some 60 Ladies were present and partook of the Barbacue, after the Repast, the Candidates for the Senate made Speachez, as a matter of course they promised much—the Candidates for the lower House also Spoke. (Pleasant Grey Genl Lewis, and Mr Jones) all promising to make the People happy in Case they are elected—Lewis's Chance in my opinion is the best for the House—for Senate (in the County) Doctor Barnett) was introduced to several Persons, whom I do not now recollect—

Friday the 18th fine weather—left for home at 3 P.M. went on as far as Cincinnatti, stopped at Hunters, got a good supper, but mean Bed

Saturday the 19th fine weather left after Breakfeast arrived at Crockett at 4 P.M. Stopped at Mr Tudds, a new large House, Mrs T. was Sick therefore I will not complain about the mean Supper, and worse Breakfeast, the *Charge* however was *good*

---

[20]Robert McAlpin Williamson, one of the colorful figures of early Texas history, was born in Georgia. A childhood illness left him a cripple with his right leg drawn back at the knee, causing him to use a wooden appendage for walking. Thus the sobriquet, "Three legged Willie." Williamson came to Texas in 1826 and was associated with several early newspapers. He was one of the earliest to resist Mexican authority, and in 1835 was given command of a corps of rangers. He fought at San Jacinto in William H. Smith's cavalry. In 1836 he became judge of the Third Judicial District, and he served in the House of Representatives in the Fifth, Sixth, and Seventh Congresses, representing Washington County. Williamson died on December 22, 1859.

Sunday the 20th fair weather, passed Masters's—& McLeans's found Mr Peck still here, sick, also Mr Gill, both however are getting better, the latter is sick (or relapsed) in consequence of his imprudence in eating water mellons—stopped all night at Mr McKnight's

Monday the 21st fair weather, in the morning, Cloudy the rest of the day—left after Breakfeast, accompanied by one of the young McKnights—arrived at home at 1 P.M. found all well— during my absence received a Letter from Thos Ogilvy dated at Savannah Georgia, in consequence of this Letter I shall pospone the Sale of the Land in Montgomery County, till I can write to— and hear from him again, received also a Letter from a Mr John Robinson from Rochester New York respecting some Land, and wants information respecting a claim he holds against Archibald Hotchkiss, received a Letter and 15 glls. whiskey pr David Wood from H. M. Eder of Natchitochez the Eastern Mail arrived in the Evening, a Letter from Canfield, a Red Lander—and nothing else —this day the writs of Election were signed and send out to the different Precincts—Judge Hart whose time is nearly out resigned —so as to give the People an opertunity to Elect a new Chief Justice. the Judge however is a Candidate for reelection and no doubt will be reelected—

Tuesday the 22d the weather has changed last night and is as cold as it generaly is in October, send off western mail, wrote to McDonald Huntsville. busy pulling fodder, busy in the afternoon in examining the various offices for the Claim of Robinson on Hotchkiss—found the Title all correct—

CHAPTER VIII

"Can just crawl from my bedroom to my writing table . . ."

Wednesday the 23d this morning it was so cold that we had to make a fire in the Chimney—I have a very severe Cold or a Sickness called the gripp. wrote a Letter to Mr John Robinson of Rochester New York respecting his Land eta—Mr Peck arrived from McLeans

Thursday the 24th weather same—this morning a little girl of Mrs. Harts's which was sick for some month or more died this morning at 8 A. M. at 12 oclock went up to Union Meeting House where all the Candidates for Congress of this County including Senators of the District made Speachez, Mr W. W. Wingfield came out as a candidate for Chief Justice. I am not in his favor for I do not think him fit for the office *nor for any other*. came home at 5 P. M. went to the funeral of Mrs. Harts Daughter western mail arrived, nothing new—received a Letter from G. K. Tewlon[1] Gd Secretary of the Gd Lodge of Texas inclosing an account against McFarland Lodge No 3 San Augustin wrote to said Lodge on the subject this Evening, to be send by to morrows mail, the regular mail rider did not come with the mail being sick at Terrills. Wm Culp brought in the mail—Miss Augusta Raguet & her Brother in Town to night

Friday the 25th weather not so cool—summer again. Mr Peck left for San Augustin, send off Eastern mail, pr Wm Culp— my Deputy Mr Millard is Sick—I am not very well, so that the Post office plagues me at this time, being much too far from my House—Capt Archibald Hotchkiss in Town. tells me he is ready at any time to make a Title to the Land he contracted for with John Robinson of Rochester New York—and that he will settle the $600. note satisfactorily—hope so—

Saturday the 26th warm as June— in the morning, Cloudy & a Slow rain in the Evening—Mr Millard still sick not much business in the office—Major Cesna and Lady in Town, stop at Mr Roberts's—no—news—at all

Sunday the 27th fair—a dull day—the Religious People all assembled in the Court House to hear Parson Rhodes preach but he did not come—

Monday the 28th beutifull weather—all hands are gone to Douglass where a big Horse race is going to take place. the candi-

---
[1] G. K. Teulon.

dates are all there—no doubt to make very fair promises!!—the Probate Court met. Blake & myself presiding—Judge Richardson Scurry and his Lady arrived here to day. stopped with us to night his Lady is a fine amiable and handsome *little* Lady but as a *Lady* as big as a *House*—Eastern mail came in, no news—the Folks who went to the Indian Treaty so far are disappointed as no Indians were found. hurrah—for Indian Treaties—oh—hush!!!

Tuesday August the 29th fine weather, Judge Scurry Sick this morning, but got well enough to start off at 3 P. M. all the Candidates for Congress exept Parker—were in Town to day and made speaches in the Court House—all in the old way of doing business.— the Candidates for Chief Justice also made a few remarks—which I belive Judge Hart made the most substantial and best remarks—hope he may be elected—Mr Radford Berry and Lady, old friends and aquaintances arrived to day. Mrs Sterne very unwell,

Wednesday the 30th weather same as yesterday, went up to the office but had such pain in my ankle (originating from red buggs)— that I was compelled to go home and lay down, a Mr Walling came to see me wants to purchase my interest in the Land where old West lives in Shelby County. agreed to let him all my right, title, and interest for $300.00 which he agrees to give, in a fine Horse and Notes on People of this County—Judge Hart sick—our little Laura took sick this Evening, however I hope it is only the effects of a Cold—my wife is a little better this Evening. myself dito—

Thursday the 31st fair in the morning, a fine refreshing Shower in the Evening, western mail arrived, a Letter from McDonald all well—a Letter from W. B. Goodman enclosing a draft on my office for $70.63—and $100.00 in Exchequer monay, this pays me up to this day and leaves in Goodmans favor

Friday the 1st of September fair weather send off Eastern mail my ancle hurts me so bad that I was compelled to keep the House for the ballance of the day.

Saturday the 2d—can't walk, confined to the Bed

Sunday the 3d same same same no news

Monday the 4th still confined—this is Election day, could not go out, however in the afternoon went up in a Carriage and gave my vote, Town full of People mail arrived from the West, nothing new—

Tuesday the 5th Cool bracing weather, a little showery occasionally, heard from several Precincts it will be a very close contested Election between all the Candidates exept Parmalee who had no oponents, and Mr Parker of Houston County who has beaten Muse sure for the Senate

Wednesday the 6th fine weather, my ancle getting better but yet I can not walk, wrote a letter to Mr B. Hudnal of Houston County respecting the purchase of a carriage he has for sale which I whish to purchase, send the letter by Mr Parker the Senator elect

Thursday the 7th weather same, lame, and confined yet. the mail rider Brown has changed his Route again. that is to say he got Johnson to ride this route again. he makes his Brother's his stopping place—good—settled with with [sic] H. A. Johnson, paid him up for all the trips, and Boarding the mail rider for Six trips $59.

Friday the 8th Sepr 1843 beutifull weather, I am still confined with my Leg. Eugenia & Charlie gone to Mr Radford Berry's to attend a Camp meeting—Mr F. Hoya returned last night from his western trip. he has received one Hundred Dollars for me from the Heirs of Bonzano, which will pay him the amount I owe him, for which amount he holds my note, which however remains now cancelled in his hands—(it is the only note of that amount I owe Him)

Saturday the 9th Weather same as yesterday—getting better, was well enough to ride up to the office to transact business, my wife gone to camp meeting Nelson, Isaac & Lafayette do—Mr Frizzell came in this Evening from his place (Lacys fort) paid a note I gave John Durst amount $13.00. this note was given for a debt Joe Durst had against Mrs Equies, for her I gave the note Thorn owes me half the amount for it was in part payment for the Land we bought of her (the Jose Cordova trace). she was the widow of Jaquin Cordova one of the Heirs of the Estate of Cordova—

Sunday the 10th fine weather, Town literally dead—every body gone to Camp Meeting—Kept Bachelors Hall, fared sumptously, Mr Frizzell dined with me, getting better very fast—can walk without a stick—Doctor Starr gone to Galvezton—George Clevenger very Sick—Blufford Mitchell who was severely cut by J. Graham, is getting better

Monday Sepr 11th 1843—weather fine—commenced to Shingle the House, and very nearly had a Thunder Storm this afternoon, but it had the goodness to go round us—all hands returned from Camp meeting, Mr Dwyer[2] hawled for me to day—had a long Conversation with Mr Hogg the Representative elect from this County, find him much more of an Intelligent man, then I had at first sight taken him for

Tuesday the 12th fine weather, recovered most intierly of my sore Leg. Eastern mail arrived from Sabine Town, nothing new, exept that R. Scurry & N. Darnell are reelected from San Augustin County, D. S. Kaufman Senator from Sabine Shelby & Harrisson Counties—

Wednesday the 13th weather very hot, and dry—at the Office but nothing doing, western mail arrived brought nothing—mail from beyond montgomery failed, send off Eastern mail as dry as it came from the west—

Thursday the 14th weather same, Board of Land Commissioners issued one certificate only, wrote the Certificates of Election

---

[2]Probably G. J. Dyer.

for R. Parmalee as District Clerk, and for W. W. Wingfield as chief Justice

Friday the 15th weather same, had a little shower last night but to day it is a[s] hot and dry as *ever*. R. Parmalee gave his Bond, and was sworn in as District Clerk, paid D. Rusk Sheriff $300. old Treasury notes for Taxes of 1841—

Saturday the 16th Sept had a Severe fever all night took medicine to day—

Sunday the 17—Sick

Monday the 18—do

Tuesday the 19th—do

Wednesday the 20 do 21th 22d 23—24—25 do

Tuesday the 26th can just *crawl* from my bedroom to my writing Table Jasper[3] the Representative from from [sic] Houston County came to see me, signed the late Election returns, and besides penning this and the preceeding is doing tolerable well for one so weak as I am—

Wednesday the 27th Cool & Cloudy, am recovering very fast —went out of the House for the first time since the 15th wrote a few lines to gould at San Augustin, requesting him to send me some tonics, western mail not in at dark.

Thursday the 28th weather the same as yesterday—the western mail arrived, received a Letter from Mr. Miller respecting his Exchequer monay, he talks about dollar for dollar in Alabama monay—he must be very enthusiastic for Texas, very!—

Friday the 29th rainy, cold, weather, am recovering my strength but very slowly, nothing doing—all's dull—

Saturday the 30th a tremendous rain this morning, cleared off at noon, went up to the office for the first time in two weeks, assorted all the Letters, to be published and those to be send to the Gel P. O. as dead letters— this being the end of the 3d quarter, went home and am not much fatigued

Sunday October the 1st 1843 weather rather equivocal in the morning, but at 12 Oclock the Sun shone out once more. felt very unwell in the morning—much better in the afternoon—wrote two Lists of Letters on hand in the Post Office at the end of this quarter, and went up Town on *foot*—and put them up—H. H. Edwards has returned from his Indian Expedition, dont think he has done much business

Monday the 2d fine weather in the morning, a Shower of rain after one P. M. and fair weather the ballance of the day, went to the office twice—Board of Land Commissioners met, issued only one Certificate B. Blake not present—Mr Goodman the mail contractor arrived—paid him $9.00 which makes us Square up to this day

Tuesday the 3d tolerable fair day was at the office nearly all day, Eastern mail arrived. did not bring any thing—Mr Flatau arrived from San Augustin brings nothing new

---

[3]Selden L. B. Jasper represented Houston County in the Eighth Congress, 1843-44.

Wednesday the 4th   the ugliest. coldest, rainy days we have had this fall. Kept the House and bed nearly all day. my leg and ancle that was so sore before I took the fever, has broke out again and I suffer now as much with it as ever. to day is Yom Kippur. Mr Flatau is doing Penance, nonsense, to keep up a Religion only one day in the year

Thursday October the 5th   rain rain rain—am now *fully* confined to the Bed with my Leg—Can sit up and write having my ancle elevated—Mr Flatau left for home, finished my quarterly post office returns and translated a Land-title for J. J. Simpson

Friday the 6th   the rain is pouring down as if it never intended to stop any more, I feel so unwell that I am compelled to Keep the Bed, having about half a dozen large sores on me besides my sore Leg—!!

Saturday the 7th   did not sleep all night, rained till near morning, before noon it Cleared up with a sharp north wind, Kept a large fire in the Hearth all day, and I Kept the Bed all day. am getting a little better—the Sun went down in a clear Sky, Mrs Dorsett[1] died to day, cause, inflammation of the stomach ca[u]sed by an over doze of Tartar Emetic.

Sunday the 8th   Splendid weather to day felt well enough to get up and shave, Kept up and getting better all day—Mrs Dorsett was burried this afternoon

Monday the 9th   weather same, felt well enough to go up Town, but was so feeble that I had to go home, and did not set as associate Justice of the County court, nor as one of the Commissioners of Roads and Revenues—purchased a Beef of Madame Chirino for $10.00   Killed it this Evening, very fine— Doctor Starr and his Lady are very Sick

Tuesday the 10th October 1843   very fine weather — commenced to take in the Corn to day— Eastern mail did not arrive wrote to McKechney about some stockings he ought to have send me sometime ago, gave Hoya seven bits to pay him which I owe him—send a Letter with $15.00 to Mr H. M. Eder to pay for the whiskey he send me some 3 weeks ago and also to pay for some articles I send for, Mr Hoya takes both Letter & monay—Charles 13 years old to day.

Wednesday the 11th   fair in the morning, cloudy in the afternoon with a S. wind—Eastern mail arrived, Red Lander, & nothing else, went up to the office twice—send off western mail, Judge Wingfield tendered his Bond as President of the Board of Land Commissioners but the names on it not being worth more than half the sum required in the Bond, $20,000. Mr Blake & myself did not accept of it, which made the Judge *mad.* Can't help it— such is the Law, and has not left us any discretionary Power, Mr Hoya not off yet—lost his Horse last night—Doctor Starr very Sick, send for Doctor Johnson,

---

[1] This is probably the wife of John Dorsett, who is listed on the Tax Rolls of Nacogdoches County for 1837.

Thursday the 12th rain last night, did not hurt my Corn much— a Splendid day to day, wind n. E. & N. Mr Hoya left for Natchitochez, loaned him my Saddle Horse, hawling in Corn as hard as we can—western mail—and no news—Doctor Starr is better— good—this has been once a great day here in Spanish times— this being the aniversary of the Patron Saint of the place—*our Lady of the Pillar*

Friday October 13th 1843 Cold night, most beutifull day, Commenced to Shingle the ballance of the House, Still occupied in getting in, the Corn Doctor Starr a little better—out of danger —Several San Augustin folks gone trough to Douglass, where a Race is to be run to morrow, between Sam Jurdan and Col Sparks[5] —I am recovering fast

Saturday the 14th weather same, finished getting in the Corn, made a much finer Crop then last year walked nearly a mile to day and feel very much fatigued indeed, gave Arendt & Hensley an order for the mule at Ried's

Sunday the 15th fine weather continues, some say there was frost last night, but I did not see any—nothing Stirring—race at Douglass won by Sparks—good—am recovering very fast, have an appetite sufficient for two—am however carefull of a relapse— Doctor Starr better, Mrs Starr worse.

Monday the 16th Cloudy early this morning—Cleared off Cold and had a Splendid day, getting in Pumpkins all day, Board of Land Commissioners met. Judge Wingfield took the Oath of office as President of the Board of Land Commissioners, issued one certificate wrote a long letter to General Post Office Department dated it 5th inst being the day on which the returns are dated, which I forgot to send by last mail,—the Camp Build by the Town folks three miles North of this is nearly finished,

Tuesday October the 17th weather continues very fine, finished, to day getting in fodder & Pumpkins, Eastern mail did not arrive, did not quite finish to cover the House but hope it wont rain to night, all hands from Town out at the Camp ground, some working and some looking on, of course all for the *love* of Religion

Wednesday the 18th weather same, turned warm at noon— wife & Daughter gone on a visit to Mrs John Durst Saw an old aquaintance with whom I came to Texas Mr Robert H. Smith, reminds me of old times—settled with Arendt and Hensley for S[h]wingling [sic] my House which they completely finished to day, bought a Beef of Mr Massingail for $5.00 in Exchequer Monay, Col Raguet & Son dined with me to day, Eastern mail came in near 11 oclock nothing new— send off western mail send my quarterly returns,

Thursday the 19th fine weather continues—camp meeting commenced to day, all hands gone, and going, wife & Daughter not returned from visit—Mr D. J. Toler the Chief Clerk of the Post Office Department arrived, he stops with me—an old aquaint-

⁵William F. Sparks.

ance—paid all my debts to the Department as Post master for 1842 and $25.00 on account of 3d quarter 1843—C. M. Gould returned. C. Chevelier dito—mail from west nothing in it. waters too high about Brassos and Houston that mails can not get on— received a Letter & a Set of Castors from friend A. McDonald Huntsville

Friday October the 20th weather very fine, Camp meeting going on in full glory, a great many People attending. Mr Toler left for San Augustin, he left his Horse with me to take care of till he returns having hurt him with the saddle, wife & Daughter returned from John Dursts, paid a visit to Doctor Starr to day he is getting well very fast, Mr Ford his Lady Mother in Law (Mrs Wolf) children & Servants stopped with us to night—

Saturday the 21st weather warmer then it has been for some days, cloudy— went up to the Camp meeting after dinner stayed till near sun down, Mr Becton preached, Mr Cawley exhorted, and a great many prayed, hope their prayers will be heard, and no doubt they will, provided it is sincere but there is the rub—at least I saw *some* that I rather belive can be put down upon the *doubtfull* list, saw Capt Vail, and many other aquaintances Capt Vail is not alone a very zealous Christian but a most Complete beliver in Miller's Doctrine,[6] he has a Complete set of midnight crys with him, go it Dan—

Sunday the 22d a tremendous rain last night, north wind this morning, rather too Cold for rain, my wife Eugenia, and the Boys gone to Camp meeting, Kept House with Placide & Laura, in the Evening wrote a long Letter to A S. Hamilton Rockville Ala an old friend & aquaintance of mine, near dark my wife returned with the following Company, Mrs John Durst and two Daughters Mr James Durst & Lady, Miss Marie Hotchkiss, Mrs Cessna & Daughter, and Mr Tom Barrett from San Augustin. Haden H. Edwards Esqr got married at early candle light to Miss Sarah Forbes, Eugenia is the Bride's Maid. Mr Cawley officiating Priest—

Monday the 23d weather cloudy, S. W. wind—all the visitors are gone exept Miss Maria Hotchkiss, Board of Land Comrs met issued two Certificates—made out my Copys of Appeals from my decisions to the District Court—have only two —Mr F. Hoya returned from Natchitochez brought the news that Cotton is on the rise—so is Red River—got a Letter from H. M. Eder inclosing a Bill of articles I send for which will arrive in Gwier's Waggon, amount of the Bill $22.25 I send him $10.50 so that I remain in his debt Eleven dollars Seventy five Cents—Miss Agusta, Miss Mary, and Mr Conde Raguet on a visit to us to night, Mr Hoya returned my Horse I loaned him safe and sound

Tuesday the 24th Cloudy, but no rain—Camp meeting broke

---

[6]Sterne refers to the belief of William Miller that 1843 was to be the year of the millennium. Miller, from Low Hampton, New York, predicted on the basis of Bible study and certain signs that Christ would appear on a certain day in 1843 and that all true believers would ascend to heaven. His followers formed the Seventh Day Adventists.

up. several of our Town People have joyned the Society. if it makes them better then they have been I hope they may remain so— Eastern mail, no news—a new mail rider a Mr King of San Augustin; send off western mail. was busily engaged in the office writing and issuing Executions all in favor of Mr Chevallier, Mr Holmes paid me up for all Land Certificates I signed up to this day. the Misses Raguets gone, Miss Maria Hotchkiss remains—

Wednesday the 25th October last night had a most tremendous rain during the time all hands were at the Court House where the Revd Mr Cawley preached—to day it [is] very cold and raining occasionally, felt unwell all day, which I attribute to the weather,—was at the office and done some Business, but the town is more like a grave yard then a Town—near dark Mr Chevallier received some goods from Natchitochez Mr Hoya dito—

Tuesday the 26th a most outrageous ugly, cold, rainy, weather. Mr Hoya's goods were unloaded, received all I expected by the waggons in good order, Mr Hoya unwell, western mail bags came in. no mail from beyond Crockett, it is said that the Trinity is so high as it has not been seen for ten years, the whole of the western streams are the same, and we will no doubt be without news from Galvezton and Houston for two or more weeks. send off Eastern mail, went home to get to a *big* fire.

Friday the 27th very cold but a clear Sky on the whole it was a beutifull day, Mr Hoya sick—was at the office but did not do much business, loaned Judge Hart Seven dollars Exchequer monay pr left in the office four Dollars in Silver in place of in case he can not redeem it—Hoya opened some of his goods, not all received two pair of Shoes on account of the three pair he has to deliver me for H. M. Eder

Saturday the 28 Cold, & Cloudy, wind E. and N.E. lots of People in Town to attend to a two days preaching—it commenced however last night; Mr Wilson[7] and Mr Williams[8] both Methodist Clergymen are in attendance, Board of Land comrs met issued two certificates—

Sunday October the 29th Cold, windy, rainy day, preaching in the Court House, morning, noon, and night, Mr Craig & Mr Williams striving very hard to make this a Methodist Community I cannot say that I whish them success alltogether, as I like the Presbyterians better,

Monday the 30th Cold, but Clear weather, Probate Court no accounts to settle, did not set as associate, Board of Land Comrs met—paid a note to F. R. Floyd, which I gave to J. Lussan in 1838—amount of note $50.00 also paid him $30.00 Texas Treasury notes he loaned me—

Tuesday the 31st weather same as yesterday—my Brother Isaac left here to day, he took with him a mare belonging to the widow Jose Ma Soto residing at the Adayes paid Mr Moffitt $2.50 on account of Ten Dollars I owe him for Schooling for the two

[7] William J. Wilson.
[8] J. M. Williams.

boys Charles & Joseph, Parsons Craig and Williams dined with us to day, made out my account against C. Chevallier, have not settled yet expect to fall in his debt—exchanged my Horse I got from Barrett, for Parson Williams Horse (or Pony) I think it is a fair trade on both sides,

Wednesday the 1st November 1843 rain this morning, cold and Clear in the Evening, felt like I had a dumb ague had to lay down about two Hours, feel much better this Evening, heard from Isaac, the Poney gave out as I expected, it could not stand being galloped all the time, Mr Hoya is getting better, but is still confined to his room, was at the office but did not do much business too cold—

Thursday the 2d November 1843 Weather fair & Cold—western mail arrived without anything in the mail bags purchased of Wilson Ewing a Claim, on Robert A. Burney of Alexandria, gave my obligation to Moses L. Patton for $90.00 the above mentioned claim is for $300.00 being a note which Burney gave to J. D. Nash of San Augustin and Nash sold to Ewing who lost it, and advertised it in the Journal & Advertiser San Augustin, all the Certificates to that effect I have in my possession, as well as the transfer of Ewing, I owe Burney's Estate 1000 acres of Land so that I am safe on my trade paid Moffitt the amount of Schooling I owed him exept $2.25 which I still owe him

Friday the 3d beutifull weather took medicine to day for the dumb ague, I think done me good. purchased a Beef of Martilien Vascocu for $10.50 did not go up Town till late this Evening, nothing doing

Saturday the 4th Cloudy and a little drizly rain all day, had Logs for a new Smoke House haled by Mr Dwyer, loaned Col Thorn 84 lbs Beef— sold to George Clevenger 91 lbs — and to Dwyer 85 lbs. — paid Vascocu for the Beef and credited him $4.25 Mr Gould arrived from San Augustin accompanied by Mr Austin of Sabine Town—received a letter from my Brother Isaac, his nag gave out, but went on with a waggon, took the mare with him tied to the waggon

Sunday the 5th November 1843 rain, rain, rain, and Keeps raining Translated a Deed for general Rusk, Mr Gould & Mr Austin took supper with us,

Monday the 6th rained all night, the little Bayou west of Town equal to a River, the Bayou Lanana began to rise about noon, at dark the Bridge was in great danger to be carried away; it keeps on raining but not hard, a North wind blowing Strong at dark—no Court to day, the Judge is water bound no body arrived yet. every body will have to swim to the place if they want to get here. made a Deed of the Land sold to, or contracted with N. A. Bonzano in 1837 being the half of the Head right of Maria Josefa Sanchez, made said deed to the Heirs of N. A. Bonzano Mr F. Hoya who is the Authorized Agent of said Heirs. received the said Deed; I have received full payment for said Land—

Tuesday the 7th Cold, but fair weather, Judge Ochiltree in

Town, opened Court got a grand Jury charged them and adjourned Court, all those having Business in Court not having arrived, on account of high waters, all the small Bayous however are down— Joseph Waples[9] the former Chief Clerk of the State Depart. arrived Col Coffe do—Kaufman, Wheeler, Anderson & Clark attorneys from San Augustin do. Town full of People and no entertainment for them, bad Business that—John Durst & J. J. Simpson two very old Settlers dined with us to day

Wednesday the 8th Cold and Cloudy, had a black frost last night, Court in full operation to day did not attend much at the Court House, Mr Ceasar Bossier a Nephew of the late Placide Bossier his two Sons, and a Doctor Charles arrived from Natchitochez to look at Texas and if pleased they will moove to Texas. the Doctor is an old French Soldier under Napoleon, has travelled all trough Mexico and a great part of Texas, has been amongst the Comanchez, and was at the Silver Mine shown him by the Indians. he is a very intelligent man—Mr Peck arrived and went on west, Capt Vail & Lady arrived

Thursday the 9th wind from S. W. Cloudy, but no rain, fair near dark, Mr Mayfield and Mr Henry Crutcher arrived on Tuesday last from Lagrange which I omitted to note—Court in session, the Civil Docket is got over very fast, several important Cases are laid over, amongst them the Case of James Smith vs Watkins and others, which Judge Ochiltree refuses to try, he, being interrested in a Case of Similar nature, Mr Bossier & his two Sons left for the west, the Doctor backed out & did not go, got my note for $100.00 which I gave to Hoya the 3d June 1842 also a note for $70.00 given June 1st 1843— remain in Hoya's debt about $25 or $30 and by the end of this month I expect to be even with him

Friday the 10th November warm & Cloudy, rained very hard for ten minutes in the afternoon, Eugenie & Charles gone to Capt Hotchkiss's, Court adjourned till Tuesday next, busy all day raising a Smoke House and a Hen House, done some business in the office, the mail is intierly stopped in Consequence of high waters, the trinity is higher then it has been for many years; Capt Vail and his wife left here this Morning for Natchitochez

Saturday the 11th Cold, very, cold, this morning, moderated a little towards Evening, building yet on my Smoke House and Hen House, bought a Beef of David Sanchez for $9.00 the finest Beef I have seen this year, done some Justices business in the office

Sunday the 12th Cold & Cloudy, have a large bile under my arm so that I can hardly use it, to write, gave to Mr F. Hoya $125.00 Exchequer bills belonging to Mr Miller of washington to sell at Six bits in the Dollar for Silver, or return said Bills when wanted— McFarland the Mail Contractor arrived from Washing-

---

[9]Joseph Waples, a native of Delaware, came to Texas in 1838. It was he who supervised the transfer of the State Archives from Houston to Austin. He was chief clerk of the state department and a member of the Snively Expedition. Waples died on August 17, 1846.

ton brought me a Letter from Mr Miller, he wants me to send him his Excheqquer Monay back, it being worth 80 cents at washington & Galvezton, nothing new from the west

Monday the 13th Cold, windy and occasionally cloudy—all day at Rusk's Office interpreting examining witnesses in the case of James Smith vs watkins & others, did not sleep last night my Bile hurting me so much, opened it this morning, feel relieved, heard of the Death of Mrs Y. W. Lacy, a Daughter of Col P. E. Bean

Tuesday November 14th rain, all day, Court met several Cases were tried all cleared—exept W. Plucker who was found guilty of an assault on Rafael d los Santos, also Eugene Laflor was found guilty of Cow Stealing, send to jail—acted as Interpreter for the Republic, much work—no pay—getting ready to start to Natchitochez with my wife, who wants to see her mother who is sick— mail from the East, no news—

Wednesday the 15th weather cleared of but too warm to last long; Laura sick but not dangerous—court in session— Mr A. A. Nelson paid me ten Dollars in Tennessee monay, being in payment of Boarding in full up to the 15th ult—Wm. P. Rose accused for the murder of Potter, was not tried for some informality in the Indictment—Mr Ward of the County of Red River arrived—nothing new—

Thursday the 16th rainy & warm— Court in session, settled with Mr. C. Chevallier fell in his debt $49.74¾ gave him my note for the amount— western mail arrived, rcd a letter from Mr W. D. Miller of washington, about Matters & things in general, and about the financial affairs of Texas in particular—Judge Toler arrived from North—delivered to him the letters brought by McFarland the mail Contractor, am also resolved to send Mr Miller's monay by him heard from Col Thorn, he is at R. Berrys yet, can not get away for high water,—several men in jail for gambling, eta—getting ready to start to Natchitochez—wrote a Letter to Mr W. D. Miller.

Friday the 17th Splendid weather too good to last long. last night we had a tremendous rain all the Creeks up to day, so that we cannot start—loaned to genl Rusk $600.00 old Texas Treasury notes to be returned on demand—wrote to Judge Terrell and drew a draft on him for $30.00 wrote also to J. S. Gill and drew on him for $17.50, all in favor of Daniel J. Toler, purchased of D. J. Toler a Horse for $17.50.

Saturday the 18th rain—left home at 3 P.M. in the rain. stopt all night at my old friend's Radford Berry's previous to my departure from home Mr F. Hoya loaned me $15.00 in Silver which I am to return to him in one month or account as one months Boarding for himself & his Clerk. left Miss Maria Hotchkiss to Superintend our Household affairs till our return—having forgot at the Commencement of this days Journal to say that Mrs Sterne went with me to see her foster mother, who is very sick, and who wants to see her before her Death—

Sunday the 19th no rain but cloudy—left Mr Berrys at 8 A.M. met John Sparks near Attoyaque who gave me the gold chain left by me at Natchitochez last June—arrived at San Augustin at 4 P. M. Stopped with A. W. Canfield Esqr—paid him $24.00 being for advertizing the sale of Benigno Santos' Land for Taxes, also Col Frost Thorn's Subscription to the Red Lander 3d Vol—saw Mr and Mrs Deyoung and Daughters, all well took Coffee with them had a lively chit chat, all agreable

Monday November the 20th fine weather, warm & a little Cloudy left San Augustin at 7 ½ A.M. dined at Brown's arrived at Sabine Town at 4 P.M. stopped with Judge Hotchkiss—the Judge not at home, his Lady who has not seen Mrs S. in seven years was very glad to see her, this is the second time I stop at his House & the Judge is absent—at present Mrs H. tells me he is in New Orleans

Tuesday the 21st very fine weather, left at 6 ½ A. M. met Mrs Douglass— Mr & Mrs Fowler, arrived at Joseph Clark's Public House at 5 P. M. having traveled 38 miles this day—

Wednesday the 22d fine weather—left at 7 A. M. went a new Road, came into the Town of Natchitochez from below—by Bludworth's Mills—two miles shorter then the old Road and not the one fourth as much mud as the old road— Arrived at Natchitochez at 11 oclock A.M. found Madame P. Bossier in bad health but not so bad as we had anticipated. the meeting between herself and Mrs Sterne was realy very affecting, and could not have been more so had they been *real* Mother and Daughter; Madame Felix Estrada, who is the old Ladies's Major Domo (and a very fine Lady) was well, and glad to see us; went to Town and saw many of my friends and old acquaintances who were glad to shake hands—delivered all the Letters intrusted to my care, and put some into the Post Office

Thursday the 23d Cloudy, and drisly rain—purchased several articles of Merchandize of Mr H. M. Eder—a German and a very clever fellow, paid him all the monay I had with me, and remain in his debt $145. which I intend to pay him so soon as I possible can do so

Friday the 24th fair, and cold, wrote letters to Mr Hugh Grant sending him his account which he owes to the Estate of James Ogilvy $160.00 sending him the Papers and Documents of his Brother James Grant in Charge of Mr H. M. Eder, that if Mr Hugh Grant pays Mr Eder for me as Administrator of Ogilvy's Estate said $160.00 to give him (H. Grant) up his Brother's J. Grant's papers—or else to return them to me—in like manner I wrote to D. Akin as Administrator of Oliver Akin drawing on him for $53.57¢ in like manner as the above, also on S. W. Oakey for $24.75 same as above, also on David McLeod for $59.29 same as above all which I gave together with the respective Papers belonging to all the Persons above named to Mr Eder, and if [he] collects the monay or any part of it is to account to me for it— gave mr Eder Letters of introduction eta—

— 182 —

Saturday the 25th saw Mr Henry Krabers, purchased of him one Third of a League of Land, deed and Power of attorney made out in C. S. Taylor's name but in fact belongs to Mr Bennett Blake and myself—on the purchase monay Mr Blake owes me $37.50¢ and then all the benefit resulting from said purchase is to be divided equally between us, gave H. Kraber my Bond for $100.00 payable when I get the Patent for his Land which I purchased from him. the Steam Boats Rowena—Starr, Republic and Maid of Iowa arrived and went away again—Business appears to be brisk—Streets very muddy—goods plenty, cotton rising—had an interview with Capt Peter Delmore, he is perfectly satisfied respecting our Land arrangements—want me to make out a deed to his Daughter Josefina Delmore for the Land. he paid me $35.00 which he owed me for monay advanced for him for Taxes eta for said Land— he is yet in my debt $13.50 for which he says he will send me *something*

Sunday the 26th November a most tremendous rain fell *all day* Swimming between where Madame P. Bossier lives and the main Town—so that I could not get home till a Horse was send for me to ride trough the water, went up the Hill and spent the Evening at ma's till 10 P. M. went to Bed—

Monday the 27th no rain but Streets two feet deep mud— Mr Albert Long's Waggon came in also Clevengers, waggon, Hamilton's and Franklin Sparks went Security for Franklin Sparks for a Bale of Cotton to Mr Eder. the Cotton to be delivered to me at Nacogdochez for Mr Eder within one month from this date, loaded all my purchases on Mr Albert Longs's Waggon, took his Receipt—eta

Tuesday the 28th no rain but Cloudy—waggons started, told every body good beye. purchased all the Articles for *consiuption on the Road* and had my Horse Shod before—cost $1.25

Wednesday the 29th November tremendous Rain last night— yet we started this morning at 7 A. M. rain on the road—had [t]o *walk* over Bridges. got *elegantly* wet before getting 12 miles— arrived at Joseph Clark's at 12 oclock—stopped all day.

Thursday the 30th rain, rain, rain, stopped all day, nearly dead with ennui—Joe Clark a fine fellow

Friday the 1st December left at 7 ½ A.M. arrived at the Laplace Swamp which was all under water—returned back to Joe Clark's and glad to stop all day—

Saturday the 2d December Clear Fine Skye —frost this morning— settled with Joe Clark remain in his debt $10.50 which he shall have so soon as possible, he is a good man. (a friend in need is a friend in deed)— at 12 noon Spopt [sic] at Judge Speights an old friend of mine my wife was introduced to his two amiable Daughters, left Speights at 2.p.m. arrived at the Sabine at 4. P.M. Sabine out of its Banks compelled to stop all night at Mr G. Cook's a good man but confound his accomodations

Sunday the 3d December 1843 at 7 A.M. got into Ferry Boat at McLanahan's Store and went down the Sabine landed in the

Swamp on the left bank of the Palo gacho had to wade out. (and nearly Swimming) to get to dry Land— paid Mr Cook $3.00 for our last nights Expences and ferriage—very cheap— waded trough mud, water, and morass—to Elisha Roberts's where we were once more comfortable and at home

Monday the 4th Cloudy—left at 8 A. M. arrived at San Augustin at 9 A.M. spopped [sic] at Mr Deyoung's saw several of my aquaintances—dined at Mr Deyoungs left San Augustin in a drizly rain—arrived at George Teal's at 5 P. M. stopped for the night—

Tuesday the 5th left at 8 ½ A.M. Cloudy & warm got Mr D. Earls to pilot us across the Attoyaque Swamp which was overflowed got trough safe by 11 A.M. Commenced to rain at 1 P. M. arrived at Radford Berry's at 2 P. M. wet— stopped for the night—

Wednesday the 6th rain last night all day to day—could not stirr— had to stop in consequence of high water—the Carizo being out of its Banks and Slew, swimming, bad Business so near home and can not get there, however passed the day agreeable enough with Mr and Mrs Berry who are old friends of ours—

Thursday December the 7th fair. Cold weather—left in company with Mr Berry, who was our Pilot trough the Swamp of the Carrizo—arrived at home at 10 A.M. found all the Childern well, all has gone on well since we left. Lafayette Holland who has been a Boarder with us since the commencement of the Spring left for New Orleans last Saturday. in the afternoon Mr R. F. Millard requested me to go out 4 miles to the widow Sparks's to marry him to said Lady which I accepted—and at 5 P.M. left for said Place, performed the Rites of Matrimony between said Robert F. Millard and Mrs Massy C. Sparks according to law, partook of a Splendid Supper and returned home by 8 ½ P.m. J. M. Williams D. D. stopped with [us] all night he is on his way to the Methodist E. Conference to be holden in Montgomery County, Mr Nelson started to Crockett

Friday the 8th fair weather went to the Office attended to some Business of Mr C. Chevallier's a Mr F. Hoya who started a few days ago to Crockett returned in Consequence of high waters, which prevented him passing on

Saturday the 9th Cloudy in the morning cleared off fair in the Evening— No Business, nothing doing Town dull—I am Dull —everything Dull—Dull—.

Sunday December the 10th 1843 fair in the morning Cloudy at noon went hunting to Kill time, but did Kill nothing else exept four poor little partridges—

Monday the 11th fair weather, looks however very threatening, the Bla[c]k Boy Joe and myself made the gable ends to the Smoke house, thereby saved at least $6.00 which a Carpenter would have charged. at 3 P.M. Mr Long's waggon arrived, all my purchases arrived safe to my utter astonishment because I expected every thing would have been ruined in consequence of the immence rains which have fallen, all is safe exept the Coffee is a little Spoiled—no matter all the rest is good—my Boys Charles, Joseph, and Placide gone to School to Mr Farmer,—Placide is going on account of Mr F. Hoya, who subscribed for a Scholar, and has none to send—so I agree to let Placide go for *him*

Tuesday the 12th December   fine weather—mooved all my things out of the old, into the new Smoke House was hard at work all day—attended to a Law Suit for Mr Blake, Starr vs Wm Smith F. M. C. loaned Esquire Hamilton 8 yards Calicoe which he is to return so soon as he can go or send to Natchitochez, let Mr Dwyer have 16 yards of Towels at 30 cents pr yards, to be paid in waggoning

Wednesday the 13th   frost last night, very fine weather to day, made an arrangement with José Maria Mendoza to make me 2000 rails at 75¢ pr hundred payable in merchandize, at work part of the day in improvements on the place was at the office. done but little business for Chevallier. Miss Maria Hotchkiss, Miss martha Pollitt and my Charles are gone out to Capt Hotchkiss's Place on the Moral

Thursday the 14th   warm this morning rain last night commenced to make a Room out of the old Smoke House tore down the Partition I made last Spring and now is a fine Room—Mr Jones worked for me to day, I am Still making Improvements on my Place, God Knows if it will be of any account after all—Mr Hoya again started to Crockett Mr Blake informed me that he has sold the land I purchased of Kraber when last at Natchitochez for $450.00 $250.00 payable in cotton down, and the ballance in one & two years—our absentees Charley, Miss Maria & Miss Pollitt returned from the Moral—Juan Manzola whom I Employed to work for me to day commenced his days work but was informed that his child had died after leaving home (an infant) so he Knoked off work and went home to make a Coffin to burry the Child—

Friday the 15th December 1843   rain last night, all night—raining a little this morning, finishing my Boy's Room and, finished the Hen House, it appears that if it was not for my having something to occupy me, the Blue Devils would get hold of me, went up Town late in the afternoon, and found the whole Town nearly Dead—

Saturday the 16th   Cloudy and looks very much like rain; the Bayou Lanana was out of its Banks during the night, it is falling now— 8 A. M.— Mrs Sterne sat up all night with her Sister Mrs Taylor who is very sick— much business to do at the office to day for Mr C. Chevallier, no mail has arrived since my return from Natchitochez

Sunday the 17th   fair weather once more, no business doing to day, Mrs Taylor better, went gunning in the morning, and visiting friends, in the afternoon

Monday the 18th   Cold and Cloudy, very cold towards Evening at the office nearly all day, felt sick at dark—went to bed without supper with a little fever on me

Tuesday the 19th   fair weather, cold north wind feel much better this morning—sued the Republic for a League & Labor of Land, granted by the Shelby County Board of Land Comrs and not recommended for Patenting by the Rolling Board—it being Mrs Susan Latham's Head Right—send the Petition by Mr Isaac Lee to Shelbyville—send J. M. Dorr's Headright Title for a League and Labor of Land occupied in Harrisson County by Mr J. T. Gill to be recorded in Harrisson County—signed the Deed made to Josefina Delmore for half of a League & half of a Labor of Land gave the Deed to the Clerk of the County Court to be recorded, paid John N. Elliott $2.25 on a/c of his fees as Comr to divide the Land between Mr Danl Lacy myself & the Heirs of Ml Santos—

Wednesday the 20th December weather fine, though a little Cloudy in the forenoon very mild towards Evening—paid Mr Hamill $5. on account of my note I gave him, paid Jones the Carpenter $4.00. let Latham have $1.00 in coffee, John Dorsett do—not much Business doing, no mails from any quarter, no news, no one is going or coming from any where on account of the high waters, if we lived in Siberia we could hear some news, here we hear none—

Thursday the 21st Cloudy in the morning, very fine weather in the afternoon was at the office all day arranging Papers & a—got a chill again near Evening and a hot fever which did not leave me till nine Oclock

Friday the 22d the most beutifull day we have had this Autumn felt well again this morning, but will take medicines for the fever & ague—Mr Reed from San Augustin came from that place. brought me several prospectuses for a Paper to be called the San Augustin Literary intelligencer, Edited or *Fathered* by L A. L Laird and *T. M. Flatau*, the Paper is to be a *Methodist* Paper—(oh! dear)—& to be under the management of a *Son of Abraham* verily I am tempted to belive in Parson Miller's Doctrine—wrote to D. J. Toler pr Mr Reed

Saturday the 23d December Cloudy in the morning, but turned out Splendid weather in the afternoon, held Justices's Court tried several Cases, paid Madam Encarnacion chirino Six dollars 25¢ on account of nine dollars I owe her—also two Dollars on an old account—Judge Ochiltree was in Town but went off without stopping any where—Mr Hudnall and Lady of Houston County passed trough here, tried to get them to stop with us but they went on, anxious to get home, paid albert Long, Six dollars in Coffee and sugar on account of transportation of goods from Natchitochez—having now paid him $16.00 I ought to charge him about $4.00 damages for having thoughroughly [sic] soaked a Sack of Salt, and Spoiled some of the Coffee, Sugar wet—and some of the Flour—

Sunday the 24th Christmass—most beutifull weather—received pr Cardenas—the Presidents message. it is such a Document as might be expected from President Houston. I am glad to find genl Houston this time says nothing about the Cherokee Lands, good— nor does he say any thing about the seat of government, received a Letter from D. S. Kauffman, he says the session will be held at washington, but the President *may* be instructed to remove to austin after this Session—a meeting of the Subscribers for the erection of a School house in this Town, was held at the Court house, a committee was appointed to select a good Spot to build upon, selected a beutifull Site on the north of the Town in a Pine grove, at 3 P. M. fe[l]t my chill to come on me again, had a Sevire ague for an hour, and fever afterwards which did not abate till 9 P. M. every one is merry, the whole Town is alive, and I belive I am the only one confined to my Bed with Sikness

Monday the 25th December   fine weather continues had a S. E. wind in the morning S.w. in the afternoon, but changed to the N. again by Evening— the worst Christmas I have seen here ther[e] was nothing going on exept a few drunken men having a fuss. most all hands gone to Mrs Luckets who gives a large dinner and Ball this Evening

Tuesday the 26th   Weather continues very fine—done some Business at the office, also the Board of Land Commissioners met only one case—made an arrangement with Mr Dwier to hale a Load of Cotton to Natchitochez after he hauls one Load for Mr J. F. Graham, folks come back from Mrs Luckets Party—received 86 lbs Pork from Blake & Parmalee on Account of 108 lbs of Beef I loaned them on the 11th Novr last. taking Latham's Pills for my fever & ague—

Wednesday the 27th   fine weather, white frost last night, St John's day, Lodge met to day, but did not go in consequence of expecting my ague & fever, this being the day, wrote a Congratulary Letter to the Lodge. Mr Dwier went with his waggon to Natchitochez send by him the Deed for half League Land sold to Delmau, wrote to Capt Delmau, to my Brother Isaac, & Eugenia wrote to Madame P. Bossier, I wrote also to Mr Eder, requesting him to send me a Pice of Calicoe, 1 pc of ¾ Domestic 1 pc Towels 1 Sack Salt & 5 glls whiskey and a Steel mill, gave Dwier one Dollar to purchase some *Bakers's Bread*, send all the Letters pr Mr Dwier—missed my fever & ague this afternoon it being now 8 P.M.—

Thursday the 28th December 1843   weather continued very fine, missed my fever & ague intierly, hurrah for Mr Wm Latham, and his Pills—Mr Dwier by whom I send my Letters eta yesterday did not start till to day —paid Mr. H. M. Smith $15.00 which I received from him some 18 months ago for advertising the separation of Hall's Estate—which advertizement was not inserted in the Red Lander—

Friday the 29th   fine weather all day, Cloudy & a S. wind after Sun down— wrote a few Lines to Mr Eder Pr Wm Graham, wrote a long Letter to Alexander Philipps, and to John L. Thielen of New Orleans, the Letters to be send by Mr J. H. Holland Esqr who is going to N. Orleans, in a few days—Doctor Irion & Lady are in Town, stopped at Doctor Starr's Capt Archibald Hotchkiss in Town stops with me all night

Saturday the 30th weather warm & cloudy—a drizly rain fell during the day—Doctor Irion & Lady dined with us, Board of Land Commissioners sat dispatched three cases—received my receipt from the County Clerk as associate Justice $6.00

Sunday the 31st last day of the year, weather warm cloudy, rained last night, made out my quarterly Post office report, settled with Doctor Lewis he falls in my debt $20.12 on a full settlement up to this day, a Mr Dane from Alabama stops with us to night, —Mr Thos Barrett arrived from San Augustin

CHAPTER IX

"Hurrah for ole Nacogdochez."

Monday January the 1st 1844 rain in the forepart of last night cleared up with a Strong west wind, beutifull day to day, got my military claim for 320 acres of Land from Nathan Wade, made a Location on a Lake about 4 miles above Lake Burleson 100 miles above this place being the same Lake on which we were encamped about six days after the Cherokee fight on the Nechaz. filed the certificate and Location with Albert A. Nelson County Surveyor of this County—Mr Humphries paid me 900 lbs Pork on account of One Thousand he owes me, Board of Land Commissioners met, done but little business

Tuesday the 2d Cold Clear weather—had a very fine Party at Mr Chevallier's last night, Mr Deyoung, Mr Morange, and Townsend arrived on yesterday Evening, and were at the Party— Mr Lane left here at 3 P.M. the Eastern mail arrived, first time in a month, did not get any news, Judge Brown arrived from western Texas, says that, the Eastern & Western Members of Congress have agreed to hold the present session at Washington, and remove the different offices to Austin immiditely after the adjournment of Congress—paid a note of $24.00 I gave to Thorn Edwards & Co in 1840—gave C. M. gould my note for $35. payable in 12 months from date. Jose M. Montes commenced to work for me at $15.00 pr month—

Wednesday the 3d January 1844 hard frost last night fine weather to day, had a dancing Party last night at H. H. Edward's and afterwards adjourned to our House where we had music, vocal and Instrumental, till 2 oclock A. M.— Mr Deyoung Mr Morange Barrett & Townsend left here this morning, Major James Durst & Lady remain in Town, dined with us—Mr Gardener looked at my Titles to a League & Labor of Land of which about 1600 acres belong to McLeod & Campbell of New Orleans for whom Mr G. is agent. gave him a copy of my account of outlays I had on the said Land, the part McLeod & Campbell part of the Expences being $182.75, which when collected I am to make said McLeod & Campbell a Deed for the Land—purchased of Alexander White five Hoggs at $3. a piece paid him in goods

Thursday the 4th white frost last night very fine day, had a dance at the House last night, the western mail arrived once more, brought a very large quantity of Letters & Papers, remooved my office from the former place to the End Room of Millard's grocery. rented the Old Room to James Eakin at $5.00 pr month, part of which is to be expended in Improvements on the House, received a Letter from the Grand Secretary of the G. Lodge of Texas—

Friday January the 5th 1844 very hard Frost last night—Mr C. S. Taylor gave a Party at his residence last night. all hands gone, myself staid at Home being too much fatigued from last party at my Home—Killed Seven Hoggs this morning weighing 841 lbs. Mr Humphries paid me up by giving me an other Hog weighing 100 lbs. held justices Court to day, Mr Orton arrived from New Orleans brought me a Letter from Bernard Cohen a Step Brother of mine, did not converse with Mr Orton about news eta

Saturday the 6th rain last night, cold and raining this morning, hawling logs for a new Smoke House, the one I build being too low, of which I'll make a Store room, arranging Documents in the Justices Office all the afternoon, the rest of the Family *all* Busy Salting Pork and making Sausages! arranged my office in as comfortable manner as possible, Keeps on raining at 6 P.M.

Sunday the 7th Cloudy and a little rain during the day, at the office all the forenoon putting my Papers belonging to the justices office in order, the afternoon at home reading Harry Lorrequer's Confessions, a tolerable good thing, but is nothing to compare, to Charles OMahley, or Jack Hinton; a Mr Blackburn who has lately remooved to Town received two waggon loads of goods—Mr Nelson went to Crockett on yesterday

Monday January the 8th 1844 rain, rain, rain,—busy in the office from Breakfeast till 2 P.M. County Court met, the Commissioners of Roads & Revenue were to meet to day but there was no quorum—went to the office again after the adjournment of the County Court, busy issuing summonses till 4 P.M. missed my Dinner at home, went to dine with Mr Chevallier—Messrs J. P. Henderson and K. L. Anderson passed trough here going on to Washington, gave Col Anderson a memorandum about my claim on the government, Anderson promised to pay some attention to [it] by lending me his influence in the Business. this is the aniversary of the Battle of New Orleans, Col J. H. Holland and myself took a Bumper to the old Hero's Health in a glass of Claret, for the want of something better—

Tuesday the 9th still more rain, this must Certainly be the negroes Jubilee for I have remarked that all this fall it would rain all the time exept Saturdays and Sundays, and now lately during the whole of the Christmass holidays it was very fine weather, and so soon as they Holidays were over we had rain again—during the day when it did not rain, raised the new Smoke House, got it ready to put on the Roof—the Eastern mail did not arrive as it ought to have done to day, wrote a letter to N. H. Darnell aquainting him with the *true* state of affairs respecting the Lodge of this place and myself as District Deputy Grand Master. wrote also a Letter to Richardson Scurry[1] the Speaker of the House of

---

[1]Richard A. Scurry, a native of Gallatin, Tennessee, was born on Novem-

Representatives, respecting my claim of $950.00 on the government, asking his assistance in the matter, send both Letters by Mr Wm Culp to be put into the mail at judge Terrells to morrow

Wednesday the 10th Cloudy, though the wind is N. it is warm most too much so for saving Pork. Eastern mail arrived from Sabine Town & Red River, rcd the Northern Standard, No 8 of the 2d Vol being the 1st of the 2d Vol we have received here, wrote to Demorse—send my quarterly returns pr to days mail— Col Tom Jeff Jennings was married this afternoon to the widow mason Daughter of j. H. Hyde Esqr, success attend them

Thursday the 11th Cloudy, with occasional rain, went on however with my Smoke House building—busy in the office arranging things, western Mail arrived brought nothing new. Congress in Session, doing I expect what they have allway been doing. heard of the Death of Mrs Jasper of Crockett, wife of the Member of Congress from Houston County[2]

Friday the 12th More rain, a north wester with rain at noon, looks like it would clear off— doubtfull— this morning before Breakfeast was called on to Marry a couple of Mexicans, ygnacio mendiola & a Daughter of Rafael Santos;—busy at work on the Smoke House, Mr Hoya went to Madame Terrills's nothing Stirring in Town, everything looks dead

Saturday January the 13th 1844 weather turned Cold last night, Cloudy all day but no rain, finished covering the new Smoke House, was not much at the Office to day, few People in Town nothing doing, Mr Nelson returned from Crockett, no news—

Sunday the 14th Cold rainy weather all day—did not leave the House all day, read Handy Andy[3] —no great thing—a Person at Isaac Lee's is said to be affected with the *veriolet* (so called by the Doctors) but I am afraid it is Small Pox, god grant it is not so. a Person will be send to morrow morning to Fort Jessup to get Vaccine, matter, to vaccinate all hands—Mr Hoya returned from the Angelina no news—

Monday the 15th at about 8 A.M. a western wind dispersed all the Clouds, and we had a Splendid day. the Persons at Lee's has the Small Pox without any doubt about it—some Business in the office to day—there were many Persons in Town from the Country, but so soon it was Known that the Smal Pox were in the vicinity, all hands left in a hurry— received a Letter from Louis

---

ber 11, 1811. He trained for the law, and moved to the Clarksville area in Red River County in 1836. On March 10, 1836 he entered the Texas Army and fought at San Jacinto. He served as secretary to the Senate of the first Texas Congress. On December 16, 1836 he became District Attorney of the First District, and on January 30, 1840 he was elected judge of the Sixth Judicial District. In 1842 Scurry was elected to the House of Representatives for the Seventh Congress, and he was selected as Speaker for the Eighth Congress. He served during th early part of the Civil War on the staff of General Albert Sidney Johnston. He died on April 9, 1862.

[2]Selden L. B. Jasper.

[3]**Handy Andy, A Tale of Irish Life,** by Samuel Louer, was published in London by F. Louer in 1842.

Rueg pr Mr Lacombe, Son in Law of old Cazenaue, this is the Husband of the lady who was here last year, he comes to see about the Estate left by his late Father in Law J. B. Cazenaue.

Tuesday the 16th cold & cloudy—grew colder during the day and at Evening it was Clear and a very strong N.W. wind blowing—a meeting of the Citizens took Place to day at the Court House composed of the citizens of Nacogdochez & vicinity—to take into consideration; and to adopt means to arrest the progress of the Spreading of the Small Pox, Mr C. S. Taylor was appointed chairman & A. Sterne Secretary, a Committee was appointed to assist the Phisicians to act, in fact, as a Board of Health, was appointed one of the Committee, had all those in Town —who had not been vaccinated before, or had the Small Pox vaccinated, the whole Town is in a Hubbub,—7 P. M. most bitter Cold, and a strong north wind blowing—Skye clear & freezing—send off the western mail but the mail rider returned because the water was very high at the Angelina—this is no excuse because other People cross it every day, and there is no danger, in crossing with the mail—had my Laura, Placide, the little negro Tom and the negro Joe vaccinated to day, by Doctor Starr, gave my note to Charles Chevallier for $6.50 as my dues to Milam Lodge No 2 for my last years dues—

Wednesday the 17th January 1844 very hard frost this morning, beutifull Clear weather all day, a South wind but bitter Cold at Sun down, Mr Muse left here for New Orleans, wrote by him to my Brother Bernard—the mail rider returned yesterday Evening from the Angelina saying he could not cross—send the young gentleman back to day with instruction that he *must* cross, which is practicable at John Dursts Bridge, no news of the Small Pox having affected any one yet, two Houses were prepared to day for the reception of any should there be any cases—

Tuesday the 18th Cold, frost last night, Cloudy & South wind this Evening, Committee of Sanity met but no report of any new Cases, no one hardly in Town from the country, western mail Boy came in, reports that the mail Bags for Eastern Texas were lost on the other side of the Trinity, wrote to Canfield of the Red Lander respecting the Small Pox at this place

Friday the 19th Cloudy, warm weather—rain at noon continued raining during the afternoon, Mr Thos Dwier arrived from Natchitochez, receved a Letter from Mr Eder, also two p calicoe 1 p Domestics and a Demijohn in which there had been put five galls whiskey, but arrived all broke into smash—also recd 1 doz hffs all $15.35. received some newspapers, and some music from Mr Eder—done nothing for me in New Orleans—

Saturday the 20th hard rain last night, fair this morning, fine day, but too warm for this season of the year. commenced early this morning to trim my Trees in the Orchard. worked hard all day, had fever near dark do not Know if it is the result, from over exertion, or if it is a *second Edition* of my Fever & ague.

settled with John S. Thorn, he falls in my debt about three dollars up to date—

Sunday the 21st very warm Cloudy weather, Mr H. Crutcher who went to Natchitochez for vaccine matter returned this morning; brought but very little matter not sufficient to vaccinate half those who, are realy in want of it—the other vaccine matter not having taken, being too old—Mr C. brought me some news Papers send me by Mr Eder—Mr A. W. Canfield is in Town, not having felt well all day did not go up Town, exept to go to the Office to get some Papers,

Monday the 22d, warm, cloudy, and raining all day a very hard rain at night, planted Trees to day. 50 Peach Trees—god only Knows who will reap the benefitt of it, a. w. Canfield dined with us—gave him up all the notes I had for him to collect also all the accounts exept that of Taliaferro which I could not find having been misplaced by me, but of one thing I am sure it was not paid, —Mr Canfield is on a Collecting Expedition, god only Knows how he will succeed.

Tuesday January 23d 1844 More rain last night the Bayou East of Town overflowed. the Person who was at Isaac Lee's with the Small Pox died last night, mail arrived from the East no news, in the afternoon went out to the Moral to perform the marriage ceremony between Dolores Causto and Teresa Medina—this young man is one of four Boys taken amongst the Prisoners at San Jacinto, and send by Col Potter to his Plantation on Soda Lake, but which I stopped here, where they have been ever since. got a fever again after dark which lasted on me more than four hours, this is now the third time that I have it every three days

Wednesday the 24th beutifull day, it appears that the weather is settled, not much Business doing in Town, george Clevenger's waggons arrived from Natchitochez loaded for Doctor Starr and Mr F. Hoya, by this days arrival from Natchitochez Mr Hoya received a Letter in which the Death of the widow Placide Bossier is announced, she was the Foster Mother of my wife, and a better woman exept my mother I never Knew, I have not yet broke the news to Mrs Sterne, and I do not Know how to do so, it will be most distressing to her, and might prove injurious—

Thursday the 25th fine day, arrange some little Business in the office, and after dinner went out to Mr J. J. Simpsons, with James Eakin who has a Law Suit to which he wants me to attend. stopped all night at Simpsons

Friday the 26th Cold fair weather, the trial was put off for 10 days, to be tried by S. M. Orton. after dinner left for home, mail from the west had arrived, recd a Letter from Mr Toler. he informs me that Judge Terrell has not paid my draft, in consequence of which he drew on me for $33.16—I belive that Judge Terrell is a fair Specimen of the great men of Texas—!!! Man who is utterly *faithless* in his monitary transactions, is not the man whom I would trust with the Helm of government

Saturday the 27th weather same as yesterday,—done some

— 193 —

Business in the office to day, had a hot fever again last night, commenced to take medecine to day. Mr Eder arrived from Natchitochez, brought me a Letter from David F. Tabor, informing me of the Death of Madame Placide Bossier, that she died on Sunday morning the 14th Inst at day light and was burried on the next day at noon—Mr Tabor mentions that the Deceased made a will a few days before she died, in which my wife and Daughter are remembered—

Sunday January 28th Cold night and morning, had a most splendid day to day made out twenty one Executions to day for the Estate of E. M. Eakin dated on yesterday, this being Sunday—Col K. L. Anderson arrived from washington, brings no very particular news, exept that there was a Bill passed in the Senate repealing the Cherokee Land Bill—good—if the Bill passes and is signed by the Executive; this County will be a Sam Houston County again, Col Anderson also brought me a Commission as a Deputy District grand Master of this District for the next year, signed by general N. Darnell as grand master

Monday the 29th fine weather—the Board of Road Commissioners met, was reelected associate Justice of County Court, also overseer of Streets and Roads within the Limits of the Corporation

Tuesday the 30th warm weather, Cloudy, but no rain. had an other fever and ague last night, took more medecine to day, sat as associate Justice of the Probate Court, the negro man who nursed the person which died of the Small Pox, was taken with the same desease, and it is very much feared that Doctor Starr is affected,—the old negro in my Possession sick but not Small Pox—Doctor Lewis attending on him

Wednesday the 31st South wind, Cloudy, but no rain, the old negro sick yet, my Son Charles has a fever nothing serious however—Doctor Starr very Sick, it is thought he has the Small Pox—there is an other case on the Hill at Lee's, nothing transpired in Town, Eastern mail arrived, send off western mail,

Thursday the 1st February 1844 rain last night rain till 11 oclock to day, Bayous rising, and Roads as they were before, a Strong team could not bring 600 Picketts out of the woods, which in good weather is hardly a load for a pair of Horses, the western mail arrived, did [not] bring any news, Doctor Starr very Sick yet, Doctor Lewis says it is not Small Pox. hope it is not

Friday the 2d very warm South wind, raining and Cloudy all day, a Boat Loaded with Cotton belonging to Mr Robert Patton left to day her anchorage on the angelina 12 miles from here, bound for the Sabine Pass, she is not heavily loaded having only 192 Bales of cotton on Board; this is a beginning. it will shortly be Small Steam Boats to take down cotton to the mouth of the Sabine,—was at the office done some Business in the office *all* for Mr. C. Chevallier, Doctor Starr is better, and said not to be small Pox, no new Simpthomps any where—Mr Eder is here yet, and much pleased with Nacogdochez

Saturday february the 3d 1844 warm, cloudy, raining occasionally during the day, it is ascertained to day that Doctor Starr *has not* the Small Pox nor Doctor Moore who was reported to have it was in Town to day well and hearty—not much Business in Town, there is however a prospect of Nacogdochez looking up— Doctor Moore came to rent a Store and Dwelling House for a Mr Dunn who is coming here with his Family to Keep a Store, Mr Tom Barrett from San Augustin also came up to rent a Store, Hurrah for ole Nacogdochez.

Sunday the 4th wind changed last night and this morning it is clear and cold, it is getting colder every hour, and near dark it was *winter again,* answered some Interrogatories send from Liberty County in a case in which Frost Thorn and others are plaintiffs and the Republic of Texas Defendant. it is respecting some Leagues of Land the State of Coauhila & Texas made to Col P. E. Bean

Monday the 5th Cold & Cloudy fair in the afternoon. Board of Land Commissioners met, two cases disposed of—some Law Business, not much of any consequence—on a treaty with Mr Eder for my Loco Land—

Tuesday the 6th Cold nights, fine warm day—busy making a fence round the Square given to Eugenia, by gel Houston, Eastern mail arrived did not bring any Red Landers, nor other news— of any Consequence, the first members of the San Augustin Literary Intelligencer was received, it does honor to its Editor & prop[r]ietor and vise versa—send off western mail, wrote to general Houston about his House in this place, want to get it for a Store, expecting to get into Business again

Wednesday the 7th Cold & Cloudy in the morning a very strong north wind blowing all day which increased towards [dark]. worked all day on the Lot I am fencing in, did not do much business in the office to day, a negro belonging to the young man who died at Lee's of the Small Pox, died to day of the same desease. Mr Eder of Natchitochez here yet expects to leave here to morrow— gave him a note on Gill & Legrand, to collect for me which he is to give me credit for if collected;—entered into writing with Mr Isaac Reynolds who lives on a place belonging to Mrs Sterne & Mrs Mayfield, Mr Reynolds is to Keep the place for four years to Keep it in good repair and to give it up peaceable at the end of said time, gave the Instrument to be recorded in the Clerk's office —Cold as *Snow* this Evening

Thursday the 8th February 1844 Cold— Cold, Cold. Mr Eder left this morning—gave him ten Dollars on account, told him to send me a Bll of Flour, and some Iron I gave him an order for, western mail arrived this afternoon, no news, the washington mail failed beyond Montgomery, send off the Eastern mail, busy fencing in my big Lot.

Friday the 9th Cold, & Cloudy, the Speaker of the House of Representatives, gel Darnell, major D. S. Kaufman and Several members of Congress passed trough here to day on their way home, received the Captions of all Laws passed this Congress; the most interesting to this County, is the total repeal of the Cherokee Bill, which will be of immense benefit to this County, had not time to speak much with any of the gentlemen— reced a Letter from J. L. Hogg our representative, nothing was done, in my business; I expected that, the Invitation made to gel Lamar in 1841—Sticks yet in gel Houstons maw—and all those whose names were to that Invitation have fallen under his displeasure, and he will revenge himself in any way, except such a way, as is worthy of a gentleman[4]—!!! Mr Houghson from Natchitochez arrived, stop with us—

Saturday the 10th weather same, left home for Douglass—accompanied by Mr Houghson, Mr Hoya & Mr Linn, stopped at Col Raguet's took Dinner at Col R. who went with us as far as Douglass—we stopped all night a[t] Mr Moore's a son in Law of Mr Dykes—a Debating Society met, at the House of Mr g. g. Cole, Subscribed my name as a monthly member, was called to the chair to preside for the Evening, subject of Discussion: if it is more beneficial for Texas to be annexed, or not, to the United States, among those on the negative side of the question was wild Bill Sparks our last years member of Congress—he did make a tolerable good speech—and the victory was proclaimed in favor of the negative side of the question—went to *bed?* at 10—and such a Damnable sleeping arrangement *is a perfect caution to all Taverns.*

Sunday the 11th very cold, and fine weather not a cloud in the Heavens,—passed the Swamp of the angelina in the water to James Durst's very Deep wading—went to Judge Terrills's to Dinner, told Mrs Terrill about my Business respecting the Claim of $30.00 which the Judge had *promised* to pay on account of a larger sum he owes me, which he did not do, and which could have been settled trough Mr goodman the mail contractor who is indebted to Mrs Terrill, and he is the man who has the Draft on me from the Post office Department, yet notwithstanding Mrs Terrills Knowing the circumstances of the case very well, this woman is a perfect virago and Judge T. must *certainly* be blessed? in having such a wife—left after Dinner (which I regret very much to have taken) to James Boulter an Englishman, an honest man, a Blacksmith who formerly lived in this place stopped all night with him—Mr Linn & Mr Hoya having left us at Mrs Terrills.

Monday the 12th Cold & Cloudy—left after Breakfeast, passed at Mr John Durst's Bridge stopped a few moments at Mr Durst's he is not at home, gone to his place on the Trinity—arrived at home at 3 Oclock P.m. attended to some Law Business between Mr Chevallier & Mr (Judge) Wingfield, looked at some of the work done during my absense, all right, Mr John Noblett mooved into the House formerly occupied by general Douglass

Tuesday the 13th weather same as yesterday—mail from the

---

[4]The business of which Sterne speaks was undoubtedly his unsettled claim against the Republic for the $950 which he had spent during the Revolution to finance troops from New Orleans. The invitation to Lamar was to a public dinner at Nacogdoches at which those present had endorsed the then President Lamar's frontier policy.

East arrived— no news,— a Captain Todd who formerly was navy agent passed trough here to day on his way west— very busy all day fencing in the Square commenced on, some days ago, Mr Houghson is here yet trying to collect debts—I think he has succeeded tolorable well, considering the bad times.

Wednesday the 14th Clear & Beutifull weather, South wind in the afternoon, but the sun went down clear Mr Hoya returned from Nechaz, the ferry Boat is sunk at the Nechaz, Mr Houghson returned home to day, some business in the office to day, all my *family* are engaged in *fixing* the gardens, have a mexican to work in the garden opposide the House does very well—the School house which was Contemplated to be build, was put up so far as the Body of the House is concerned, the Roof is to be put on to morrow or next day—

Thursday 15th fine clear day—South wind in the forenoon— north wind after dinner—worked in the garden all day exept to send off the Eastern mail and open the western mail, which Did not bring any news,—several gentlemen from the United States in Town to day, the Ex governor of Mississippi Hiram g. Runnels was in Town, did not see him, he went off early this morning, some little to do in the office

Friday February the 16th 1844 fine Spring weather had a frost last night—wind changed and blows from the South at dark —received a Bll of Irish Potatoes from Mr Eder, commenced to plant them 15 minutes after receiving them worked hard all the afternoon, have all hands employed in making fences, and improving the Place; received pr Albert Long a Letter from Mr Pierce the Clerk of Mr Eder, he send me a new york Herald—thank you Mr Pierce—Mr Chevallier received some goods to day which were attached to Natchitochez by Mr Sanks— come rather too late for winter—

Saturday the 17th frost this morning, fine weather all the rest of the day, planted Irish Potatoes all the forenoon, and planted Trees in the afternoon I planted 20 accassias— (Black Locusts) *god Knows who will rest under their Shade*, am getting the place in *tolorable fix* as the saying is—Mr Wortham of Crockett arrived here to day, he is going to reside here with his Family, he is going to follow his trade—a Brick maker, and Brick Layer, is to build a house for Mr F. Hoya, and one for C. Chevallier; and if all Ends meet I'll build one myself, at least I shall build one bake oven, and underpin my house

Sunday the 18th February 1844 Cold last night very fine Spring weather to day, all the Peach Trees are in Blossom, and if we should happen to get hard frosts again, our hopes for fruit will again be destroyed, wrote a Letter to Alexander Phillipps of New Orleans and packed up all the Papers concerning the League and Labor of Land of the Heirs of Juan Clemente Cortez out of which I intend to give Mr Phillipps his 880 acres, I inclose in the Package the Patent for the Land, which Mr Hoya is to bring back with him—I only send it for the satisfaction of Mr Phillipps, so that he sees that all is right—there have been so many bad claims sold in New Orleans that they are now very particular about Land and Land Claims—I also made memorandum or addition to the Letter I wrote to John Thielen in December last which I intended to send by Mr Holland, and did not send, because Mr Holland did not go—

Monday the 19th— weather moderated, but does not look like rain, hard at work planting Trees in the new fenced in Lot, Major greer, the Senator of San augustin came here on his way home, dined with us and went up to Mr Orton's to stay all night, Joe the Black Boy is sick with fever and ague, got medecine's for him from Doctor Starr, Doctor Irion dined with us he is going to move into Col Raguet's House, very good—

Tuesday the 20th February 1844   rain last night, and a gentle rain all day to day, does not do much harm to anybody— or any thing, but is of great service to the Trees I have planted yester-day—wrote a long Letter to Bernard Cohen, and gave a list of articles which I want Mr Hoya to purchase for me in New Orleans, packed up all my Correspondence I had written and the Docu-ments send to Alexander Philips and gave them to Mr Hoya—set-tled up with Mr Hoya, and after all Demands and offsetts are shown, I remain in his debt only Six Dollars and seventy five cents.

Wednesday the 21st   rain last night, rains a little this morn-ing, but not enough to prevent me from working in the gardens; where I was employed nearly all day, was at the office only a short time, received a Letter from gel Houston, by a Mr Clay-brook, who went on by way of San Augustin to Shreveport, Doc-tor Lewis and Judge Hart who have been at variance for some time made up all matters to day, very good—

Thursday the 22d   fine weather—Mr Nelson settled with me to day gave me his note payable in 60 days for $54.75 went on to Natchitochez, wrote a Letter to Mr Oliver Rouquier and to Mrs Hunt or Bernard Cohen, to be delivered by my son Charles who goes on to New Orleans with Mr Hoya and Mr Eder of Natchi-tochez, gave all the Papers and Documents I had to send to Mr Hoya—they started off at 11 a. m.—the western mail arrived at 2 P. m. received a Letter from a Mr Salzman of New Orleans re-specting his Claims on the Estate of James Ogilvy decd. Comes most too late for any good—the Houston Thelegraph says we be-long to the United States *quien sabe* hope to god it is so—re-ceived a letter from the Post Master general, advising me that the draft I drew on Judge Terrill has been Payd ($30.00) and placed to my Credit

Friday the 23d   Splendid day, real Spring weather, all the vegetation is putting forward even the fig trees are budding, if we have a frost again this year, adieu to all fruit, and to most of our vegetables—busy at work in the garden all day, planting apple trees, and arranging my Terrasses, which are in a fine State of progression was up at the office and done some business for Mr Chevallier as Justice of the Peace, It appears that there is a revival in this Town, every one of the Old Settlers are Improving their Property, Judge Taylor, Judge Hart Mr Roberts, Col Thorns, H. H. Edwards and myself are all busy in doing some thing to improve our respective premises

Saturday the 24th of February 1844 fine weather busily engaged in the garden or rather gardens for I am at work in three gardens— went up to the office for a short time done some business as Justice of the Peace—received and send off Northern mail (Henderson). Mr gould who I thought to be in the Island of galveston, arrived this Evening from San augustin, brought me a Letter from Mr Eder of Natchitochez, Eugenia gone on a visit to Mr John Durst's

Sunday the 25th weather continues very fine, wind changed to the South to day—Mrs S. feels a little unwell from fatigue, having worked too much in the garden—Mr Thorn returned to day from Natchitochez, accompanied by Capt Vail, Col Thorn having come as far as the Sabine and returned to Red River— brought me a Letter from Mr Eder, which he received from New Orleans, dated 13th inst—announcing the fact that our commissioners have made arrangements with Mexico for an Armistice for 10 years—also that genl Murphy[5] the united States Minister at our seat of government is the Bearer of a treate of annexation of Texas to the united States *ojala*

Monday the 26th February, 1844—weather rather *uncertain* cloudy, warm, sunshine, and a little Sprinkling of rain—sun went down clear—worked in the garden nearly all day, with the Exeption that I was compelled to be in the office, Judge Terrell is in Town, settled with him the $33.16 drawn on me by the Post office department, he has also paid for me on account what he owes me $284.00 in old Texas Treasury notes.—the ballance which I belive to be $150.00 in old T. T. notes he is yet in my debt, he however thinks otherwise. n'import—paid David Muckleroy $22.62½ for Mr Wm B. Goodman for Keeping his mail rider and Horse from the 20th october 1843 to date, paid said recipt to Judge Terrell who held the draft and paid him the Ballance in monay, so that at this time I owe nothing at all exept $12.50 to the general Post office Department also, exepted, the present quarter which commenced the 1st January Last—no further news from the west, or East, about annexation or armistice—Bob. Patton was in Town to day, just returned from a very successful trip Down the angelina, nechaz, to Sabine Pass and back, brought a Cargo of Coffee, Sugar, Salt, Iron, and flour,—good

Tuesday the 27th February 1844 fine Spring weather hard at work in the gardens, Eastern mail failed—the old negro Charles

---

[5]William Sumter Murphy was born in South Carolina in 1796. He had a legal and military background when he was appointed in 1843 to be the United States minister extraordinary to Central America and **charge d'affaires** to Texas. He played an instrumental role in implementing President John Tyler's policy of annexing Texas. He died in Galveston on July 12, 1844, of yellow fever.

I put up to day in the Service of T. J. Jennings Esqr where he will serve on account of the fee J. M. Watkins owes him on account of the estate of Wm Cabble dcd, Sowed Rey to day, it is a little late, but it will make a good Pasture,

Wednesday the 28th weather continues fine, and very warm all the Trees are budding out, still hard at work in the garden, sowing Reye, and ploughing up ground for Sweet Potatoes, was but very little in the office to day— Mr Wm graham returned from Natchitochez last night. he saw Mr Hoya, Nelson, and my Son Charles near the garrison 25 miles from Natchitochez on Sunday Evening last, all well; gel Henderson arrived to day from Crockett washington, Houston & galveston, brought no Particular news, received a Letter pr gel H. from David Akin Administrator of oliver Akin decd dated New Orleans 29th January 1844, he says he will pay the monay I drew on him for, if he can get his Papers, which he will receve pr Mr Eder who will no doubt receive the money and Mr Hoya will consequently bring me the articles I send for.

Thursday the 29th weather warm & Cloudy, had a very light shower to day—was a short time at the Office and renewed some Executions in favor of Js Eakin Admr of E. M. Eakin, done some business for Chevallier, and worked in the garden the rest of the day, and feel very fatigued at this present writing 7. P. m—

Friday the first March commenced to work in the garden this morning, but rain drove me out of it, rained very hard for several hours and continues to rain all day and at this time 7 P. m—had several trials in the magistrates Court no news from any quarter

Saturday the 2d Clear weather anniversary of our Independence (?) nothing going in the Place, no one Stirring—went out to Mr John Dursts, for Eugenia, who has been out there a week on a visit, She is 15 years old to day, arrived at Mr Durst's at 5 P. M. Mr Durst gone to Trinity saw Mr Washington a Lawyer from Liberty *who* stopped all night at Mr Durst—

Sunday the 3d fair—left at 9 a. m. Arrived at home at 12 oclock found all well, Mr Joost returned to day from Natchitochez, Charley was well. Mr Hoya & Nelson gone to New Orleans. was introduced to a Mr Frather of Natchitochez

Monday the 4th March 1844 fine weather rather cloudy Mr Barrett returned from New Orleans, dito Mr gardiner, Mr Barrett brought me a Letter from Bernard Cohen, and a Package containing several late novels—Mr Gardener informs me that he has not done any thing in my Business with Mr Campbell, but offers me a Certificate of 640 acres of Land, which I dont think I shall take. the Board of Land Commissioners met to day and done some Business in some 7 or 8 cases—Mr Barrett commenced to Board with me

Tuesday the 5th white frost last night, but Dont think it done much damage to fruit trees. paid my Taxes to day as Administrator of genereux Benard, Patricio de Torres, and as agent of P Delmore, & for Mrs Sterne and myself, all amounting to $72.25, which I had great trouble to get— this much for a government to which I am paying Taxes to protect me in my rights and it is the very one that is swindling me out of $950.00 but n'importe—I assisted to raise the *thing* so I must not or at least ought not to grumble

wednesday the 6th Cold night but not much of a frost as I expected their would be—some busines at the office, Mr Barrett received some goods to day, graham dito, the Town is looking up— a Mr Blackbourn returned last night from new Orleans reports that all in that city are for Anexation—good—he also states that the Steam Boat De Soto ran afoul of the Steam Boat Buck Eye and sunk her, and that 100 or more lives were lost by this sad accident. Mr Hoya and Mr Nelson were on Board when this accident happened (That is on Board of the De Soto) hope that my Son Charles was not on Board and from what I can learn from Mr Joostt Charlie is in Natchitochez

Thursday the 7th heavy dew and Cloudy in the morning, sun very warm in the afternoon, worked in the garden most part of the day—

Friday the 8th warm this morning very heavy dew, cleared off fine, worked all day without intermission in the garden, Sowed Rice, and Sowed, and planted all kinds of vegetables,

Saturday the 9th warm but clear last night—a Strong North wind is blowing this morning, fine weather the ballance of the Day, was up at the office, and attended to some Law Business, was introduced to a Mr Wardlaw, from Missoury, nothing new—

Sunday the 10th cool weather n. E. wind blowing very strong all day, received some Pear and white mulberry trees from my friend Radford Berry. Planted them, occupied myself at doing something all day, received the Red Lander of the 9th inst, pr private hand, nothing of great interest in it—

Monday March the 11th 1844 rain last night, rained very hard occasionally untill 3 P. M. when it cleared up, warm, the Eastern mail arrived brought a great number of Red Landers some Marchall times⁶ and a lot of *Back* numbers of the Northern Standard. Jessy Walling Esqr who came from the west brought me $35.00 in Exchequer monay also my draft paid which I drew on T. J. Gill for $17.50 on the 17th Nov in favor of Daniel J. Toler all of which is to be credited on a note I hold against Gill for $150.00

Tuesday the 12th March very fine weather, every thing is coming up in garden and growing fine, worked in the garden, was at the office, wrote to wm Pierpont also to Messrs Root & Taylor of Independence, respecting my claim for $500.00 I hold against S. B. Eves's Estate. made up the western mail but no one to take it away, gave Judge Hart a claim of $35.00 against the County

---

⁶Sterne possibly refers to the Marshall **Review**, the successor to the **Sabine Advocate** at Pulaski. It was published by L. A. W. Laird, who was formerly associated with the **Red-Lander.** It was issued between January and December, 1843.

which he noted and filed to be paid when its turn comes, and when there is monay in Treasury

Wednesday the 13th Cloudy last night, commenced to rain very hard about 10 oclock A. M. continued to rain all day—paid David Rusk Sheriff and Tax Collector Thirty Dollars Exchequer monay, Doctor Lewis returned from Rusk County no one, as yet to take away the mail which was made up for the west yesterday morning.

Thursday the 14th very hard shower of rain last night. Clear this morning, worked a little in the garden sold *Dap* a Poney I purchased of Dan. J. Toler to Mr Parsons *to pay my debts.* Mr Barrett who had gone to San Augustin returned this Evening. my old friend Elisha Roberts stops with me to night from his place on Trinity, on his way home.

Friday the 15th Clear day, too wet however to plough, grew colder every minute towards Evening, gave orders to make fires under the Peach Trees,—Doctor Wm G. Lewis gave me an account to collect for $92.00 as his medical Services to Wm B. Hamill decd and also a negro who belonged to same—which amount when collected I am to account for to Doctor Lewis. Stephen B. True arrived from Natchitochez this Evening, says that Nelson is on the Road coming back from New Orleans

Saturday the 16th Cold north wind blowing but no frost last night, made fires in the Orchard, and Killed some Peaches thereby —which otherwise would have done well—Mr Nelson arrived, brought me a Letter from Mr Eder's Clerk— Charlie is well— Did not go down to New Orleans,—am glad of it— for he would have been on the Boat De Soto when she ran over the Buck Eye— got a few late Papers—the half of the Cabinet officers of the united States have been Killed by the Explosion of a *mammoth* gun[7]

Sunday march the 17th 1844 Saint Patrick Day—!!! beutifull day, had a very little frost last night,—Mr Becton preached at the Court house this morning, nothing else stirring

Monday the 18th had a heavy white frost last night dont think it done much harm—Mr Rynolds who lives on my place, is in Town, dined with us—good old Fellow—returned Mr A. A. Nelson his note he gave me for $54.75 and took a note on Wm C. Edwards of San augustin for $57.75 payable next 25th December gave nelson my due Bill for $6.75 being the Ballance due him on Settlement as above stated. nothing new in Town—

Tuesday the 19th no frost last night, very warm all day. a little cloudy towards Evening—not much doing in Town, at home

---

[7]On February 28, 1844 an explosion occurred aboard the U.S.S. **Princeton** in a trial run to test a new, twelve-inch cannon, the "Peacemaker." The explosion of the cannon killed Secretary of State Abel P. Upshur and Secretary of Navy Thomas W. Gilmer. Upshur was even then negotiating the treaty of Annexation with Texas. He was succeeded as Secretary of State by John C. Calhoun.

nearly all day, the western mail was taken away for the first time under the new Contract

Wednesday the 20th fine fair weather—wrote to Mr De young of San Augustin and send him $27.87½ pr general Rusk, which sum I collected for him from Wm W. Wingfield, wrote to Wm C. Edwards, was introduced to Mr Ellis Surveyor of San augustin County, Mr A. A. Nelson who has been boarding with me for near two years or more, left to day to board with Judge Hart— we parted as we met—as Friends—

Thursday the 21st very fine weather—planting corn all day, nothing whatsoever stirring, in Town, a Mr Buckley arrived from the u. S. reports, no news

Friday the 22d fair & clear, a very hard north west wind blowing all day, finished planting half of the field of corn—garden suffering for rain—the western mail arrived for the first time under the new Contract— brought several Letters eta. one for myself from the County Clerk of Liberty County telling me he did not receive my Deed for my head right for record, so that the *old Scamp* wiess has not given my Deed for my head right to be recorded as agreed upon—it serves me right I Knew he is a Damned Scamp and ought not to have trusted him

Saturday the 23d a little frost last night not sufficient to hurt vegetation much—no news from any quarter, nothing doing in Town

Sunday the 24th a very little frost again last night R. Scurry passed trough from the west, did not see him. brings no news of any consequence, this day passed as all Sundays do, in Nacogdoches—stale flat and unprofitable

Monday the 25th beutifull weather, real Spring weather— worked in the garden eta, done some Business in the office, James Durst & Lady in Town, going to Shreveport, wrote a Letter by him to Mr Myers of that place, mail come in from East, received a Letter from C. W. griffith of New Orleans respecting some Land he owns here, purchased of A. Emanuel

Tuesday the 26th march 1844 very warm, rain to day—a very welcome visitor, rained just enough to make *things grow.* wrote a long Letter to Mr griffith of New Orleans respecting his land Claim in this County, on the Lanana Creek—an unfortunate difficulty happened to day between M. S. Orton and Bennette Blake, the first tried to Kill the latter with a Bowie Knife, Mr J. S. Roberts, and Wm Johnson are intitled to much credit in preventing this sad Catastrophy—Blake was wounded in the Head but not dangerous, I can say no more on the subject, as the case is to come before me to morrow as a magistrate

Wednesday the 27th tremendous storm last night Hailed very much but did not do any Damage here, sat as Judge in the case of Orton—bound him over in the sum of $1500.00 to appear at the next District court, Orton Made friends with Blake, trough the instrumentality of Judge Taylor—good—no news—

Thursday the 28th Cloudy last night, finished planting Corn to day, and immidiatly afterwards it rained and hailed severely, but did not do any damage. the Brothers of Mr Hensel who died at Lee's of Small pox came on here to settle their Brother's Estate. nothing more of importance happened to day

Friday the 29th March 1844 Cloudy last night a north west wind commenced to blow this morning and continued all day growing colder and colder untill it was as cold as Siberia, the western mail arrived at 6 P. M. not much news, received the new Post office Law—Postage is reduced to one half of the last years Postage—Robert A. Terrill in Town, Judge Ochiltree is in Town, gone home this Evening—San Augustin Court adjourned

Saturday the 30th a tremendous North wind Blowing all day, at sun set calm, and clear and all appearance of a hard frost to night, wrote to Bernard Cohen, and to Charles W. griffith of New Orleans, send the letters by S. M. Orton. a Mr Coon a Taylor has mooved up to this place from San augustin, occupies Mr Brichta's House

Sunday the 31st wind Calmed at sut [sic] set last night and we had a very hard white frost, Killed Beans and several other vegetables which had come up— but apparently did not injure the Peachez a[t] twelve oclock last night, Mrs S. *send me after a midwife* did not find Mrs Willbourne but got Doctor Lewis whom I had also engaged in case of accident, but who now will have to perform all the duties of midwife—this evening at sun down no news yet—Mrs S. appears to do tolorably well 6 P. m at ½ past 7. P. m. was delivered of a Daughter, Dr Lewis in attendance—all well.

Monday the first day of April 1844 White frost last night, splendid weather to day, Mrs Sterne and child are well, Doctor Lewis has been in attendance all day, all well at Sun down to night Board of Land Commissioners met and dispatched many cases—Rinaldo Hotchkiss is in Town Just arrived from Matamoros, where he has been for two years—

Tuesday the 2d April Cloudy, weather moderate. Mrs Sterne and infant are well, nothing new stirring—

Wednesday the 3d warm and somewhat cloudy, no news from any direction—busy at the office all day

Thursday the 4th warm weather. Mr Hoya, and Charles returned from Natchitochez to day, Charlie has been Sick, but is convalescand at present—he informes me that the late Madame P. Bossier, in her will bequeathed $500, to Mrs Sterne and $500, to Eugenie, Mr Hoya has not attended to any one of the messages he promised to attend to for me—Doctor Franklin told the truth when he says "that, if you want your Business well attended to— go and do it yourself, I shall in future allways endeavor to follow the Sage's advise, received a letter from B. Cohen and from H. M. Eder of Natchitochez, Mr Eder writes he will be out here soon

CHAPTER X

"... Well I can grin but must bear it- ..."

Nacogdochez February 2d 1851—*Sunday* After a laps of very near five years I again commence to Keep a diary, partly because it amuses, but more, because I found my old diary occasionally a very usefull refference of passed events.

I arrived at home last night in the Western Stage, from Austin, Wharton, & Houston, delivered to R. Parmalee all the Documents he delivered to me on my departure, failed in accomplishing the Business he send me to transact. Parmalee's Brother James, of Durham Cont arrived last night, a fine man, he treated me when at his House last april like a friend, found that my wife has sold one of her negroes, well done—Deposited the monay $850.00 with her Brother in Law Judge Taylor—well done again—saw Mrs Taylor to day, she has been Sick for 5 weeks and I am very fearfull will never recover. went up Town, received a letter from my Son Charles dated Town Bluff Tyler Co Jan 1851—a letter from John W. Overton Dated Dallas Texas December 22d 1850— respecting some Land, letter filed and answered, a Letter from Mr C. E. James dated cheneyville La. inquirring about gel mason's Lands, filed & answered, to day a letter from T. H. Patterson dated Fort Jessup La wants information about Dan Keller's land. answered and filed to day—this was a very wet, cold day, and raining now. 9 P.M. my wife is up with her Sister who is very low.

Monday feb. 3d 1851 Cold, rainy day, arranged my papers, wrote a Letter to Chief Clerk of gel Land office inquiring about business, left in the office during the last Extra Session of the Legislature, my Son Joseph went to Messrs Linn & Culp's Drug Store to day, for a month or more. Mrs Taylor a little better this morning

Tuesday Feb 4th 1851 Cold & Cloudy in the morning— Cleared up at noon and had fine weather, worked in the garden all day spend the Evening at Mr Bondies's paid Madame Bonamie $15 for Laura's Schooling, also $10 to Mr nickerson[1] on account of Placide and Rosine's Schooling, Mrs Taylor better—

Wednesday feb 5th 1851 This was a most beutifull day, had a little white frost last night, but the whole day was equal to may— worked all day in the garden, with the exeption of a letter I wrote to Wm R gallagher of New Orleans, handed to Horatio nelson a

---

[1]Thomas Nickerson was president of Nacogdoches University in 1850-51.

receipt in full from C. Chevallier owner of a Judgement against me in favor of Jacob Davis, spend the Evening at Col Thorns

Thursday feb. 6th 1851 as beutifull day as we have had for a long time, worked in the garden nearly all day. agreed to go to Sabine Town to morrow for Mr Parmalee. received a Letter from S. A. miller of Crockett asking me about some documents he send by me to austin more than a year ago, I delivered a Package to Mr Shaw the Comptroller, and dont Know what were its Contents, answered the Letter, in rather *short meeter.* Mr C. Hopfeldt arrived yesterday which I forgot to mention, he stops with us. Spend the Evening till 11 P. m. at a dancing party at the widow Hart's

Friday February the 7th 1851 left home at 9 a m dined with Mrs Barrett[2] at melrose, staid all night with J. N. Fall at chirino. this is a new village and is situated in a fine healthy location near the River Attoyaque, found my old friend Capt D. H. Vail and his Lady. this was a fine day, but clouded up at Sun set.

Saturday Feb 8th Cloudy, and looks like rain;—left at 8½ a. m. arrived at San augustin at 12, Stopped at the City Hotel, visited several of my friends, spend the Evening at Wm m. Simpsons,

Sunday Feb 9th rained very much last night, all the creeks are overflowed, stopped all day, took Tea with Mr and Mrs Phillips, Mrs P. is a sister in Law of my Eugenie, spend the rest of the Evening with Wm M. Simpsons Family, to day it rained till 12 oclock, fair in the afternoon

Monday the 10th Cold, and Cloudy, Cleared up at noon, purchased a Claim of $75.00 (late Republic debt), from J. M. N. Murray for $22.00, Arrived at Sabine Town at 5 P. m. heard of the death of D. S. Kaufman our Representative to Congress;—this is a great loss to Texas, and I do not Know if an other one can be found to supply his place, Stopped with Doctor Dewees,

Tuesday the 11th fair weather untill Sunset, when it cloudet in the west—left Sabine Town at 7½ a. m. arrived at San augustin at 3 P. m. this day I purchased two more claims one for $73—and one for $119 paid $20—and $35, spend the Evening playing whist—

Wednesday Feb. 12th 1851 fine weather to day—very warm, cloudy towards Evening—remained here all day—send a communication to the red land Herald signed fair play, giving the road overseers a Small hint about the bad roads in this County eta

Thursday the 13th rained trem[en]dously last night, and still continues this morning, gave up my Horse to one of Parmalee's drivers, and took the Stage home, left at 11 a.m. found Mrs Luckett, Mr mithel of Cherokee County also Floyd Kendal, and Houston Terrill returned from California, whither either has much of the Dust—quien Sabe, upset once, and broke down once, rained nearly all the time, and after getting mudy all over got home at

---

[2]Here Sterne is probably referring to his daughter Eugenia, the wife of Thomas C. Barrett.

10 p. m. found all well received a Letter from J. S. mayfield informing me that his wife and self have empowered Judge Taylor to act for them in the sale of the Boden tract of land, received a Package from genl land office containing various Documents—

Friday the 14th fair weather, looked like rain early in the morning—some rain at 8 P. M. Cold towards midnight, worked in the garden all day. Judge Ochiltree a candidate for Congress in Kaufman's place, Judge Taylor a Candidate for District Judge— Mr James S. Linn placed a Miss ann gilchrist to go to School to Miss Tompkins—she boards with us—

Saturday Feb. 15th 1851 rained last night, very cold this morning, wrote a letter to S. A. Miller of Crockett an other answer to his letter of 2d inst—one do to wm Daugherty of cherokee county, inclosing Certified Copy of Riddle's field notes of his Head right league Land on Nechaz one do to J. M. Swisher requesting him to let me Know about S. A. Miller's papers—also one to gel land office on same business—One to g. w. Smyth about my Headright leagues, and in answer to his letter of 29th January last, received a letter from A. S. Ruthven[3] Houston, nothing new. went to the Division in the Evening, remained till 7½ P. m. —spend the rest of the Evening at my Daughter's House,

Sunday the 16 a little cold in the forenoon, beutifull weather the rest of the day, wrote a Letter in answer the one received on yesterday from A. S. Ruthven, wrote a Letter to the Deputy u. States marshall at Henderson, enquiring about the Sale of a League & labor land sold on account of the Execution in favor of the Messrs Piersons of New York,

Monday the 17th white frost this morning, cold all day, notwith standing the Sun Shone bright, worked in the Orchard, hard work—trimming Trees—wrote a letter to C. S. Taylor giving him an account of the land affair between Mr Silverberg's Heir of mississippi & myself, went up Town in the afternoon and saw many People from the Country. had an interview with Mr Hayter, respecting a claim of mine on the Loco Creek, he wants to purchase it—it is however in the hands of Chevallier & Bondies as purchased at Tax Sale, Chevallier told me he will give it up at the price he paid for it, and the Interest, We agreed on that. mail arrived, confirms the news of Kaufman's Death, we also heard the sad intelligence of my old friend John Durst having died at galvezton. had a small Soiaré at the House till 11 P. m.

Tuesday February 18th 1851 cold this morning, but very fine pleasant day in the afternoon, moderated, and a little rain at dark. trimmed fruit trees, and worked in the garden till Dinner, wrote a Letter to Z. Wms. Eddy of Jasper on Judge Taylor's behalf, one do to Sol Adams of Trinity County on my own behalf, one do to Mr Issac Towsey of Cincinnatti Walker County, one dito to general Bates United States marshall at galvezton inquiring about

---

[3]A. S. Ruthven was Grand Secretary of the Grand Lodge of Texas, Ancient, Free and Accepted Masons.

the sale of a League & Labor of land in vanzandt County, sold by that Theif David Ayers Deputy Marshall

Wednesday the 19th rained last night very hard, cloudy all day, worked in the garden till dinner wrote a letter to my Son Charles sent it pr Charley Carroll, wrote also to the Clerk of the County Court of Vanzandt County for information respecting my land sold by Ayers—

Thursday the 20th Rained nearly all night, and at or a little after day light a tremendous rain fell which was, "The clearing off shower" had a very fine day, worked some in the garden, all or near all the peach trees are blossoming, and I fear we will not have any fruit again this year—received a letter from John H. Reagan of Buffalo Texas—informing me that Jacob Huffer is willing to give me 196 acres of Patented land for a debt he owes me, answered the Letter, and Instructed Mr Reagan to take the land.

Friday 21st a beutifull day, worked most all day in the garden wrote a letter to my son charles to be send by Mr Chamabadut, who goes to marry John Fort to Miss Carroll. went to the funeral of Mrs Harlacher, gave A. Davis of Angelina County permission to land his flat boat on the East side of angelina River opposite marion— gave Davis permission to clear & Cultivate a field on the land.

Saturday February 22d 1851 Very warm, but cloudy—worked all day in the garden. Eastern mail arrived—no news, received the Red land Herald the first time, since its new Editor A. H. Evans has been in the Sanctum— This is the anniversary of the birth of the Father of his Country george washington—but I am realy very sorry to record that it passed off unnoticed,—nineteen years ago this day (being the Centenial anniversary I was at Fort Jessup with Col Jose de las Piedrass, the then, Commandante of this Frontier, we were treated most Cavallierly, and Piedress intended to give to general Levenworth (the then commanding officer of Jessup) and his officers a splendid féte on the 16th September following, but on the 2d August, we had a fight with Piedress's Command, and forced them to evacuate the place, Piedress himself was made Prisoner and his Regiment *escorted* to the Rio grande, *Sic transit eta*

Sunday the 23d very warm and Cloudy all day, rained very hard about 9 P. m. nothing new,

Monday the 24th Cold, and a little Cloudy in the morning, a very beutifull afternoon, Probate Court in sesion, saw many persons from the Country, Charles Hotchkiss placed his son with us to board, gave him a bill for lumber to build a dining room 21 feet by 14, was occupied all day at work repairing fences, new gates to Stable lot, and divers other things; went to the Lodge in the Evening; Reinaldo Hotchkiss returned from the north.

Tuesday the 25 very fine weather, pr last nights mail I received a Letter from my friend gallagher of New Orleans also a Letter from the Deputy U. S. Marshall at the Town of Henderson in answer to my letter of the [blank] day of [blank] inquiring about the vanzandt Tract of land sold by David Ayers, passed the Evening with my friends Parmalee & his family—

Wednesday February 26th 1851 Very warm day, this was realy a spring day without intermission, repairing fences, making new gates to my Horse lot, am much fatigued, did not go up Town till after supper, nothing new

Thursday the 27th warm night rained very hard about 4 A.M. turned Cold at 12 oclock, and rained tremendously, done some work to the fence round Horselot—Wm C. Stanley of Angelina got me to attend to his land certificate which he gave to a Wm. H. Jenkins to locate, he has not heard from it since—wrote about the matter to Comr of general land office inquiring if such a certificate has been returned, wrote to County Clerk of Houston County where the Certificate was issued asking the number & Date of it—wrote a Letter to my friends, gallagher, and Jim Durst, inclosed Durst's letter in gallagher's it is quite cold. 4 P. m. and is still a raining—Capt. Hotchkiss, and several Ladies & gentlemen passed the Evening with us—

Friday 28th had a severe frost last night. it is Sleeting this morning—good bye peaches for this year,—it is now the third year that we had no fruit, it cleared up about noon, had a fine afternoon weather had moderated very much, it is still cold, but not near as much as in the morning, done a little work on Horse lot was in Town in the afternoon, nothing new, went to a party in the Evening at Col Frost Thorn's.

Saturday March 1st 1851 big white frost, fine day, discovered that more then a third of the peach blossoms are not Killed so that we may have some fruit yet—worked all day on the fence between Orchard and the Horse lot, mail from East nothing new— the mail for the west can not cross the Angelina bottom Nechaz & Trinity are also impassable on the State route

Sunday the 2d white frost again—a beutifull day followed wrote a Letter to gel Land office requesting a copy of a Certificate & transfer originally granted to woodson Henry, agreed to go to Leon County to attend to some business for C. S. Taylor, in return, he is to attend to a land suit of mine in Shelbyville. expect to start on Tuesday next, This is the 15th aniversary of the declaration of Independence of Texas, it is hardly remembered—

Monday the 3d very fine weather, finished the fence eta round Horse lot, worked a little in the garden and showed Tom what was to be done during my absence, M. B. Erwin arrived to day from austin with Hartley's Digest of the Laws[4] of Texas, he also brought the bey laws of our Lodge which I had printed at

---

[4]Oliver Cromwell Hartley, A Digest of the Laws of Texas, to which is subjoined an appendix containing the acts of the Congress of the United States on the subjects of the naturalization of aliens, and the authentication of records, etc., in each state or territory, so as to take effect in every other state or territory; and to which are prefixed the constitutions of the United States, of the provisional government of Texas, of the republic of Texas, and of the state of Texas. The Digest was published by Thomas, Cowperthwait and Company in Philadelphia in 1850.

Austin last time I was there, a Ball and supper at the widow Hart's in honor of the 2d of March 1836, danced till 2 oclock, of the

Tuesday the 4th left home for Leon County on business of Judge Taylor's Crossed the Angelina at David Rusk's ferry, and stopped all night at John Hearn's in Cherokee County.

Wednesday March the 5th 1851 left after Breakfeast, to Rusk to dinner this place is flourishing very much, it has sprung up from wild woods to a fine village in 4 or 5 years, left at 3 P. m. to Mr Jno Acock's stopped all night

Thursday the 6th rained tremendously all night, and did not stopp till 12 oclock today, left after dinner and crossed the Nechaz at Cannon's Ferry and had to stopp at Ben Cannon's on account of a Creek which was overflowed.

Friday the 7th left after Breakfeast—crossed the swollen creek with some difficulty, arrived at Palestine to dinner, this is a new Town and improving very fast, went to Magnolia on the Trinity stopped all night, this place is also new, it is the present head of navigation of Trinity and is an Exelent place for a large business, and if it once gets the start, must become the principal point on the River, such, as Shreveport, is on Red River, but it is very sickly, and for that reason would not like to reside here with my family; stopped with Mr Hagood.

Saturday the 8th very fine day, crossed the River had a mile to ferry, passed over a most dreadfull road to a lake which I ferried, here I found that I could not proceed further on my route on account of the large Creeks which I had to cross, to get to my point of destination, I finally concluded to go up to their heads, and Cross—after a great deal of deep wading, and bogging down in the mud, stopped all night, at a Mr Roberts, on the Springfield road

Sunday March the 9th 1851 beutifull day—left very early and went about 17 miles up the road towards springfield, here I turned in towards the left, and with much difficulty crossed the main Kitchy Creek, and three other of its branchez, stopped all night after a hard days travel at one of the most filthy Houses I ever was in in Texas, I shall forbear mentioning the name—

Monday the 10th left early, passed Julian Sanchez, and Lewis Sanchez's Houses, and arrived at the new County seat of Leon County at 1 oclock P. m. attended to business I went for, and left at 2 P. m. to Mr Tom garner's stopped all night—(a good House)

Tuesday the 11th left after Breakfeast, arrived at the old Kikapos Bluff (Haylet's) on Trinity, got into the ferry-boat at 12 and landed at Hall's Bluff in Houston County, at ½ past four P. m. arrived at Crockett at 8 P. m. Stopped at Longs Hotel.

Wednesday the 12th Court in session, saw the People in regard to the Election of a State Senator, find that I have no opponent in this County, and will probably not have any, saw several of my old friends, and got much encouragement—left after dinner and arrived at murchisons at sun set. s[t]op—

Thursday the 13th rained all night very hard, Keeps on raining and it is now 12 oclock—left in the rain at 1 P. m. and rode till I was stopped in my further progress by a large Creek, which resembled more a large torrent then a little stream. was compelled to stop, at a wedding—rain, a small House, large company— very comfortable of course—slept in a heap of cotton Seed—good Bed.

Friday march 14th Cloudy and warm. left after Breakfeast, crossed the creek by swimming my Horse, and walking over a log myself, very very bad roads crossed the nechaz at Cannon's ferry, and arrived at Rusk at night—stopped at the widow Brackens—

Saturday the 15th rained very hard last night—left at day light, Creeks nearly all swimming, crossed the angelina, and had to go by the way of Douglass to avoid swimming the little loco and the creek at garretts—arrived at home at ½ passed 4 oclock, found all my children with the whooping cough

Sunday the 16th beutifull day, Bishop (methodist) Orsenith Fisher preached in the Court House twice today, nothing new stirring in Town— wrote to L. F. Ardry in answer

Monday the 17th Saint Patrick's day—and a very fine day it was—worked in the garden, and Orchard all day mail arrived, Cotton rising—nothing new—

Tuesday the 18th very fine weather worked, and superintended the work in the garden, planted some corn. My Son Charles arrived from Town Bluff Tyler County on a Keel Boat, which he brought up in 11 days for P. M. Fort & Co his Employers, he is not in good health—Sold to Harlacher and Suter a lot belonging to P. gorman of New Orleans as his Agent—for $200—out of which is to be deducted my fees—recording fees, Taxes since 1837, and making out Deed to purchasers. Mrs Parmalee, Mr Rankin, and Mr Robinson spend the Evening with us

Wednesday march 19th 1851 Very fine Spring day, however the sun went down cloudy, worked in the garden, part of the day, went fishing—not much luck—received a Letter from A. g. Walker of Dallas brought by a Mr Keen, all the big fuss about the Cuba Expedition has ended as it should have ended— in Smoke— a nolle prosequi has been entered against gels Lopez, Henderson Quitman and others—thus the Mountain (u.S.) has labored and brought forth a *little bit* of a mouse.

Thursday the 20th very fine day, continue to arrange my gardens—wrote to C. G. Keenan of Huntsville in answer to his letter of 15th inst—wrote a Letter of Introduction of H. L. Rankin to Stephen Crossby, and milton Swisher of Austin, and one to Trow Ward & John Carrollan of San Antonio—mail arrived from East, no news— Dan Culp returned from the north, brought under his protection from Washington City to Sabine Town, the widow Kaufman and her childern, Spend the Evening at a Soiree at Madame Bondies's.

Friday the 21st a Warm cloudy day, planted Irish Potatoes, trimming Shade trees, and working in the orchards & gardens generally. saw general James Smith of Rusk County in Town, he is a candidate to represent his District in the Senate of the State,—Mr James Hill Surveyor of Smith County is in Town, informs me that a lot of mine in Tyler Smith County which cost me about $25 is now worth $150.00 am very glad to hear, that, that part of old nacogdochez County, formerly (and not long ago) was the *Indian Nation* now contains some 10000 Inhabitants—had a conversation with Doctor J. H. Starr respecting the claim of gardner norcom & Co. Made an arrangement with him satisfactorily to both of us—received a Letter from Mr gallagher of New Orleans. very great prospect for rain at Sun down—

Saturday March 22d 1851 We had a very hard rain and Thunderstorm last night but this morning it was clear, and had a beutifull day worked in garden—agreed to go to Leon County again for Judge Taylor, handed in my resignation to the Sons of Temperance— I do not quit this good and noble Institution for the purpose of again to indulge freely in the cup of intemperance or intoxication, but because I am compelled by the rules of the Order to act as it were a Kind of Spy on my Brother, and this is the only feathure I dislike in the Order, and whenever this is stricken out (as I hope it will be) I shall join again; and for ever—. Eastern & western mails arrived—received several Papers, and a certificate from the County clerk of Houston County that W. C. Stanley's certificate No 173 for a League & labor was issued by the Board of land Commissioners of Houston County on 4th October 1838, wrote a long Letter to E. E. Lott, to be send by James Hill to morrow

Sunday the 23d very cold, but clear day—went to church (catholic) nothing very new Stirring.

Monday the 24th cold, but has not done any damage to vegetation, worked in garden, commenced my new room for my Library. went to Lodge to night, a Mr Wheeden[5] was innitiated, had a fine supper at the Stage House Hotel

Tuesday the 25th warm, cloudy—worked in garden, made ditches eta. agreed to go to Leon County again for Judge Taylor, My Son Charles has left the Services of Messrs Fords, he will do business hereafter for himself,—perhaps in Douglass, wrote to Mr King the Pianist of Henderson, to come down to arrange the Piano—

Wednesday March 26th 1851 fine day—left home in company with Mr C. Hopfeldt who goes to the Rio grande, got a Horse from C. S. Taylor on whose business I am going to Leon County to attend the Sale of a tract of land. Stopped at night at Mr Shaw's 28 miles—

Thursday the 27th Cloudy, left early, and Stopped at Crockett at night 33 miles, got from the Clerk of the County Court a Certificate that Thos. W. Adams got a conditional Headright for 640 acres, said Adams is at Loredo, I send it by Hopfeldt to get the unconditional certificate for Jacob Masters who owns the Headright

[5]Roland Weeden.

Friday the 28th very fine day—left after breakfeast crossed the Trinity at the old Kikapoo Bluff, and went to Mr garner's 25 miles—

Saturday the 29th left at 7 oclock a. m. weather warm and cloudy, arrived at Centreville at 10 oclock, went to Leona at which place I found the Tax collector, paid him $9.90 to redeem ⅓ of a league land which had been sold for Taxes, belonging to F. T. Phillipps, which is the land to be sold on next Tuesday—here Mr Hopfeldt left me, he is going towards austin and I went to the Residence of the widow John Durst.

Sunday the 30th _Cloudy—accompanied Mrs Durst, Lewis Durst and his wife, to a Mr Hunts 4 miles below on Boggy creek, went a fishing, spend the day very agreably, returned to Mrs Durst's at dark when it commenced to rain very hard, and the wind blew allmost a tornado

Monday the 31st rain, rain and more rain, cleared up at noon, went to Leona, and returned to Mrs Dursts at dark.

Tuesday april the 1st 1851 Cloudy, but no rain, after Breakfeast, Lewis Durst accompanied me to Centreville saw the Sheriff who informed me that three appraisers had been appointed, who have appraised the land to be sold at $1.50 per Acre, it not bringing two thirds of its appraised value, it was not sold—and then I levied an other Execution on it in favor of Turner & woodruff, and returned to Mrs Dursts'

Wednesday the 2d cloudy, and looks like rain, left early in the morning, Crossed the Trinity at Robbin's Ferry and arrived at Crockett near Sun set. 45 miles

Thursday the 3d rained very hard ever since 3 oclock this morning, and now 9 A.M. it is still raining. cleared up a little after dinner, Started to go on, but there is so much water and is again raining. I stopped at Joseph rice's. 5 miles

Friday the 4th Clear & Cold—left at 6 oclock a. m. got to the nechas at 11 a. m. rising very fast, got over safe. found the angelina out of its Banks and all over the bottom, got a guide to pilot me through, and landed safely at McKnight's at sun down. 42 miles. here I found Judge O. M. Roberts, and Judge Taylor both bound for Linnwood where there is a large meeting expected to morrow to devise plans for clearing out the angelina to said place—Judge Roberts is a Candidate for Congress, and Judge Taylor for the place resigned by Roberts as District Judge—there are now Seven Candidates in the field for the Seat in the united States Congress vacated by the death of the lamented David S. Kaufman

Saturday April 5th 1851 rained hard last night, but has cleared up fine but Cold this morning—this is the 49th anniversary of my birth day, (confound it I am getting old) the water in the Swamp rose so much last night that Judge Taylor declined going over—Roberts went piloted by Conde Raguet, and Taylor went on home with me—stopped at Douglass till after dinner. saw the

— 213 —

Sovereing People here, and received much encouragement in my canvas for a seat in the State Senate, have no opponent as yet—left after dinner and arrived at home at 5 P. m. found my family all well—found my new room (Library) enclosed but not finished inside. found a Letter from Reddin Andrews of Lagrange who wants me to inquire about a man by the name of Juan Tabar if he had ever lived here—also a private Letter from S. Crossby of Austin, also a Letter and accompanying documents from gel land office, the letter is in answer to mine dated 15 february, and was one month a coming from Austin

Sunday the 6th Cold but fine weather, answered the Letter of Reddin Andrews wrote also to Capt Crossby acknowledging receipt of his Letter private, and Official eta wrote to Doctor jowers about a supposed misunderstanding between us, want him to send me an explanation, cloudy and warm this Evening.

Monday the 7th rained hard last night accompanied by a Thunder storm clear this morning, wrote to Wm R. gallagher, geor[g]e Dirmeyer, and Bernard Cohen of New Orleans, to introduce my Son Charles who will leave here on wednesday next for that city to try and get into some business. he can learn more there then in a country Store and will Know a little more of the world then he can at Town Bluff on the nechaz—tried to get a Carpenter but failed, so I turned in and Sealed my Library myself to day

Tuesday April 8th 1851 very cold clear morning — *nearly frost*— at work on my Library—wrote to Patrick gorman of new Orleans and send him $100 by my Son Charles, on account of the lot I sold for him to Harlacher and Suter, settled up with Charles Chevallier, and for the first time in ten years am intierly out of that man's debt and if god lets me live shall remain so for ever—settled with P. N. Ford & Co gave my note for $97.00 payable in 7 months, and this is about the last debt I have to settle in Texas—I am now less in debt *in the State* then I have been for the last 12 years, and if I live two years more expect to be clear of debt intierly

Wednesday the 9th very Cold Morning again but no frost, a beutifull day—this morning my Son Charles Started in the Stage for New Orleans, papered my Library—received a lot of plank from Mr C. Hotchkiss, wrote a letter to Mr Jessy Duren of Houston County respecting the Claims of the Boden Family—Col Johnson spend the Evening with [us], he is M. T. Johnson the Candidate for Governor. he was formerly a resident of Shelby County, has allways been in the Service of his Country, he is a perfect gentleman, and as brave as a real Texean. may success attend him—we have now two Candidates in the field for Representative of Angelina and nacogdochez, Mr Pollock[6] a young Lawyer, of this place and Squire Ambrose Eubank of Melrose, no one is running for the County yet exept Bill Hardeman, have agreed to go up to

[6]William C. Pollack.

Tyler on Friday next to convey Mr Chaubert, of New Orleans, to that place, purely out of accommodation to Mr C. that I go—having to put one of my Horses in a Stage with an other Horse, in order to get along

Thursday the 10th April 1851 Cold morning, warm, & Cloudy in the Evening, still at work on my Library, and will have to leave again before I complete it, having made an arrangement with a Mr Chabert of New Orleans to go up to Tyler with him, Judge Scurry is in Town he is an old aquantance of Representatives of the u. S. he stands a good chance of being elected—. paid Mr Muller the carpenter $12 for work done to my new room

Friday the 11th rained since Midnight, and is cloudy & raining now, 9 a. m. started at 10, in company with Wm. F. Herer & Mr Chabert in the Stage & R. Hotchkiss on Horseback,—roads very bad— stopped all night at Mr Branch's 20 miles—

Saturday the 12th rained very hard all night till 9 this morning, every Creek Swimming, started at 10 went a circuitous route to avoid Swimming Creeks, after a very hard days labor arrived at Henderson at sun set, 26 miles

Sunday the 13th very fair day, left after breakfeast, took a circuitous route again to avoid Swimming arrived at Mr McKean's Sun Set 27 mile—

Monday the 14th beutifull day—waters falling very fast, left very early, and got to Tyler at 10 A. M. —Supreme Court in Session, and everything has a thriving appearance—but a Town is not going to grow *very large* because the Session of the Supreme Court is held in it once a year, sold two lots for $160.00 which I consider a good Sale, for it is nothing but a Country village at best, and I think lots are higher now, then they will be in a year hence—got a miserable dinner and left the place—returned by the main Henderson Road to a Mr Stephenson's 12 miles,

Tuesday 15th left at day light, stopped at Henderson to get a Horse shod, and came out 5 miles to a Mr Morriss's having travelled to day 30 mi.

Wednesday april 16th 1851 very cold morning, but a splendid day—left at day light and arrived at home before Sun Set having made 37 miles— found all well—found a letter from Jas. H. Durst written in New Orleans and brought by Mr Remley, one do pr H. L. Rankin from my old friend Carrollan & Ward of San Antonio on private Business—one do from gel Land office advising me that Wm. C. Stanley's certificate for a League & Labor of land has never been returned to the gel Land office

Thursday the 17th very fine day—wrote a Letter to Editor of Red land Herald inclosing an advertisement for Wm. C. Stanley's Headright certificate, Eastern & western mails—received *a lot* of newspapers among them the New Orleans weekly Delta for which I subscribed for a year, received a Letter from yoacum & Mc Criaree of Huntsville advising me about 640 acres of land of mine amongst A. Macdonalds papers is the Patent for the same, received a letter from M. B. Erwin of Austin—

Friday the 18th good Friday—fine weather till towards noon when it clouded up and looked like it was going to rain very hard but the Storm passed over—every thing looks in its *holiday clothes.* vegetation flourishing, a fine prospect for plenty fruit, and without an accident we will have a fine year for every thing, for crops of all discriptions look well and flourishing—wrote a Letter to Messrs Yoakum & McCriaree of Huntsville telling them how McDonald came in possession of the Patent, which is mine. I have retained a copy of the Letter, wrote to gel land office for a certified copy of Francisco Acosta's Headright, 640 acres, which is the patent in possession of Messrs Yoakum & McCriaree. wrote to Charles G. Keenan in answer to his letter of the 5th inst. Erwin's Letter received yesterday needs no answer, send an order to grand Ecore pr Thos Ford to get a load of groceries expected to be there, send by my Son Charles from New Orleans, he is to receive 2½¢ pr lb delivered here, and charge if he finds no goods there

Saturday april 19th 1851 This was a real Summer day, the heat was as intense at 5 P.m. as it is in June, wrote to my son Charles, and to James S. Cartwright of Houston county, this last is an Electioneering letter.

Sunday the 20th Rain last night, fine weather to day, looks a little like rain towards Sun Set—this being Easter Sunday passed the day, in arranging and fixing my Library all my Books are now *concentrated* in the Library in stead of being in every room & Corner of the house

Monday the 21st [April, 1851] very cold, had a fire in the room, all day, this is the 15th anniversary of the Battle of San Jacinto, nothing doing to commemnorate it—Well!—received a letter from David Ayers of galvezton, filed, and answered, send letter pr to morrow's mail, send a Letter to the Comptroller and Auditor inclosing one receipt in favor of William A. Corder for $6, one for $16 and one for $56 all for provisions furnished to the troops of the late Republic of Texas, wrote also about the claim of Mr Rainer and J. J. Simpson, Mail from the East arrived no news—

Tuesday the 22d rained last night, and has rained all day more or less it is as cold as winter—arranged my Library and papers went up Town—saw my old friend Col Reiley—fine day for transplanting vegetables, availed myself of it by transplanting half the day,

Wednesday the 23d Cold & Cloudy, Clear towards Sun set, continues cold wrote to J. W. Hampton of Austin requesting to send me the Laws of last two extra sessions, which I left to be bound in the gazette office. wrote also to Tom F. McKinney for proceeding of the consultation, at last finished my Library, and arranged all my papers, Col Reyley & Doctor Starr dined with us to day, gave a due bill for $17.50 to J. J. Simpson, on account of Mr. Nickerson, being a ballance of Schooling for Placide & Rosa

Thursday the 24th April 1851 Fair weather till late in the afternoon, commenced to rain at about 5 P. m. wrote to my Son Charles to be send by the Misses Lillia & Mary Raguet, who are to leave for Ohio to morrow morning, received of Mr F. Hoya a Patent for 240 acres land situated in Harris County originally granted to F. Booker, with a chain of Title to Mr Hoya and a Power of attorney from Hoya to me to sell the same, the proceeds to go to me in payment of my share in the Soldiers Claims we purchased together—received this morning from the Post Office, a Certificate from the County Clerk of Houston County, respecting Wm C. Stanley's Headright Certificate, no news from New Orleans.

Friday the 25th beutifull day, Col greer the candidate for governor of that name, is in Town, saw several persons from the County who have moved in during the last two years, who all Know me, but I am aquainted with but few, my prospects are good so far, settled up with Mr Francis Hoya in full. Mr Rohte who arrived last night from San Augustin reports the Small pox to have broken out at that place. it was brought there by a stranger who came from Cincinnatti (on Trinity) and passed through this place. God grant we will not be visited by such a terrible Calamity—I preferr the Cholera of the two evils

Saturday the 26th a beutifull day worked a little in the garden, read, and arranged my papers in my Library, agreed to let Sam Hayter 100 acres land for $62.50 he will be in Town next Wednesday to close the trade, had a final Settlement with Mr Francis Hoya to day, we part in a day or two friends, and we dont owe one another one cent—purchased a Claim on Charles grayson at Administrators sale for $........ [blank] also one on Ezekiel Ables—both bad chances, but they cost almost nothing, so I can not loose much. mail from East & west, received a letter from J. M. Swisher Auditor of the State of Texas, and a Copy of a Letter directed to S. A. miller of Crockett, respecting said millers claims against the govt, send by me in 1849—received a Letter from my Son Charles date 18 inst and one from Mr W. R. gallagher New Orleans, Charles goes into E. Reiley's Store on trial for a month or more—am well satisfied with the Situation

Sunday the 27 April 1851 very fine warm day, went fishing this forenoon, had good luck. dined with Judge Taylor, answered gallagher and Charles's Letters—Judge Taylor gave me two notes to collect against Sol wolfe of angelina County—

Monday 28th fine summer weather, passed tne day as usual, in my study, and part in Town electioneering—mail from East arrived, brought a Letter from James P. Kay a former Clerk of Kelsey H. Douglass's of this place, he requests me to write to his Sister the widow Delmore to inform her respecting lands owned by her late Husband, complied with the request and answered the letter—recd a letter from my Son Charles inclosing Invoice of goods he purchased in New Orleans, answered— red also a letter from L. Skipper & Co Grand Ecore advising me of the arrival of the goods at that place, letter answered and filed—went to the lodge, and assisted in Innitiation of three candidates a Mr Loper—

Doctor Strode, and a Mr Dameron.[7] My Daughter Eugenia her Husband and children are with us to night—

Tuesday the 29th fair day, till 3 P. m. Clouded and is now raining, 7 P. m. mailed all my letters to go pr to morrow mornings mail, County Court in Session, Chief Justice not here. continued my *only* case I had in the probate court by the associate Justices.

Wednesday the 30th rain all night, cloudy and sprinkling rain during the day. set out plants of every description, delivered to Mr. Sam Hayter the Deed of Dan Lacy to R. Parmalee of 100 acres land, and Parmalee's deed to J. J. Hayter, he is to bring me in Town next time he comes $62.50— my Son Joseph's 19 birth day aniversary; rd a Letter from gel land office one dito from Huntsville, of McCriaree—not important—

Thursday May 1st 1851 May day— and a beutifull day. it was the balmiest day the most mild of the Season, had a beutifull ceremony performed on the mound North of the Town, on the commons by the female Students of Miss Mary Thompkins School, appropriate Speaches were made, and the happy little cherubs looked as though the whole path through life will be strewn with roses, as was the approach to the mound, this perhaps has been to many of those dear Innocent beings the Happiest day of their lives. God grant they may see many and many as happy, and when their dream of this world is at an end may they appear before their maker in as white a garb and as innocent in Heart as they appeared on the mound to day. spend the evening at a party given by Col Thorne—Mr & Mrs Hoya who have been residing with us for several months, left to day for the north and, perhaps to Germany, may the[y] have a happy trip of it—

Friday the 2d a fine day but rather a little to cold for vegetation. paid $14.80 Taxes to day on Mrs Sterne's Property and on a House & Lot of Laura's on the Square, nothing new astir exept a show, Slight of hand tricks, eta

Saturday the 3d Cloudy, rained from about Sun down till 10 oclock P. M. wrote to the Comptroller about a mistake made respecting the payment of Taxes on James Maffitt's land in Angelina County which is entered as James Mayfield—want the Comptroller to Correct it—send him also a Claim against the Republic in favor of J. Pate as witness, to be audited—my little girls gave the may queen and her subjects a party this Evening, the little cherubs amused themselves to their hearts content

Sunday May the 4th 1851 fine weather, rather a little too cold, wrote to C. Hopfeldt at Lareda, day passed of rather dull

Monday the 5th a beutifull day, Mr Hardeman,[8] my colleague in the last Legislature is in Town, paid me a visit, he is a candidate for the County representative, and I belive thus far has no opponent. he went to Douglass from here—send a letter by him to M. F. Heinhardt, requesting him to give me information about

[7]J. J. Loper, Alvin F. Strode. and J. W. D. Dameron.
[8]Thomas Jones Hardeman. He represented Bastrop in the Second Legislature, State of Texas, 1847-48.

field notes he send me pr mail during the last Session of the Legislature belonging to a Mr Brewer, send him inclosed G. W. Smyth's Letter to me in answer to one of mine about the same business—wrote to Messrs Yoakum & McCriaree of Huntsville, requesting them to send my Documents of the Acosta Claim by the mail on the 13th inst—or else keep them till I go to Huntsville—Judge ochiltree the Grand M of the Grand Lodge of the State informs me, that a petition has been send on asking for a Dispensation for a Chapter of R. A. Masons for this place, and that my name has gone on in the list of Petitioners; all right—mail from East arrived. brought nothing but a Letter from L. Skipper & Co, grand Ecore, advising me that the goods send by my Son Charles from New Orleans, were send by them on the 2d inst pr Thomas Ford. was at a Party given by Mrs. Hart. did not get home till after 11 P. M.

Tuesday the 6th Fair weather, Sold a Horse to T. C. Barrett for 25 Blls Corn payable in the Fall, and a note on a Mr Jones of Cherokee County better known as Rucky Chuch Jones for $30.00. received my Horse I purchased from Mr David Mucleroy, purchased a Saddle of a Mr Weeden for $20.00. paid him $10 cash down, the rest payable in 60 days—Sale day to day of property by Sheriff's Sale. not much property sold, our County is not in debt much—

Wednesday May the 7th 1851 rained last night, continues to rain 9 a. m. Stopped at noon, but is still Cloudy—at Sun set—planted Potatoe Slips, eta Mr Parmalee left this morning for the north my old friend Capt vail and his Lady arrived in Town

Thursday the 8th Cloudy, had the roof over my new room removed and put on anew, rained a little towards evening, went up Town after breakfeast, but had to return home on account of much pain in my leg. Col Thorn & Lady started for the hot Springs in arkansas, If my Rheumatic pains increase as they have done for the last four days, I am thinking I shall have to go to some place or other to get cured. Mail arrived from East no news —Mr Thompkins, Brother of the young Lady which resides with us arrived pr Stage from San Augustin he stops with us

Friday the 9th Cloudy nearly all day, did not leave the House all day, passed the day reading, and looking over the journals of the House of Representatives of last Session of the Legislature. Miss Mary Thompkins has announced her determination to go on home, and that this was the last day of her teaching in this place,

Saturday the 10th very warm cloudy weather, went up Town and had the galvanic battery[9] applied to me, alleviated my pain

[9]The galvanic battery was invented by Luigi Galvani, a professor of physiology at Bologna, Italy in 1786. This battery produced one volt of direct current and was used to relieve pain due to rheumatism or arthritis when the electrodes from the battery were applied to the joints. The tery usually contained a zinc and copper electrode that was surrounded by cloth which was soaked in a sodium sulfate solution. However, any

so much that I could walk the ballance of the Evening, Eastern mail brought Miss Charlotte Thompkins and nothing else—western mail arrived full of emptiness—my old friend Col Mallard is in Town—the waggon with the groceries from grand Ecore arrived this Evening and camped in Town, saying he could not find any residence, all right I preferr his unloading to morrow morning

Sunday the 11th warm & cloudy—Thos Ford delivered his load of groceries all in good Order, paid him $63.75—Kept the House all day, my Rheumatic pains returning again, well I can grin but must bear it—

Monday the 12th May 1851 very warm & Cloudy—received $62.50 of Sam Hayter, for a small tract of land—went on Horseback to gel Rusks. had a two hours conversation with him about matters and things in general—Mail from East arrived, no Letters, rd the Delta and a few other papers—

Tuesday the 13th very warm day, rode once, and walked up Town once. wrote a long Letter to my Son Charles, wrote a Letter to mitchel Editor of the Masonic Mirror of Masonic Signet at San Louis Mo inclosed $2.50 in gold send him also six subscribers to wit, N. J. Moore, J. H. Muckleroy J. S. Linn, James Hart Wm W. Barrett, and Jno T. Shanks Sr—wrote him a long communication respecting the negro Lodges existing in the united States.

Wednesday the 14th This was a true Summer day, rather a little too warm. took a ride to day, and feel much relief from my pains—mail from west did not arrive till very late, received nothing but some Austin & Houston papers, containing no news—

Thursday the 15th Summer has set in for good, and Shade and cool Breezes are in requisition, received a Letter from Mr Walker of Dallas, he did not send me the Certificate I wanted, nor did he send me the one send up to him by Mr Keen, Walker is a queer chap certain—wrote a Letter (Electioneering) to Henry Ward of Trinity County, and a Letter to the Editor of the Masonic Signet Sant Louis, with J. S. Thorn & R. Weedin as new Subscribers the young men in Town are getting up a party to be given to the Misses Thompkins—mail arrived from new Orleans brought letters from Charles & Mr gallagher—it is not far past midnight the last of the party are just departing—Wrote a letter to James H. Durst Rio grande City—send it via New Orleans

Friday the 16th very warm day, read, nearly all day, took a ride and applied the galvanic battery to my Rheumatic leg. affords me relief, my old friend Capt O. M. Wheeler in Town

Saturday may 17—1851 an other fine Summer day—wrote a letter to the Comr gel land office. inquiring if Conrad Eigenauer Headright was recei[ve]d at gel land office—wrote to Mr A. g. Walker of Dallas in answer to a letter of his dated 15 April, wrote to Jno H. Reagan inquiring about the debt due me by Jacob & Saml Huffer, also to my Son Charles send letter by Mr. W. H. Thompkins

---

acidic solution could be used. When the strength of the current weakened the user could add salt water to recharge the battery.

Sunday the 18th weather changeable, had a little Shower to day, not enough however to wet the ground, sat up nearly all night, waiting for the Stage to leave, Mr and the Misses Thompkins's left, regretted by all their friends—pr last nights western mail I received a Letter and a copy of Francisco Acosta's Title for 640 acres land from the gel land office—Slept off more then half of this day—

Monday the 19th very warm weather, County Court in Session, spend most of the day in Town, Mr Thouvenin arrived on yesterday lodges with me, Eastern mail arrived nothing new, brought me a letter from my Son Charles, and one from Mr Castro, which had been missend and forwarded from Natchitochez. rd a Letter from Fred Aeschelman

Tuesday the 20th very warm & Cloudy, Judge Webb a Candidate for the Supreme bench in Town, dined with me to day—a Mr Pistole from Leona County arrived, has business with Judge Taylor, stops with us till Taylor returns from Jasper County.

Wednesday the 21st Cloudy but no rain, very warm, received a Letter from A. M. Keen of Dallas, respecting some land he wants to purchase. reced. pr western mail, a bound copy of the Journals of the House & Senate of both Extra Sessions, also the laws of dito, all bound in one vol. reced a lot of Electioneering Documents from greer & Crossby Candidates for governor & Comr gel land office. they are in English, Spanish, and german—go it my Candidates—

Thursday may the 22d 1851 Weather is rather tantalizing, we want rain very much indeed and looks like rain all the time—and dont rain— rode up Town, saw Mr Young Lacy & Mr Duren, commenced making a Ditch in a piece of rich bottom land below my orchard, a fine place for a garden—mail arrived from the East rd a letter from New Orleans (from Charles) wants to come home very bad.

Friday the 23d weather same as yesterday, rain wanting very much—received a letter from Kennedy & Fisher New Orleans respecting Lindley's Lands in Rusk County, Col Wallace one of the Candidates for Congress is in Town;—our Town is improving. two large two Story Houses have been raised on the Square within the last 10 days

Saturday the 24th had a fine rain last night, cool day—Col Wallace and L. Dale Evans made Speaches to day in the court House; I dont think Evans will get many votes here—good many people in Town. Eastern & Western mails arrived, no news in either—

Sunday the 25th a little rain last night, like all Sundays this was a very dull day

Monday the 26th Started at a little after sun up, in company with Mr Horatio Nelson, to Marion Angelina County, Judge Clark overtook us on the road, got to Marion at 12, after dinner the District Court was opened by Judge Clark, after empannelling, and Charging the grand Jury, Mr Pollock, a candidate to represent angelina & Nacogdochez, and myself, got possession of the Court House, and addressed the citizens of that County then in Town (about 60) I belive. I am authorized to flatter myself, in beliving that I'll get nearly a unanimous vote in Angelina, whither I have opposition or not, paid my friend Doctor Young a visit,—I find that a ride of 20 miles has not done my Rheumatic pain any injury, but feel better then I did before I left home. Stopped at the House of a Mr Davis—all three candidates for District Judge are here—

Tuesday May 27th 1851 beutifull day—left Marion after day light—arrived at home at 10 oclock. last nights mail brought a letter from Charles dated 18th (New Orleans) still homesick. Mr Bondies has returned home after a very long absence to Sabine pass—our Priest Mr Chambaudut[10] has also returned from galvezton—Mr Edward Plant arrived during my absence, have not seen him yet. My Rheumatism has allmost left me—

Wednesday the 28th weather same, Mr Bondies transferred to my wife his half of 1500 acres land situated on the Loco Creek. Mr Silverberg, of Canton Miss arrived at my House, Mr Plant and myself had the following arrangement about my new york debts—to wit—I am to confess Judgement on all the debts, provided there is a Stay of Execution till March 1853. this will enable me to pay in the mean time to the Agent Doctor Starr such monay as I may have from time to time, this also will enable me to do some Kind of Business without being disturbed every day by different Suits, and will therefore enable me more to pay up then it would otherwise—western mail brough[t] me a letter from Doctor Keenan, also one from James B. Shaw State Comptroller— inclosing a Certificate for John Pate for $14.51 as Juror in 1841-42, also returning me the Tax receipt on James Maffitts land in angelina County; lots of Papers from the west. the Congressional Canvass between gel McLeod & Volney E. Howards runs high, and they appear to pay one an other very poor compliaments.

Thursday the 29th warm & occasionally cloudy—entered into an arrangement with Mr James Plant, as follows—Mr P. is to send on here all my notes given to Individuals in new york in 1846 which are yet unpaid and not in Suit—when all are here in the hands of Doctor Starr (who is to be the agent for the creditors)—I am to confess Judgement upon all of them, (but if possible all notes ought to be made one Suit of) with the express understanding that no Execution is to issue till Novr 1852, but then no levy is to be made upon said Execution untill March 1853, in the mean time I am to pay to Doctor Starr such amounts as I chose from time to time, got a Copy of the agreement filed away, my son Charles arrived pr to nights Stage from grand Ecore having quit New Orleans for the Summer—answered the Letter of C. g. Keenan, and acknowledged the receipt of J. B. Shaws

---

[10]L. M. C. Chambodert, listed in the Census for 1850 as a Roman Catholic Priest, aged 28.

Letter, requesting an answer to my letter respecting the claims of Corder, send on sometime ago

Friday the 30th may 1851 Summer day, very warm, Mr Plant left this morning for New york, and Mr Silverberg for home in Mississippi our old friend Levinson returned—on a visit—gave O. L. Holmes our County Clerk Chevallier's & Bondies's Deeds to my wife, for the Loco lands to be recorded, also a Suplementary Schedule for same as required by law. Judge Ochiltree returned last night from galvezton, informs me that it is probable that I will have an opponent in Col Long of Crockett—I am willing & ready

Saturday the 31st very warm, rain wanting very much, Crops commence to Suffer for want of rain;—attended the probate Court to day, got four months on the Estate of Conrad Eigenauer to settle in—wrote to Messrs Kennedy & Fisher of New Orleans in answer to a letter received of them in relation to Mr Lindley's land in Rusk County, advising him to appoint an agent eta—wrote a letter to A. S. Ruthven. and one to M. B. Menard, on private matters, wrote to gel Cazenau about the land on the Carrizo Creek, offering him a thousand dollars for the land, inclosed the letter to Trow ward and John Carrollan of San Antonio to [be] forwarded to him as soon as possible. paid C. Chevallier $7.75 for paint and oil—and to Davis the Carpenter $9.50 for painting; Eastern & western mails arrived, a letter from C. Newman New Orleans inquiring about a Mr greenwood, who owes him a large amount of monay, also a letter from that Thief Ayres,

Sunday June 1st 1851 very hot & dry Weather, a lazy day— spend the day reading

Monday the 2d hot & rain wanting very much, this is the 23d anniversary of my marriage, all Sun shine yet, few dark clouds have obscured our matrimonial Hemisphere. all our childern are now here, god Knows how long we may be permitted to remain together in peace,

Our District Court commenced its session today, not many cases will be disposed of, as it is doubted whether Judge Clark is a Constitutional Judge, or not wrote to David Ayres in answer to his letter of the day before yesterday, the lodge met this Evening, and afterwards had a preliminary meeting of the Royal arch masons, for the purpose of forming a Chapter, was appointed a committee of *one* to procure all things required for the chapter, answered C. Newman's letter

Tuesday the 3d very warm day—Court adjourned untill next Monday purchased all the articles required for vails of the Chapter, and other paraphernalea, omitted yesterday to mention on my diary that I gave O. L. Holmes a draft on David Mucleroy for $25. for fees due him as probate clerk—

Wednesday the 4th wether still the same, garden in an awfull fix, wrote to adjutant gel requesting him to inform me what land or monay is due to leonard Tomlinson for military Services up to 18 June 36. wrote to James B. Shaw & Jno. M. Swisher as

Comptroller and Auditor of the State, inclosing Jno F. graham's Discharge as Quarter master & Commissary in 1840 of mine & Barcley's company, send also Reuben Webb's Joel Walker's and and [sic] Spener Adams's Discharges, to get audited and certificates for.

Thursday the 5th Hot & dry, made a Deed to gel Rusk for 640 acres of land, as administrator of P. de Torres's Estate, R. Scurry is in Town, Eastern mail arrived, nothing new, received a Letter from Mr gallagher, inclosing one I send to charles dated 20 May.

Friday the 6th went to Douglass to a meeting of citizens, respecting a[n]gelina navigation

Douglass— *Saturday June 7th 1851* a large number of citizens of the Surrounding Country, and many from Nacogdochez were present. general Rusk addressed the meeting in a lengthy and very appropriate manner, upon the subject of improving the navigation of the Angelina. Judges ochiltree and Scurry, gave us a political entertainment, Doctor C. g. Keenan, a Candidate for Leiutenant governor made a few appropriate remarks, next followed Edwards, Pollock, and Eubank all three Candidates for floating representative of Nacogdochez & Angelina, I made a few remarks, and this Closed the entertainment—Doctor Keenan went home with me, he informs me that Col Long of Crockett is a Candidate opposed to me, all right—Ezekiel Able gave me a Power of attorney to collect his monay as a mounted ranger in 1840 in my Company, arrived at home at 9 oclock P. m.

Sunday the 8th Hot, hot, and no rain, every thing in the garden is nearly gone. Bishop Freeman & Parson Samson preached to day, did not leave the House to day—

Monday the 9th had a severe Storm last night, it rained for over an hour, the rain appears to have been a general one, and it certainly came in good time—Court in Session—our Royal Arch Chapter was duly installed to day, and we were up in the Hall till Supper

Tuesday the 10th Court in session, was up in the Chapter last night after Supper till near three oclock this morning, and I am half sick—conferred the mark M. Degree on three this morning, and set up nearly all night for the purpose of conferring the Royal Arch Degree on Ben Rusk, Wm Barrett, Jess Muckleroy, J. Hart, H. White & Sam Kirk—Mr Hillencamp who has been here about two months left to night in the Eastern Stage for Europe—

Wednesday the 11th June 1851 Hot weather—up in the Lodge Room, conferring degrees till I am realy sick, am not able to go up to night. send Charles to Hayter's to Know if he intends to trade for Mrs Sterne's land on the Loco or not—send me word he will be in Town to morrow—

Thursday the 12th rather cool morning—received a Letter from J. H. Reagan about the Huffer's Claims—answered the letter immediately—receid also a letter from Doctor Jowers, (Politics) answered also, immidially—

Friday the 13th left home, on an electioneering tour, as well as to be at Huntsville Walker County on the 22d of this month to attend the Convocation of the grand Chapter of the State as a Delegate from this Chapter—passed through Douglass, and Linnwood to John Connor's in Cherokee County—got a power of attorney from Connor as administrator on J. S. Thompson's Estate to collect, on halves, all that may be coming to said Thompson as a Sergeant in my Company of Rangers in 1840, gave Connor a receipt accordingly, stopped all night

Saturday the 14th left early after Breakfeast in Company with Mr Ashcroft—arrived at the Town of Rusk at 10 a.m. Town full of the Sovereign People listening to Candidates making *all Kind* of Speaches, went home Joe Ables, stopped all night

Sunday the 15th left after Breakfeast Crossed the Nechaz at Stinson's ferry saw Mr W. W. Pharr of Anderson County, he gave me a Claim of $27 against the late Republic of Texas to collect being for wittness fees in a State case vs Saml Stivers—arrived at martin murchison's sun down—stopped—

Monday the 16th Commenced electioneering in good earnest. visited about 15 or more Houses, belive my chance good on San Pedro. stopped all night with Friend J. S. Carthwright.

Tuesday June 17th 1851 Left early, met Capt D. C. Ogden at the Pine Spring. arrived at Jacob master's at noon, stopped for the day and all night—rained very hard this afternoon, done much good, but it did not extend far—the Stages from Nacogdochez, and Huntsville arrived, this being the half way House

Wednesday the 18th left early, arrived at Crockett a noon, dined at my opponent's—Col Long's, left after dinner in company with Judge Randolph a Candidate for the lower House for this, Trinity and Anderson Counties, went to Cook's mills where we parted, I went to Col J. J. Hall lately married to Mrs Sharp. lately, she was miss mahela Roberts whom I Knew as a little girl— stopped all night, and was treated, as a man generally is, treated at a true gentleman's House,

Thursday the 19th left early, saw many persons to day, mostly Relations and old friends of Col Longs, stopped all night at Mr H. grey's on the Cincinnatti Road— a good public House

Friday the 20th left early, stopped at noon at the widow Thompkins arrived at Cincinnatti at 6 P. m. stopped at my old friends uncle george Hunter—he is a prince of Landlords for *men*, but god help the Horses—

Saturday the 21st left early, arrived at Huntsville at 10 A. m. stopped with the widow Keenan, send Mr W. W. Pharr's certificate for $27 to the Comptroller and Auditor at Austin to be a[u]ed eta. Mr Pharr resides near sand spring P. O. Anderson County

Sunday the 22d very hot, dull, lazy day, many persons arrived in Town to be in attendance at the grand Chapter and the grand Masonic fraternity, preparations on a large Scale going on for a public Dinner, under the Trees, and a Ball at the Court House in the Evening of the 24th

Monday June 23d 1851 The Town and our Hotel is fast filling up—at 3 P. m. the grand chapter of the State met, Saml M. Williams presiding, after receiving credentials, and appointing committees adjourned—saw Messrs Yoakum and McCreary they gave up to me the Patent of F. Acosta for 640 acres land which was found among A. McDonald's Papers—gave them a receipt for it in case of accidents—but it [is] all right, the Patent *is* mine, there is no necessity to say why it was among McDa. Papers *he is dead*—resquiat in pace—paid a visit to general Houston, he and his Family are in good health—Forrest Lodge of this place appointed me Marshall of the day for to morrow

Tuesday the 24th Saint John's day—and a hotter day we certainly did not have this Summer—G. Chapter met, done some business and adjourned, at 10 Oclock formed the Masonic bodies in procession, about 150 Masons being in the procession marched to the public square, where the Female School of Miss crawford, the male accadamy, Ladies and citizens generally, joined the procession, and marched up to the Hill where the colledge[11] is erecting —the road is a deep sand, the Sun pouring down its meridian heat, when the procession arrived at the top of the Hill, and after arriving at the Building, I was nearly fainting from Fatigue, heat, and thirst, water being to scarce that I gave a negro a dime for a glass full of the pure beverage. after the ceremony of laying the corner stone Professor McKinney, delivered an oration suitable to the occasion, after which all who could eat, found a most bountifull supply, but there was *no shade* over the Tables which prevented many from participating in that feast, I could not eat, and felt very much like having a fever—send for my Horse, and formed the procession again, and returned back to the Town. at 4 P. m. the grand Chapter met and went into the Election of officers for the ensuing year, when the following were elected and appointed— E. B. Nichols, G. H. P., W. M. Taylor, D. G. H. P., H. R. Cantmell, G. K., Sam McClarty G. S., A. Neil G. C. H.—J. C. Harrisson G. P. S. — A Sterne G. R. A. C. — C. G. Keenan G. T. —A. S. Ruthven G. Sec—G. M. Patrick, and J. M. Hall Grand visitors— James L. green, J. D. Geddings and W. H. Cushney G. M. of the veils, Wm H. King g. guardian— R. Brewster and J. McMillen g. Stewards, J. B. Robertson g. Marshall L. P. Rucker g. Chaplain—H. Yoakum G. O. D. D. Crumpler g. Sentinel, and at 8 P.M. the Installation took place, Nacogdoches Chapter received her charter under the number 13—when the chapter adjourned dancing was going on at the Court House, but I felt so much fatigued that I did not go even to look at the dance—but went to bed unwell—

---

[11]Austin College, sponsored by the Brazos Presbytery of the Old School Presbyterian Church, was located at Huntsville after that community donated $10,000 for the project. Samuel McKinney was its first president. After an initial prosperity, the Reconstruction era brought the college to near collapse and it was moved to Sherman by the Texas Synod of the Presbyterian Church in 1876.

Wednesday the 25th June 1851 feel better this morning, having a good night's rest—the Grand Chapter met again, and finished all the business before it, and adjourned—visited the subordinate chapter of this place which worked this Evening—did not get to bed till midnight—

Thursday the 26th left after dinner, in company with gel Hatch one of the candidates for the lower House of this County—arrived at Cincinnatti at 6 P. m. stopped at Hunters, gel Nichols (of the firm of Rice & Nichols) stopped also at Hunters, made an arrangement with him to employ my Son Charles, to commence in September or october next, gel McLeod made a speach here this Evening—

Friday the 27th crossed the Trinity, and took a good Electioneering Tour and stopped all night at Col Seldon Tryon's

Saturday the 28th left early, went down the River a most desolate dreary country—arrived at the widow McDonald's. not at home, put up with the overseer—what a contrast—her splendid mansion—and his little hovel—well—I was well treated, and was satisfied,

Sunday June the 29th 1851 left early—and after getting lost a couple of times got at last to Capt Sol Adam's (Duncan's Ferry on Trinity) took Dinner with the Captain, and went on 10 miles to Mr Upton's stopped all night—

Monday the 30th left early, arrived at the County Town? Sumpter the Seat of Justice of Trinity County, as yet in the woods only one family living here, the *log* courthouse is began but not finished—having seen *All* the People of this Town, I left and went to Mr Jno C. gallien, dined—and went down the River through as fine a Country as there is in Texas, this is a very thick settlement for 10 or 15 miles down the nechaz—stopped all night with allbritton.

Tuesday the 1st July 1851 left after breakfeast, forded the River Nechaz, oppos[i]te to Cornelius Dollahite—stopped all night with my old friend Otho Siggenberger—

Wednesday the 2d left early, saw several People. crossed the angelina at the Shawnee Crossing, and arrived at home near Sun down, found all my family in good health during my absence. I received letters from, the Editor of the Masonic Signet of St Louis, one from Charles newman New Orleans, inclosing account against geo greenwood, and a power of attorney to collect it—but the Bird is flown, and Mr Newman's Chance for his monay is rather dull—a letter from D. Ayers telling me more lies. the letter dated June 10—filed—a letter from J. S. Beers respecting Lucretia B. Sturges's land—one from A. g. Walker of Dallas, respecting the Certificate I send him by Mr A. M. Keen—One from M. B. Menard, in answer to mine of 18th April, One from R. D. Rutherford, about Ma Del Carmel's Labor of land, One from Com gel land office, in reply to Eigenauer claim—said claim is not in the office—

Thursday the 3d July 1851 Wrote to John D. Gann of Angelina County, informing him that Louis wilworth has received his

pay and donation land up to 4 Novr 1837, but that 640 Acre Donation land is due him which he can get by applying to Capt Kimbro
for a Certificate that said W. was in the Battle of San Jacinto,
wrote to C. Newman of New Orleans respecting his claim on geo
greenwood, his man is gone, and nothing left of the goods—answered J. S. Beer's letter respecting Lucretia B. Sturges Claim—
eta wrote to A. g. Walker of Dallas, in answer to his letter of 3d
June requesting him to send me Eigenauers Certificate pr mail at
my risk—wrote to Mr James Plant in answer to his Letter of 5th
June, telling him that I will give my creditors 5000 acres of land
for the debts I owe in New York, exclusive of Edwards and the
Piersons—wrote to Mr Allen Harrington of Trinity County, telling
him that J. S. Roberts wants to sell a part of the land adjoining
H. being a part of Charles Roberts's headright, this was a very
hot day. went up Town near Sun down, nothing new—

Friday July 4th Cool pleasant morning—wrote a letter to
adjutant general inquiring about Rosswell gorman's pay in Capt
Dolson's Camp in 1841, also about B. B. Sturges's Claim as a
member of the Santa fee Expedition, wrote to gel land office inquiring about Elenor gallien's Head right, wrote to Edward Tyler
Cincinnatti respecting Theresa Tomlinson's Headright, wrote to
Wm C. graham of Rusk inclosing him a copy of certificate of
woodson Henry Head right, from gel land office, wrote out a number of Tickets for the Election to be send to the different Boxes
in the District. this was a very dull 4th of July indeed, there is
a Ball in town to night but think it will be a meager affair, saw
John D. Gann in Town to day, he got the letter I wrote to him
out of the Post office, made an appointment to address the People
of melrose next Saturday, and those of Chirino on Saturday week,
at Douglass on the next Saturday following and at Nacogdochez
on Saturday the 2d August next—

Saturday July 5th 1851 very hot weather—went to gel Rusk,
spend a hour, conversation, Politics Presidential canvass eta—several angelina men in Town, wrote Tickets all the afternoon, gave
them to Jno D. Gann to distribute—wrote a Letter to F. L. Brauns
Counsel general of Wurtemberg at Baltimore to be taken on by
C. Chevallier who starts in the morning for New York, eta, authorized Mr Brauns to pay Chevallier any monay he may have in
his possession belonging to Mrs Sterne. made an appointment to
speak at melrose on Saturday next, at Chirino on Saturday week,
at Douglass the Saturday following

Sunday July 6th 1851 Cool morning, wrote to Yoakum & Mc-
Creary Huntsville about the Acosta land, Authorized them to sell
it at $1.25 pr acre—wrote to John Long my opponent in the Can-
vass, informing him that the Candidates will meet at Melrose next
Saturday, inviting him to attend, wrote to my friend Wm R. gallagher of New Orleans, on matters and things in general

Monday the 7th very hot forenoon, cool & Cloudy towards
Evening with a little sprinkling of rain, wrote a long letter to

the Editors of the Signet St Louis, Judge Ochiltree returned from his Electioneering tour up the Country, in good Spirits,

Tuesday July the 8th very hot Weather—general Memucan Hunt made a Speach to day in the Court House about his Claim against the late Republic of Texas, after he got through I was called on to state what was the action of the last Legislature in regard to this Claim, did not give my own opinion but Stated mere facts—which seemed to be satisfactory to the Audience, and I dont think that Representatives of this County will be instructed to pay the general what he Claims,—there were many People in Town, all say I am *doing very well* everywhere

Wednesday 9th weather less hot then yesterday, wrote to adjt gels office respecting J. F. gilbert's Claims, 640 San Jacinto 320 Bounty & his pay wants to Know if morris may has received it—western mail come in brought nothing but Papers, barren of news—

Thursday July the 10th 1851 weather same—as yesterday, wrote to Thos H. W. Forsyth of Trinity County, inclosing Tickets for the election in august next. wrote to P. young, and J. S. Cartwright of Houston County, and one to Franc wright, inclosing in each Tickets as above—wrote to John Carrollan of Bexar (requesting him to show the letter to Mr Truehart) about Patricio de Torres's land in this County, wrote a letter to C. g. Keenan Huntsville Texas Eastern mail arrived, recei[v]ed a Letter from James Robinson of Durham

Friday the 11th very hot forenoon, had a very fine rain in the afternoon, being the first good rain here in 11 weeks—answered J. Robinson's letter

Saturday the 12th hot as usual—left after Breakfeast went to Melrose and at 2 P.m. addressed the citizens of that place and its vicinity, no other Candidates exept Mr Pollock being there, Dined with old Lady Barrett, returned home at sun set, having made an arrangement to address the People of Chirino on Saturday next, wrote a few lines to Major Sam Flournoy to that effect, send a copy of gage's bill quiet land titles, which did not pass last session, to Isaac Parker at Rusk—

Sunday the 13th Weather same as yesterday—my opponent Col Long is in Town this morning, Bill Hardiman do—wrote to Col Ben Holt of Angelina County respecting Leonard Tomlinson's Survey near or on, Odle's Creek angelina county that the field notes & the conditional certificate is here in the Surveyor's office ready for Patenting if the unconditional Certificate is produced. received a Letter from James Cook of Rusk whishing to Know something about a lot of mine in the Town of Rusk, Concluded to go to Rusk to morrow—wrote to Thos F. McKinney acknowledging the receipt of a Book he send me

Monday 14th gave out my trip to Rusk, wrote to Jim Cook, and to S. P. Donley about the lots in question, Col Ward Candidate for Comr gel. land office is in Town;—Odd Fellows going to organize a Lodge here—

Tuesday the 15th July 1851 very hot day—12th anniversary of the first day's fight with the Cherokee Indians—a man named Tom Griffin was dangerously wounded in several places by Mr Joel willburn last night—principal Cause was whisKy—Col Thos. William Ward addressed the People to day at the Courthouse—did not go up to hear him—

Wednesday the 16th very hot day—Col Matt Ward Candidate for Liut govr in Town—Col Long dito—western mail arrived, receivd a Letter from N. W. Faison of Lagrange inquiring of me respecting a Juan Tobar that once resided here who is said has a tract of land in Fayette County

Thursday the 17th Hot & dry as usual—wrote to Sol Adams, and Thos H. W. Forsyth of Trinity county, and to Isaac Towsey of Cincinnatti, nothing new—

Friday the 18th very hot—left after dinner, for Melrose—stopped all night with old Lady Barrett—

Saturday the 19th Weather exesively hot—left after an early Breakfeast, and went to Chirino, Addressed the Citizens of that place and vicinity, dont think I shall lose many votes here—after the Speaking went with Asa Yarborough Esqr to his House, took Supper and went over to Isurr Pantaleon's House to a dance, found about 30 voters here, stopped till moon rose and arrived at home on

Sunday the 20th a tremendous rain fell yesterday at, and near, melrose, but not a drop fell here, Asa yarbrough gave me the order for James M. gullatte for his Discharge and his pay in 1840—

Monday the 21st Hot, Hot, hot! Mr Pistole, and McClennan of Leon County arrived purchased land of judge Taylor, they stop with me—The R. A. Chapter met to day, conferred degrees on Doctor Bockin, on Newel and Hulen B. Crain, was in the C[h]apter till 3 hours passed midnight — saw many persons from the country, *prospect very bright*

Tuesday the 22d July 1851 was at the Lodge from breakfeast time till after 12 oclock—conferring the Mark and Past M. Degrees on Archibald Hotchkiss David Rusk & Thos C. Barrett, — the Sons of Temperance had a procession in which our Lodge joined by invitation, the Revd Simpson Shepherd delivered an address at the Temperance Hall. My Son Charles, and my little grandson Charles are sick with the fever, I hope not dangerous—gel J. Pinkney Henderson is in Town, I gave him a patent for 240 acres land lying in Harriss County originally granted to [blank] Booker, Henderson is the attorney of Aaron H. Bean of New York to whom I owe a debt of about $350, I gave him this Patend, to see if Bean will take it as whole or in part payment of said debt—Ambrose Ewbanks a Candidate for the Legislature for Nacogdochez & Angelina is with us to night—

Wednesday the 23d Weather tremendously hot—was in Town for a short time. wrote Tickets for the Election nearly all day—each Ticket for this County having 13 names on it—the Sick Children are better—western mail arrived, recd a letter from Mr Conley of Rusk informing me that Mr Clark had transferred my lots in said Town— right— also a letter from gel land office respecting Elenor galliens head right— send the letter inclosed in mine to J. C. gallien, for his information—one from adjutant gel in answer to my inquiry respecting Roswell gorman's Soldiers Claim for pay in Dolson s Company to repel Vazques— and in reply to an inquiry about B. B. S[t]urges's claims, he refers me to Starr & Amory rece[iv]ed a large lot of Papers—

Thursday the 24th wrote to Roswell gorman, inclosing the letter from Adjutant gel. with a request to send it back to me after informing himself of its contents— Capt Crosby is in Town— wrote to Jacob Masters, and J. H. Bracken Esqr inclosing Tickets for the Election, wrote a letter to Wm. F. Allison of Houston County, mail from East received a letter from R. Parmalee from New York—

Friday—July the 25th 1851 much appearance of rain all day, but it is dry—at Sun set— Judge Taylor returned from his Electioneering tour. he is in good Spirits, Capt Crosby dined with us to day—received from W. W. Barrett a Certificate belonging to Mrs Emily Thompson to be forwarded to Austin for the signature and seal of the Secretary of State, filed till I get her Power of atty to be send on with the Certificate, for its authentication, My Son Charles Sick—not dangerous—

Saturday the 26th Cloudy—no rain—went with Anastacio Caro to his House on the Attoyaque, found a Considerable number of People, found two other Candidates there, Mr Pollock & Ewbank all of us (the candidates) addressed the crowd, and dancing commenced immidiately after, and I returned home—previously however I got a Power of attorney from Robt Mays administrator on the Estate of James Shields to collect the monay coming to said Chields [sic] for Military Services rendered in 1840—on my arrival home I found my Son Charles very sick, having had a Congestive chill, send for Doctor Irion at 11 oclock at night—the Eastern mail arrived very late, rd a Letter from Wm. R. gallagher, received several papers

Sunday the 27th Charles a little better, Doctor Irion pronounced his chill last night to have been Congestive—at last we had a tolorable good shower of rain, wrote a letter to Joseph Herrington the Chief Justice of angelina County, send by Judge Taylor

Monday the 28th Probate Court—got the Case of Joseph Polvador Admr on José Santos's Estate laid over till next Court— many persons in Town, Translated a Deed for Simon Wiess—Lodge met, was up till midnight,

Tuesday 29th very hot—send a lot of Tickets to Melrose & Chirino. Charles is recovered from his fever, getting well—

Wednesday July 30th 1851 Weather Cool & pleasant this morning, wrote a Letter to W. Larkin of Bastrop inquiring about J. P. Brokman, requesting him to get me a Power of atty to get B.s Pay for services in my Comp. in 1840. wrote a Letter on same subject to Jno Brown (red) about John Park, the afternoon of this day was as hot as any day we had this Summer; was told by Larking Lee that John Cochran one of my Soldiers of 1840 was in Arkansas

Thursday the 31st Weather same as yesterday— my wife, Charles, and Laura went on a visit to Melrose this morning—received pr last nights mail a Letter from Adjutant gel informing me that Morriss may obtained John F. gilberts donation claim for 640 acres Land—received a Letter from Edward Tyler respecting Thresa Tomlinson's Headright—re'd. a Letter from J. M. Swisher Auditor of the State with the following par fund certificates: Elisha Tubb for $120.00—Joel Walker $72.00, Reuben Webb $74.00, Wm A. Corder $62.40—Sam W. Rainer $160.00 Wm Vince's Heirs for $228.00—J. J. Simpson $13.46 J. F. graham $325.33—. W. Pharr for $27.17 and the following certificates belonging to S. A. miller of Crockett to wit— Christopher Brimer, Durham Avent John Adams S. A. Miller John Bowen & John W. Thomas the latter Six mentioned Certificates I have send this day pr mail to Miller, to Crockett—Received also a lot of Documents belonging to J. J. Simpson—wrote to W. W. Pharr at San Spring Post office Anderson County, inclosing him his certificate for $27.17—wrote to Elisha Tubb of Cherokee inclosing to him a blank Power of atty for him to sign for me to collect the certificate recd to day from the Auditor's Department—Dr Keenan in Town

Friday the 1st August 1851 last night was the hottest we had this Summer, mail from East, brought letter from Major Durst dated Rio grande City July 2d 1851— he is doing good business— Mr O. W. Randal of this County returned last night from California, did not see him—wife returned from Melrose—wrote a letter to Auditor Swisher, requesting him to give me some information about to whom the $228 claim of Vince's heirs belongs. it was send to me last mail, but is not mine

Saturday August the 2d 1851 Cloudy, left home at day light, arrived at Douglass at 9 stopped at Clute's, did not address the citizens as I contemplated, —had a very fine rain in the Evening— went to the Lodge—have a severe cold—determined to remain here till monday—

Sunday the 3d Fine day—my old Rheumatic pains are returning on me, on account of the cold I got, can hardly walk

Monday the 4th Election day—about 150 People in Town—I received 95 votes — my opponent 28— my Rheumatic pain very severe, so much that I cannot ride, send my Horse home by J. C. Morrisson, have to remain here for the Stage on wednesday—

Tuesday the 5th Can not walk—heard from the different precincts, my vote in the county is near 500, that of my opponent a little over 100

Wednesday the 6th my Rheumatics increasing—Stage arrived from west, got the returns from crockett— my opponents residence, he received 122 votes mine 42—in angelina County I got nearly all the votes—so that my Election is sure beyond a doubt—

got into the Stage at 3 P. m. arrived at home at sun down, found all well. got a Letter from A. g. Walker of Dallas, also one from Doctor Daken of same place, all about land matters—filed— one from Cordova about the Eigenauer Estate— One from Mrs. Cazenau (Mrs Storms Eagle Pass—in answer to mine of 30th may last, she will send a Power of Attorney to sell her land on the Carrizo —one do from R. gorman, he will send me his papers soon to enable me to get his pay as a volunteer in 1842.

Thursday the 7th am confined to my bed, David Ayers paid me a visit, and if there is any trust to be placed in him at all, I have made a satisfactory arrangement with him for the ballance of the Judgement he holds against me for J. S. Pierson & Co. the proposition I made to him, and to the Messrs Piersons, are filed, and also copied into my Letter book—I feel easy now for I think he will no longer trouble me—

Friday the 8th August 1851 very hot weather—am streched on my Bed, and have to write on my back—got my Son Joseph to write out three advertisements to sell 640 acres of land of Jose Santos Coy's Estate on the 1st Tuesday next month, put up one at the Court House, send one to Douglass & one to Melrose,— Judge Taylor returned, he is beat for the Judgeship— his opponent Hicks is elected,—

Saturday the 9th am not any better, wrote to the Editor of the Masonic Mirror St Louis and send him on the following Subscribers living at or near Douglass, Saml H. Borem, Amos Rallason, Saml Rogers, A. C. Derritt, Wm H. Derritt, Graves Scott, M. F. Reinhardt & J. S. Murphy. wrote to gel James Smith inclosing him a claim of Danl Woodlan for a Horse, to be approved by him, and to be send back to me, to get it audited—Eastern & western mails arrived, brought nothing new—

Sunday the 10 very hot—am rather worse to day— got Doctor Martin to treat me for Mr Rheumatism, Mrs Sterne had Several Ladies to dine with her; — they *all just dropt in* all right

Monday the 11th took medcine last night, feel week this morning, getting very tired of being streched on the Bed—our Daughter Laura Commenced [going] to School this morning to Madame Bonamie, again—Mrs Sterne received a Letter from a Mrs Beveridge now at San augustin, wanting to board here, she has a Daughter and an other young Lady with her—they are Teachers—

Tuesday the 12th have to Keep my bed—one comfort is that J can read—

Wednesday the 13 very hot day, took medicine last night, feel very weak. the western mail arrived, rec'd. several Papers, and a Letter from Mrs Cazenau (Mrs Storms) informing me that she has sent a deed to James Shaw for the Carrizo land, which is left at Austin with Mr. J. B. Shaw—this does not suit exactly as I wanted it for my friend Wm F. Storms, I must attend to this as soon as I get well— re'd. a Power of atty from Elisha Tubb to collect some monay for him due by the late Republic of Texas

Thursday the 14th 1851 this was as hot a day as we have had this Summer—am still confined to my bed, but am getting better, mail arrived from the West—brought nothing from beyond grand Eccore, this is two weeks we have been without a New Orleans mail, there is something wrong—

Friday the 15th an other hot day, am getting much better, but can not walk yet— I have now been confined to my Bed more than a week, yet none of my masonic Brethren have been to see me yet;

Saturday the 16th Can Walk a little, but it fatigues me, and hurts me much. Doctor Starr came to see me on business, showed him Mrs Cazenau's Letters respecting her land on the Carrizo, he has some papers in his hands respecting a claim I purchased from Berry Smith, which is mine, but is among F. Hoya's papers, he promised to look for it and give it to me— received the Papers from Doctor Starr, and gave him a receipt for them— mails arrived, brought nothing from beyond grand Ecore,—Mrs Beveridge and her Daughter arrived and Stopped at our House, they expect to teach music and take a female School—

Sunday the 17th very hot—Thermometre 99 in the Shade! feel rather worse to day, took more medecines, — am very much pleased with Mrs Beveridge, and her Daughter.

Monday the 18th passed a very bad night, Robert Mays administrator of James Shields sold me his claim on the govt for $73 paid him $15 in cash, and gave him my note for $21.50 payable after the govt pays off the Troops which were out with me in 1840.

Tuesday the 19th weather same—passed a bad night— Mr Epperson of Red River in Town, he is defeated whig candidate for governor, he is a very fine young man— he held a joint note of mine and Judge Ochiltree's for $150—for which I gave him my Saddle Horse, we have not had a mail from new Orleans in three weeks—the cause—Red River low, and no positive contract pr Steamboat from New Orleans to grand Ecore —very annoying indeed— particularly as I can not do any [thing] else but read at present—

Wednesday the 20th had a fine rain this afternoon, cooled the air considerably—am not getting much better,—Mr Harrisson at our House Sick—western mail arrived. brought nothing for me but a few newspapers, with Stale news—

Tursday the 21st got me a pair of cruthes—cant get along very well—Eastern mail arrived again with out a new Orleans mail—had a very hard rain last night, wife and the two Boys gone to a Dance at Mrs Harts

Friday the 22d fine weather this morning—Mr Harrisson who was here a few days left this morning for home, Mr William Daniels gave me a Claim for a Hundred Dollars to collect, also a Claim on the government as one of Burton's *Horse Marines*, for having taken (in 1836) the Schooner Watchman, and two others— laden with provisions and ammunition for the Mexican army—gave me a power of atty to collect the monay, and he agreed to give me one third of all I got on account of the claim on the vessells and cargo, from which he never received any thing—

Saturday the 23d   very hot weather, begin to feel a little better, can walk a little—got Charles to write to J. N. Fall inquiring of him news in regard to the whereabouts of Joel Walker—To Elisha Tubb of cherokee acknowledging receipt of his Power of atty and inquiring about Reuben Wells to A. C. Caldwell of Marion inquiring about Lemuel Caldwell to J. M. Swisher inquriing about a claim of $228 he send me in favor of Wm Vince's Heirs,— I Know nothing about this claim received a Letter from Doctor Jowers inclosing to me Deeds from Robert Earl to Albert Emanuel, and from Emanuel to James Plant, no New Orleans mail yet.

Sunday the 24th   fine breeze all day—answered Doctor Jowers's Letter and acknowledging receipt of the two deeds, mentioned yesterday— Mr Cahoon arrived from San Augustin—Stops with us— am getting better very rapidly

Monday august 25—1851   weather more pleasant, Jacob Mast, gave me a lot of receipts for provisions and provender furnished to the troops of Texas in 1838, send them to the auditor and comptroller—he gave me also a discharge of A. C. Bullock, who served as a substitute for mast, in 1836, send it to the Adjutant gel,— wrote to Sam Rainer directed the Letter to Collin County— inclosed a power of attorney for him to sign—three of the Representatives elect paid me a visit to day— to wit— Wm M Hardeman, Doctor Jowers, and Mr Pollock—rd a Letter from J. H. Reagan, informing me that he got a Deed from Huffer for about 200 acres land near Kickapoo Creek in my favor, for a debt Huffer & his Son owed me—re'd a Letter from Judge Herrington of Angelina, informs me that Wm. C. Stanley has not removed from that County, but lives near the Nechaz, on the Woodville road—

Tuesday the 26th   weather very warm—Mr Parmalee came home from the North last night, brings no news

Wednesday the 27th   a little rain last night—damp day feel my Rheumatic pains again,

Thursday the 28th   warm & damp—received pr last nights mail, a letter from W. Larkins Bastrop inclosing a power of atty from J. P. Brockman, to receive his pay as one of my soldiers in 1840 rd a letter from E. E. Lott, Tyler—on land business, *and Elections* one do from B. F. Tankersly, Houston—wants to be speaker of the H. of Reps—and one or two more from candidates for offices in the Senate, answered Tankersley, and Lott's letters. the Eastern mail arrived again without a new Orleans mail received a Letter from Mr. Lindley of Powhatten ark. about his land in Rusk county

Friday the 29th   weather moderate,—can walk about the House a little, nothing new stirring—

Saturday the 30th August 1851   nothing new—getting better with a vengeance, can not walk five minuttes at a time before I am compelled to lay down again—western mail arrived, rd a Letter from David Ayers, wants me to send him a Copy of a deed from

Manuel Procela to J. J. Linn given to me by Judge Buckley, to get the Heirs of Manuel Procela to make a new Deed—did not succeed in getting the New Deed, received also a letter from a Mr Bell of Austin County, and Plasters of grimes, both want to be elected officers of the Senate — no Eastern mail

Sunday the 31s August dull day—read all day with the exeption of a letter written to David Ayers, inclosing him the Deed of the Manuel Procela League of land.

Monday September 1st 1851 fine day getting better very slow —a mail has arrived at last from New Orleans, recd a lot of *old* news papers, and a letter from my friend James Robinson of Durham— one do from Mr James plant of new York dated July 21st— rd a letter from F. B. Brown of Marion, Angelina C. inclosing two claims against the late Republic of Texas one for $ [blank] in favor of Mr galloway claims filed—(though they are too late) answered the letter to Brown wrote to the yankee Blade telling them that I paid Horatio Nelson four dollars—

Tuesday the 2d well, I went up Town in the Buggy, and attended as agent of Joseph Polvador to the selling of 640 acres Land out of the Estate of José de los Santos Coy's Estate and David muckleroy to bid it off at $500. there being an understanding about it—inasmuch as the Debts of the Estate are only due to Polvador & myself, the land which is realy not worth the $500, is to be reconveyed by Mucleroy—to me or Polvador or both of us, as Polvador and we can agree, I have Polvador obligation among my papers

Wednesday Sept 3d 1851 cool night, and morning—Rd a Power of Attorney from W. A. Corder to collect monay due him by the late Republic of Texas—gave me his discharge for a month's Service in Hayley's company in 1839— wrote to Auditor & Comptroller and inclosed the discharge, recevd a Letter from J. B. Shaw Austin advising me that a Deed is in his hands for me from gel Cazenau and wife for 1283 acres of land the same I sold to his wife when in new york in 1846. she was then Mrs Storms—re'd. a letter from E. Tubbs of cherokee giving me information about Mr Reuben webb, re'd. several Letters from Candidates for offices in the Senate

Thursday the 4th fine weather,—answered the Letter of J. B. Shaw, and wrote to Reuben webb (in duplicate, send one to Karrissa and one to Jacksonville Cherokee C.) inclosing a blank Power of Attorney for him to sign— wrote to J. P. Wallace of Bastrop informing him that Joe is a candidate for the same office (Engrossing Clerk) eta Eastern mail arrived, no news

Friday the 5th weather very warm, walked to Mr Parmalee's to day and back—being more then I could do for a month past—

Saturday the 6th hot day, wrote a Letter to Fred. Fountleroy Jasper in answer to one recd. from him, western mail brought a Letter from gel Sam Houston, on business—Letter filed—rd a Letter from gel E. B. Nichols— says he dont want Charles till the

River rises—that is not Keeping word gel nichols! we made a different arrangement at Cincinnatti on the 27 June last—

Sunday 7th weather hot & Cloudy—wrote to A. J. Mcgowan Editor of the Texas Presbiterian,[12] requesting him to send the Bye Laws of our Chapter, if printed to W. W. Barrett, who has the money to pay him for them, answered Nichols's Letter, dito gel Houstons, read wacousta,[13] by Major Richardson—good—commenced to read Consuelo[14] —by geo Sand—good again used Bartine's Lotion for my Rheumatism, helps me very much

Monday September 8th 1851 very warm day—Mrs Beveridge commenced her Semenary to day, she teaches in the old university, send my little Daughter Rosine to her, wrote a letter to gel E. B. Nichols galvezton about my Son Charles—received a letter from gel J. S. Mayfield recommending a Young man as a candidate for one of the Clerkships in the Senate.

Tuesday the 9th warm, till 12 oclock, had *a young* Storm without Rain—put a new Roof to the Kitchen—answered gel mayfield's letter recd yesterday. rode up Town on Horse back, Mr Pollock our Representative very sick,

Wednesday the 10th Cloudy—rain after dinner till near sun set—Wrote a letter to Mr Kellough and wife, inclosed the letter to Doctor Jowers requesting him to send it to the Kelloughs—wrote to James Plant of new york, respecting the same business he being Perkins's Agent, mail from west & north rd a letter from R. Scurry our Representative to Congress elect

Thursday the 11th cloudy weather, a little rain, in the afternoon—wrote a Letter to Col James Truit, and an answer to R. Scurry send off the negro Boy Tom with the waggon after a load of Corn due by Mr Perry of Douglass, Judge Joseph Herrington of Angelina County was here to day. brought me my Certificate of Election as Senator of the 11th District. Joseph gone to Cherokee County

Friday the 12th fine day—wrote a letter to J. H. Reagan Palestine requesting him to send me the Patent and Deed from Mr Huffer he obtained for me. wrote to Joshua, B. Hanks of Plenitude P. office Anderson County—inquiring about T. g. Hanks—send also a blank power of attorney for Archer Browning to sign, if he is in that County—send a Power of attorney to the widow Caldwell to sign to get the pay for Service for her late son Lemuel Caldwell—who was in my Company in 1840. wrote to Doctor Daken of Dallas Texas in answer to his letter of [blank] July last about a League & L. certificate he wants to purchase

---

[12]Several newspapers have used the name **Texas Presbyterian.** This refers to the paper published first in 1846 in Victoria by A. J. McGowan.

[13]**Wacousta; or The Prophet, an Indian Tale,** by Major John Richardson, was originally published in 1851 by Dewith & Davenport of New York. It subsequently appeared with the subtitled changed to **A Tale of The Pontiac Conspiracy.**

[14]**Consuela** was written by Mme. Dudevant under the pseudonym George Sand. It was translated by Francis G. Shaw, and published in Boston in 1846 by W. H. Ticknor & Company.

Saturday September 13th 1851 fine weather—wrote a petition to the corporation of Nacogdochez praying for payment of $25 and 7 years Interrest thereon, for the amount advanced for said Corporation made an agreement with Robert Mays of Shelby County for Jackson Shield's pay as a volunteer in 1840, did not have the requisite transfer agreed to send my son to Mays House next Monday to get the necessary Documents—advanced him $5. on account of said Claim. made an arrangement with John S. Roberts, and Casimiro Garcia, for said Casimiro's claim on the Republic of Texas for Services rendered in 1835—Roberts is to advance the purchase monay to Garcia which is to be refunded to him out of the proceeds of said Garcia's pay or land warrants he may get—to which getting I have to attend, and after Roberts is refunded his outlay, we are to divide the rest between us—the said Roberts and myself

Sunday the 14th fine day—rather *warm*—the western mail was brought in on Horseback last night (Paper mail left behind, Letter mail arrived only) Judge Ochiltree and his family arrived from galvezton. a Mr Tinnin Deputy Surveyor of Vanzandt County was here—made an arrangement with him to Survey the Sherman League of land into small tracts as it may be needed, he is also to offer it for sale eta

Monday the 15th fine day—was up Town,—commenced to repair my field—Judge Joseph Herrington brought me the Power of attorney of Mrs Mary Caldwell, to collect Lemuel Caldwell's pay for Services in 1840. she gives me half of all I can get. send Charles to Shelby county to get Shield's Power of attorney—Eastern Mail came in brought nothing for me. Chapter met—could not go up. Tom Barrett and J. Herrington rd the R. A. degree.

Tuesday the 16th Was up Town, nothing new Stirring—exept the sad news of the intire failure of the cuba Expedition—*Lopes Garroteado* all hands prisoners or Killed—the Revolution at an end—

Wednesday Sept 17th 1851 fine weather—got a receipt from Judge ochiltree the agent of Alford Edwards & Co of new york—against a Judgement they had against me in the District Court of this county filed the receipt among my papers—by advise of N. J. Moore the District clerk—western mail arrived—re'd. a large lot of Papers—rd a Letter from D. Ayers acknowledging the receipt of a Deed sent to him the 30th August last—also a letter from J. M. Swisher the Auditor—acknowledging the receipt of mast's Claims send 23d August last, also the receipt of Wm Daniel's claim and Wm A. Corder's discharge—none of them acted on, advising me also that the claim of Vince's Heirs was filed by me for Capt Snell of Houston—

Thursday the 18th fine day a little cloudy in the morning—inclosed the certificate of vince's Heirs to A. S. Ruthven of Houston to hand it to Capt Snell if it belongs to him, or Keep it for me till we meet at austin next winter—wrote to R. H. Peck of Austin, about a Certificate of Mrs Fanchers

Friday the 19th mail arrived last night from the East, brought no Letters nor papers, several young men from this county arrived from California; —was in the Lodge till midnight conferring the Degree of good Samaritan on Mrs Barrett (my Daughter) and Mrs Emily Thompson, also on Mr Hood of Cherokee and John Paine our Sheriff

Saturday the 20th fine weather—this was the 3d anniversary of the establishment of the sons of Temperance in this place, it was celebrated in fine style the masonic fraternity was invited, and we marched in procession to a beutifull grove near the Town where ample preparation were made for the reception of 700 persons who were present, a Bible was presented by Miss Fanny Simpson an address by Mr. J. C. Harrisson, after which all partook of a fine *rural* dinner (Barbecue). in the Evening a Ball given by the widow Hart to all who can shake a leg—unfortunately I am fatigued and full of pains, so I can not go—Mrs Sterne is unwell so she Keeps me company at home all the children exept Rosa gone to the Ball, old Lady Barrett paid us a visit to day, Town full of People from all parts of the County and from San Augustin

Sunday the 21st Sepr 1851 weather very fine, did not go up Town—Daniel Culp and Lady dined with us, Mr Nelson who has been absent for two weeks as a boarder returned to day—wrote a Letter to T. T. gammage in answer to one re'd. from him last night,

Monday the 22d fine weather—too fine— for rain is wanting very much fixing fence round field—Mrs Barrett and Mrs E. Thompson spend the day with us, was up Town, saw Mr Sam Hayter wont be ready for our land trade till the end of this week. no U S. mail again!!

Tuesday the 23d The ground is literally parched up, it is like a rock, the sand in the Street is ancle deep, and the dust is intolerable, god Knows what the poor Cattle will do if rain dont fall soon—a Mr Henry Sossaman of San augustin who lately moved up here, a Silversmith by trade—in a fit of mania a potu jumped out of the upper story window of Simpsons Hotel on Sunday night, he died this morning at 4 oclock A. m. and this afternoon late was burried—it is a very strange thing which I have now observed for the last 24 years men who come here drunkards dont live long here—I think I have seen 15 or more that came here, having been drunk for years, and before many days, some weeks but none lived a long time after they got here; this poor Devil had joined the Sons of Temperance, but it was no go—his two Sisters—very amiable girls having heard of his reformation came up to be present at the last Saturday's festivities, but alas, they saw their last brothers grave opened to receive him, the worst of all graves—a Drunkards grave—my wife had a cooking Stove put up in the Kitchen—is very much delighted with it—and so am I, because she is—the widow E. Thompson of Melrose, put her little Daughter Laura to school to Mrs Beveridge. she boards with us—

Wednesday the 24th Sepr 1851 fine day, but no rain—was in

Town—not much stirring—western mail arrived—receivd my regular files of Papers, and a Letter from David Ayers—I do not
Know how to take that fellow exept as I first did—that he is an
infernal rascal and nothing Shorter—!! rd a letter from E. B.
Nichols about my Son Charles—rd a Power of attorney from Reuben webb of Cherokee County to collect his claim against Got
[government] for Services under my command in 1840—Power of
atty filed with claim—rd letters from W. Larkins, and Wallace of
Bastrop—J. B. Long, and M. B. Erwin Austin—Electioneering
letters—

Thursday the 25th very Cool morning a fire not at all disagreable, wrote an answer to genl. E. B. Nichols of galvezton—
one to W. Larkin Bastrop—one to Lone Austin—requesting him to
get me a Room for next winter, wrote to the U. S. Deputy Marshall requesting him to inform me the result of the sale of the
Quintus. C. Nugent League of land which is to take place 1st
Tuesday of next month, also wrote to him that the Sherman
League is for sale at $2000. wrote to David Ayers galvezton about
the Pierson Business and the very last Letter I'll write—!! wrote
to Maurice Barnett Jr of New Orleans inclosing a Power of attorney he gave me to sell 640 acres land granted to Edward O'Connor
sold by O. C. to said Barnett of 7th Novr 1838 located in upshur
County, said Power of Attorney was attested before J. H. Holland
as Texas Comr but he did not put a Seal to it as required by law—
want him to acknowledge it before a Texas Comr in New Orleans
and to be send back to me

Friday the 26th very hot and dusty—my Son Charles Sick—
paid Horatio Nelson four dollars for two years subscription to the
yankee Blade rct filed, was twice in Town to day—not much doing

Saturday the 27th cool morning & Evening—charles better—
Eastern & western mails no news—nothing from the East—rd a
letter from Tankersly Houston, at bed time it was very cold—

Sunday Septr 28th 1851 This morning it was as cold as winter, and a fire in the chimney indispensable, Mr Cahoon arrived
last night, Mr S. M. Orton also returned from the north, bringing
with him a Daughter by a first marriage Mr O. has purchased a
large stock of goods at the north, so has Chevallier, so have the
Messrs Raguet's so has Bondies & Co well I am fearfull before a
year passes round I shall have more Company besides P. H. Ford
& Co however I sincerely hope not—but—quien sabe—

Monday the 29th Thermometer fell to 51½ this morning, and
every body is as cold as if it was December—I am the worst suf-
ferer, for my Rheumatism has returned on me as bad as ever, and
am laid up once more, I grin, but have to bear it—Mr Joseph
Polvador came to have his probate business arranged about the
Estate of Jose de los Santos Coy's Estate send him to Judge Taylor who attended to the matter for me, Eastern mail arrived,
brought nothing—

Tuesday the 30th Cold weather, my Rheumatism not any

better; Sale of 640 acres land to D. Mucleroy, from Jose Polvador admr of J. de los Santos Coy was ratified by the Probate Court an appeal was taken but was all o. k. sale to Mucleroy in my posession—

Wednesday the 1st October Weather moderating, still confined to my Room. Western mail came in, re'd. my usual number of Papers also a letter from A. S. Ruthven acknowledging the receipt of the Letter of the 19th ult inclosing the audited Claim of $228.00 of Vince's Heirs, Mr Ruthven says Capt Snell who gave me the Claim to be Audited is not now living in Houston, but on the Rio grande. he is expected in Houston soon, rcd a letter from Roswell Gorman, about his land, receivd also a letter from the U. S. Deputy Marshall, in answer to mine of the [blank] ult, and one electioneering letter, but the writer has not paid the Postage, *so much for it*—Mr Evans of St augustin arrived from N. Orlean by the western Stage—Red River dried up—

Thursday October the 2d 1851 fine day, getting a little better —Eastern mail nothing new—

Friday the 3d fine weather, our Daughter Laura's birth day she is 11 years old, our youngest, Rosine took fever to day, hope it is not dangerous—my neighbor Bondies is very sick with the fever, Charles is gone to San Augustin to see Mr Hurt about a situation—Cahoon left this morning on the Stage for San Augustin —Robert mays of Shelbyville was here, brought me Jackson Shield's Power of atto to collect his pay for 1840—advanced him $10 more which makes 15 dollars—gave him my due Bill for $22.50 which however is not payable till the claim is collected, and the ballance of the claim is mine,—I feel much better to day, I think that gum guiacum which I now take regularly, has done me more good then any thing I have tried felt so well that I walked, (or rather limped) up to the new Post office, to see our *new Post master* Mr Thos Hubert, Judge Coon having resigned— he has been the best Post master we ever had here, and I hope Mr Hubert will do as well as Coon,

Saturday the 4th weather same, walked up Town twice to day—Judge Buckly send me a Letter pr D. Ayers he wants me to make a Deed to a League of Land sold in 1836 to J. J. Linn Trustee of Belden & Folger New Orleans can not do it, till I see Judge B. Dont want to get into any more scrapes about land— mails arrived, rd a commission from Canton Miss. to take Saml Flournoy's Testimony in a number of cases in which J. Silverberg's Estate is plaintiff, Flournoy gone west, rcd a Letter from Mrs. Cazenau Eagle pass about her land on the Carizo near Patonia, a Letter from P. de Cordova respecting Ergenauers Estate, rcd a Letter from a Mr Wm R. somebody (I can not make out the name) New Orleans, about some land in which James Sampley was concerned in 1836. this land is claimed by different persons—and I am willing they should fight it out between them, without my assistance

Sunday October the 5th 1851 weather fine, rain wanting—inasmuch as water is getting very scarce for stock—wrote a Letter to Mr Buckley send it by D. Ayers, telling my reasons for not signing the Deed he wants—my little Daughter Rosine better—Kept House all day exept a very short time I was in Town heard of a tremendous riot in Smith County three persons Killed on the spot two more mortally wounded, one severely wounded (the Sheriff of Smith County) and several others are wounded but not severely or mortally, and from information it is not going to stop there, this is bad business, *certain*—

Monday the 6th 8 oclock a. m. looks like rain—and I *feel* like rain—wrote a letter to E. Silverberg Canton Miss acknowledging the receipt of the Documents rd pr last mail— one to Thomas ward Austin about getting my room ready—one do to Doctor Jowers Palestine telling him the day I'll start so that he can meet me in Crockett on the 18th inst—one, to J. J. Hall of Crockett telling him to get his Petition and papers ready for me to take on to Austin (he wants a League of land as his headright)—drew off my account with our chapter, I owe the chapter $6.20 and the Chapter owes me my expences in Huntsville last June as the Representative of the chapter at the grand chapter of the State. Eastern mail arrived, brought a few papers only, re'd. an appointment as a member of the American Legal Association New York for the term of two years, provided I send on five dollars quien sabe—rd a letter from Judge Joseph Herrington Angelina County including Petition eta of Wessly W. Hanks to be presented to the Legislature, Mr Perry of Douglass in Town, wrote a letter to Capt Crossby of Austin inclosing one from my Son Joseph—

Tuesday the 7th warm weather again, no use to say any thing more about rain,—was up Town twice—arranged some of my papers to take on to Austin, returned to Col Jeremiah Strode a claim he gave me last fall to collect against the govt, said claim not sufficiently authenticated—also returned some papers to Wm D. Hayter, which belonged to him, both through the Post office

Wednesday the 8th cloudy, yet no rain, saw Wm N. Hardeman going on west on his way to austin, he has been at Burkville, had not much time to converse with him, Ochiltree and Henry W. Raguet are appointed on the permanent Committee and Com of Correspondence,—translated a Land Title of Zacheus gibbs, loaned Parmalee & Coe 46 planks 10½ feet long 1½ inches thick and 14½ inches wide, to be returned so soon as the Mill's can saw the same quantity got Jno F. graham's Power of attorney to collect his monay for services in 1840. Western mail arrived, brought my usual number of news papers, received a Letter from J. M. Long Austin, advising me that my room will be ready for me, with a Stove in it—good news that—

Thursday the 9th weather very warm, looks like rain all the time but still dry. rd a letter from Mr Pollock, who is at present at J. J. Hayters—he wants to come in Town, send word to him by Sam Hayter to come to our House—Sam Hayter told me at last that he would take the land, and will arrange it in a few days—veremos! Eastern mail. rd nothing but Stale news—received a list of Lawyers belonging to the American Legal association! John Border who is going on to Houston says the Trinity river has risen a little wonder whence the water came? it has not rained here this five months—do any good—

Friday the 10th Weather in Status quo—very cloudy, no rain —our Charles is 21 years old to day, good heavens how time flies, it appears to be only as yesterday since he was born, there is a considerable stirr about the House, cake baking eta going on looks very much like a frolic *going to happen*—at last about noon had a very fine rain, the best one we have had for Six months, at dark, the House is lit up in every corner 8 P. m. guests arriving, *thick.* feel allmost intierly recovered from my Rheumatism, hope to god it may never be any worse then it is now—Col F. Thorn returned to day from the hot springs Arkansas, he has derived much benefit from them, he looks in fine health.

Saturday October 11th 1851 Rain, and cold, at 8 a. m.—had a very pleasant party last night, danced till about 2 oclock this morning, and all went away, Satisfied—rained a little all day—Mr Pollock came in to day from J. J. Hayters, he is convalescent but is very weak and not able to travel yet, saw a Captain Rogers from Mississippi going on west with his family, they stop here in Town for the present—wrote to Editor of the Red land Herald, requesting him to send me Wm C. Stanley's advertisement of lost land certificate published in the Herald sometime ago.

Sunday the 12th beutifull day—was in Town twice—but nothing going on, wrote a letter to Thomas ward Austin, to engage boarding for Pollock also wrote a letter to Ben F. Hill in answer to one rd by M. B. Erwin, respecting Lee's Business

Monday the 13th Cool night & morning, but a splendid day, saw Sam Hayter this morning says that his Father will be in to see me to morrow morning *certain,* send Charles to Angelina County to see Wm C. Stanley to get the land business between us arranged—Judge ochiltree gave me some Documents relating to a Head right of Ramon Sanchez to be attended to at Austin (see my memorandum of Austin business)

Tuesday the 14th very beutifull weather—received J. B. Reed's power of atty to collect his pay as a volunteer in 1840 on halves—I received several Documents to day about claims to come before the Legislature—paid Voight & Rennely $36.51 my a/c up to date—well, what shall I say about Hayter, that I have been shamefully deceived is the *least* I can say if ever men made a firm trade, it was made by Saml Hayter & myself he acting for his Father—to day the Father came in and I found that Mr Saml Hayter either deceived me on his own hook or I was deceived by both Father & Son—but they are rich men—and rich men can do wrong with impunity—for Dollars will set them right if ever so wrong—I would not after this take the word of either for 2 *bats*

Wednesday October the 15th 1851 weather very fine—preparing to start to Austin—recevd several Documents to day from various Individuals of business to be attended to at Austin—Charles returned this Evening from Angelina County, brought me the Power of attorney and other Documents from Wm C. Stanley respecting his Headright; —Mr Cheatham of angelina County was here to day, he resides on Mrs Sterne's and Mrs Mayfield land in angelina County, the Headright of James Maffitt, Mr Cheatham wants to rent the place—Judge Taylor who is the agent of Mrs Mayfield has no power to rent, but only to sell—so the matter *rests* in Status quo—paid Rennely & Voight $36.51 for various articles furnished the family—western mail arri[ve]d

Thursday the 16th Cool nights & morning—fine day—send a notice to J. J. Hayter & Wm D. Hayter by the Sheriff not to cut wood on the loco land owned by Mrs Sterne. wrote to Yoakum & McCreary Huntsville, about a Section of land I want to sell in walker County—wrote to Wm A. Hagood magnolia, about a land certificate he wants to purchase—to T. T. gammage Marshall and J. C. Hill Tyler about same business to L. E. Tipps Henderson on same business—

Friday the 17th Weather same—business to be attended to at Austin is flowing in from all parts—shall have my hands full this winter—Camp meeting at, or near, Melrose, every [one] gone to it—Charles made an arrangement with Bondies Rohte & Co for a year Service as clerk—

Saturday the 18th Weather still, fine not much doing in Town, all hands gone to the Camp meeting at Melrose—mails from East and west rd a letter from James Plant, my proposition was not reced on the 24th Sepr the date on which Mr Plant wrote—

Sunday the 19th Weather Splendid—Town intierly deserted —well if all that have gone to camp meeting had Religion in view all's right, but that I doubt very much, to see, and be seen I think had more to do in the matter then Religion. Mr Pollock, and Charles returned in the Evening, arranged Papers to day, getting ready to leave on Monday night—John Pate transferred a claim against the govt to me for 14.51—told him he might have the land on Kikapoo Creek I got from Huffer for a dollar an acre—

Nacogdochez *Monday October 20th 1851* fine day—getting ready to start—visited the Chapter in the Evening bid all good-bye, my children and grand children are all at the House, and at 2 ½ A. m. on

Tuesday the 21 took an affectionate farewell of all my dear Family, and together with Mr Wm C. Pollock started on the mail Stage, and arrived at Jacob Master's Jr at dark—

Wednesday the 22d left at 4 A.M. passed through Crockett and Cincinate and arrived at Huntsville at 8 P.M.—saw Doctor Keenan and several other friends—

Thursday the 23d left at 4 A.M. passed through the fine and flourishing Town of Anderson in grimes County and arrived at Washington at sundown—

Friday the 24th The Stage from Houston brought up a full *load* of Passengers, among them my *friends* Mrs Prentiss and her amiable Daughter who are going up to Austin to remain during the winter, and we will board at the same House,—the Stage started at 4 A. m. *Crowded, full.* my blanket was lost here by the negligence of the Hotel Keeper who is also Stage agent—arrived at Lagrange at 8 P. m.

Saturday the 25th the weather has been very fine and pleasant ever we left home—started this morning at 3 A. m. passed through Bastrop and arrived at Austin at 7 oclock P. m. Mr Pollock stopped at Browns Hotel and I went to my old quarters at old Squire ward's the Father of Mrs Prentiss—

Austin—*Sunday the 26th* feel exedingly fatigued from my journey, but am allmost recovered initerly from my Rheumatic pains—my Room is not quite ready for me but will be to morrow —was introduced to some of the Rio grande members of the Legislature, and saw a great many of my old friends who were glad to see me—some for selfish and other *perhaps* pure friendship—

Austin *Monday October the 27th 1851* windy and boisterous day—went to the general land office and deposited John Reeds land papers—also Judge C. S. Taylor's papers for a Labor—also a memorandum from Wm C. Johnson for two Patents (Originaly [blank] Eakins's), also deposited Wm C. Stanley's papers—went to the Adjutant gel's office and deposited O Peterson's papers for Bennett Blake—also Jno J. Simpson's claim for land of Chism, also Isaac Lees claim for Jno Blair—The Claim (San Jacinto) of Jno F. Gilbert was issued to Morriss May as agent—I have to see the adjutant gel again about this claim. Casimero garcia rcd 320 acres and his pay for services in 1835 under Capt J. S. Roberts, which was delivered and paid over to Wm newel as his assign, 640 acres Donation Claim must be obtained before the Legislature if it is obtained at all, the Claim of Jno F. Chairs belonging to Doctor george H. Livingston was presented and paid to B. A. Mudd as assignee of Thos B. Huling—the Affidavit that Chairs was in the San Jacinto army must be countersigned by a Superior officer —Presented Doctor Johnson's Claim which could not be admitted to be audited, because the certificates were signed in October being *after* the time for presenting Claims had expired—left the Claim in the Auditor's office on file—presented Mrs Emely Thompson's Power of attorney and Clerks certificate of Henderson County at the State Department to procure to State Seal to them—presented D. O. Norton's Letter to the governor asking an appointment of Notary Public for Wood County—saw many of my old friends to day—and got fairly installed into my old Room. saw my friend Lewis Knight of Nacogdochez County to day, also Joseph Shanks a son of major Jno T. Shanks of our Town—wrote to Mrs Sterne—to J. S. Roberts notifying him that Casimiro garcia rcd pay and 320 acres land for the services in 1835, to Doctor Livingston of Sumpter A. County that Jno F. Chairs recd 320 acres land, and send him back the affidavit of Chairs to get either gel Rusk, or general Sherman's signature that Chairs was with the army at San Jacinto wrote to W. W. Barrett, that the 20$. draft given to me by Mr Scruggs on Geo W. Grant for Nacogdochez Chapter was not paid, but accepted by Grant. took a Box No 121 at the Post office, wrote to my son Joseph after midnight,

Austin, *Tuesday October the 28th 1851* very warm weather, many members arriving to day, Doctor Jowers and Col Cannon came in, was introduced to a Host of persons of all Kind and discriptions, and after this I shall not undertake the task of putting down in this Journal every thing that passes, as the Journals of the Senate will answer such a purpose, but shall only note down such things as may directly interrest me or as may be of importance—to Day I wrote an agreement between Robert Mays of Shelbyville and Louis Knight of Nacogdochez, Mays sold to Knight 320 acres (choice) out of the East half of said, to be surveyed by the County Surveyor of Travis County, see memorandum left with me—paid a visit to Mrs Col Thos wm Ward—the adjutant gel gave me back the claim of Bennett Blake for 320 acres land of Oliver Peterson said land having been taken out by geo. w. Smyth as assignee

Wednesday the 29th very warm weather— feel bad—received from the gel land office John Reids Patent, and certificate for the ballance of his land inclosed to him, and send it by Robert Mays and Lewis Knight—wrote Bennett Blake that the claim of O. Peterson of 320 acres land, Bounty warrant was issued to geo w. Smyth ass. of said Peterson—wrote to Judge Taylor inclosing to him again his field notes for a labor of land with statement of Comr gel land office—wrote to Wm C. Johnson respecting the two Patents of J. M. Eakin—they can not issue till unconditional certificate is send on here send Joe's Letter written yesterday, and one written to My wife by R. mays—& L. Knight—a number of members of both Houses have arrived, *and still they come.* wrote to Doctor Price of washington about my Blanket I lost at washington on Friday morning the 24th inst—wrote to Jacob masters Crockett about my memorandum book I lost at his House on the night of the 21 to 22d inst—

Austin *Thursday the 30th October 1851* very warm weather — mail from the East brought a letter from Andrew Caddell, he wants the assessor & Collection law changed, to make assessment roll and return funds eta at the same time—in place of on the first June and 1st July. went to the gel Land office and Adjutant gel's office and found out the way in which manner B. Blake's certificate for 320 acres land O Peterson's bounty warrant was issued to a Mr Keaghey of Jasper, got a certified Copy of Keaghey's oath that he lost Peterson's Discharge and a certified copy of the Discharge and transfer to Blake from Auditors office and inclosed both to Blake—wrote to Elisha A. Evans of Angelina County, telling him that his Survey conflicts with Anastacio Varela's headright and can in consequence not be patented—members coming in fast—wrote to John Reid inclosing a patent No 752 issued to Isom R. Chisum which was send for by me by James

Read last session. said patent is for 320 acres land—wrote to Doctor Johnson of melrose telling him that his claim was not issued in consequence of his vouchers not having been signed previous to 1st Sept 1851—wrote to Mrs Sterne, and to Placide.

Friday the 31st Weather continues to be the same a quorum of the House of Representatives has arrived, and there are about 12 Senators in the City—candidates enough to stock a good Plantation for officers of the Senate & House of Representatives—saw so many of my old friends to day who arrived from all parts of the Country—that I can not particularize, all seem glad to meet one an other here again, and many cordial shakes of hands have been done to day, and no doubt sincerely so at least I can say as much for myself, for I did not take one of my old associates by the hand, but my Heart was with it—

Austin Saturday November the 1st 1851 weather is oppressively hot after 11 a. m. till dark—wrote a Letter to Mrs Sterne, wrote an affidavit for Mrs Sterne's & Mrs Taylors Relationship in germany eta a large number of the Representatives and Senators arrived to day, they are most all here now—and I expect that we will be able to go to work on Monday morning next

Sunday the 2d Weather still same—dull day—went to the Methodist Church where Mr Becton formerly of Nacogdochez County preached, the Eastern mail arrived, brought Petition eta of old major Hyde of our Town,—to go before the Legislature—rd an other letter from A. J. M. g.[owan] who wants to be chaplain of the Senate—no go—rd a communication from A. Huston respecting a tri weekly mail from washington to Nacogdochez

Monday Novr 3d Cold nights and very warm day—the Senate met to day elected its officers, House at 12 oclock has not elected a Speaker. received the Duplicate certificate for a League & Labor of land for Wm C. Stanley of angelina County, feel simptoms of returning Rheumatism—

Tuesday the 4th weather very unfavorable for Rheumatism, it is raining a little—Pollock very Sick—wrote to Mrs Sterne

Wednesday the 5th weather cool—Pollock better wrote to W. W. Barrett inclosing two documents for Mrs E. Thompson to which I got the State Seal—feel unwell—

Thursday the 6th fine weather, wrote to Taylor and Tom Barrett, Mat Carthwright here, introduced Bills for the relief of Solomon Allbright, Heirs of Joseph Rutherford, W. S. Music and Eli m. Thomason

Friday the 7th cool but very pleasant, the governor is Sick, and will not send in his Message till Monday next. both Houses hard at work—Pollock getting well

Austin *Saturday Novr 8th 1851* Cloudy in the morning but fine in the afternoon—to day the votes for govr and Liut govr were counted out, Bell is Elected by near 10,000 votes over greer, and J. W. Henderson has a majority of over 2000 votes over any of his competitors[15] —wrote a letter to Charles—mail arrived and brought me a Letter from the dear ones at home, it is a great pleasure to me indeed, received a letter from Doctor Livingston of Sumpter, respecting the Chairs Claim—wrote to him sometime ago on the subject, recd a letter from M. F. Reinhardt inclosing affidavit of E. Ables—filed with the Power of attorney he gave me sometime ago to collect his pay for Services in my company in 1840, also a Letter from Frank Brown of Marion angelina County, he wants a notery publicship for Mr Nash of his place—wrote to Mrs Sterne at midnight

Sunday the 9th Cloudy in the morning—fair in the afternoon weather, cool in the morning and hot as June during midday— went to church (the Episcopal) heard a very exelent Sermon by the revd Mr Fontain. wrote to my wife in the afternoon—also to Laura, and Eugenia

Monday the 10th rain about daylight—cold weather rained towards Evening—heard the governor's Message to day, wrote to the Post master of Nacogdochez about matters and things in general, to Judge Herrington, Andrew Caddell in answer to his letter of 19th October—to Mrs Sterne and T. C. Barrett—

Tuesday the 11th rained hard last night—rain more or less all day—very cold wrote to C. S. Taylor Inclosing the affidavit of the Heirship of Mrs Taylor to her mother's Estate in germany—Wrote Isaac Lee respecting his claim —

Wednesday the 12th rain last night & this morning—fine afternoon, wrote to Capt David Muckleroy J. S. Linn, and J. T. Shanks on matters and things in gel—and to R. Parmalee on business

Austin Thursday Novr 13th 1851 weather cool but pleasant— delivered the memorandum of Luis Knight and Robt Mays to Robt Pace the Surveyor of Travis County, he will give me an answer in a few days if he can do the work—wrote to R. Parmalee and to my family—send also a letter to Mrs Sterne by a Mr Likens of Rusk County.

Friday the 14th beutifull weather, been busy all day in the Senate in the morning and on committee in the afternoon, wrote a letter to W. W. Hanks Sumpter Angelina County, advising him that his land clas [claim?] has passed the Committee to day for ⅓ league land—

Saturday the 15th we have beutifull weather again, nothing of importance took place to day—The Judges of the Supreme Court, and the Judge of the U. S. District Court are here ready to go to business on Monday next.

Sunday the 16th beutifull day—went to church, and heard a splendid discourse on Education by the revd Mr Fountain, wrote

[15]P. Hansborough Bell became governor on December 21, 1849, and retained that post until November 23, 1853, when he resigned to assume a seat in the United States House of Representatives. He was succeeded by Lieutenant Governor J. W. Henderson, who served the remaining month of the term as governor.

to Mrs Sterne to Laura, Placide, and Miss Cummings—rcd a letter and pe[ti]tion from Edward Tyler also one from James R. Arnold and one from J. A. Ragan of Natchitochez also a letter from gel Rusk—who wants me to send him the names and residence of the Senators—to send them Documents from washington

Monday the 17th beutifull weather, warm—sold Wm. C. Stanley, certificate for $460.50 to Hamilton & Mancock—introduced a Bill for the relief of the Heirs of Haden Arnold decd one for Casimero Garcia, the Petition of Theresa Tyler, the Memorial of Mr J. A. Ragan of Louisiana who offers to dry up all the Lakes in Texas and render them tillable—wrote to charles

Tuesday the 18th rain last night—fine day to day—got a Patent for a league of land out of the land office for Edward Tyler and inclosed it to him pr mail to day—introduced a Bill for the Relief of Charles Chevallier assignee of Napoleon Davaltz.

BIBLIOGRAPHY

The following list of books and periodical selections were most helpful in preparing the notes. The interested student is referred to them for more complete information concerning the several characters and events. No attempt is made to rank them in order of usefulness or value, and the editor's debt to these and other sources consulted which may have been omitted from this list is gratefully and completely acknowledged.

Biographical Directory of the American Congress, 1774-1961, Government Printing Office: Washington, 1961.

Biographical Directory of the Texas Conventions and Congresses, Book Exchange: Austin, 1951.

Carter, James D., *Freemasonry in Texas, Background, History, and Influence to 1846,* Committee on Masonic Education and Service: Waco, 1955.

Greene, Glen Lee, *Masonry in Louisiana: A Sesqui-Centennial History, 1812-1962,* Exposition Press: New York, 1962.

The Handbook of Texas, 2 vols., Texas State Historical Association: Austin, 1952.

Kemp, Louis W., *The Heroes of San Jacinto,* Anson Jones Press: Houston, 1932.

Kemp, Louis W., *The Signers of the Texas Declaration of Independence,* Anson Jones Press: Salado, Texas, 1944.

Smithers, Harriet (ed.), "The Diary of Adolphus Sterne," *Southwestern Historical Quarterly,* vols. XXX through XXXVIII (October, 1926-January, 1935).

Warner, Ezra F., *Lives of the Confederate Commanders, Generals in Gray,* Louisiana State University Press: Baton Rouge, 1959.

White, Gifford (ed.), *The 1840 Census of the Republic of Texas,* The Pemberton Press: Austin, 1966.

INDEX

— 259 —

Hyde, Munroe: 152, 162, 247
Hyde, Mrs.: 158

Southwestern Historical Quarterly: iii, 89n
Sparks, Franklin: 183
Sparks, John: 182
Sparks, Hawkins: 48
Sparks, Massy C.: 184
Spark's Settlement: 26
Sparks, Wm. F. (Wild Bill): 75, 112, 113, 114, 139, 176
Speight, W. R. D.: 156, 183
Springer, J. B.: 2
Stage House Hotel: 212
Stamps: 22
Stanley, Wm. C.: 209, 212, 215, 217, 235, 243, 244, 245, 247, 249
Starr, James Harper: 3, 6, 22, 23, 25, 31, 40, 52, 59, 63, 65, 68, 70, 76, 84, 87, 92, 101, 105, 106, 111, 112, 113, 117, 126, 132, 136, 141, 145, 158, 160, 163, 164, 167, 173, 175, 176, 177, 183, 185, 187, 192, 193, 194, 195, 197, 212, 216, 222, 231, 234
Starr, Mrs.: 159
Stedham: 63, 128
Steevens: 21
Stephenson, Mr.: 215
Stevens, Nancy: 89, 92, 95, 100, 112, 126, 131
Sterne, Adolphus: iv, viii, 4n, 41, 42, 45n, 50n, 69n, 75n, 126, 192, 226
Sterne, Charles Adolphus: iii, vi, 1n, 6, 22, 68, 77, 99, 103, 130, 134, 152, 161, 162, 173, 175, 179, 180, 194, 198, 200-02, 204, 205, 208, 211, 212, 214, 216, 217, 219-222, 224, 227, 230, 231, 235-238, 240, 241, 243, 244, 248, 249
Sterne, Eugenia: v, vi, 30, 51, 63, 67, 68, 77, 83, 92, 98, 100, 102, 103, 118, 139, 144, 156, 157, 173, 195, 199, 200, 204
Sterne, Emmanuel: v
Sterne, Mrs. Eva Rosine: iii, 3, 4, 5, 6, 9, 12, 16n, 71, 72, 76, 77, 78, 91, 110, 117, 121, 141, 150, 172, 181, 182, 185, 193, 195, 199, 201, 204, 233, 239, 244, 245, 247, 248, 249
Sterne, Joseph Amador: vi, 77, 95, 99, 101, 113, 121, 122, 134, 152, 153, 179, 185, 205, 218, 233, 242, 246
Sterne, Isaac: 8, 21, 47, 131, 133, 157, 178, 179, 187
Sterne, Laura J.: vi, 28, 40, 59, 63, 65, 76, 108, 109, 161, 172, 177, 181, 192, 233, 241, 248, 249
Sterne, Placide Rusk: vi, 10, 28, 30, 40, 58, 59, 67, 80, 177, 185, 192

Sterne, Rosine: vi, 39, 42, 52, 241, 242
Sterne, William Logan: vi
Still: 137
Stille, William B.: 9
Stivers, Samuel: 225
Stockman, Mary Celeste: 14n
Stoddard, J. B.: 9
Stone House (Old Stone Fort): vi, 4n, 11, 17, 25, 26, 39, 78, 80
Storms, Wm. F.: 233
Stringer, F. L.: 100
Strode, Alvin F.: 218
Strode, Col. Jeremiah: 242
Strong, Alexander H.: 3, 86, 87
Sturges, B. B.: 228, 231
Sturges, Lucretia B.: 227, 228
Sublett: 62, 137
Sublett, Henry: 54
Sublett, P.: 70
Sugarloaf Mountain: 18, 74
Summergrove, La.: 14, 15
Suter, Mr.: 211, 214
Sutherland, John: 8
Swisher, J. M.: 207, 211, 217, 223, 232, 235, 238
Swisher's and Smith's Hotel: 18n

— T —

Tabor, David F.: 161, 164, 167, 194
Tabor, Juan: 214, 230
Taliafero: 134, 162, 193
Taliaferro, C. E.: 133, 164
Taliafero, Massingail: 134
Taliafero, Ned: 90, 91, 95, 102, 105
Tankersly, B. J.: 235, 240
Tarrant, Edward H.: 46, 53
Tavern Bill: 19
Taylor, Charles S.: 1, 16, 19, 25, 33, 37, 46, 63, 68, 87, 100, 101, 111, 132, 137, 139, 141, 145, 164, 165, 183, 185, 190, 199, 201, 203, 205, 207, 209, 210, 212, 213, 217, 221, 230, 231, 233, 240, 245, 246, 247, 248
Taylor, Mrs. C. S.: 3, 4, 91, 99, 185, 205, 247, 248
Taylor, W. W.: 31, 226
Teague, Mich: 2, 45, 111
Teal, George: 137, 140, 143, 144, 157, 184
Tennille, Ben: 59
Tenoxtitlan, Texas: 19
Terrill, George Whitfield: 28, 29, 43, 44, 46, 49, 53, 64, 67, 69, 70, 71, 72, 74, 75, 76n, 77, 99, 100, 101, 115, 121, 131, 134, 135, 138, 141, 147, 149, 158, 166, 167, 181, 191, 193, 196, 198, 199
Terrill, Mrs. G. W.: 76, 119, 131, 191, 199

www.ingramcontent.com/pod-product-compliance
Lightning Source LLC
Chambersburg PA
CBHW060042100426
42742CB00014B/2669